Keegan
and Dalglish

Keegan and Dalglish

Richard T. Kelly

**SIMON &
SCHUSTER**

London · New York · Sydney · Toronto · New Delhi

A CBS COMPANY

First published in Great Britain by Simon & Schuster UK Ltd, 2017
A CBS COMPANY

1 3 5 7 9 10 8 6 4 2

Simon & Schuster UK Ltd
1st Floor
222 Gray's Inn Road
London WC1X 8HB

www.simonandschuster.co.uk

Simon & Schuster Australia, Sydney
Simon & Schuster India, New Delhi

A CIP catalogue record for this book
is available from the British Library.

ISBN: 978-1-4711-5475-1
Ebook ISBN: 978-1-4711-5477-5

Typeset and designed in the UK by M Rules
Printed and bound by CPI Group (UK) Ltd, Croydon, CR0 4YY

Simon & Schuster UK Ltd are committed to sourcing paper that is made
from wood grown in sustainable forests and support the Forest Stewardship
Council, the leading international forest certification organisation. Our
books displaying the FSC logo are printed on FSC certified paper.

For my father

'*We are the ones who carry out the dream. The dream that the supporters will never achieve because they can't play. So they live through us. But we have dreams we can't realise, too.*'

Kenny Dalglish, 2010

CONTENTS

Introduction   1

PART I

1 Kenneth Mathieson Dalglish 1951-67   19
2 Joseph Kevin Keegan 1951-67   31
3 The Big Leagues 1967-71   39
4 Almost Famous 1971-73   54
5 Technique 1973-74   69
6 Changes 1974-77   81

PART II

7 Make It Anywhere 1977-78   105
8 Force of Will 1978-80   120
9 The Top, and Staying There 1980-82   132
10 Last Orders 1982-84   152
11 'The English Disease' A Diagnosis   166
12 The Stakes of the Game 1984-85   171
13 After the Fall 1985-89   182

14 Hillsborough 1989   196
15 Keeping It Together 1989-91   207

PART III

16 Sleeping Giants 1991-94   227
17 'That's Bottle Out There!' 1994-95   255
18 Nemesis 1995-97   265
19 Succession Problems 1997-98   281
20 Gambling 1999-2000   304

PART IV

21 The Cost of Everything 2001-07   321
22 The Game in Black and White 2008-09   342
23 The King Is Alive 2009-12   348
24 Unfinished Business 2013-17   361
    Conclusion   368

    Acknowledgements   374
    Bibliography   375
    Index   382

INTRODUCTION

There's something inherently sad about an autograph book – 'sad' in both senses of the word. Probably any sort of memento has a certain melancholy to it, but this one's a little pitful, too. Look at the state of those stale pages, devoted to dashed and oft-illegible 'signatures' – dubious evidence that you once grabbed the briefest encounter with some kind of a hero.

That's only, mind you, if one has managed to keep something so organised as a 'book'. It's not to speak of the sorts of autographs that get scribbled onto stubs, old receipts or whatever else you could produce from your pocket before the hero in question got away from your clutches, out the door or into the lift or VIP enclosure. Autographs are for kids, really, you would think – on paper. And yet the habit persists into the adult world, much like all sorts of youthful practices. People in queues at book signings aren't so far removed from this curious fever – they seek the excuse to have a moment with someone special, and something tangible to take from it.

We all know that on some basic level a passion for football is boyish: it makes juveniles out of grown men, renders them prone to a terrible sentimentality. Go to any professional football training ground, into any changing room, and the hairy fug of testosterone and banter will leave you in no doubt that football remains a man's game. It's not massively more polite out in the stands. And yet, from whatever perch the modern fan looks out, the following of football seems to endure into adult life as a vehicle for somewhat arrested emotions – what the psychologists call latency, or projection, or displacement.

This is by way of preamble to the confession that I have, in my time, stood and waited breathlessly for footballers' autographs; and that, as a boy, the signature I coveted above all was the King's.

It was July 1980, I was nine years old, and the setting was Jurys hotel in Dublin, at that time one of the fancier spots in town, where the Liverpool FC squad were staying in advance of a pre-season friendly with Dundalk at Lansdowne Road. My father had guessed rightly that I would love the chance to fill up my autograph book, and we found the foyer at Jurys crawling with young Dublin lads who clearly had the same idea as me. There were easy pickings to be had from assorted Liverpool first-teamers and squad resting at ease in the plush seating – no bother spotting the permed heads of Phil Thompson or Terry McDermott. The roaming pack of boys into which I folded myself, though, went single-mindedly in search of Dalglish. We didn't even need to say as much – it was implicit. 'Kenny' was the big prize, the ubiquitous schoolyard hero, the top Panini card in the pack, no question.

What was it Dalglish had, the way he did the thing he did? Is it shallow to admit that he looked great? In my childish mind that was part of the deal, for sure. The Umbro Liverpool kit of that era had a terrific lustre. I'd never seen it look finer than in the Charity Shield match of 1979 when Liverpool tonked Arsenal 3-1, those red shirts aglow in the light of August, the white V-neck collars so pristine as to seem clerical. The scarlet of Dalglish's shirt found its analogue in the flush of his cheeks under his straw-coloured barnet; and stamped on his back was '7' – the luckiest of numbers, the one he'd inherited from Kevin Keegan two summers before, Keegan having moved abroad to 'better himself' at SV Hamburg.

What really counted, of course, was the football, and above all the goals – not just that Dalglish scored so many, and in such style, but also the unalloyed joy he clearly derived from it. His delighted celebrations – arms aloft, big beamer of a grin – were a major, major part of his appeal. As sportswriter Aidan Smith would reflect, years later, in the *Scotsman*, 'No one ever looked happier for having achieved the dream of every lad.'

Still – back to the aesthetics – it did seem even to my juvenile self that you had to have a bit of the artist in you to truly savour the special finesse of Dalglish's goals. Always, he chose placement over power: he seemed to just stroke the ball towards the net, yet there was audacity and nervelessness in how he bet on himself to catch the keeper out. One of his best finishes was in that Charity Shield game against Arsenal, where he ran at goal, hotly pursued, only to check right – so dumping a defender down onto his backside – before clipping a perfectly measured side-footer to the far right corner.

Watching the game, in the flurry of the moment, it seemed to me that Dalglish's placement was magic: I imagined it was a gift – as opposed to a craft, the result of long practice. I should have understood better the reasons why Dalglish was so often able to repeat the trick. In a game against Crystal Palace, for instance, surrounded by four hostile white shirts just a yard inside the box, Dalglish had dug the ball out of that mess of defenders and chipped it past the keeper onto a spot maybe six inches inside the right-hand post. Back then I just couldn't see the degree to which Dalglish actually depended on defenders to obscure the goalkeeper's sight of the ball, so that he could curl it around the whole lot of them. (I couldn't know that Dalglish, when himself a nine-year-old, had learned the trick by studying Ian McMillan, inside forward for his beloved

Glasgow Rangers.) But then, aged nine, I didn't realise Kenny Dalglish had been a professional footballer longer than I'd been alive. I could see, though, that he was at the height of his powers.

Beyond the goals, Dalglish's precise passing was a wonder, too – inspiring just as many artless playground imitations as his shooting. Then there was the inimitable way he could keep the ball at his feet with his back to goal, warding defenders away. Just five-foot-eight, Dalglish simply wouldn't be tackled until he was ready to lay the ball off to another red shirt.

Maybe the most thrilling sight, though, was when he got on his figurative bike with the ball and pedalled towards goal: supremely balanced, arms out at his sides as if ready for flight, surrounded by some sort of force field that could cause brawnier opponents to bounce off him – like Derby County's Vic Moreland who, first left for dead by a Dalglish turn, was then deposited on his backside as Dalglish shrugged him off and used his left peg to strike a rare power shot past the Derby keeper. The grin he showed us after that bravura effort was extra-radiant.

Dalglish's sunshine face, it should be said, was reserved only for such accomplishments. In football, the forward's facial expression is usually a weather vane for how his team is faring, and Dalglish's could be a grim sight if Liverpool happened to struggle. Evidently he hated to lose, so it was a good thing Liverpool didn't lose very often. Kevin Keegan had left the club having made them champions of Europe, but Dalglish had gone on to match that feat and by 1980 he seemed already, remarkably, to have eclipsed his predecessor. It wasn't just us little autograph hounds for whom Liverpool *was* Dalglish.

That night in Dublin the hunting pack of which I was part succeeded finally in cornering the great man, alone in a corridor as he emerged from his room, subdued, in a lemon-yellow V-neck sweater. (This was still the era before footballers were style icons who posed for billboard ads in little Armani pants.) Very probably he'd been asleep – his standard preparation for a game of any sort. We all knew from diligent study of *Shoot!* magazine that Dalglish was the consummate professional, a man of regular habits, a home-loving, teetotal non-smoker who prized his private peace and quiet above all else. Even so, regardless, we fell upon him, our books and scraps and pens thrust in front of his quizzical frown.

He was much like his legend had suggested – polite, terse, not hugely happy, and yet he signed for everyone. Reminded of our own manners by his, perhaps, we took our turns, accepted our trophies, then made ourselves scarce. A few hours later at Lansdowne Road, Liverpool won the Dundalk friendly 2–0, Dalglish on the scoresheet, and all was as well as it could be in the nine-year-old world.

It's December 2014, the venue a private members' establishment in central London, the occasion a 'corporate hospitality' bash – and the King is signing autographs again, though what the punters put before him is finer fare than the paper scraps we urchins presented 30-odd years ago in Dublin. This afternoon Dalglish is signing high-priced souvenir shirts, and hardback copies of his latest memoir, *My Life*.

Dalglish is over 60 now, and in decent shape, though the years are there around the eyes and the renowned ex-teetotaller looks a tad rubicund in the cheeks. It's been 25 years since his playing career formally ended, and the game has seen a few new generations of hero since. As blogger Daniel Storey has put it, 'To a generation of supporters, Dalglish will only be the Liverpool manager between Roy Hodgson and Brendan Rodgers.'

Still, when a sporting life is done there is an appreciable afterlife to be enjoyed, so long as you are the owner of a good name which has been carefully tended. For the organisers of hospitality events such as these, there is pretty good coin in offering proximity to the greats of football, or golf, or cricket.

The punters get a ringside seat for the revisiting of the legend's memories, and their own, of great and shining moments in sporting time. 'Everybody likes to hear stories,' Dalglish admits with a wry smile. All this, plus three courses and wine.

Dalglish tells the gathering that he counts himself lucky to have made his name at two great clubs, Celtic and Liverpool – clubs where he scored more than a hundred goals apiece and won trophies as a manager, too – clubs that also, in the end, would wind up hiring and then firing him as boss, having become businesses of a different sort in the years since his playing glories. It could be considered a hard day's work – playing this circuit, having to live up to the mantle of legend. You're not exactly facing a tough crowd; but then no one has ever regarded Kenny Dalglish as a born raconteur. Sean Fallon, the Sligo-born coach who discovered the teenaged Dalglish and brought him to Celtic, considered the boy to be 'something of a loner'. Phil Neal, who captained Dalglish at Liverpool and ended up having notable disagreements with him, pronounced him 'a quiet, complex sort of character'. His Liverpool and Scotland teammate Graeme Souness spoke early of Dalglish's tendency to be 'civil to those in football but dreadfully suspicious of anyone he did not know'.

Outside of his family, what Dalglish has appeared to know and loves above all is football and its peculiar culture. He's a player's man, and prefers the company of other footballing men – among whom he does not count the majority of the football media who have never kicked a ball with any distinction. Accordingly, journalists always struggled with Dalglish the player, lumbered with the task of trying to embroider his terse utterances. It got harder still after Dalglish graduated to management, where media duties are compulsory and men who were legends on the pitch can suddenly find themselves exposed to an awful lot of low-cost criticism.

The toll of all this on Dalglish, judged by his own famously high standards, was pronounced. It was at Anfield in May

1995 – when the Blackburn Rovers team he had managed for four tumultuous seasons clinched the league title at the latest possible moment – that the wider public got to see Dalglish's delighted grin in its pure state for perhaps the final time. Three years later, at Newcastle United, where Dalglish's legend suffered its first significant tarnish, the support dubbed him 'Miserable Kenny'.

'I know he was seen as a sourpuss,' his old accomplice Terry McDermott has said. 'Yet nothing could be further from the truth. Kenny was – and still is – a funny, funny man.' Let's agree that some of the funniest people we know don't always seem that way to strangers. Let's agree, too, that when it comes to evaluating the wit of footballers you probably have to be there to get it. Dalglish is certainly known to have a deathless love of the game's obligatory changing-room pranks and 'banter', though Graeme Souness has rated his gags as roughly on the level of the *Beano* or *Dandy*.

Before the corporate crowd, though, Dalglish shows himself adept at winning a laugh, not least when he's prompted to recall Scotland's failed heroics against Holland in the 1978 World Cup. Observing ruefully that one more Scottish goal that day would have earned a famous against-the-odds progression to the next round, his face corkscrews into a grin. 'So we made sure that didnae happen . . .' This crowd are delighted by the diffidence of the legend. At one point he gestures to the mounted corporate displays behind him, adorned by portraits of previous legends who have taken their turn in this format. 'Following on from Kevin again,' Dalglish observes of one such. 'He's been here before me, like he was at Liverpool . . .'

February 2016, and it's a reasonably big night out at the Ramside hotel, County Durham's top golf and spa destination. A lot of beefy lads have smartened up in dark suits, and their lasses are dressed 'glamorous', just like the formal invitations decreed. Tonight's guest of honour at this corporate-charity shindig is 'King' Kevin Keegan – a man who was a Liverpool immortal, and twice European Player of the Year at Hamburg, yet who is venerated above all round these parts for his stints as player and manager of Newcastle United, where he won precisely nothing. This, then, is a night for staunch Newcastle fans, who remember and celebrate 'legends' in the absence of any actual silverware.

Those punters who shelled out for top-whack tickets are invited to pose for a personal photo with the great man. Keegan, grey-suited and versed in these matters, waits patiently while the queuing customers nurse their tall fizzy five-quid pints and a big lad frowns and fumbles with a big digital camera. Then Keegan welcomes each fan in turn, throwing an arm round the shoulder of every one, jabbing a finger as if to say, 'He's the man!' He jokes easily with those who are most conspicuously taller than him, and gibes the occasional fan of Sunderland AFC. (This, after all, is County Durham, debatable lands when it comes to football loyalties.) Keegan's manner, though, is an index to the local esteem of him. Newcastle fans saw him as firmly on the side of the crowd: as their boss he was wont to give impromptu sermons on the mount to gatherings of support, and at times he seemed to want to put his arms around them all.

The Ramside dining-room suite is set for 30-odd tables, all of them filled. An auction of memorabilia will follow the evening's main event, prizes on offer including a Liverpool shirt signed by Kenny Dalglish. Guests have been invited to submit questions in writing for Mr Keegan, but the comedian emcee warms the room with a few of his own invention.

'Why did you leave Liverpool for Hamburg?'
'Did you used to get your perms done for free?'
'Would you like to smash Alex Ferguson in the face?'

Keegan mounts the stage to big applause and proceeds to deliver a well-rehearsed PowerPoint presentation of his life and times. Even as a player he had a lucrative sideline as a performer, and performance is the bigger part of what Keegan does these days. If Dalglish famously says little, Keegan is effusive, available, loquacious, sometimes emotional. Having made a success of most things in life, he has now, unsurprisingly, become an accomplished cabaret-style public speaker. He swears frequently – 'fooking' this and that – but only in the style of a northern comic: an affable 'Would you believe it?' punctuation in the tale of his rags-to-riches rise.

Keegan's family history being such a part of his bond with the locality, he stresses his north-east roots, how his grandfather was a coalminer from nearby Stanley who conducted himself heroically at the scene of a terrible pit disaster. Young Kevin had Durham coalfield relatives, he knew pitmen and their dialect, and he knew they were Newcastle United fans. He talks about how, as a lad, his small stature saw him struggle to get a try-out with any serious football side. He shows a snap of the contract he signed at Pegler's Brass Works, for whose reserve team he was playing when Scunthorpe United came knocking with professional terms. Keegan's was quite a life to have come from, no question: you have to say that he pulled himself up by his bootlaces. But the reason it really happened for him, he insists, is Bill Shankly, who took him to Liverpool. And the reason for their bond, he is equally adamant, is 'because Shanks was a miner' – one of four brothers raised in Glenbuck, all of whom followed football as a path to a better life. 'He felt an affinity with me,' Keegan argues. 'He maybe wanted it for me.'

This is the heart-and-soul Keegan who makes plain he hasn't forgotten where he came from. And yet, here we approach a paradox. Keegan was already a wealthy man when he came to Newcastle as a player in 1982; wealthier still when the millionaire property developer John Hall hired him to manage the club in 1992. When he riffs on a photo opportunity he shared with Tony Blair in 1995, or breaks into fluent Spanish during an anecdote about volatile Colombian striker Faustino Asprilla, anyone can see this is a successful and accomplished individual. Keegan winds up his act with a bit of motivational blather for the corporate audience; and one is reminded that he's working tonight – also that he has always seen himself as an entrepreneur businessman, at ease in this kind of company.

Thus, a certain oddness when Keegan has a go at the corrupting influence of money in football, and is keenly applauded for it. He slates Newcastle's sponsor, the payday moneylender Wonga, and its owner, the dubious sportswear billionaire Mike Ashley, and the world governing body FIFA ('THIEFA', as he dubs it). This is Keegan the moralist, wont to mutter darkly about 'the morals' of the men now running the game. 'I just see football for what it is,' he told the *Independent* in 2007, 'which is all about money.' But in casting the stone, is Keegan himself without sin?

Keegan's conspicuous roots come in handy when he talks of the traditions of the game and their supposed integrity. He is comfortable in praising the olden days. Keegan reckons the weekly quarter-of-a-million quid paid nowadays to a Wayne Rooney or a Yaya Toure is beyond the pale. 'When I played,' he told the *Guardian* in 2011, 'you never felt disconnected from the fans because you were earning maybe two to three times more than them.' But then, as a player Keegan famously had a very refined and fairly impatient sense of what his skills were really worth.

Keegan was English football's first millionaire, a pioneer in turning success on a pitch into money-printing licences on the side. Thirty years before David Beckham sold Armani pants, Keegan did his best in an era of lesser opportunity, promoting everything from football boots to Brut aftershave, breakfast cereals to road safety. Footballers just didn't have the shop-window presence in Keegan's day, the pick of channels and outlets; but, such as these were back then, Keegan filled them. Where George Best squandered all such opportunities in his unquenchable thirst for white wine, Keegan was a solid pro who caused no trouble, even inheriting some of Best's contracts.

The bonus clauses of the Premiership era clearly irk Keegan; and yet when he signed for Newcastle in 1982 he negotiated a cut of the gate money for himself. He frequently laments the ruination of the English game by overpriced foreign players; and yet his transfer record as manager of Newcastle and Fulham and Manchester City shows that his deeds don't quite match his words. Keegan might not like Rooney's wages but he was happy to have shares in Proactive, the domineering agency run by Paul Stretford that represented Rooney and fought remarkably hard for that privilege.

Keegan was and is a speculator, a good capitalist – an honest trader, for sure, but selling his skills at the best rate the market can offer. The Keegan philosophy has always been that you shouldn't begrudge a man for making a success of himself. The man himself has on many occasions made clear he doesn't expect people to obstruct him in the honest business of getting ahead. Steadfast in charity work to benefit the less fortunate, Keegan has nonetheless endorsed 'the message that life is about the survival of the strongest and the fittest'. Is there a contradiction there? Or is it all of a piece with making the best of oneself?

During a stint as columnist for the *Daily Mail* Kenny Dalglish wrote of wishing 'to reassure supporters that despite the financial rewards, no player starts out in football for money rather than enjoyment'. While making plain that players should be rewarded for success, Dalglish stressed that '[t]he only way to put in the time and dedication to be a professional player is for the first motivation to be a love of the sport, not financial'. Keegan, though, has done his utmost to suggest to the world that he thinks differently – that the sport was a vehicle for him, one for which he was utterly committed, but ultimately a business. Reflecting in his 1977 memoir on life at Liverpool he wrote: 'Football was not everything to me then, and never will be. I see my life in broader terms.'

What of Dalglish's part in the new business of the game? In his memoirs he has spoken fondly of the 'family ethos' of Celtic and 'the Liverpool way' of doing things to which he was drawn – simpler times when deals were honourably done between conscientious clubs and the working-class parents of young talent. The parasitical fug that now attends the signing of a promising youth was witnessed at its thickest back in 2002 around the figure of then-Everton prodigy Wayne Rooney. But who was the influential figure who, a court was subsequently told, allegedly discreetly advised Rooney's family to pass their boy into the care of Stretford's Proactive for representation? That would be Kenny Dalglish, while employed by Stretford in an advisory capacity.

This is no new breed of disgrace: footballers have always liked money, no more or less than most of the rest of us do. But if some kind of rot has set in – if, as Keegan asserts, the game is now 'all about money' – it has to be said that neither Keegan nor Dalglish have gone greatly out of their way to cast out the thieves from the temple. Rather – to extend the analogy – they have been decently remunerated for their respective roles in ensuring that money has kept trading across the tables.

Across 50 years the careers of Keegan and Dalglish have shadowed and mirrored one another, both for good and for ill. Now in their mid-sixties, they are elder statesmen – resemblances to their shaggy-haired Panini portraits of the 1970s long faded. Keegan now wears a trim crown of grey and a perpetually rueful mien, while Dalglish has grown a face of quintessential Glaswegian cragginess.

They are two highly talented, quietly complex men from equally unglamorous backgrounds, born in the same year, who ascended to superstardom almost in tandem. Their playing styles were notably different, as thumbnailed cannily by Dalglish: 'He ran onto flicks, while I went about my work slightly deeper.' But though as players (and again as managers) they were on opposing sides, they served the same clubs at different times and seemed not 'rivals' so much as exemplary figures in the game, capable of inspiring youngsters and fans not just by heroic feats on the pitch but by rigour and dedication on and off it. Keegan and Dalglish were football royalty, sporting kings – as intensely revered as any players these isles have produced. And yet, having made their names and reputations in the 1970s and 1980s, they would become recognisable to the next generation as top managers – albeit more fretful, troubled figures, given to big gestures and stunning departures. Both men acquired airs of enigma, as a consequence of strong-willed decisions made in private then dropped onto the heads of a startled public.

What had kept them both in football so long? The love of a club, and a principled, even romantic vision of how the game ought to be played? That's what some hardcore supporters believe, and there's evidence in their favour. But the desire to remain a big player on a big stage, the interest in a big paycheque, the resumption of old rivalries and unfinished business – these things, too, may have had their pull, serving to draw both Keegan and Dalglish into a Faustian pact.

Money had changed the game, no question. The Premiership era had seen the throwing of cash at raw talent, wagering on more-or-less instant first-team dividends, and teenagers paid lunatic sums just to warm the bench. Older fans like to evoke a lost world when football's revenues were loyally through the turnstiles, and for players there was an ineluctable process of serving time, earning one's place, a long polishing of rough talent, careers forged in old boots on old pitches in front of standing support who religiously took up their places behind metal barriers. These were careers begun on antiquated time-served business terms, years in the making: a working-class calling, the rewards of which came chiefly through the acclaim of crowds composed of people very much like oneself.

On Saturdays Jackie Milburn would work a shift at Ashington colliery then take the bus to St James' Park to play for Newcastle United. Milburn's memoir *Golden Goals* (1955) is a study in the virtues of graft, sacrifice and gratification endlessly deferred. The scholar Joyce Helen Woolridge writes with a nicely acid touch of how Milburn conjures 'the cobbled idylls of Ashington and dressing rooms populated by grand fellows who were always pals'. Football drew huge crowds yet players only saw a fraction of those gates in their pay. Football's maximum wage was capped at £20 a week, £17 in off-season. Moreover, once registered with a club, a player could not sign for any other without the permission of the one already holding his registration. This was known as the 'retain-and-transfer system', and it meant that a player was at the club's disposal, told who they were joining.

But in 1961 the players' union voted down football's wage ceiling: a sudden show of player power, a sign that players had a notion of what they were worth. (Fifty years on, Dalglish would profess that 'a career in the game has taught me the debt of gratitude we owe to those who fought so hard'.) Big-city clubs could now turn their huge gate receipts into wages: Johnny Haynes of Fulham became the first £100-a-week footballer. In 1960 George Eastham went on strike at Newcastle to force a move to Arsenal, and his PFA-sponsored legal fight finally had retain-and-transfer declared an 'unjustifiable restraint of trade' in the High Court. In this time of flux, the priorities of football's traditional support were not static either: in the 1960s a lot of the labour force had new leisure-time options, displacing the rituals of the job, the pub and the match. Still, crowds came, paid cheaply for tickets, and piled into the old, groaning terraces. From here, though, the relationship between the man on the pitch and the man on the terraces was changing, too.

Keegan and Dalglish were working-class boys, both with significant distances to travel – from Protestant Glasgow and Catholic
Doncaster – in order to realise their ambitions. As fledgling
players they were scouted and recruited and apprenticed at clubs
under respectful, well-founded systems directed by great and
doughty managers – Bill Shankly, Jock Stein.

'All players are born. Anyone who tells you that they can
make players are very stupid people.' Thus spake Shankly. But
was 'Shanks' ever wrong? If we take Kevin Keegan on his
own terms then the great Liverpool boss was certainly wide
of the mark (if not, indeed, calling Keegan stupid). In his early
memoir Keegan promoted himself unabashedly as the product of application and dedicated toil. 'If someone said I was
the greatest player in England, I would not accept it, because
I know that it isn't true ... My game is completely centred
on my work rate. I get involved for the full ninety minutes.'
The legend runs that Keegan 'made himself into a player',
whereas Dalglish's natural gift shone as if perfectly formed
from the get-go – that Dalglish was marked out for success
while Keegan had to scrap his way to it. The truth is subtly
but importantly different.

Kenny Dalglish really had to graft, but he was a thinking
player, too. He did an awful lot of hard thinking. Footballers
are easily dismissed as thoughtless yobs, and Dalglish has always
liked to recall himself as a dead loss at school. But there is such a
thing as football intelligence, and it doesn't just live in the feet,
nor can it be learned from books. It begins with watching, being
a student of behaviour on the park, comprehending that any
game of football is an ebb and flow of influences upon which
a player can assert himself. Dalglish grew up watching football
just like any other fan, with the fan's turbulent levels of anxiety
and excitement. But it wasn't long before the computer in his
head was doing a more advanced kind of processing, and he was
learning how to put choices into practice out in the hurly-burly
of a real game.

On top of this skill, though, was application, the keeping of the head, the cultivating of the body, the desire to improve and keep moving forward, even as talented contemporaries faltered or fell. 'You might not be good enough,' Dalglish would write, 'but that doesn't mean you cannot apply yourself properly and see where that takes you.' On this score, too, Dalglish was to show that he had what it took.

PART I

1

Kenneth Mathieson Dalglish

1951-67

'Our Object is: The advancement of Christ's kingdom among boys and the promotion of habits of obedience, reverence, discipline, self-respect and all that tends towards a true Christian manliness.'

Motto of the Boys' Brigade movement established in
Glasgow by William Alexander Smith (1883)

'I have always believed in discipline . . . Discipline must prevail at home if children are to behave outside. My mum and dad brought me up to believe in fundamental principles, like having good manners and knowing right from wrong.'

Kenny Dalglish (1996)

Kenny Dalglish maintains to this day that he is a lucky man, since from an early age he was looked after, encouraged in life and in sport, and taught, too, the golden rule of looking after others in turn. That as a boy Dalglish was 'football daft' is only the prerequisite for what he would make of himself: no lad can hope to get a start in football otherwise. Importantly, though a working-class boy, Dalglish was not from an unusually poor family – he had material support from his parents, disciplined people who respected both his aspiration and application.

He was born on 4 March 1951 in the Dalmarnock district of Glasgow's East End, within the so-called 'Cuningar Loop' made by the River Clyde. He had an older sister, Carol: thus, as four, they were the nuclear family. His father Bill was a diesel engineer for a motor company, with a routine as sure as the turning of the earth: 'He'd come in from his work every night,' Dalglish remembered, 'have his tea then have a sleep on the couch or in the chair.' Bill entrusted his pay packet to wife Cathy, who managed the household. It was a domestic arrangement that Dalglish was to reproduce.

Bill Dalglish was, at least, in the right line of work. Victorian Glasgow had known prosperity by the manufacture of ferries, passenger liners and steam locomotives – the city then had a shout to be the shipbuilding capital of the world. But by the 1950s the coming industries were those of the motor car, the diesel train and long-haul airliner. Patterns of both work and residence were undergoing transformation: postwar Glasgow was considered 'slum-ridden', in need of major schemes of housing clearance and reconstruction. 'Glasgow folk have been through hell,' the city's housing convener James Duncan announced in 1951. 'We are going to build so many houses that this second city will be a housing paradise on earth.' Whole inner-city districts were razed, and 100,000 new houses arose on Glasgow's peripheries. One such was Milton, and it was here – in early 1952, Kenneth Dalglish just ten months old – that his family moved north to a rented social home, a cladded apartment house. The streets of the Milton scheme were all named after Scottish islands, and it was Mingulay Street for the Dalglishes.

'Deserts wi' windaes' is how Billy Connolly characterised Glasgow's new estates in one of his early one-liners. Milton was not a superbly engineered community. It had shops and a public park, but no pubs or cinemas or other such leisure amenities, all of which were a bus ride away. But the Dalglish family had a back garden, a big deal for a boy who loved to kick a ball, as Kenny was doing keenly around the scheme from roughly the age of five. He started at Miltonbank Primary School in Scalpay Street but school, for him, would only ever be 'a way of playing football for my school team'. He was mad for kickabouts day and night – it ruled his young world.

'Everybody played football, good, bad or indifferent,' his future teammate Danny McGrain would recall. 'You'd play in the playground and you'd come home from school and end up playing in the back garden.' If not the garden, then the venue was the local park, where Dalglish and his pals had the use of a set of collapsible goalposts constructed by someone's dab-handy father out of conduit plumbing pipes. Glasgow being football daft suited the young Dalglish fine, though it meant that what he could do with a ball would have to really shine if it was to stand out.

Bill Dalglish had played the game keenly himself until an accident in which a lorry ran over his ankle. He subsumed his passion into being a staunch fan of Rangers FC, and took his boy along to Ibrox as soon as he could. Thus Dalglish became a boy bluenose, inducted into the ritual of match day – down the same passageway, to the same crush barrier, there to meet with Bill's workmates and their own boys. This was the Rangers of Sammy Baird and the South Africans Don Kitchenbrand and Johnny Hubbard. But Bill Dalglish's favourite was Ian McMillan, who signed in 1958 – an old-school inside forward, playing in 'the hole' just behind the front man, linking play between midfield and attack.

Dalglish attended a Boys' Brigade like all his peers, but in early 1963 he switched troops just so he could play for his school in the morning and Possilpark's Boys' Brigade in the afternoon. He was now at High Possil Secondary School, which had a decent football team though no pitch of its own. He drew the attention of Bobby Dinnie, a keen local coach and scout who ran Possil's YMCA team at Glenconner Park. The club had a link to Arsenal, and their scout Joe Hill came one day to have a look, identifying Dalglish as one of six promising boys worth an invite to trial at Highbury. But, as Dinnie recalled, Bill Dalglish stuck to the view that Kenny 'was his only son and he wanted to see him staying in Scotland'. This close familial instinct was to recur: Bill Dalglish had firm ideas about what his boy ought best to do.

Dalglish was 14 in 1965 when the family moved south to Broomloan Court, a new high-rise estate of 21-storey tower blocks in Govan. It was a step up as moves go, but more importantly for Dalglish the estate – hemmed by an arterial road, Ibrox, and a greyhound and speedway track – was situated right next to where Rangers trained.

The team had been dominant in Scotland, treble winners of 1964, driven by their skilful wing-half Jim Baxter. An ex-apprentice cabinet-maker and coalminer, Baxter had a penchant for taking the mickey out of opponents on the park, and some part of that 'swagger and arrogance' was impressive even to Dalglish. In a choice of heroes, though, Dalglish favoured Baxter's Scotland teammate Denis Law of Manchester United, who scored regularly and with relish but retained about him the air of his austere Aberdeen upbringing.

Dalglish undoubtedly hoped hard that Rangers, his team, would show an interest in him as a football prospect. Their chief scout Jimmy Smith had taken a few looks, but no offer was forthcoming. Rangers had a certain preference for big lads, or else lads with an obvious turn of pace; and Dalglish, despite his promise, had neither of those easy attributes. He was going to need something else to impress the talent-spotters.

Nearly finished with formal education, Dalglish made the most of its sporting options, turning out for a Glasgow Schools XI that won the national Under-15s trophy, and attending national schools trials at Glasgow's Pollok Park. Danny McGrain, also invited, would remember 'this wee guy with a bright red face . . . looking as if he'd just run a marathon'. Dalglish did not, however, make the final cut, and the manager of his Glasgow Schools team, irked on his behalf, pitched him into a game against the Scottish Schools XI, where his exertions belatedly earned him a place in the team. In May of 1966 he got run-outs in Victory Shield matches against the home nations. Playing right-half against Northern Ireland at the Glentoran Oval in Belfast, he scored twice in a 4–3 victory, and was in a 1–1 draw against England at Ibrox. The *People* newspaper picked him out as 'a brilliant ball-player'. That August he was pleased to receive an invite for a week's trial down south with Liverpool FC at Anfield, alongside his teammate George Adams. Liverpool had just become English league champions, for the second time in three seasons under the management of the former Glenbuck miner Bill Shankly.

Shankly had taken charge at Liverpool in December 1959 and instantly asserted himself, clearing out the playing squad and rebuilding it. 'I had problems trying to convince the directors that you couldn't get a good player for £3,000,' Shankly would say. But he convinced them to sanction the influential signings of Ian St John and Ron Yeats. He also initiated the redevelopment of the Anfield stadium and Melwood training ground. ('If you'd seen Anfield when I came, it was the biggest toilet in Liverpool.') His football fixations were soon clear to his players: physical fitness, and a game based on 'pass and move'. He and Liverpool were badly in need of silverware, and it took a while to come, but Shankly's obsessive, coaxing style of man management began to pay off, while TV coverage helped to make the Spion Kop end of Anfield famous – a site of tribal singing and swaying the like of which football had not seen. Once Shankly got going, his mouth and his cocky version of wit suited the Scousers rightly. They loved his bold strokes – such as putting the team into an all-scarlet kit, worn for the first time in November 1964 for a game against Anderlecht: 'Christ, the players looked like giants,' Shankly would recall in his characteristic cadences. 'And we played like giants.'

Dalglish the teenage triallist first pulled on the red shirt of giants for a Liverpool B team against Southport on 20 August 1966. His account of the trial has shifted a little down the years. He makes little of it in his first memoir, published in 1978, whereas in later versions (by which time he was recasting his career as one essentially consecrated to Liverpool FC) he speaks of Shankly giving him a lift back to digs, encouraging him to stay a few days – showing keenness to make a deal. Whatever were Shankly's impressions, what is certainly true is that Dalglish didn't stick around. Homesickness was one factor. He also had another trial in the bag at West Ham. But he couldn't stand to miss Rangers hosting Celtic in a Glasgow Cup tie on 23 August, so he caught the train back up from Lime Street and went straight to Ibrox.

He was among 76,456 that night. Rangers had spent big on Dave Smith of Aberdeen and Alex Smith of Dunfermline. But Celtic were purring on the back of their first Scottish league title in 12 years, and they handed Rangers a hammering, driven by their midfield pair of Bobby Murdoch and Bertie Auld. Billy McNeill came up from defence to score Celtic's first, after which the pacey inside forward Bobby Lennox bagged a hat-trick. For Dalglish and the Rangers support, this had begun to seem a dispiriting habit. The balance of power in the Scottish game was shifting, to the new-model Celtic being made by Jock Stein.

Stein had been an average sort of a player, for non-league Llanelli in Wales, when Celtic first recruited him in 1950 with an eye to having a reserve centre-half on the books. Stein was a Lanarkshire Protestant, though his Catholic wife had loyally 'turned' to his faith. But his father, a rock-solid Rangers man, did not favour Jock's signing for the enemy. Stein's view was that he would go wherever would save him from South Wales, better still if he could rejoin his wife and child in Scotland. Such friends as forsook him when he signed for Celtic were friends he came to count as not worth the bother.

Still, there was no wishing away the gulf between the two Glasgow clubs, nor the fact that it made football somehow less than good sport. Rangers was the club of the Queen, the Union, Scotland's Protestant majority and the Calvinist culture of the kirk, founded by Freemasons and members of the Orange Order, strongly tied to the shipyards of Govan. Glasgow Celtic was the team of Irish Catholic patriots, revolutionary Fenians and Home Rulers, begun as a charitable organisation by one Andrew Kerins from Ballymote in Sligo (subsequently 'Brother Walfrid' of the Marist order), a teaching missionary who had witnessed the Irish famine of 1845–49 and saw football as a vehicle for social work in Glasgow's East End, a means to bolster the faith and keep the flock out of the clutches of Protestant soup kitchens.

Then, as now, the sectarian hostility between Glasgow's Old Firm of Rangers and Celtic bore no real relation to church-going habits, spiritual pieties or doctrinal difference. But it was clearly a great deal to do with tribe, assumed ideas of virtue, and clinging to a fantasy of superiority – having some lesser other to hate. Thus could fundamentally non-religious people be tarred as 'Orange' or 'Fenian' varities of 'bastard', by fellow non-religionists who, as Simon Kuper deftly puts it, were 'not about to give up their ancient traditions just because they no longer believe in God'. Danny McGrain has labelled the Old Firm antagonism 'a mutual loathing society', 'a social disorder which used football to express itself'.

The antagonism was glaring, and yet when it came to recruiting players Celtic had an ecumenical view, welcoming men of whatever denomination. Until the First World War, at least, Rangers fielded Catholic players without much fuss. It was during the long tenure of manager Bill Struth, though, that Rangers scouts got into the hardened habit of asking young prospects what school they attended. Celtic's relative openness on this score gave them a competitive advantage; and to ask what would have become of Glasgow Celtic had they spurned the services of Jock Stein is to look down into a long, dark drop.

It took a full-blooded injury crisis at Celtic for Stein to get into Celtic's first XI, but once there he proved himself and retained his place. Indeed, club skipper Sean Fallon – tough, speedy, and a Sligo man like Brother Walfrid – came to pick Stein as his vice-captain, well aware that the two of them were in the autumn of their careers, wanting 'to prove to the other lads that players his age weren't washed up'. Inheriting the armband from Fallon, Stein led Celtic to a league and cup double in 1954. But three years later his playing days were ended by an ankle injury. For reasons more than Stein's ill luck, seven barren years for Celtic ensued.

Stein committed himself to pursuing a career in management, but deduced that he was unlikely to progress in that direction at Celtic, and served his apprenticeships at Dunfermline and Hibernian instead. He was a diligent student of the game, travelling to Milan to study Helenio Herrera's famous Internazionale side, impressed by the rigour of their routines if not so much by their negative football. In March 1965 Celtic, in a state of some desperation, made an approach to Stein and he became the boss, only the fourth in the club's history and the first non-Catholic.

Stein found his consigliere in Sean Fallon, whom he appointed as his assistant. Celtic already had notable players, such as the small, flame-haired crackerjack winger Jimmy Johnstone. Fallon soon showed a knack for spotting young talents such as David Hay. The player Stein liked above all was Bobby Murdoch, unfussy, composed and a peerless passer of the ball, and he moved Murdoch and Bertie Auld into a centre midfield pairing, quite an engine in the middle of the park. But Stein felt that if Celtic were to really start firing then they needed the smack of a Herrera-like stickler. He took a stiff broom to Celtic Park, imposing himself on every aspect of preparation and regimen. Fierce and inflexible, he was to become a formidable presence on the training pitch, clad in a trademark black tracksuit. He put the fear of God in the players, whether by a hard stare, a low growl, or a kicked door if it came to it. Bobby Lennox never forgot a 'pasting' Stein dished out to the whole team in the wake of a 5-1 loss to Dunfermline: 'The walls of the stadium must have been shaking ... He kept blasting us and seemed to grow bigger as he did so. I could see the big frame swinging his arms and cursing and swearing. It was terrifying.'

By 1967 the sands were running out somewhat on Kenny Dalglish's hopes for a break into football. He'd had his trial at West Ham, and their teenaged midfielder Harry Redknapp was one who noticed him – his lack of pace ('but that didn't matter') and his talent for retaining possession ('He could hold the ball as well as any man twice his size'). Still, there was no offer of provisional forms. Done with schooling now, Dalglish bounced around a few odd jobs – delivery boy, warehouse packer – before getting himself apprenticed to a joinery business five minutes' walk from home. But he was still making his big bet on football.

He had been recruited to Glasgow United's Under-16 side by manager Bob Keir and plied his trade on the club's red ash pitch at Cambuslang. It was there that Celtic's Sean Fallon came to have a look at one of Dalglish's new teammates, a forward named Victor Davidson, whose mother had written Fallon a letter in praise of her boy. Fallon saw plenty to like in Davidson, but a fair bit, too, in Dalglish – the ruddy-faced work rate, the balance, that obstinate gift for not relinquishing the ball.

Then Dalglish got a chance to play for United under the lights at Celtic's Barrowfield training ground, a game against a Celtic

XI of juvenile 'provisional signings', and his team came out on top, a 3–2 win in which he scored. Stein and Fallon were watching, and Dalglish was aware but not overawed by the presence of the big bossman. Bob Keir passed on to Dalglish an invitation from Fallon to train with Celtic at Parkhead. And yet Dalglish fought shy of relaying this offer to his father, Bill – an impatient Keir was moved to contact Bill Dalglish himself the following night. Still, Celtic's interest was not a simple matter: it was no small thing for a bluenose to sign for the Hoops. In time, Kenny Dalglish would make very clear he had no truck with the 'tens of thousands of bigots who chant at Old Firm games'. But the different complexions of the two clubs were undeniable.

'We weren't Orange but we were staunch': thus Hugh McIlvanney recalls Jock Stein describing his family's view on the Protestant faith. Stein's biographer Bob Crampsey would thumbnail his mission at Celtic as one to 'bring the virtues accepted in Scotland as Presbyterian – industry, attention to detail, consistency of performance – to a club which had all too faithfully conformed to the stereotyped image of the Gael, volatile, variable, a touch feckless'. The enduring idea of a 'Protestant work ethic' may be no more than a self-consoling fantasy. If there's anything especially Protestant about hard-earned worldly success, you hardly need to be a Prod to prize such a thing, though it may be that Prods are more inclined to give themselves points for that. Still, to propose that someone is 'culturally Protestant' – not notably observant yet somehow informed by the creed – is to say there is something about them that prizes frugality, self-discipline, hard graft and just reward; someone who might be seen to nod sagely at certain old proverbs: 'Look before you leap', 'A penny saved is a penny earned'. And culturally Protestant is what the Dalglish family surely was. Thus it was going to be a serious step across a threshold for Kenny Dalglish to accept the overtures of Celtic.

Bob Keir having met with Stein and reported back to Bill Dalglish, Sean Fallon then paid a visit to the Dalglish house.

Stein was the gaffer, but Fallon was agreed by all to possess the more facile human touch. Fallon had, in fact, promised his wife Myra an outing for their wedding anniversary, to Seamill Hydro, the fancy Ayrshire hotel to which Celtic traditionally decamped in advance of big games, or to unwind after. Fallon told Myra they would need to stop off en route, though not for too long. But at the Dalglish place Fallon entered a domestic environment he felt to be 'a bit tense' – a Rangers house, a lion's den, if you will – and so spent an hour talking round the houses while Myra fumed outside in the car. Fallon even picked up the sense that Bill Dalglish might rather his son pursue the apprenticeship in joinery.

What was the size of the lingering attachment to Rangers? Most likely Dalglish had decided that just wasn't going to happen. Rangers had been a dream for him, no doubt, and his father must have felt similar. But in later life Dalglish was to express a sanguine line that showed both his unregarded wit and his sense of priority: 'My dream was to become a professional footballer. The location was just a detail.' His father took the view that 'life is no rehearsal' and appreciated, moreover, 'the sort of footballing education I would receive under Jock Stein at Celtic'.

On 4 May 1967 Dalglish signed provisional forms with Celtic. Two days later Jimmy Johnstone scored twice for Celtic at Ibrox in a 2-2 draw that saw Celtic retain the Scottish league title.

Dalglish's contemporary and pal Daniel Fergus McGrain had also made an impression on professional scouts, yet the man from Rangers had discounted him as a prospect under the mistaken impression that McGrain's full name meant he was a Catholic. Once again, Celtic benefited from Rangers' set of blinkers. Sean Fallon enticed McGrain to Parkhead a couple of weeks before Celtic played Internazionale in Lisbon in the European Cup final, on 25 May 1967.

The game had a mismatched look: Inter were strapping specimens of Mediterranean manhood while Celtic's all-Glaswegian XI looked more than a little wan and undernourished. But Stein lined them up formidably: 4-2-4, with Auld and Murdoch in midfield, centre forwards Wallace and Chalmers dropping deep, and wingers Johnstone and Lennox drifting inside, making space for Craig and Gemmell to push up from full-back. They hammered Inter 2-1, a triumph of attacking football over the defensive Italian style known as *catenaccio*.

Days later, Rangers narrowly lost the European Cup Winners' Cup final to Bayern Munich. Sixteen-year-old Kenneth Mathieson Dalglish felt this as a blow, no doubt, but having joined the newly crowned champions of Europe he had consolations to spare. Now he and McGrain would be cleaning the boots of Celtic's 'Lisbon Lions'. It was as Celtic men, then, that Dalglish and McGrain attended the Old Firm game at Parkhead on 30 August 1967. Rangers got in front but then squandered a penalty chance. Celtic equalised, and McGrain cheered. Dalglish, still a bluenose at heart, couldn't feign any such enthusiasm. And things got worse, Celtic running out 3-1 winners. Yet, like Jock Stein, to whom he was now apprenticed, the young Dalglish was a pragmatist – a hard thinker, a tough decision-maker. He had correctly surmised 'what it took' to be a professional, to get to where he wanted to be. If he had not been handed his ideal pick of things, nonetheless he had made his choice, and crossed his personal Rubicon on the Clyde.

2

Joseph Kevin Keegan

1951-67

'Scunthorpe United can by no means be considered one of the country's most glamorous clubs.'

J. Staff, *Scunthorpe United Football Club: The Official Centenary History*

'When I discovered that Dad worked underground I imagined that if I dug far enough down in the garden, I would meet him in the pit. In no time the garden was scarred with my potholes, and whenever I got under Mum's feet she would say, "Why don't you go and look for your dad?"'

Kevin Keegan, *An Autobiography* (1977)

Born in Burnbank, Lanarkshire, in 1922, Jock Stein played his first serious football for Blantyre Victoria Juniors, and in 1942 he joined Albion Rovers as a centre-half. But the game could not be a living in itself – merely an aspiration. Aged 16, Stein had become a coalminer, a proper job, and he would graft like so for 12 years, a thousand feet underground, chiefly at the Bothwell Castle pits on the banks of the Clyde. In the years of his later fame Stein always recalled his time as a miner in tones of warmth and pride. ('I knew that wherever I went, whatever work I did, I'd never be alongside better men.') He was only voicing a familiar sentiment among coalminers: that to work underground was to share in a remarkable sense of camaraderie, solidarity and mutual dependence. The pit, as Stein saw it, was 'a place where phoneys and cheats couldn't survive for long'. Such integrity gave coalmining an unlikely romance, of sorts.

At the same time to be a miner was – clearly, and for very many men – a bloody awful and dangerous job. To work so deep in the earth was to know every day a true and terrible dark: the claustral pit shafts and vulnerable pit roofs were giants to be faced daily. The sportswriter Ken Jones has written feelingly of how his father Emlyn, a gifted footballer at 17, still couldn't live off what Merthyr Town paid him and so was forced back to the mines that he feared and hated: 'I cried because it seemed that I would have to go back down that hole.' The black seams discoloured your skin and silted their way into your lungs. In the cramped and filthy blackness, heavy with dank, fetid odour, men shared space with grinding, pitiless machinery. Coalmines got men and boys maimed, killed, mangled, mutilated – including men whom Jock Stein worked alongside.

It was remarkable how brave people could be underground. One February day in 1909 at the Burns colliery in West Stanley, County Durham, a faulty pit lamp blew up and ignited the methane-heavy atmosphere of what was known to be a 'gassy pit'. The explosion was heard and felt above ground, then flames shot from the pit fully 1,500 feet into the air. The catastrophe was plain; but there were no emergency services, no special equipment – local people just raced to the pit to do what they could, forming impromptu search parties, knowing themselves to be in danger from the flames and the carbon monoxide, having no clue of who would be where in the inferno. Frank Keegan was one man pulled out to safety, and yet, having been rescued, he went back down the mine with others and helped to bring survivors out. After 14 hours' work 30 men had been saved. 168 miners had died. But the awful day had brought forward a number of heroes, and one was Frank Keegan, grandfather of Kevin.

Any young man with his wits about him, considering all the misfortunes that might befall a man underground, would surely wish for some other road in life. But what choices were available to young men in pit villages? Bob Paisley, second oldest of four brothers, was from one such Durham village, Hetton-le-Hole, the sort of place that seemed adept at producing footballers. Bob's father Samuel worked at Hetton Lyons pit, and didn't want any of his boys to follow him down there; but viable alternatives were few. And so Bob, aged 14, began a surface job at the pit. He was there on the day his father was carried up to the surface after a bad accident. Samuel Paisley was unable to work for five years; and after Hetton Lyons was closed Samuel wouldn't let Bob go near another pit. What saved Bob Paisley was footballing ability: he was taken on first by Bishop Auckland, then, in 1939, Liverpool. War, though, intervened to put a stop to his nascent career.

For Jock Stein, the vital national duty of keeping the pits productive during wartime spared him the call to uniform. Nonetheless, as Bob Crampsey notes, Stein 'belonged to the very last generation of boys who would go down the pits in the nature of things'. The war kept the pits open, and postwar nationalisation was a reprieve for a declining industry. But when Stein went to Llanelli in 1950 it was because the Welsh club could offer him a full-time contract – football as a proper job.

Joe Keegan – son of Frank, hero of Burns pit – followed his father into the mines; and furthermore followed his dad by being a fan of Newcastle United. Hetton-le-Hole, Bob Paisley's patch, was where Joe started work, but with so many Durham pits closing down he joined a large exodus at that time and moved to Armthorpe in Doncaster, finding work at Markham Main Colliery. He had his war exemption but didn't take it, serving with pride in Burma. He and wife Doris had their first child, a daughter, in 1948; then in 1951 along came a son, born on Valentine's Day, christened Joseph Kevin. Home was a small terraced house with a coal cellar and gas mantles, a zinc bathtub in an outhouse and a toilet at the foot of the garden, by a brick wall that offered a decent surface against which to bang a football, for all that the thudding made a pain in the neck for Mrs Wild next door.

Kevin Keegan came to regard his dad as 'a typical miner', fond of a pint and a bet on the horses, a man who 'never had a bank account as long as he lived'. He was more or less addicted to his Woodbines, though chronically bronchial and short of breath – a condition that rendered him unable to work for periods, so requiring Doris to take cleaning jobs. There could be boorishness and even a bit of aggression towards his wife; but Joe Keegan was a patriot, a Labour voter, no moaner, and the owner of a particularly north-east form of assured taciturnity: he didn't say much but you always knew what he thought. Keegan would remember his dad's life lessons to be roughly these: stay out of the mines, make your own way, and look after yourself because nobody else will. 'My dad once said to me, "You're never going to go down the pit,"' Keegan remembered. His mature view of coalmining was that nobody 'should have to work that hard and risk so much danger to make a living'.

Keegan credits his father for instilling in him a self-belief; and self-belief was certainly needed. As a child, plainly titchy, Keegan suffered from croup and a wheezy chest and his family were advised to stop him playing sports. It took him quite a while and no little effort to overcome these deficits, to get to where someone would notice him, to become by some distance the greatest footballer to emerge from Doncaster, albeit via Scunthorpe.

Keegan had developed an early fascination for his dad's pit wage packet, and also understood that money was in short supply. Aged seven, eager to supplement the household income, he asked for a paper round, expressing readiness to stand on a crate so as to reach the high letterboxes. He washed cars with a pal, and sold firewood. In 1961 the family – and Kevin now had a two-year-old brother, Michael – relocated in a manner typical of the times, from Joe's miner's cottage to a spruce council house on Waverley Avenue in Balby. It was a step up, but Keegan was already resolved to keep forging ahead.

He attended St Francis Xavier Catholic Primary School, Balby, and became the class clown, borderline passer of exams, but keen on all sports and, by the age of 10, 'football daft'. Another figure who spurred him on was the headmistress, Sister Mary Oliver, who liked a kickabout herself, her habit whipping around her knees. He taught himself to jump and head by tying a football to a clothes line. His Uncle Frank gave him an old leather ball, and his first pair of second-hand Winit football boots was paid for by his dad with the proceeds from a win on the horses. There was a zeal about Keegan: it settled on an ambition to play football professionally.

The year 1961 was a meaningful moment in the history of such ambitions, which had found a forceful champion in Jimmy Hill, chairman of the Professional Footballers' Association. Hill was quite certain footballers deserved to extract more value from the sweat of their labour: 'I uphold the professional's prerogative,' he declared, 'of squeezing every penny out of his situation.'

The PFA were threatening strike action, seeking the abolition of both the £20-a-week maximum wage and the retain-and-transfer system. A landmark meeting of club delegates was held at Manchester's Grand hotel in early January of 1961. The Bury FC delegate argued that a strike on this issue was wrong, partly because he earned a good bit more than his coalminer father – that players, in other words, ought to be content with their lot. This occasioned a memorable riposte from the Bolton rep Tommy Banks, himself an ex-miner who had graduated to playing for England and advertising Gillette razorblades on the side. Banks stood and declared that coalmining was one thing – a thing he knew well – but it was quite another to pull on boots and play before avid crowds of 30,000, 'trying to stop Brother Matthews here'. Banks was gesturing to the man sitting beside him, the great Stanley Matthews, 'Wizard of the Dribble'. Banks' point was that no one's skilled labour was being properly remunerated. By all accounts Banks had a powerful effect upon the room. Liverpool FC had bussed their players to the meeting expecting them to vote down a strike, but the players caught the prevailing mood. On 18 January, Hill shook hands on a deal with the football authorities signalling the end of the maximum wage. Retain-and-transfer had a-ways still to go, but things were changing.

Keegan moved up to St Peter's Secondary School and kept playing football – also cricket and cross-country running whenever the goalposts were down. He was anxious for his chance at a trial with a proper club, but the clubs that ran the rule over him invariably decided he was just too slight and diminutive. Doncaster Boys gave him a chance, but two other lads from St Peter's got the nod. Then he was offered a trial at Coventry City, and yet his school's sports master, Mr Gormley, advised the headmaster that it was hardly worth Keegan taking the time off school 'because he will never make a footballer as long as I live'. Undeterred, Keegan went to Coventry, stayed with his Uncle Frank in Nuneaton and spent six weeks among two hundred other boys. He made it to the final two; but only one was taken on, and that was Brian Joy, not Kevin Keegan.

After this knockback Keegan had some dark nights. 'My size was beginning to haunt me. Everyone seemed to be telling me

I was too small, not strong. But I was determined not to give up.' He had found a role model, at least, in Alan Ball, whose titchiness didn't detract one bit from what he could do for Blackpool and for England. Keegan was furiously resolved in himself, quite clear whom he had to prove wrong. Adversity would be the making of him. 'My parents taught me to work for things,' he wrote in 1977, 'and I hate getting something for nothing. I never appreciate anything unless it has cost me some effort.'

He attended the local Enfield House youth club, for the football and the table tennis and the pop music clubs; and, though he found the ambience a bit rough and unnerving at times, he noted in some of the larger lads there just what a difference could be made to one's physique by diligent exercise with free weights. Keegan's readiness to pitch in was a hugely powerful engine in him. When a chance arose to undertake a sponsored 50-mile charity run from Manchester to Doncaster he was at the head of the queue to volunteer, the sort of spirited lunacy that evinced his dedication. On the day, he broke down a mile outside of Barnsley, but took his lesson from the experience and did it all again, successfully, a few months later.

Keegan left school in 1966 with O-levels in history and art, though the school hadn't thought him fit for entry given how much he messed about. Still, once again, he showed them. In July, he took a job at Pegler's Brass Works: a store clerk in charge of bathroom taps, earning £6 a week. He kept up his football with Pegler's reserve team on Saturday morning, the youth club side in the afternoon, plus a regular game for Lonsdale Hotel in the Sunday League. And that was how things went along for a year or so, until September 1967, when a young Sunday League player for Woodford Social, a furniture salesman named Bob Nellis, so admired what he saw of Keegan on the park that he spoke of him to a friend called Jeff Barker, who scouted for Fourth Division Scunthorpe United. Barker took a look at Keegan and he, too, liked the cut of the youngster.

Scunthorpe was a clean, neat town that was all about its steel-works, and had been so since 1899 when it came into being as the marriage of five villages, its football club likewise an amalgam of smaller local sides. Steel grew the town, and it grew Scunthorpe United to the point of admission to the Football League in 1950. To mark the event, the club dubbed itself 'The Iron'. In 1967 the steelworks still employed around 40 per cent of the town's population, though that summer Harold Wilson's Labour government renationalised the steel industry to form British Steel, and Scunthorpe saw change, its three main producers (Appleby-Frodingham, Lysaght's and Redbourn plants) folded into one with the attendant rationalisations. But there were still jobs. And if Scunthorpe United was going nowhere fast, the team had a support of 10,000. The club meant something to the town. It meant plenty to the fiercely focused Kevin Keegan, in his quest to prove wrong that teacher who reckoned he should stay on another two years at school and get his A-levels. There were to be plenty more in line for the same treatment.

3

The Big Leagues

1967-71

'This Keegan is a sharp, brave little lad. He gets up in the air ever so well for his size and he's as brave as a lion!'

The judgement of Tony Collins, scout for Bristol City, on watching Keegan play for Scunthorpe United in 1971

'I remember watching a [Celtic] reserve game at Lesser Hampden and this boy with a big arse and red cheeks being the standout.'

Jim Kerr, Simple Minds vocalist, on his first impressions of Kenny Dalglish

Though Celtic had taken a provisional punt on Kenny Dalglish, Jock Stein was of the view that the boy needed 'hardening'. And so, from August of 1967, Dalglish was farmed out for a season to semi-professional Cumbernauld United, a side that played on a borrowed, harrowed pitch bounded by lonely metal rails. These sorts of secondments were the Celtic way for young bucks: Danny McGrain went to Maryhill, and Dalglish's Glasgow United teammate Vic Davidson to Ashfield.

Dalglish's mission, which he had no choice but to accept, was to have lumps kicked out of him by journeymen players near their journey's end and players who had tried the big leagues but since been discarded – by has-beens and never-weres, in other words. Dalglish, the bright spark with the burning-ember cheeks, offered an obvious target for resentment. But he was plenty hardened already; shovelling shavings in the week as an apprentice joiner, and having to suck up a fair amount of hilarious banter from his elders in that line, too. Dalglish was never going to make a carpenter of any competence, but at Cumbernauld he scored 37 goals, and each time he made a keeper fetch the ball out of the net he was staking his claim at Celtic.

Come springtime Dalglish was pressing for his full professional forms, but not getting anywhere: Stein envisaged him serving out one more season in the muck and nettles at Cumbernauld. The gaffer's reservations were a lot to do with pace. Dalglish was not conspicuously 'slow', but nor was he lightning. Sean Fallon was more of a Dalglish fan, possessing at least one quality Stein lacked, namely patience. Stein 'wanted things to happen right away', was Fallon's view. 'Some boys develop more slowly than others.'

When Bill Dalglish went to Stein to press his son's case, he was issued with a veiled warning, Stein observing that Kenny would face stiff competition to start in Celtic Reserves, a side of such quality that Stein was lobbying for them to be admitted to Scotland's Second Division. Bill Dalglish's response was one that could have been foreseen by anyone familiar with his son's already notable implacability: 'I accept what you are saying, Mr Stein, but if Kenny is going to have a go he's going to have a go now.' The boy's resolve must have impressed Stein to some extent – if only in the slowly head-shaking respect of one who had decided that the dogged applicant ought to be allowed enough rope to hang himself.

Dalglish signed full professional terms with Celtic in April 1968. Cumbernauld United were readying to bid farewell to the old metal rails and open a new ground, the Ravenswood stadium. In May, Stein brought a Celtic XI along to bless the endeavour, and in his programme notes he gave an honourable mention to his new signing, Dalglish. On the park Celtic won 4-1, among the goalscorers one Luigi 'Lou' Macari, a star of Fallon's young reserve side that was also exuding promise in the likes of David Hay and George Connelly – founding members of a talent pool dubbed the 'Quality Street Gang'.

Dalglish's pal Danny McGrain successfully pressed his case for professional forms around the same time. In June the two got smart haircuts and smart blazers in order to travel with Celtic's Under-21s to the prestigious Casale Monferrato international youth tournament in Italy. In close season, too, they stuck together, meeting up in Drumchapel to kick a ball around on the blaes pitches provided by Glasgow Corporation: blaes being compacted dried red clay that was hard-wearing through the seasons if eye-watering on a windy day. Dalglish had a particular issue on which he wanted to work: how to deal with a defender harrying him from behind as the ball came to him with his back to goal. As McGrain put it, Dalglish was most fastidious about 'what kind of pass he wanted if some defender was up his backside'.

Dalglish's backside was proving to be no small thing in his development as a player. His lower centre of gravity surely contributed to the quality of balance he had, coupled with the strength in his hips and thighs, helping him to crouch possessively over the ball, shielding it, legs apart, elbows wide, destabilising his marker. If his back were to goal, what next? Try to turn with the ball at pace, or lay it off precisely to a teammate? One thing that became clear to him on the blaes pitch, with its sharp-etched summer shadows, was how to use the sun in his decision-making. Dalglish realised he could study the shadows on the ground to judge which side he would be tackled from. And if he spun away in the opposite direction, that notable backside of his made a barrier to help him leave his marker behind him in the dust.

Scunthorpe United was under new management as of October 1967 when former Norwich City player-manager Ron Ashman took charge. Ashman recruited a few of his old Norwich players to the cause, but it wasn't enough to prevent Scunthorpe's relegation to the Fourth Division in May 1968. If Kevin Keegan was to make it to the top in football, he was now going to have to do so from the league's bottom tier.

Still, he had his models and mentors. 'The thing that impresses most people about you,' first-team coach Jack Brownsword told Keegan, 'is that you are a one hundred per center . . . you always want to be first. Never lose that, because it's the biggest thing you've got going for you.' Brownsword had been a formidable full-back for The Iron, an ex-miner and a late starter in football, but one who, having made it, soldiered on into his forties, playing in 1962 when Scunthorpe finished fourth in Division Two (the champions that year Shankly's Liverpool). A hard taskmaster, Brownsword found plenty to admire in Keegan's obvious zeal.

Scunthorpe put young players through a regimen. They scrubbed boots and lavatories, cut the grass and swept the terraces, painted turnstiles and burned rubbish behind the stands. On one occasion Brownsword came upon Keegan and another lad playing head-tennis, and berated them over the proper work they should have been doing. ('You aren't here to play football!') Even in training they were often obstinately denied a ball, made instead to concentrate on fitness, a strange English fixation. Keegan found a like-minded teammate in Derek Hemstead, as keen as himself on cross-country runs, and got in the habit of running up and down the steps of the Glanford Park terraces with weights in his hands, consecrated to bulking himself up physically.

Come the summer, Keegan's pay fell from £25 per week to £15. Following the lead of older teammates, he took a plate-laying job at Appleby-Frodingham steelworks, but he would remember the way work got done in the nationalised industry as an affront to his industrious instincts: 'There was no incentive; it didn't make any difference to the workers whether they produced a million tons of steel a week or half a million tons.' (The following summer Keegan would take his summer work as a porter in a Doncaster hospital for the mentally handicapped, where he felt he could make himself properly useful.)

He made his league debut for The Iron in mid-September 1968, aged 17, on the right wing against Peterborough. A few weeks later he was pitched into a League Cup fixture with Arsenal. Gradually, he became a mainstay in the side, nearly ever-present. Gerald Sinstadt came from Granada TV to interview the promising whelp, still breathless from training, heavily accented and politely guarded about how he had found the demands of the big league. ('At first very tough, couldn't do much right, to be honest. But, the more I've played, easier it's come, y'know?') He resisted the notion that a move to a bigger team was on the cards: 'I'm getting first-team football here. Should think if I went First Division I'd struggle a bit . . .'

At the St Leger Fair in September 1970 he got to chatting by the fairground waltzer with a girl who had caught his eye: Jean Woodhouse, 16 years old and studying for her A-levels. Keegan, three years older, told her rather bashfully that he was a steelworker, since Scunthorpe United didn't seem quite the thing to impress. He guessed right: Jean's idea of a proper footballer was George Best. Keegan was saving his money and had bought himself a smart Cortina, but he wasn't getting anywhere terribly fast. Still, he ran into Jean again at the Top Rank Suite disco in Doncaster, and he set his cap at her.

Dalglish's first try-out for Celtic Reserves came against Greenock Morton, in a side largely composed of players who had, like himself, just come home from being farmed out. But Greenock were the better side, and at half-time Jock Stein barrelled into the changing room, closed each of its small windows, then erupted in a Vesuvian show of displeasure. Part of coming of age as a Celtic player was receiving the rough edge of the boss's tongue: Stein could dish out dog's abuse, the wrath sometimes physical, certain recalcitrants getting manhandled a little if it came to it. Dalglish, fastidious and a trier by nature, was aware nonetheless that he should take extra care to avoid being the object of the big man's opprobrium.

In September 1968 he had a bow for the first team, as a second-half substitute in a dead-rubber League Cup win over Hamilton Academical. (Connelly, Hay and Macari got on, too.) In the reserves, though, he was one lad among a promising batch, without an obvious best position. Vic Davidson was getting noticed by banging in the goals. Dalglish, however, was tasked by Sean Fallon with extra shooting practice, given a bag of balls and an empty goal. But he took the chore seriously, as he took everything about his football seriously, and he began to improve, with the 'single-mindedness' Fallon had noted, of which Stein could only approve.

No cocksure talent could rest easy at Stein's Celtic in the belief that they had it made. The gaffer demanded commitment and discipline, needed to see that his players recognised that and embraced it. Though Stein was a keen gambler (his best mate Tony Queen was a bookmaker) he was a strict teetotaller who invigilated his players' social habits and relied on other eyes since he couldn't be omnipresent. ('The Big Man's got spies everywhere,' lamented Jimmy Johnstone, a prime candidate for such a watch.)

Booze was a part of footballing culture, no question. Fondness for a beer wasn't an absolute bar to excellence or glory, but the game offered cautionary tales of how talent could get washed away on tides of drink. Rangers hero Jim Baxter had been indulged by a club that even settled his bar bills, but when the toll on Baxter's body became all too clear in training he was shipped out to Sunderland; and after 1967 there was little more to Baxter's career beyond the pub, a sorry waste.

Celtic's younger players, lesser targets for Stein's scrutiny, could still get up to high jinks. But Dalglish, if not totally out of this, gave the boss no cause for concern. 'Sometimes,' sportswriter Kevin McCarra would marvel years later, 'I wonder if this marvellous performer can actually have been Scottish at all, so unrelated was he to the hell-raising, self-destructive virtuosos that were once a speciality north of the border.' Fallon saw that Dalglish 'stayed away from the drink and was always focused on his football'. In time, his teammate Macari would rate Dalglish as 'an example of the way Jock instilled virtues in his players that gave them lengthy careers'.

Dalglish was still a reserves player in 1969–70, but he scored 19 goals as they helped themselves to the league and cup double. That October Stein gave him a game in midfield for the first team against Raith Rovers, and though he was nervous (in the changing room Bobby Murdoch wryly observed him pulling a boot onto the wrong foot) the vociferous support in Celtic's north terrace – locally known as 'The Jungle' – indicated approval of the new boy's passing and ball-winning.

He also travelled with the first team for European Cup fixtures, and after Celtic outclassed Don Revie's Leeds in the semis he got to go to Milan for the final against Feyenoord, carrying bags and making up the numbers in training. Celtic were well fancied to win a second European title in the San Siro, but found themselves overrun in midfield and thwarted by Feyenoord's pressing game, based on stamina and movement. The Dutch side bore down when the ball was lost, running and hunting it, yet regrouping so as never to be hit on the break. 2–1 losers on the night, Stein's great Celtic side suddenly looked to be slipping down the other side of the peak they had scaled back in 1967. They were not a poor side overnight – the likes of Murdoch, Lennox and Johnstone were still delivering the goods. But around them would have to be the lineaments of a new Celtic team. In Dalglish, Hay, Connolly, Macari *et al*, Stein surely had the materials.

There was a question, though, over whether he had the hunger to undertake the rebuilding. Matt Busby had approached Stein about the possibility of succeeding him at Old Trafford, and Stein was seriously tempted, albeit conflicted. Celtic went from Milan to a tour of the US, Canada and Bermuda, including a game in Toronto against Busby's team, Dalglish lining up against George Best. But in the midst of a subsequent match with Bari, Stein turned to Fallon in the dugout and announced that he was 'away home'. In Stein's absence the tour party's discipline cracked, and Fallon sent Bertie Auld and Tommy Gemmell home for inappropriate behaviour that the teenaged talents such as Dalglish were not meant to see.

For Dalglish, as for Keegan, as for any player who set himself proper ambitions, the pursuit of football success was a narrow path and near enough all-consuming. Yet around any corner could be moments to make all such personal goals look insignificant, and one such moment pulled Dalglish into its orbit at Ibrox on Saturday, 2 January 1971.

It was an Old Firm game and Dalglish, not in the Celtic side, was loyally in attendance in the away end, amid a crowd of 80,000 people packing the concrete-terraced stadium and behaving largely irreproachably. (Police would report only two arrests.) The game was scoreless nearing the 90th minute, when Johnstone headed Celtic in front; still, Rangers managed to bundle in a leveller. Just before the final whistle the numbers of supporters seeking to leave swelled in the standard manner. Stairway 13 was one exit point at the east end of Ibrox: five flights of steep stone steps down to the Copeland Road, split into seven lanes. It had been the scene of accidents before – a couple of fatalities, even, in 1963 – but the provision remained unchanged.

On this Saturday, as the shuffling and pressing intensified, something happened. Some would say that a child hoisted up on his father's shoulders fell off, causing a chain reaction. But whatever the cause, people toppled onto one another down the steps. One eyewitness reported that the crowd 'caved in like a pack of cards', as if 'falling into a huge hole'. Within moments, the simple ritual of exiting a football match had become a scene of suffering and death. People were crushed and asphyxiated, the breath forced out of them, some dying upright. There were 66 fatalities in all, 200 or more people injured. Dalglish had left the game at the other end of the ground and, like many, was unaware of the scale of the tragedy until the evening. His thoughts were likely similar to those of Sean Fallon: 'Everyone who had been there that day would have gone home and just thanked God their own family was safe. And you never forget about it. How could you?'

What ensued from the Ibrox Disaster was a Fatal Accident Inquiry in Glasgow, and a government-commissioned review of safety and conditions at British football grounds generally. It was a moment, too, that cast a shaming light on the sectarian acrimony between Glasgow's two great sides. The staff of both clubs had done their best on the day to help the injured and attend to the dead. Rangers players and staff attended a requiem mass given at St Andrew's Cathedral. Jock Stein reflected that the loss of life made 'bigotry and bitterness seem sordid little things'. But there was to be no great epiphany or redemption, no lasting transformation of the easy and deep-running hatreds between Rangers and Celtic. If life was bigger than the game, the game still had a driving force all of its own. 'People cared about the game before the disaster,' Daniel Harris would observe astutely in a *Guardian* retrospective, 'and people cared about the game after the disaster, because it was, and is, impossible for them not to.'

Jock Stein's courtship dance with Manchester United had become something of a minuet by February 1971, and Celtic's board, wised up to what was going on, were increasingly thin-lipped, expecting Stein to respect the money he was on and show loyalty to his club. The players were spooked, and Billy McNeill was deputed to let Stein know so. In mid-April Stein and Matt Busby met at a motorway service station where terms of the succession were more or less agreed. And yet, within 48 hours that deal was off, to Busby's considerable pique. Jock's wife Jean didn't want to leave Glasgow; but then nor did Jock.

Celtic Reserves wrapped up a league and cup treble, Dalglish bagging 23 goals in a free-scoring side, getting four of the 10-2 aggregate that the team inflicted on Rangers in the Reserve Cup final. He was emerging from the shadow of Vic Davidson and Lou Macari – though Macari wrote his name in lights with a fine opportunist goal in a replayed first-team cup final that Celtic won 2-1. All goals were to the good, but vital goals put a sign on a player. Still, Dalglish was taking the big chances that came his way. In the first team for a testimonial at Kilmarnock, he played up front and grabbed a double hat-trick – a rash of goals Stein could no longer ignore. He was marked for the first team now.

Scunthorpe's young Keegan was still being watched keenly, the lower leagues being a perfectly viable pool of talent for top clubs to replenish their squads. The local papers continued to look for eye-catching links between Keegan and First Division outfits, but the strongest declared interest was from Preston North End, soon to be Division Three champions but not so very much higher in the football stratosphere than The Iron.

As it happened, Preston couldn't get their money offer quite up to scratch, so Keegan's wait endured.

Would anyone come in for Scunthorpe's number eight? Or was he 'just another busy midfield player', as Everton manager Harry Catterick had pronounced? Jack Brownsword believed Keegan was top-flight quality; and Ron Ashman believed in Keegan's value to the club as a sell-on if nothing else – he could see £25,000 there, for sure. Still, as the spring of 1971 rolled round, Keegan was moodily of the view that his big chance might have gone by, that there was no one else left to take a look at him. In fact, he had already been seen, weighed in the balance, and judged worthy.

The scouting operation at Liverpool FC consisted of Andy Beattie, whom Bill Shankly had once assisted as manager of Huddersfield, and Geoff Twentyman, an ex-wrestler doggedly ready to drive Shankly's old and dilapidated orange Cortina up and down the country in pursuit of a tip on a promising player. Twentyman kept a detailed ledger, with data and terse observations of the prospects he watched. Scunthorpe's Keegan he had quietly seen and rated as having 'a lot of promise'. Andy Beattie added a note to the ledger, that the lad would be wasted in midfield: 'No 8 might be better as a forward.' Shankly knew of Preston's interest in Keegan because he rated their scout Peter Doherty. He took a look himself when Scunthorpe came to Goodison Park to play Tranmere in an FA Cup tie on neutral ground. And for Shankly, Keegan ticked a lot of boxes. He was looking to replace Ian Callaghan in midfield. Twentyman felt Shankly preferred 'locally based lads', northerners who could settle quickly in the area and with the fan base; and Scunthorpe wasn't so far away if you shoved Manchester and Leeds out of the road.

By 1971 Shankly had masterminded many successful changes at Liverpool, but he had also gone six years without winning anything, and the team was now looking at a fifth-place finish. A team such as Liverpool – the Liverpool of Shankly's grand dreams – could only mark so much failure down to the cost of transition. Shankly's big gambits in the transfer market, though, had proved to be dicey. In 1967 he paid Chelsea near a hundred grand for their target man Tony Hateley; but Hateley was not the target man Shankly needed. The following year he splashed £110,000 on Alun Evans, Britain's most expensive teenager, but three years on the investment hadn't matured.

It was a humiliating loss to Second Division Watford in an FA Cup quarter-final in February 1970 that proved the crux. Shankly had been loyal to the side he had built, shy of dropping or disappointing players he had brought along. But that side was ageing: Ian St John, Ron Yeats and Peter Thompson were at the tail end of their careers. Bob Paisley, Shankly's right-hand man, felt that Liverpool needed to slough off a bit of excess sentiment.

In Ray Clemence they had a quality keeper. The defence of Chris Lawler, Alec Lindsay, marshal Tommy Smith and big stopper Larry Lloyd was sound. Emlyn Hughes had promise, though he needed to find his best position. Steve Heighway, a gifted young winger who also carried the relatively cerebral air of a college graduate, had just come through, and he and Brian Hall gave the midfield width. But up front, goals were a problem for Liverpool. In November 1970 they paid another £110,000, for Cardiff's John Toshack, and he was soon scoring against the big sides – Everton, Leeds, Arsenal. But Toshack needed a strike partner.

On 3 May 1971 Scunthorpe accepted Liverpool's offer of £32,500 for Keegan. Ron Ashman took his departing player on the four-hour drive over the Pennines. Keegan had smartened himself for the big day, buying a new tie, and as it transpired he looked a good deal smarter than Anfield, where the main stand was undergoing renovation and club business was being conducted in Horsa huts out in the car park. On arrival, Keegan had nowhere to sit but on a dustbin; so he perched there, chit-chatting with Ashman, awaiting his audience. Eventually Shankly hastened out of a hut, pumped Keegan's hand, then drove him down to the dockside for his medical. Shankly personally invigilated this procedure like a canny headmaster who wouldn't be fooled. But when Keegan tugged his shirt off, Shankly – with his youth leader's regard for boys who kept themselves in shape – was properly stunned by the young man's physique: 'Jesus, son, but you're built like a tank!' Keegan's long hours spent hefting weights and running up and down stone steps were at last repaid, with interest.

In terms of the financial package, Liverpool's offer didn't feel to Keegan like so very much of a step up from Scunthorpe: he was emboldened to ask Shankly for £5 more per week. 'I have to better myself,' he stressed, and Shankly took that on board. Shankly liked his players to have passion, and the right character, and Keegan's seriousness struck him as being of that sort. Keegan very quickly felt that he had met someone whose concern for him could prove transformative – who recognised all the virtues he had consecrated himself to, whose avidity was a full-blown and florid version of his own. It was an auspicious day for a young player, no doubt, a meeting with a remarkable man. And yet it was equally true to say that Bill Shankly had never before met anybody quite like Kevin Keegan.

That weekend Liverpool met league champions Arsenal in the FA Cup final, and contested it keenly, but could not prevent the north London side completing the double. Keegan watched the game, with his girlfriend Jean Woodhouse at his side, conscious of being still on the threshold of the big club he had joined. Shankly's manners, at least, he could understand. Liverpool's losing team came home to huge crowds at St George's Hall, where Shankly surveyed the gathering and remarked that it was 'questionable if Chairman Mao of China could have arranged such a show of strength as you have shown yesterday and today'.

Once pre-season was under way at Melwood, Keegan found himself under the scrutiny of a new drill sergeant: Ronnie 'Bugsy' Moran, a pugnacious Crosby-born ex-captain of the first team, who had joined Liverpool's coaching staff on retirement and now had the reserve side under his cosh. Keegan soon got a typical Moran tongue-lashing for not being a proper mid-fielder, not tracking back. Where he won points, however, was by making a mark in an advanced role. Like Jack Brownsword, Moran could see that Keegan had a great engine in him – a buzzing player who scrapped for every ball, who left nothing in the locker and everything out on the park. At times he ran with his tongue out, a natural trait that affirmed his image of hound-like enthusiasm. But just as impressive were the skills – the quick turn, the handy touch with the outside of his right boot. Moran told Shankly they had an attacker on their books, and in the final 'bounce game' of pre-season Keegan started for the first XI against the reserves and bagged a hat-trick.

Liverpool were to host Nottingham Forest on opening day, and Shankly surprised everyone, including Keegan, by picking his new Fourth Division recruit to start. 'I have not the slightest doubt about playing him,' he told reporters. In the event Keegan nearly missed his big day, having crammed his whole family plus Jean into his Cortina only to misjudge the journey time to Anfield – more accustomed to the easy drive to Scunthorpe, caught unawares by the size of the throng around Liverpool's ground. But he made it with a few minutes to spare, Shankly forgave him, he pulled on the red number seven shirt and ran out to face the roar of the Kop that, already, was chanting his name.

3.12pm, Saturday, 14 August 1971, Anfield

From the first whistle Keegan was running, looking to get into the game, to get on the end of something. With 12 minutes on the clock he was poised on the edge of the six-yard area when Peter Thompson crossed from the right. Keegan readied himself for a strike fit to burst the net – but the contact he made wasn't true and the ball only bobbled off his shin. It bobbled, still, clean past the Forest goalkeeper and across the line.

'Jammy bastard!' was heard amid the cries of general delight from the terraces. Keegan leapt and punched the air, his own fledgling trademark – for they all count, however they're scored, and when after the game a reporter suggested there had been a big slice of luck Keegan was as cheerful about the aspersion as one who had lately felt the fortunes moving his way. 'Don't say that! It went into the right place, didn't it?'

4.25pm, Saturday, 14 August 1971, Ibrox

Celtic were at Rangers in the League Cup, leading 1-0 when John 'Yogi' Hughes was felled from behind in the box – penalty kick. Much to his surprise Dalglish was told by Billy McNeill to take it. The portly photographers duly shambled and clattered their way to positions behind the goal, where Celtic's away support were making the expected din. For them, of course, the penalty award was in itself a goal to the good. *Gotta score, better score, dinnae ya miss it ya bassa . . .* 'I was nervous to say the least,' Dalglish would remember of the build-up.

Having placed the ball on the spot, he suddenly stooped to retie his laces – an act rarely seen outside of Pelé at the 1970 World Cup. But Dalglish had, as ever, done his homework: he knew that Rangers keeper Peter McCloy defaulted to dive to his right for a right-footed penalty taker. Dalglish jogged forward and side-footed the ball to McCloy's left. The net billowed – Dalglish's first senior goal for Celtic, his arms immediately up in delight, living the dream of every young lad.

4

Almost Famous

1971-73

'The whole commercialisation of footballers is still in infancy. Nobody yet realises the millions of people out there, all fanatics, all untapped, all interested in anything to do with a famous footballer.'

An associate of Tottenham Hotspur's Martin Chivers, quoted in *The Glory Game* by Hunter Davies, 1971

'Part of Liverpool's success in the 1960s and 1970s was built around the socialist ethic of collective effort with equal wages and no prima donnas. Liverpool supporters warmed to this all-red "political correctness". There was no room for anyone thinking he was above anyone else.'

Andrew Ward with John Williams, 'Bill Shankly and Liverpool', in *Passing Rhythms: Liverpool FC and the Transformation of Football* (2001)

There was plenty of good football to see in the English First Division of 1971-72, and yet an increasingly troublesome minority were coming along to the games not to watch but to goad and fight with elements of the other team's support. For some time the problem had been sufficient to provoke questions in the House of Commons. 'I am somewhat tired of making statements on this subject,' declared sports minister Denis Howell in October 1969, 'because, personally, I do not believe that this indiscipline and crowd hooliganism has very much, if anything, to do with sport in general and football in particular. It goes much deeper than that.'

Violent incidents at football matches were increasing steadily: menacing rowdiness by groups of fans in or around the ground, rucks on the special trains carrying fans to games, the rituals of antagonistic chanting, weapons other than fists employed, including missiles thrown at the pitch or the officials. On Friday, 20 August 1971 Anfield played host to Arsenal versus Manchester United, since United were banned from playing their first two home matches of the season – punishment for those violent elements having thrown knives into an away section at the end of the previous season.

Young men banding into gangs for the express purpose of fomenting violence was not some new breed of disgrace in postwar Britain. 'Youth culture' had thrown up a number of variants already. But by 1971 a new sort of problem attached to football was uncomfortably clear. The question was aired publicly, in newspapers, in the House of Commons. How could grown men carry on like so? Where did this aggression come from? How could the exercise of authority, or self-respect, have sunk so low? Sociological studies were soon trying to find 'the roots of hooliganism' within wider social problems, such as adverse economic conditions. Most hooligans who made themselves available for interview resisted that explanation. They spoke of loving a piss–up and a punch–up. Braggadocio or not, this was the language of young men who prized toughness above all else, and made it the price of admission to a gang, a self-sustaining homosocial group that didn't recognise any supposedly wiser or disapproving heads. The gang was the model, its bonds strengthened by a hatred of rival gangs, exemplified by defence of territory. The great stage for this, then, was awayday. In April 1972 Manchester United's travelling fans, the 'Red Army' or 'Stretford Enders' (self-styled 'best fighters in the land') came to London for an Arsenal game and ran amok in north London. If a lot of 'hooliganism' was swagger and front and exhilaration, real violence certainly happened, and a real solution was required.

Under Shankly Liverpool had built among staff and players a way of doing things, a 'Liverpool way' founded on continuity of staff and a commitment to fostering best practice. Behind Shankly and Bob Paisley were Ronnie Moran, head of youth development Tom Saunders, and chief coach Reuben Bennett. It was a machine operation of sorts, and that machine began to put hours into Kevin Keegan, as willing and apt a vessel for the process as could be imagined.

The players' routine was well established: report to Anfield, get on the bus to Melwood, get stripped and ready, whereupon – as team captain Tommy Smith would recall, amusedly – 'We got fit and played five-a-side, five-a-side ...' Shankly was fiercely focused on a handful of principles: giving and receiving the pass, instantly controlling the ball, being aware of your place in the game, and making yourself an option going forward. The five-a-sides were more than just a competitive kickabout (though Shankly was always tracksuited and looking to get in the game). The desired outcome was that everything be faster and sharper, each player twisting and turning on the turf like a boxer. It was typical of Shankly that Liverpool fans were permitted to observe proceedings at Melwood, though they saw little in the way of magic. The point was that the courtesy cemented Shankly's remarkable communion with the support, of which Keegan became especially conscious on train journeys between London fixtures: Shankly 'would bring fans into our carriage and talk to them all the way home. When we kidded him on about the supporters disturbing our rest, he would roar: "That is who you are playing for, boys. Those people are what this great game is all about.'"

Next to Paisley and Moran, Shankly was not so much a trainer of players as a motivator. After three games in the number seven shirt Keegan was assured by Shanks that he would soon be playing for England. It was partly power of positive thinking, but a perfectly reasonable prediction, too. A goal in a win over Leicester, Keegan barrelling home a Toshack header, pointed to the prospect of the two making a useful collaboration. With other teammates, though, there was an edge. Keegan's irre-pressibility saw him attempting an occasional wisecrack during Shankly's orations at Friday team meetings. For this he was dubbed 'Andy McDaft' by Tommy Smith.

The skipper, nicknamed 'Smidge', son of a Liverpool docker, had survived the post-Watford cull of 1970 to become the rock of the side. Indeed, Shankly had said of Smith that he wasn't born so much as 'quarried'. He was known to intimidate on the park, and also around Anfield, where he pointedly ensured that no player got above themselves. Keegan, accordingly, crossed his sights. Keegan, in turn, felt that Smith was 'the club bully'. In due course they came to blows at Melwood one day, Keegan not backing down, showing himself tough enough, though he would admit to feeling relief that the fight was broken up by others.

With Shankly in his corner Keegan had all the support he really needed. There was, though, a small matter between the two that blew up at an early stage. 'Good players don't get injured,' was one of Shankly's homilies, and Liverpool could get remarkably uninterested in players who made themselves una-vailable for selection. In advance of a game at Stoke, however, Keegan felt a niggle in his left foot, such that he declared himself unfit, and Shankly let him know he thought this was feigned. Keegan, though, felt the insult to his marrow and walked out of Anfield directly; only a talking-to from his dad got his head straightened sufficiently to return. Shankly, the man manager, seemed to realise that he had run into something irreducible in Keegan: he pretended nothing had happened, proposing instead that the club do something about the clutch on Keegan's recently acquired Ford Capri. It gave them both a laugh, a story, for later years. And yet, a real issue about Keegan's *amour-propre* had been made clear.

Keegan's first season was one in which Shankly was uncommonly desperate for silverware. They entered the Cup Winners' Cup as a result of Arsenal's double but drew Bayern Munich, managing a goalless draw at Anfield but losing at Bayern. Toshack was out with injury for a while. Then after Christmas came a slump in form. But once Toshack was repaired, his partnership with Keegan began to look like a really potent pairing of little and large: Toshack holding the ball up or knocking it down; Keegan anticipating and darting about in order to latch on, or else dive fearlessly into low headers of his own. Keegan had made a big difference to Liverpool.

In April of 1972 they thumped Manchester United at Old Trafford, and went on to run Derby to the wire for the league title, which would have been theirs if they had beaten Arsenal at Highbury on the last day. It was to no avail: Toshack suffered a disallowed goal two minutes from time. But the travelling fans could see Keegan busting a gut. His first Liverpool season ended trophy-less, then. But he hadn't joined a club groaning with silverware – he wasn't under pressure that way. He had made a fine start, and intended to bring winning ways of his own to bear. In the summer of 1972 he got engaged to Jean Woodhouse. She moved west from Doncaster to digs in Liverpool, found work as a tax collector in Bootle, and resolved to pass her driving test. It was serious.

Keegan's first run-out in England colours came soon enough, albeit at under-23 level: a game against Scotland at Derby's Baseball Ground on 16 February 1972, two days after he turned 21. The pitch was a horrendous mud heap, but the game a decently fought 2-2 draw, Southampton's Mick Channon scoring a brace for England. Scotland's replies both came from Kenny Dalglish, whose performance was rated by watching experts as a thing of notable grace in bog-standard conditions. One such was Shankly. 'Christ, what a player!' he told a confidant. Afterwards, Norman Giller of the *Daily Express*, hanging about in hope outside the changing room, collared Dalglish to get his opinion of that poor pitch. 'Nae comment,' was all Giller got for his efforts. 'Well done,' observed Giller's fellow pressman Ian Archer of the Glasgow *Herald*. 'You got two words out of him, which is a record.'

The goalscoring prowess was a mark of how Dalglish had found his first-team spot at Celtic as an inside forward. League goals were coming easy to him, including a hat-trick against Dundee: he would have 23 by season's end. His first chance of pro silverware went begging, though, when Celtic took a 4-1 beating off unfancied Partick Thistle in the League Cup final, and Dalglish won plaudits – but no self-satisfaction – by scoring the elegant consolation. Over in Malta for a European Cup game against Sliema Wanderers, Dalglish was told by Stein that he had been selected for the national squad by Scotland's new boss Tommy Docherty. He got his first full cap as sub in a 1-0 win over Belgium in a European Championship qualifier.

Celtic motored towards a seventh consecutive Scottish league title; the Scottish Cup was added in May with a 6-1 whalloping of Hibs; and yet the key test for the club, the standard they had set themselves, was the European Cup. They made it to another semi-final after a fine lobbed goal by Macari got them past Ujpest Dozsa. Inter Milan, the old enemy, awaited, and the tie was decided by a penalty shoot-out, Dalglish unable to participate since he had been replaced by Dixie Deans, who fired Celtic's first penalty far over the bar – a miss that proved decisive.

Despite the disappointment, the Celtic players felt they had achieved enough to merit a cash bonus – a grand, perhaps. They got nothing. Macari, feeling fairly confident, sought a meeting with Stein about a new contract. He got a £5 raise on his £50 a week. That was decent money in Glasgow; but in England you had footballers earning 10 times that at clubs sporting not a shred of Celtic's successes. The hard truth was that footballers just got paid better down south. As of September 1971 Celtic had a new chairman in Desmond White, who gave no sign of wanting to put more of the club's turnstile revenue onto the pitch or into the players' pockets.

Dalglish was not yet pressing his case in the manner of Macari: he remained focused on his self-improvement. His presence off the pitch was recessive; he still lived with his parents, drove a modest car, and ruled himself out of the heavy-duty drinking sessions into which likelier lads such as Dixie Deans tried to draft him. If he did join the lads on the regular Monday night jaunts to Joanna's Disco, invariably he dropped a shoulder early doors. He was comfortable, though, at the Beechwood Bar near Hampden Park, where the Celtic squad would eat lunch. Stein and Fallon had adopted the Beechwood as it was only down the road from their homes in King's Park. The landlord was Pat Harkins, and his teenaged daughter Marina helped out round the place on occasions. She caught the eye of Dalglish, an interest that was returned, and shortly after her 17th birthday the two had their first date, Dalglish giving it the works – a Disney movie, *The Million Dollar Duck*, followed by a fish supper.

Scotland were booked to tour South America in the summer of 1972 and Dalglish – along with teammates Macari, McNeill, Murdoch and Johnstone – got the summons from Tommy

Docherty. Jock Stein, though, thought the trip too far, the itinerary too long: he wanted his boys properly rested in close season. And so the Celtic cohort stayed put in Glasgow – except, that is, for Macari, evidently keen on asserting himself. Out in Brazil among a Scotland squad bristling with players who now plied their trade in England – 'Anglos', in the parlance – Macari picked up that scent of how much better remunerated were the men down south.

November 1972 brought Dalglish's first goal for Scotland, two minutes into a World Cup qualifier versus Denmark: George Graham squared from the left and Dalglish swung a left peg to convert. The qualifying group was an oddity, just three teams and winners take all, but Scotland were now well set to go through and Dalglish was repaying Docherty's trust. The following month, however, Manchester United poached Docherty, having found Frank O'Farrell to be not quite the substitute for Matt Busby they had hoped Jock Stein would be.

Docherty's first target for acquisition was Macari. Liverpool were interested, too, Shankly offering Macari £180 a week plus 5 per cent of the transfer fee. But in January Macari signed for United, bagging £200 a week and his 5 per cent of a Scottish record transfer fee of £200,000. Stein had done good business. But the Macari move suggested that clubs in a hurry to get somewhere looked to buy quality players off the shelf rather than develop them within their own ranks. And Desmond White's Celtic were not buyers; rather, they suddenly looked like a selling club.

Celtic's season was good but not ideal. In Europe, Dalglish scored a composed brace in a 2-1 home win over Ujpest Dozsa, but Celtic were done 3-0 in the return. He bagged a trademark low thumper in the League Cup final against Hibs but Celtic lost; and he scored against Rangers in the Scottish Cup final, too, yet Rangers pinched that 3-2. The consolation was sizeable: in the league Dalglish scored 41 times, the last at Easter Road on the final day, a 3-0 win that secured the title over Rangers by a point. Dalglish was a star now. Sportswriter John Rafferty hailed him as 'the very epitome of the old fetch-and-carry inside-forward'.

On 14 February 1973 Scotland's new boss Willie Ormond led the side into the Scottish FA's centenary match against England at Hampden Park. Ormond's team, however, was a largely 'Anglo' selection, with five players from Manchester United alone, and captain Billy Bremner at Leeds. There were only two domestic league players, with Dalglish the sole Celtic man. Keegan had got a couple of starts for England in World Cup qualifiers against Wales, but for this game Mick Channon took Keegan's place in a forward line alongside Allan Clarke and Martin Chivers, and the three of them filled their boots. On a brutally frosty surface Scotland were seen off 5-0. The Hampden Park crowd – routinely hostile to any players they saw as not pulling their weight for Scotland, and to Anglos especially – made their displeasure felt.

In his first forays with England, Keegan had soon learned just how different were its requirements to the Liverpool set-up he knew – how club men had to fit themselves into the unfamiliar format of a national team, sometimes in the manner of square pegs. Keegan, though, liked to play his preferred game, and the England dispensation had him hankering for Liverpool and Shanks. Still, he was proud to make the big step up and wear the shirt: it was Sir Alf Ramsey who picked him first in November 1972, for a side still captained by Bobby Moore – umbilical links to England's World Cup victory six years previously.

Making the acquaintance of Moore was to have a galvanic effect on Keegan's fortunes, for reasons only tangentially to do with football. In the TV era, the game now offered considerable opportunities for players who had the right profile and were keen to exploit it. Moore had done much careful cultivating of his image, and wasn't ashamed of that. 'The song says: Who wants to be a millionaire?' Moore wrote in his first memoir. 'Well, I do. And don't you too?' Keegan, by now a recognisable figure to local and national press, was certainly interested, and wanted the attention.

Years before Keegan wheedled an extra fiver a week out of Shankly, Moore was 'one of the first to ask West Ham for more money', and was proud of that fact. He had the extra assets of a newspaper column, endorsement deals, other bits of business outside football (the resultant revenues directed through Bobby Moore Ltd); and he evinced a love of the finer things that a boy from Barking, Essex, might spend his money on: a white Jaguar, a wardrobe of sharp suits, above all his purpose-built home, 'Morlands', in Chigwell, with its porch of white classical pillars.

Moore, seeing Keegan was a coming man, advised him to get his business affairs in good order. As Keegan recalled, 'He told me: "You're going to get lots of offers, I had three businesses myself. I had a nightclub. Didn't do well with it. I had a leather business. Didn't do well. I had a sports shop next to the West Ham ground. Did well with it. Always stick to what you know."' Moore had an endorsement deal with the toy maker Mettoy, and put in a good word such that Keegan soon had his printed signature on a line of plastic footballs for kids.

The existing glamour figure at Liverpool, chief beneficiary of endorsement opportunities, was Steve Heighway, a presentable fellow whose game was lit up by flair. Heighway, though, had noticed Keegan's desire to cut a *bella figura* in the fashions of the day ('flared trousers, huge collars and platform shoes'). He read this as an index of a deeper desire to be noticed. 'Kevin's ambitions were far beyond what mine were,' Heighway later observed. 'He was far more confident in his ability than I was and believed he could achieve anything that he set out to achieve.'

To make himself into a business, though, Keegan needed business associates. The first man he trusted to run his affairs was Victor Huglin, boss of a Liverpool carpet warehouse. But Huglin's clout only carried so far. Keegan began to run his own fan club out of the Liverpool junk shop of a man called Lennie Lisbon ('Lennie the Junk') and formed his own company, Nageek Enterprises. In November 1972 he released a pop single: a rather plodding, mournful number about the pressures of fame, entitled 'It Ain't Easy'. He had secured a ghosted newspaper column for the *Daily Express*, and was exhibiting great readiness to jump in his car and open supermarkets countrywide.

None of this was what Bill Shankly usually permitted of his players. 'Shanks didn't want Kevin spending all his time opening shops,' Ian Callaghan recalled. And yet teammates could sense that the gaffer was more or less turning a blind eye to Keegan's extracurricular activities. Shankly 'never said a word to Kevin', in Steve Heighway's recall. 'But then he always treated him like his adopted son.' That attitude would surely have been sharply different had off-field fripperies begun to take a toll on Keegan's performances in red. But Keegan gave Shankly no such cause for concern – or, to put it another way, he was not George Best.

Best had taken Bobby Moore's example to another tier in his successful modelling career, his string of fashion boutiques and endorsements for hair tonic, chewing gum and 'Stylo Matchmaker' boots. But Best's incentives weren't really money or material things. His true tastes were traditional working–class Belfast, itemised by novelist and Best biographer Gordon Burn as 'the bird, the boozer, the puzzle book and the gee-gees'. If this added up to an ideal life for a certain type of lad, it wasn't what Best's image was meant to be selling. Moreover, one of those pastimes was becoming consuming – and it wasn't 'screwing', as he charmingly called it. Rather, Best's addiction to alcohol was about to swallow up everything else, his ambitions dissipating as the monotonous habits of the drunkard took charge.

In May 1972 Best had repaired to Marbella and briefly threatened retirement. That November, in a nightclub fracas, he fractured a girl's nose. The press could smell that he was going off the rails. His decline made a vacancy for a new pop star sort of footballer, one who knew better how to stay out of bother. That same November Keegan signed with agent Paul Ziff and the sports PR firm Public Eye Enterprises, stepping up the promotion of his personality for commercial purposes. 'My name is everything I've got,' Keegan would write, with the zeal that marked him out.

Liverpool led Division One from mid-September 1972 until mid-February 1973 when back-to-back defeats saw them slip to second. But Keegan scored a winner over Ipswich that got them back on top, where they stayed. When his strike five minutes from time sealed a 2–0 win against Leeds at Anfield on Easter Monday, the job was all but done, for Arsenal could overhaul them only on goal average. The following Saturday, a 0–0 draw with Leicester was sufficient for Liverpool to win their third league title under Shankly, Keegan's first piece of career silver.

The chance for a second followed hard upon, as Liverpool faced Borussia Moenchengladbach in the two-legged final of the UEFA Cup. The first game at Anfield in early May was washed out, and Toshack, lately sidelined, had not been picked to start that one. But he was recalled for the rearranged tie, and it was his dependable flick from a cross that allowed Keegan to hurl himself headlong and open the scoring. Toshack next knocked on an Emlyn Hughes header for Keegan to net the second, and Larry Lloyd headed in a Keegan corner to make it 3–0. It finished like so, Keegan even missing a penalty, which didn't seem so crucial until the return leg when Borussia – a far sterner proposition at home, directed by midfield supremo Gunter Netzer – went 2–0 up in the first half. But Tommy Smith led a rearguard action, the Germans ran themselves out, and Liverpool got home.

A crowd of 250,000 welcomed the team back to the city, and Shankly outdid himself in praise of them, 'the greatest fans in the world'. Keegan was now familiar enough with Shankly's actorly, preacherly style, but on this occasion the boss surpassed himself. 'The reason we have won,' Shankly told his congregation, 'is because you believe and we believe – it is faith.' There was something to that, if not quite so much as Keegan's goals and Smith's thou-shalt-not-pass defending over the two legs.

A triumphant season's work, then. And yet with regard to the fruits of his labour, Keegan felt 'bitterly disappointed'. His bonus reward for 10 months of graft in which he had made a substantial contribution to putting two trophies on the table was £2,000 – £400 after top-rate income tax. Keegan was only just beginning to reckon with the tax liability from his first season in Division One, and didn't care one bit for the size of bite that the government was taking from his pay packet – its cold-water effect on the thrill of doing well and bettering oneself.

Among the footballing profession Keegan's views were in the majority. The young Tottenham defender Steve Perryman had different and 'very strong' views on tax ('It's got to be paid') – or so he told the author Hunter Davies, who had spent the 1971-72 season at close quarters with Bill Nicholson's Spurs team for a book-length study entitled *The Glory Game*. Three-quarters of Perryman's teammates, however, were inclined to vote Tory, albeit in an 'apathetic' manner, and most intended to send their children to fee-paying schools. While footballers remained uniformly the products of working-class upbringings, most didn't plan on keeping to their station in life. Once they had set themselves to achieving certain ambitions, it was no small thing to tell them they shouldn't.

In his 1977 memoir Keegan would muse that he thought Bill Shankly could have been 'a great socialist leader'. No doubt he was gesturing to Shankly's working-class manners, his wit and popular touch. But motivating a team of elite sportsmen to defeat rival teams of elite sportsmen bears no relationship to the game of politics. Shankly himself conceded as much: 'The socialism I believe in is not really politics. It is a way of living. It is humanity. I believe the only way to live and to be truly successful is by collective effort, with everyone working for each other, everyone helping each other, and everyone having a share of the rewards at the end of the day.' Keegan, while respectful of the working-class solidarity to which Shankly was gesturing, did not want to live in that world – at least, not every day. If Shankly's Liverpool had been in any real sense a 'socialistic' enterprise committed to 'equal wages and no prima donnas' – as some academics would later fantasise – then Keegan would likely have walked out of that club forthwith.

Come the summer of 1973 Keegan was bumping into George Best a fair bit, and he took careful note of how the older man was managing his career. He noted Best's curious aloneness, and how he seemed to have stumbled into the state of everyone wanting a piece of him. Best had just opened a Manchester nightclub called Slack Alice's, a roaring success, where he set about drinking the proceeds. Keegan's first memoir would feature a chapter entitled 'Lessons from Bestie' in which – while stressing his respect for Best the player – Keegan made clear a top professional shouldn't squander his talent as a barfly, and that any contract a man entered into ought to be honoured. 'As soon as I was in demand to attend functions or endorse products,' Keegan wrote, 'I set out to conduct myself differently from Bestie. I tried to learn from his mistakes. If I said I would go somewhere then I went.'

In November 1973 Stylo the bootmaker decided Best was no longer a suitable front man, and replaced him with Keegan – keen, reliable, high profile, and a pro. Six months later, Best was finished at Manchester United, his career effectively shot at 27 – that age of rock-star notoriety at which Jimi Hendrix, Janis Joplin and Jim Morrison all died.

Thirty years later – after scarcely imaginable tides of cash had coursed through British football – Keegan would tell the

Guardian: 'For us, it was never about money. At Liverpool the best-paid player was Tommy Smith, and he only got 30 quid a week more than me.' But 'never about money' was just not credible. In 1973 football was beginning to offer some vertiginous examples of personal gain. That August, Ajax agreed the transfer of Johan Cruyff to Barcelona for 60 million pesetas, or £1.6 million. Cruyff's annual salary would be nigh-on half a million pounds. Many readers of the back pages of the *Sun* and *Express* surely shook their heads and called that crazy money, while considering it nice work if one could get it. Keegan quite possibly saw Cruyff's deal as a not unrealistic aspiration.

5

Technique

1973-74

Since 1958 Scotland had been missing from the World Cup finals, an exile that had turned the summer 'home international' against England into the main obsession for team and fans (so making losses such as the 5-0 gubbing of 1973 especially grim). Manager Willie Ormond lost five of his first six games in charge, but none were World Cup qualifiers; and Tommy Docherty had left the team well placed in their cushy group with Denmark and Czechoslovakia. If Scotland could beat the Czechs at Hampden on 26 September they would be through to the finals in West Germany.

Ormond's first-choice XI was heavily reinforced by Celtic: Dalglish, Hay, Connolly, McGrain, Hunter in goal. Billy Bremner and Denis Law were unusual as Anglos, and Ormond's restoration of Law to the side caused Dalglish a certain anxiety – to be playing alongside a hero, for one, but also to be partnering the great goalscorer up front. Goals were a little rarer for Dalglish at Celtic, simply because he was playing more with his back to goal, bringing other attacking players in. Spearheading a Scotland attack with Law at Hampden Park, though, put Dalglish under a yoke of expectation.

On the night, the stadium was crammed and devoid of any

visiting support from behind the Iron Curtain. It was a physical game and Scotland laboured against an encamped Czech
defence. Then a speculative shot by Zdenek Nehoda went clean
through Ally Hunter's slippery grasp. Scotland clawed back:
defender Jim Holton headed an equaliser. Dalglish, though,
seemed to weary and Ormond replaced him with Joe Jordan,
who repaid the chance with a winner. Three weeks later
Scotland went to Bratislava and lost meaninglessly – arguably
more interested, and not kindly, in whether England could get
the win they needed at Wembley that same night in order to
get past their opponents Poland and book their own place in
West Germany. But Poland won it, with Keegan forced to watch
from the bench, a trial he would remember as 'agony' – though
Sir Alf Ramsey felt the wound more directly, and would resign
thereafter.

Anglo-Scottish resentments had more to them than just the
game. Like Lou Macari before him, David Hay had found in
Scotland duties an intolerable reminder that he was earning several times less than teammates playing in England. Having spent
a while out of the Celtic team through injury, he realised he
had been denied win bonuses over that time, and in the winter
of 1973 he took the radical step of going on strike as a protest.
It was the maturation of Celtic's long-standing problems with
relatively low salaries and the lure of England. Dalglish, too,
was beginning to consider his options.

Celtic still secured another league and cup double, the title
their ninth in succession. Again they reached the semi-final
stage of the European Cup, but the tie against Atletico Madrid
was stunningly ill-tempered: three Atletico players were sent
off in a goalless draw at Parkhead that Dalglish would describe
as 'without doubt the worst game I have ever played in as far
as violence is concerned'. In Madrid Celtic lost 2-0. There
seemed to be a ceiling on Celtic's attainments, and therefore on
Dalglish's, too. A restlessness was growing. The World Cup, at
least, offered him a big stage.

Liverpool, too, were back in the European Cup, a competition in which they had previously been dealt lessons at the hands of Internazionale and Ajax. In November 1973 they ran into Red Star Belgrade and lost both legs. At home Red Star were fast and skilful in possession, dominant yet patient – making Liverpool look leaden by comparison with their quick, smart passing, often from out of defence, often in maddening triangles. They scored two fine goals, though Liverpool grabbed one back. But at Anfield Red Star scored a cracker to make the tie look unsalvageable. Keegan managed to poke a shot through the keeper's legs and fractionally over the line, but amid the defensive mêlée the goal wasn't given. Red Star then wrapped it up, deservedly, with a superb free kick. Liverpool had been outthought, outclassed.

In the wake of the humbling loss, Shankly, Paisley, Moran, Tom Saunders, Reuben Bennett and reserves coach Joe Fagan – the brains trust of the club – met to pick over its lessons. They held their session in a small, shabby, windowless room under the main stand where the players kept their boots on hooks, and beer crates doubled as seating. Paisley and Fagan had made this an HQ of sorts, but now the circle was widening. Their conclusion was that if Liverpool were to beat the best in Europe, they would first have to join them, by way of a more 'continental' approach. At centre-half big Larry Lloyd suddenly looked too conventionally a 'stopper'. Liverpool needed converted midfielders there, to keep possession and break out of defence. On the upside they had Phil Thompson and Emlyn Hughes, who could surely do just this. Liverpool would soon be defined by a patient passing game tailored to Europe – but under new management. It was to be Bob Paisley's way. But it wasn't to be Kevin Keegan's.

The FA Cup threw up one of its headline-ready pairings when Liverpool were drawn at home to Doncaster Rovers, Keegan's old hometown club, which had wanted no part of him back in 1966 and now sat last in the Fourth Division, 91 league places below Shankly's Reds. Naturally, one newspaper strove to induce some collywobbles by trumpeting the 'home game that Kevin wants to miss'. On the day, and within minutes, Keegan headed Liverpool in front; but Donny Rovers showed what they had come for by striking back, then taking the lead. It took a second Keegan header to salvage a replay and a trip back to their Belle Vue ground (for what had to be an afternoon kick-off during the 'three-day week' imposed by the Conservative government to conserve electricity and coal stocks during a strike by the National Union of Mineworkers). This time Liverpool did the business 2-0.

The efficacy of Keegan and Toshack was proven, 30 goals between them that season, but injuries again cost Toshack, even sowing doubt over whether he would return. Keegan, however, was ever-present, and Liverpool never worse than second in the league. But Don Revie's Leeds – with their Scottish spine of Harvey, Bremner and Lorimer – were imperious, unbeaten for 29 games from the start of the season.

Liverpool would have run into Leeds in the FA Cup quarter-finals, too, had Revie's side not fallen surprisingly to Bristol City. But Keegan had the look of wanting to power Liverpool to the cup all by himself. He scored in a fifth-round win against Ipswich, and in the semi-final versus Leicester he executed a superb lob over Peter Shilton's head to set up a final with Newcastle United, a team that had a fair bit going for them, not least a rampant goalscorer in Malcolm Macdonald. When it came to respective approaches to the big game, though, Newcastle entirely lacked the rigour that Shankly had instilled in Liverpool. On the day, the TV summariser adroitly observed Newcastle to be 'looking just a little disorganised'. Liverpool, however, were a fluent wonder to watch, the only anomaly being how it took more than 45 minutes for Keegan to fire them ahead. The second goal was academic, and the third one con-summate, the outcome of an imperious bout of knocking the ball around, Keegan spreading a huge cross-field pass to Tommy Smith then finishing the move for his second of the game.

At last Shankly had the FA Cup; yet he was removed from the jubilation upon the final whistle, repairing to the dressing room alone, testifying later to a sense of stunning enervation: 'I didn't go running around celebrating with the team. I didn't get carried around. I let the players have the arena. I was satisfied and I was tired.' Keegan was perhaps the only Liverpool player who really took notice of this wilful seclusion on Shankly's part, though he may have been reluctant to accept what it meant.

Keegan had found another champion in England's temporary boss Joe Mercer, who made him a regular for the summer's home internationals. Against Wales in Cardiff Keegan scored his first international goal in a 2-1 win. But he had to make way for Martin Peters in the match against Scotland, who were bound for the World Cup but taking some stick in the papers for an incident on the Ayrshire coast that had seen the inebriate Jimmy Johnstone adrift in an oarless rowboat, beyond his teammates' help and requiring rescue by the Clyde coastguard. As if stung by such ridicule, Scotland were much the better side against England: Dalglish looked to have hit form and had a shout for the team's decisive second goal, his strike deflected past Peter Shilton off defender Colin Todd.

Scotland had two more games to warm up for West Germany. Keegan and England, thoroughly disconsolate, went on tour to the east for matches against East Germany, Bulgaria and Yugoslavia. But after the team had landed in Belgrade from Sofia, Keegan was subjected to an extraordinary indignity: grabbed in the baggage retrieval area by airport security men, hauled into a back room and badly roughed up, on the grounds that he was suspected of having assaulted a stewardess during the flight. It was a baseless charge and FA officials finally managed to extract a bloodied Keegan from the mêlée. He scored in England's 2-2 draw, as if to prove he would not be intimidated. Still, Belgrade was, in every respect, just not where Keegan wanted to be in June of 1974. He believed his talent deserved a bigger platform, and would vent his frustration later that summer: 'I didn't go to the finals and I didn't watch a single game on television. I'm not a good watcher.'

Scotland's World Cup preparations had time for one more needless mishap following a friendly in Oslo, where Johnstone and Bremner were found to be worse for drink in the team hotel. Dalglish came on late in that game but got the winner, wrapping up his case for a starting place at the finals. Nonetheless, within the Scotland squad he still cut a somewhat recessive figure, in no way bolstered by the authority that his performances for Celtic would have suggested.

In West Germany Scotland undoubtedly felt the weight of expectation. It was etched on the faces of the team that lined up against group minnows Zaire: a game that Scotland were expected to win, convincingly. Hay, Lorimer and Jordan all looked purposeful and acquitted themselves well, as did fullbacks Danny McGrain and Sandy Jardine, the skilful Rangers captain. Dalglish, however, looked a little anonymous, and felt as much in himself. He was substituted 15 minutes from time, and Scotland had managed only a 2-0 win, their approach arguably overcautious.

Next came the reigning world champions, Brazil. It was the consensus of the squad that Dalglish ought to start, and in a forward role; yet he just didn't seem to work there, and withdrew a little deeper. It was not a game of sinuous skills: the Brazilians cut up remarkably rough. But Scotland fought well and were just the wrong side of the post away from a famous victory. Questions were being asked in the press, though, about Dalglish. Come the crunch game against Yugoslavia, which Scotland had to win to ensure progression, his selection looked like a bit of a luxury. Ian Archer charged him with lacking the confidence to press sufficiently far forward. Hugh McIlvanney rated him 'fading, sadly unconvincing' in the time he had on the pitch before being subbed by winger Tommy Hutchison. Scotland managed to draw the game, but they were out.

Dalglish would admit that he had not met his own standards and in time would testify to 'a very real regret which still gnaws away at me ... there were occasions when I was frightened to try things in case they wouldn't come off'. Previously it had been asked of Dalglish, for all his Celtic stardom, whether he was liable to fade in the second halves of seasons. Was there, maybe, a stamina issue? Possibly the great stage had awed him a little bit, too. But it had not produced that effect in Dalglish's Celtic teammate David Hay, who had excelled. Come July, Hay was off to Chelsea for £250,000. Celtic had brought forth a Scottish World Cup hero; but Hay had got too big for Celtic and Desmond White was fully ready to cash in.

At a press conference hastily convened on 12 July 1974, Liverpool chairman John Smith announced that Bill Shankly had informed the board of his wish 'to retire from active participation in league football' and that the board had 'with extreme reluctance accepted his decision'. Shankly then spoke, describing the delivery of that decision to Smith in jarringly bleak terms as 'like walking to the electric chair'.

He had made up his own mind, refusing an offered extension on his contract. He left knowing that he had not been able to emulate Jock Stein's European Cup triumph, and would have had to wait another couple of years in any case. He left, too, in the afterglow of that consummate display at Wembley, with a squad in good nick, Keegan in premium condition. But that candid comparison of his resignation to capital punishment made plain that within Shankly there was no outright positive spin he could put on his decision; and he must have known that regret would continue to gnaw inside even as he threw the switch on himself.

Shankly's intimations of the end had been aired before in the company of those who knew him best, yet he hadn't really been believed: nobody was braced for it – least of all the support around Liverpool, who were plunged into a version of bereavement by the news. Shankly was felt to be irreplaceable. When Bob Paisley was then promoted internally to the boss's job, Keegan was not alone in doubting the step-up. Paisley gave every sign of doubting it himself. Leading the first training session after his appointment, he advised the players he was 'only looking after the shop until a proper manager arrives'.

Still, Paisley's personal story was one of remarkable toughness and perspicacity, though the man himself would have insisted – outwardly, at least – that it was really nothing so special. If he appeared a mild sort, though – all self-effacing County Durham, turned out as for the working men's club, hair brushed off the temples with tonic, chunky zip-up cardigan over shirt and tie – Paisley had steel in him. He had served Liverpool loyally as a player yet had known the bitterness of being dropped for the FA Cup final of 1950, an experience that had taught him to get on with it, and to expect the same of others. When his playing days ended he had taken a correspondence course in physiotherapy, and the nous he acquired gave him another string to his bow by the time he became Liverpool's reserve coach. The man had many sides. But for Keegan, who felt the loss of his mentor more keenly than any, the main thing of note about Paisley was that he wasn't Shanks.

The Football Association had made a tradition of a 'Charity Shield' match to launch a new football season, contested by the current Division One champions and the FA Cup holders. The 1974 edition brought a novelty: the match, between Leeds and Liverpool, would be played at Wembley and broadcast live on television – a big curtain-raiser, and an advert for the English game. But proceedings on 10 August 1974 ran according to a different sort of script.

The Liverpool team were led out by Shankly, a show of respect to the great man. Striding along beside Shankly was the new Leeds manager, Brian Clough. Don Revie had just quit to take over the England team from Joe Mercer and Clough, arriving at Elland Road, had been typically outspoken in his disparaging view of the Leeds brand of football. It soon became apparent that the Leeds players hadn't cared for that: having been stigmatised thus, they were about to make a great show of holding up their bloody stigmata.

Keegan's views, expressed in his 1977 memoir, were even more radical than Clough's: 'I hated Leeds and everything they stood for.' From the moment the Charity Shield game kicked off, Revie's team seemed to fancy a scrap. Soon the game became one big niggle. As Johnny Giles would tell the *Guardian* with relish, 'Keegan was quite an emotional lad and he was in one of his moods that day.' Giles and Billy Bremner were happy to buddy up for a sort of tag-team toughness: together they helped to make Keegan's afternoon a misery, and Keegan felt he was getting no help from the ref.

Around the hour mark, incensed, Keegan pursued a loose ball and went through Bremner, then hared after Giles, who felled him with a right-hook. From the resulting free kick the ball went up into the Liverpool half, but Keegan went after Bremner. 'I have Irish blood in me,' he would write, 'and sometimes my temper rips.' He and Bremner exchanged blows in front of the ref, and though Keegan protested when they were pulled up together he surely knew he was for the early bath. He stripped off his shirt and flung it away. Bremner copied him, though he might have thought twice about showing his pale gut alongside Keegan's ripped and muscular torso. Joe Keegan was in the Liverpool changing room to console his son, and when Bremner entered to make an apology Keegan's dad told him to bugger off.

The game went to penalties, but the story was already written. 'Football itself has been dragged shamefully through the mud,' wrote Geoffrey Green of the *Times*, 'leaving all thoughtful people to fear for its future.' The TV audience, after all, had clearly heard the fans' choruses of 'You're gonna get your fucking head kicked in'. It was the sound of an exhilarated crowd, unbothered by the impression they were giving – terraces full of young men quite full of themselves, wanting a buzz, baiting the away fans from whom the police had tried to keep them.

'Trouble' had come to seem an ineradicable part of the game. Worse, it had acquired a certain organisation, firm versus firm, bad scenes on match day at the railway station and in the city centre, clashes in and out of the ground, infiltration of the away end. On the last day of the previous season, Manchester United's relegation from Division One had resulted in a pitch invasion so gratuitous that the FA had instructed the club to install steel fencing at the front of the terraces behind the goals. But Division Two clubs were not looking forward to the visits of the Stretford Enders.

Weeks later Tottenham had played Feyenoord in Rotterdam in the second leg of the UEFA Cup final. Spurs were second best and a section of their so-called support made trouble as if in pointless protest. Manager Bill Nicholson had used the PA to tell them they were a disgrace, and he would resign early in the following season – five days after 17-year-old Blackpool supporter Kevin Olsson was fatally stabbed by a rival fan behind the Kop at Bloomfield Road during a match against Bolton. There was a growing feeling that home and away support would have to be more firmly segregated at English football stadia. It was going to require fences, for all that this would give a claustral sense of caging, with no mind to how it would feel to the regular fans who came to watch a football match rather than live out fantasies of prowess in combat. With all this to be borne in mind, however, the notion that Kevin Keegan had brought football into disrepute by his reaction to the organised bullying of Leeds players seemed a fantasy all of its own.

Keegan would be made an example of – fined and banned for 11 games. In the aftermath of the game, clearly not quite himself amid the turmoil, he chose to drown his sorrows in beer. He awoke blearily to the unwelcome news that he was required to play in Billy McNeill's testimonial on Monday night and had to get himself up to Glasgow. It was a big occasion, and Keegan roused himself to set up Toshack for Liverpool's goal in a 1-1 draw. Kenny Dalglish's contribution to the Celtic performance was muted – a further letdown for his many admirers after that indifferent World Cup. Ian Archer wrote more in sorrow than anger of 'how tired and jaded' Dalglish seemed. But if he was still shaking off the summer's letdown, Dalglish's football brain was engaged. He could see and appreciate the quality of Liverpool's passing game, Emlyn Hughes now settled at centre-half and Phil Thompson passing across the back. Liverpool certainly had it in them to kick on without Shankly. But did Keegan want to be part of the project? Changes had been made to things he had trusted and invested in.

It was a moot point, too, as to whether Shankly was truly ready to let go. When the Liverpool players reported back to Melwood for pre-season training they found Shankly also showing up daily, using the facilities to stay fit, just as all former staff were entitled to do. But Shanks was also circulating among the players, seeming to relish the banter. At some wrenching level, Shankly's regret over his resignation was plaintive. The bigger problem, though, was that the players found themselves confusedly calling him 'Boss'. Paisley could not be at ease with this, and John Smith had to ask Shankly to stay away – an unacceptable situation thus ending with a stunning affront. Keegan, while seeing Paisley's predicament, felt Shankly's pain more keenly and would blame the club for the situation having arisen: 'They didn't get it wrong very often but they did that time.' He had chosen his side, in other words, and to that extent Keegan was no longer quite 'with' Liverpool FC.

6

Changes

1974-77

'You need a good family life. It allows you to go to work knowing everything's good.'

Kenny Dalglish

'What George needs is to find himself the right girl and settle down and get married.'

Matt Busby's lament for George Best

Lumbered with his five-week ban from the Charity Shield debacle, Keegan turned out on Liverpool's opening day win at Luton but would not feature again until October. With time on his hands, he worked to improve his golf, having caught the bug of the prosperous man's game, and also spent time with his parents in Armthorpe. Joe Keegan was plainly unwell – his son urged him to see a specialist, and a tumour was diagnosed. Advised that an 18-month wait for NHS treatment was quite likely, Keegan paid for his father to receive private medical care, thinking it his filial duty (though he would profess to be 'annoyed with the system').

For his part Joe Keegan – possibly from a residual loyalty of his own to the idea that he had conceded a point of principle – made a special plea to his son to get himself married. Parents, like football managers, are usually of the view that their charges are better off wed, domesticated and cared for in a stable home environment. Keegan, moreover, had stayed close to his dad, taking his parents' views to heart. On 23 September 1974 Keegan wore a white leather suit for his wedding to Jean at St Peter-in-Chains Roman Catholic Church, Doncaster. The newlyweds then moved into a farmhouse in Cilcain near Mold in North Wales, an hour's drive from Anfield.

In Keegan's absence Liverpool had started well, but September saw three league defeats, and Paisley had to weigh up more than one selection problem. Phil Boersma had been drafted in from the cold to deputise for Keegan up front. New signings Phil Neal and Terry McDermott had to bed in, as did Ray Kennedy, recruited from Arsenal in Shankly's final days, ostensibly as Toshack's replacement. Upon Keegan's return, though, he and Kennedy didn't combine too well from the off. If Kennedy's task really was, à la Tosh, to win the ball in the air, harry defenders and create space – that wasn't happening. Keegan made his dissatisfaction known: the partner he preferred was Toshack, for whom the case was clear on past evidence. Still, that November – after Liverpool went out of the League Cup at Ipswich and the Cup Winners' Cup to Ferencvaros – the club accepted £160,000 for Toshack from Leicester; only for Toshack to fail his medical and return to Anfield, determined to fight for his place. But Liverpool could only muster four wins between November and mid-March. Any hope of Paisley capping his first season with the league title had gone.

The boss had continued to intimate his own style: team talks that let the players into his thinking rather than Shankly-esque rhetorical flourishes. He wasn't interested in showboating for the press, and he didn't mind the players having a drink. Keegan wasn't averse to this, but it wasn't Shanks. 'There was nothing wrong with Bob Paisley,' he remarked down the line, 'but he just didn't motivate me like Shankly could.'

Dalglish followed Keegan, come the autumn of 1974, by tying the knot with his steady girlfriend. 'He didn't actually propose,' as Marina Harkins recalled of the great moment. 'He just asked if I'd like to go with him to buy a ring.' They were married on her birthday, 26 November 1974, at Netherlee Church of Scotland, and they moved into their marital home in the well-heeled Newton Mearns suburb south-west of Glasgow. Dalglish had got himself set up like a manager's dream. Drinking, gambling and women were the common indulgences by which a promising player squandered his gift, but Dalglish was well clear of such traps. His teetotalism was entirely professional. He was not inclined to fritter a penny of his hard-earned pay. (Indeed, a certain reputation for parsimony was afoot: 'Kenny likes a penny' became a saying.) His marriage to Marina, meanwhile, seemed to bear out Paul Newman's adage that a man would hardly run out for a hamburger when he had steak at home.

On the pitch, Dalglish was partnered up front with Paul Wilson, whom he had known since boyhood and whose game he understood. But Dalglish was now inclined to lie deeper, seeking more to orchestrate play. Sportswriter Kevin McCarra, a longtime Dalglish-watcher, would look back on this passage in his career as one marked by 'spectacular virtuosity' at times. But then, by McCarra's reckoning, Dalglish was having to raise his game partly as a one-man response to Celtic having 'slipped back a little from their European Cup-winning peak'.

In October they thumped Hibs 6–3 to win the League Cup, but that same month they were dumped out of Europe in the first round by Olympiacos. Despite their routine qualifications Celtic had not got past a team of note in Europe since Leeds in 1970. And if the club was not feeling sufficiently introspective, Rangers picked their moment to end Celtic's nine-season supremacy in the league, the emblematic scuppering coming at Ibrox in the first week of 1975. Rangers' 3-0 win was larded by two late goals, but Wilson had created enough chances for Celtic to win, and Dalglish was one of several to have a fruitless day in front of goal. It was only Celtic's second league defeat of the season, but they would lose seven more and trail home second, consoled only by a Scottish Cup win over Airdrie.

With the team's ambitions on a plateau Dalglish was looking increasingly to personal opportunities for advancement – turning his mind to business, broadly understood. If he was not an operator on Keegan's level (and the Scottish game offered few such opportunities in any case), Dalglish had figured out that his good form and good name carried weight, and that his wage deserved a supplement. His father-in-law Pat Harkins set a compelling example in business, albeit the licensed trade from which Dalglish kept a healthy remove. Harkins had teamed up with Jock Stein's big bookmaking buddy Tony Queen to open a couple of American-themed joints: The Virginian bar-restaurant in Glasgow, and The New Orleans in Rutherglen. In 1975 the cautious Dalglish dared to invest alongside Harkins in an Airdrie-based whisky maker.

Dalglish also capitalised on his friendship with Rangers captain and Scotland teammate Sandy Jardine. Both of them well known yet diffident, perhaps needing one another for support, they formed a double act to do supermarket openings and radio ads for Lorimer's beer. Moreover, with the experience of recording Scotland's World Cup song behind them, they cut a single of their own under the stage name of The New Firm. The 'hit' side was called 'Each Saturday' ('Each Saturday would not be the same! / If we couldn't get along to the game!'). But really the tune was carried by some sprightly female session vocalists, with its nominal stars making only gruff and fitful contributions until a spoken-word exchange over the fade-out:

JARDINE: Eh. Whit team d'ya play for, anyway?

DALGLISH: What d'ya mean, whit team do ah play for? You knae who ah play for, ah play for Celtic. Who d'*you* play for?

JARDINE: The champions!

DALGLISH: The champions? You've only got it on rent . . .

All knockabout stuff; and no one could have expected a sudden flowering of a musical talent. (Even the Radio 1 disc jockey John Peel – in time, arguably Dalglish's most ardent public admirer – would admit, 'As with most footballers, Kenny's musical taste is deeply suspect.') The truly telling thing about The New Firm was the reticent Dalglish's readiness to cut this sort of profile, these kinds of capers, for a bit of extra cash.

Finally, after four years of solid graft since Shankly's first prophecy, Keegan was a fixture in the England team. Having attained the mountaintop, he duly walked out of the national squad in pique. It was Tuesday, 20 May 1975, and Keegan had learned that he was to be dropped from the starting XI for the following day's home international against Wales. Keegan had been feeling a little raw because of other circumstances: his father Joe remained in very poor health, and Jean was away in Cornwall. But 'the emotional lad' had shown, again, how things could rattle him.

Informed of Keegan's departure, Don Revie was forced to ring the Cilcain cottage – forlornly, since Keegan had gone directly to Anfield to get Paisley's advice. Thankfully, Revie reached his wounded and recalcitrant star there, and Liverpool arranged for Keegan to be driven back to the England base for a face-to-face with the boss, whereupon things were hammered out, Revie reassuring Keegan that he had only wished to rest a premium performer for one game so as to keep him sharp after a long season.

Paisley, though, decided to speak to the press about the incident and was remarkably candid, making plain that he considered Keegan a special case who required personal explanations in the event of any such exclusion – not just as a courtesy but because he considered Keegan 'so temperamental', 'terribly mixed up and upset', 'a lonely boy at the moment'. (Another cause of upset Paisley pointed out, with maximum lack of tact, was the tendency of England teammates 'to go on about their wages'.) Keegan would later describe his actions as 'bloody silly'. He realised he had made a big fuss out of virtually nothing. But this tightly wound tendency to walk away from affront, even from the national side, was on his record now.

Still, if Revie had meant to keep Keegan keen, that plan worked to perfection. He was back in the side to meet Scotland (and Dalglish) at Wembley, and the day turned into one of the worst-ever Scottish failures in the fixture. Gerry Francis opened the scoring with a swerving shot that Scotland's keeper Stewart Kennedy ought to have sighted sooner. Fighting back, Dalglish made one flourishing run on goal only to be checked by a foul. Then Keegan put a cross onto Kevin Beattie's head and Kennedy, misjudging the flight, managed to wrap himself round a goalpost. Again, Dalglish led a rally, streaking through the centre, playing a wise weighted pass that was wasted. But England got a third from Colin Bell that lit up all the question marks about Scotland's hapless goalie. It was 5-1 at the finish.

For Dalglish, some sort of confrontation with Celtic had been looming awhile. There were big matters to mull over: the club's prospects, his own ambitions, the responsible promptings of marriage and family – for Marina was pregnant with their first child. Stein and Fallon had surely helped to make Dalglish a player, but a player he now undeniably was, and he wanted away. There had been rumours of interest from Everton and Leeds.

Stein's rule of iron over the playing staff had been challenged and eroded by the departures of Macari and Hay, and it surely couldn't hold much longer. But circumstances would not make a parting of ways so simple for Dalglish.

Stein took his summer holiday of 1975 on Minorca, in the company of his wife Jean, Tony Queen and Bill Shankly's brother Bob and his wife. But Stein was soon itching to be home, as was his way. On 5 July he was driving the party back from the airport, nearing Dumfries, when his Mercedes was rammed head-on by a Peugeot coming down the wrong side of the dual carriageway. The Peugeot's driver, one John Ballantyne, was found to be far over the alcohol limit on whisky and lager. But Stein suffered chest wounds and fractured ribs plus other injuries to his hips and feet.

He was to spend four weeks in intensive care at Dumfries & Galloway Royal Infirmary. Despite Celtic's predicament, however, Dalglish did not feel he could delay raising the matter on his mind any longer. 'I'm sorry to be adding to your worries,' he told Sean Fallon in the meeting where he put in his request to leave Celtic. Fallon was a sympathetic figure, the one Dalglish was closest to – the man who had, after all, recruited him to Celtic when no other club was making a concrete offer, and who had championed his cause when Stein was more circumspect. Fallon now exerted his influence: Billy McNeill having retired, the captaincy was vacant and Fallon offered it to Dalglish. A small pay rise was also arranged. It was enough to persuade Dalglish that this was not his moment to depart.

The 1975-76 season was the first in which the Scottish Football League split into three, the top flight known henceforth as the Premier Division. It was not, as it turned out, a great season to be captain of Celtic. Dalglish would finish as top scorer with 24 league goals, but Celtic lost the League Cup final to Rangers, who went on to retain the league title. Sean Fallon's reward for having tried to steady the ship in Stein's absence was to be demoted to chief scout, as Davie McParland was appointed to be number two. Stein returned to work having taken a full year to recover, but things could not be the same again.

In mid-May Scotland met England at Hampden, the England team sporting a Liverpool spine of Clemence, Thompson, Kennedy and Keegan. But Dalglish was everywhere that day as Scotland took the game to their old enemy. With the score tied at 1-1, he controlled a Jordan cross masterfully, only to scuff a weak shot at goal – but the ball squirmed through Clemence's legs and in. It was not one from Dalglish's top drawer but, as Keegan would say, it went in the right place. Keegan himself was anonymous in the game, possibly preoccupied. Like Dalglish, he had come to a big decision about his career, and he did not intend to be talked out of it.

After September 1975 Keegan didn't score for 10 matches, and Liverpool were among a tight bunch of clubs vying at the top of the table. But soon he was ramming in the goals again. Against Manchester United in November Liverpool's travelling support displayed 'Killer Keegan' signs; and, like old times, Keegan squared for Tosh to slot home, then Tosh headed on for Keegan to dive in. Liverpool motored to the semi-finals of the UEFA Cup to meet Barcelona at the Nou Camp, and won with a smart strike by Toshack. Keegan was in awe of Barcelona's set-up, not to speak of Johan Cruyff's salary; but not so awed that he didn't fancy a piece of it.

He had come to see Liverpool as parsimonious in its dealings with its players – this even before the Labour government's top-bracket tax rate was applied to his earnings. Income tax and its drag on incentive had become a Keegan obsession. 'I had reached the point where, because of taxation, there was no incentive for me to go any further in England,' he would write. 'I became conscious that I was not fulfilling myself. I was ambitious, so why shouldn't I aim for the very top, both financially and for my own personal satisfaction?'

Liverpool were certainly prudent on the spending front, albeit in the manner of the time. The club had a bank account with no overdraft facility. The job of general secretary Peter Robinson was to budget correctly, so Liverpool spent no more than it was taking through the turnstiles and season tickets. Robinson had, though, begun to muse in public about the need to market the club more effectively – the possibilities of merchandise, sponsored games, perimeter adverts. Like Keegan, Robinson had sensed a direction of travel. The club's commitments, however, were more complex than the player's.

Some loyal servants of Liverpool FC felt that Keegan's priorities were wrong. 'I stayed with Liverpool for fourteen years and never once asked for a rise,' Ian Callaghan would later assert. 'The manager would come to you if he was going to give you more money.' But Keegan was not prepared to settle for that, and didn't believe he ought to. 'A man who does not know what he is worth is not worth anything,' he wrote in his memoir, 'and I knew what I was worth to Liverpool.'

Keegan's ever-growing roster of product endorsements had now surpassed even the high bar once set by George Best. Its apogee came in 1976 when Brut 33 toiletries put him in a TV advert where he swapped locker-room banter and compared chest hairs with Henry Cooper. A good gig, for sure, but Keegan was gripped by the bigger instinct of securing his financial future. To do so, he decided that he would have to surmount the challenge of succeeding with a foreign side, a task that had bested Denis Law, Jimmy Greaves *et al.* But the fact that successful precedents were so few was not one to deter Keegan.

For the first leg of the UEFA Cup final against Bruges at Anfield, Paisley lined up Toshack, Heighway and young David Fairclough in an attacking trio with Keegan just behind. Within a quarter-hour Bruges were 2-0 up and Paisley cut his losses, bringing Jimmy Case on for Toshack and moving Keegan up to

lead the attack. Within five inspired minutes, Heighway set up
Ray Kennedy for a rasping left-foot strike; then came another
fruitful foray down the left, Keegan executing a brilliant turn
and lay-off to Kennedy who hit the post, leaving Case to knock
in the rebound. Heighway then won a penalty running in on
the left again, and Keegan converted, bottom right.

Before the return leg Liverpool clinched their first title under
Paisley with a 3-1 win at Wolves, Keegan setting them on their
way with a typical scamper onto Toshack's flick-on. In Bruges,
though, a certain *froideur* arose, Keegan critical of the club's
travel arrangements: Shankly had been invited along but was
put up in a separate hotel to the main party. As for the match,
a penalty put Bruges ahead on away goals but Keegan scored
from a tapped free kick: a low scudder blazed along the turf.
For Liverpool the second half was a long rear-guard action, but
they emerged with their second league and UEFA Cup double.
Keegan, however, seemed to feel little for it. His true ambitions
were driving him elsewhere.

His summer was frenetic, per the extraordinary demands
he made on himself. In late May he went with England on a
US tour, followed by a World Cup qualifier in Finland. After
a visit to the Isle of Man, he did a TV summarising stint for
the European Championship final then, on the following day,
played an exhibition game in Paris, arranged by Piet Keizer,
a former Ajax player who now ran an agency for representing
players, Inter Football. Watching from the stands was the boss
of Real Madrid, Miljan Miljanic, in search of a replacement
for the influential midfielder and World Cup winner Gunter
Netzer. Such a player would need more than just skill: they had
to be a star in the manner of Netzer, a collector of Ferraris and
owner of nightclubs who took his blond hairdo very seriously.
On this level, it was hard to see past Keegan as the man Miljanic
sought; and Piet Keizer was keen to bend Keegan's ear on how
he could help to progress matters. Back in Liverpool, Keegan
met with John Smith, who told him that an offer from Real

was expected, and Keegan could go quietly – if he undertook to give Liverpool one more season of service. Keegan reflected, and thought this fair.

Off he went again, then, to open a summer fete in Rhyl just as he had agreed, then to Bracknell in Berkshire for the filming of the BBC's *Superstars* series: a decathlon-type contest pitting sportsmen from various fields against one another. For Keegan to subject his body to such strains in close season was a real anomaly in professional football, even more so at Liverpool where Bob Paisley, a physio by trade, didn't even like to see his players tramping round a golf course in case they bent themselves out of shape. But Keegan couldn't be told what to do; any more than Shankly could stop him opening supermarkets.

Keegan felt comfortable in most of the *Superstars* events, save for cycling, but his competitive instinct drove him on. He got in the saddle and set off like the clappers, only to tip off onto the red shale track, taking skin off his back and shoulder. Despite the wince-inducing grazes, he swallowed some painkillers, got bandaged up and back on the bike, completed the heat and won the competition, scooping £2,800 and celebrating with champagne and a steak, even as his wounds began to throb. The lunatic folly was exposed by the time Jean was driving him home: he was as sick as a dog and they detoured urgently to Northampton hospital, where Keegan would spend four days in bed and earn himself a stern talking-to from the doctor. Possibly the lesson Keegan took most to heart was that he needed to find ways to earn more of what he fancied for less work and fewer scrapes. He was still in the hospital bed when the press reported that Liverpool had received and knocked back a bid from Real Madrid of around £650,000.

Rested and repaired for the new season, Keegan was still talking like a Liverpool player. ('There's a tremendous ambition among all the lads to win the European Cup.') Since he was resolved to move, however – and since the process was clearly going to be complex – he decided to make public that at the

season's end he would be off. But to where? By now, with
Real Madrid's interest known, Bayern Munich and Borussia
Dortmund were sniffing around. Even Keegan grew perplexed
by the game of chess going on around him. Piet Keizer was still
pushing to represent him, but something about the very idea
of agents riled Keegan: his feeling was they just didn't deserve
the money – business needed to be done between the clubs, the
revenues properly split. Having made his big choice, Keegan
wouldn't be cheated.

It was Charity Shield day when the news broke that Keegan
had given Liverpool notice of his intention to quit. Within a
week the club had signed Ipswich striker David Johnson, an
England international, in no way a replacement for Keegan,
but a sign that life would go on. Keegan's publicised plans
engendered resentment among certain teammates. His single-
mindedness, the restless manoeuvres that served to keep him at
the centre of all things, were bound to be a little irksome now.

Although Keegan could never be considered a lame duck,
he had doomed himself to a season's worth of interviews in
which he would be forced to remind the Liverpool support that
he was leaving in order 'to better himself'. That simply hadn't
happened before; and it made for a slow ebbing away of the love
Anfield had for 'King Kev'. A segment of the support would
now believe that Keegan was a far bigger fan of himself than of
Liverpool FC. The chant of 'Kevin Keegan walks on water' was
decommissioned. If Keegan was just one player in a great side,
he was by common consent its single most vital component; and
now it seemed likely he would go and make some other side
great, too. The dilemma was summed up in mid-September at
Derby, Keegan getting dog's abuse from some travelling fans yet
scoring Liverpool's winner. The impending problem was clear.
Whoever could replace King Kev in the red number seven?

Kenny Dalglish scored his hundredth Celtic goal against Motherwell in November 1976. Jock Stein was back in the chair, the team back on title-winning form. But their engagements in Europe amounted to a 2-4 aggregate loss to Wisla Krakow in the UEFA Cup. Dalglish now rated Celtic's European campaigns as 'disappointment all the time'. He and McGrain were the last umbilical links to the Celtic of the late 1960s, when they had been but boys. Marina was pregnant again, expecting their second child. He told Stein definitively that he wanted to leave, and it made for renewed tension. 'I'd no crib with Celtic when I decided I wanted to leave them,' he would tell the *Sunday Express*. 'It was simply a question of wanting to try something else. Perhaps that is a bit selfish but if you don't try, you don't know.' The ex-Rangers forward Alfie Conn was signed from Spurs in March 1977, Stein anticipating Dalglish's departure even if he hadn't approved it. But Dalglish was clear in his head that he ought to be at a club that could compete with the best in Europe. The shortlist for such a move was going to be short indeed.

In Turkey with Liverpool for a European Cup tie with Trabzonspor, Keegan was advised by Peter Smith of an offer from Juventus: a perplexing buy-and-lease-back deal whereby he wouldn't actually join the Italians until 1978. A few weeks later England were in Rome for a World Cup qualifier and Keegan played so poorly, marked out of a 2-0 defeat, that he feared he had heard the last of any Italian interest.

On 4 December 1976 Keegan's father Joe succumbed to the cancer that had blighted his latter years, dying at the age of 71. Liverpool had a game that day at Ipswich, and Keegan stoically turned out, but was unsurprisingly nondescript as Liverpool lost, and he cared little for what the crowd thought. The emotional man was feeling raw, and off his game for umpteen reasons. For his own wellbeing, he needed to make his deal.

In February 1977 Real Madrid lodged another offer for Keegan. Liverpool were making great strides in the European Cup, scrapping past Saint-Etienne and FC Zurich. Gunter Netzer urged Keegan to go with Real, but the Spaniards were impatient with need, weary of waiting. They bought Ulrich Stielike instead, leaving Keegan feeling powerless and frustrated. He kept up his form, scoring four in five to keep Liverpool on course for the league title. And when Liverpool beat Everton in the semis of the FA Cup it meant the domestic double – a season's treble – was on, too. Keegan was doing as much as he could to keep himself in the shop window, but the customer remained elusive.

Five days before an Old Firm Scottish Cup final, with Celtic champions again, Dalglish was presented with a new contract since his existing deal was due to expire. Though he had no intention of committing to the club for the long term, it was a fact that he could not play in the final for Celtic unless he was a registered player; and both he and Stein knew that if Dalglish were absent on such a day then the press would draw conclusions. For the sake of appearances, then, and on the understanding there was nothing else to it, Dalglish signed the contract. The game, before a disappointing crowd, finished 1-0 to Celtic. Dalglish refused the chance to take a penalty (a test he had come to dislike) but Andy Lynch did the honours. Back at Celtic Park the following Monday Dalglish sought to reopen talks with Stein about his move; Stein expressed surprise that a player who had just signed a new Celtic contract should speak of such a thing. But Dalglish had no time for Stein's dummying-up over a temporary fix they had conceived together. Politely but firmly, he stood his ground.

A goalless draw with West Ham confirmed Liverpool as English champions again (though a rowdy swarm onto the turf by fans at the final whistle denied the players their expected lap of honour round Anfield, to Keegan's irritation, and the Kop let the offenders know they ought to 'get off the fucking pitch'). Liverpool's FA Cup final against Tommy Docherty's Manchester United was a week away. Suddenly, a new interest in Keegan showed its face: SV Hamburg, one of West Germany's oldest clubs, fresh from victory in the European Cup Winners' Cup. Now, on the eve of the game with United, Hamburg's officials sought a meeting with Keegan.

Since the founding in 1963 of West Germany's national Bundesliga, Hamburg had been top-flight makeweights; but recent years had brought improvements – league runners-up, a domestic cup, and now a European success. They were a wealthy club with a big ground, the Volksparkstadion, which held over 60,000 fans after modernisation for the 1974 World Cup. Japanese electronics giant Hitachi, moreover, was paying Hamburg £125,000 annually in sponsorship. The club's general manager was an entrepreneur named Dr Peter Krohn, who bubbled with ideas to buoy the club's profile, even getting the team to turn out in pink jerseys. Krohn was offering Keegan £90,000 a year, and the club had money to put into a big transfer fee that would otherwise go straight to the taxman. In several key respects, then, this was a club in Keegan's image; and it didn't hurt that his wife had A-level German. If Hamburg lacked the gilt edge of some of Keegan's earlier suitors, their numbers added up, at least.

The FA Cup final was an indifferent game that got lively quite suddenly in the second half: a goal by United's Pearson, equalised by Case, prior to a flukey Macari deflection off Jimmy Greenhoff that crawled across the Liverpool line. Keegan was an easy target for stick as Liverpool's treble hopes fell; but the defeat hadn't been his fault. He remained in London overnight to finalise contractual terms with Hamburg. What the support may have considered bad form was, to Keegan, just business.

Liverpool regrouped in Rome in midweek to go for the grand prize against Borussia Moenchengladbach. Keegan started in a deep role behind Toshack, man-marked by Berti Vogts. And yet, remarkably, everything Liverpool did with the ball seemed to go through Keegan, who was soon pulling Vogts all over the place, winning every header, losing his man as if at will. So rigid was the German system that once Keegan had lost Vogts then no other player dared to break shape and get after him. Liverpool ran out 3-1 winners and Keegan had enjoyed probably his best game of the season. Afterwards Vogts sought him out and solemnly offered to buy him a beer.

The Liverpool support chanted Keegan's name, for all that he felt he hadn't heard much of that throughout the season – that those fans had shown him just a little fickleness, since the season's record revealed that he had managed 20 goals in 57 games and was leaving them as champions of Europe. In his 1977 post-Liverpool memoir, Keegan took an unprecedented step in querying the fidelity of Liverpool's support, wondering whether the fans, so 'hard to please', had been 'spoilt by years of success' and would melt away from the club if things ever got tough. This was certainly a novel way of making a clean break from the famed traditions of Anfield.

That weekend Keegan flew to Hamburg for a medical and a look around with Jean, and then returned to London to complete the paperwork and speak to the press. He shook hands with Paisley and John Smith with some genuine regret, and Paisley struck a serious tone. ('Obviously, it's a sad day for Liverpool.') Once Keegan got talking, though, he was adamant in his tone: 'Financially, this move has set me up for life . . . I'm no traitor . . . I'm simply doing what I want to do – and that's all that matters to me. If I had spent my life doing what others wanted me to do, I would not be where I am today.' Questioned, understandably, about the sort of player Liverpool might seek to take over his

vacant jersey, Keegan offered that they would probably want a
player much like himself – someone who would fit well with
Tosh, of course.

Amid the hurly-burly of the Hamburg deal, Keegan would
have no part in the home international against Scotland at
Wembley the next day. The stage, then, was set for Dalglish, a
lonely Scottish League man in a changing room alongside Asa
Hartford and Willie Donachie of Manchester City, Gordon
McQueen and Joe Jordan of Leeds, Bruce Rioch of Everton,
et al. But Dalglish played a blinder. Liverpool's Phil Neal,
deputed to mark him, was soon throwing up his hands. ('The
idea was to get Kenny, but I couldn't get near him.') Reduced
to the crudest measures, Neal fouled Dalglish out on the left,
and Asa Hartford's free kick found Gordon McQueen's considerable forehead: 1-0. Fifteen minutes later came a Scottish
break that ended in Dalglish forcing the ball past Ray Clemence
after two tries – a Keegan-esque toiler of a goal. Following the
final whistle the jubilant Scottish fans swarmed onto the pitch,
bounced on the goalposts until they broke, and carved out
souvenir squares of Wembley turf – terrific fun for them, but a
picture of alarming disorder to anyone looking in on television.

In good spirits Scotland went to South America at the invitation of the military junta of Argentina, host nation of the 1978
World Cup, condemned to friendlies in the meantime. England
were there, too, but their tour was overshadowed by the seeming
end of their World Cup qualifying hopes (as Italy got a result that
took a grip on their group); and by the sacking of Don Revie
(who was found to be engineering a move to the United Arab
Emirates, and would shortly be replaced by Ron Greenwood).
Scotland ignored the politics of their position, learned about the
climate and the venues, and played well. Dalglish was meant to
go on with Celtic for a pre-season tour of Australia from 13 to 31

July. But in Dalglish's mind the tour had become the last-chance-saloon moment of his need to leave Celtic.

On the eve of the team's departure Dalglish told Stein he wouldn't travel. Stein talked him round, assured him that on their return he would ring around selected clubs about a transfer. But on returning home Dalglish discussed things with Marina and decided that his giving in was just a waste of everyone's time. He returned to Celtic Park that afternoon without his boots. 'Your career,' a glowering Stein informed him, 'has just taken a big backward step.' Remarkably, Stein managed to get Dalglish to say that he would show up to Glasgow airport, one last chance; but he must have realised the pointlessness, for in the morning he phoned his player and told him not to bother. The episode had been a little dance, driven along by Stein's residual sense of his authority, and Dalglish's of loyalty and propriety. Neither of these could be sustained. As soon as the press had done the headcount of Celtic's squad at the airport, Dalglish's house in Newton Mearns was under siege from the media. While his teammates were airbound for Australia, Dalglish took his boots and went to train with Celtic Reserves.

In early July, Keegan, Jean and their two sheepdogs made the big move to Germany, having offloaded their cottage in Cilcain. Keegan got the family sorted for wheels with a new Jaguar XJS and an Allegro for Jean: good Leyland cars, none of your Audis or Volkswagens. Fancying a new image for his unveiling as a Hamburg man, he had his hair done in a dewy, curly perm that reduced his wife to a scoffing heap of hilarity.

The Keegans' first German home was an unappealing room high up in the Plaza hotel on Hamburg's outskirts. This constituted a contract violation: Keegan had asked for a proper house with a garden, since they had their dogs to think about, whereas the hotel room hadn't so much as a balcony to offer. For the moment, Keegan let it ride – unusually, for one so precise about how he should be treated; mindful, perhaps, of not kicking up a fuss too soon. But already, more than one thing was not as he had bargained for when he signed for the club. Hamburg had parted company with manager Kuno Klotzer, who had wrangled with Peter Krohn. The new gaffer was a well-travelled veteran, Rudi Gutendorf.

Keegan reported for training alongside fellow new boy Ivan Buljan. The pre-season games brought illustrious opposition. Hamburg warmed up with a 6-0 stroll against Barcelona, Keegan getting a tap-in, then entertained Liverpool and won 3-2, Keegan scoring the first (nearly clattering Clemence in the process) then setting up the second for the team's leading influence, midfielder Felix Magath. Duisburg awaited Hamburg as their first Bundesliga fixture, for which Peter Krohn was full of puff. 'With God and Kevin Keegan,' he trumpeted, 'we will win in Duisburg.' In fact, they were well beaten, 5-2, and Rudi Gutendorf was as much perturbed as Keegan, later suggesting that his team, resentful of the new Englishman among them, had sought to 'sabotage' the result ('I saw that my players didn't like to win'). Keegan, a hater of cheats, was suddenly facing an extraordinary test.

For sure, the Hamburg players had been happy and settled as a side that had won the Cup Winners' Cup with a manager, Klotzer, whom they respected. They had not wished to see a successful formula discarded. But Gutendorf had been drafted in, and some players believed Krohn's hire had been made on Keegan's behalf – Gutendorf spoke English, for one. And, like Gutendorf, Keegan was seen as Krohn's man; a flashily needless addition to a well-run side that had shown its worth. 'If you put this little English guy in, we don't want to work with you' was Gutendorf's recall of the message brought to his room one day by a delegation of players. 'We won the cup and we don't need him and we don't like him.'

Felix Magath was among the most forthright on this score. Magath considered Keegan to be 'just like a businessman' – a description Keegan might have endorsed, but which didn't suit Hamburg. Keegan's definition of professionalism just didn't chime with his new team. The Hamburg players were keen to show Keegan that they were not nothing – that their play was not going to be geared to him, for sure. And so, for Keegan his German adventure was not turning out like the brochure had advertised.

With the Scottish season about to begin, Dalglish remained an anomalous reserves player – and not even their captain, for all that he remained the club skipper in name. He was at Celtic only in body, but still he couldn't be sure where he was going to. Seasoned members of the press, though, were well used to Jock Stein's wiles, and a few of them were keen to impress Dalglish with whispers that Liverpool FC, flush with the money they'd got for Keegan, would be in for him soon enough. On Tuesday, 10 August 1977 Dalglish ran out at Dunfermline for a friendly, the small crowd studded with journalists, who were fly enough to notice that Bob Paisley and John Smith were also in attendance.

After the game Dalglish repaired to Pat Harkins' pub in Rutherglen with Celtic keeper Peter Latchford, sitting over his usual cream soda while Latchford sank a pint. It was there Marina reached her husband on the phone, with news that Stein needed a word. A little before midnight Dalglish was driving to Parkhead, where lights burned only in the gaffer's office and in the boardroom: Messrs Paisley and Smith were being entertained. Before the introductions were made, Desmond White had a last go at suggesting to Dalglish that his contract could be improved. 'Mr White,' Dalglish replied, 'it is not a question of money.' Liverpool settled with Celtic at £440,000, a British record fee, about which Paisley had no doubts.

The next day Stein drove Dalglish to the lodgings of the Liverpool party, and the two men had their Glasgow version of an emotive farewell. 'All the best, you wee bastard,' said Stein, giving his departing golden boy an affectionate cuff. And with that, Dalglish was headed south, more or less directly into the whirlwind: a first training session at Melwood, and a photo opportunity at Anfield (where fences were being erected to prevent future pitch invasions of the kind that had taken the shine off the title win clinched in May).

'The Liverpool fans will like Dalglish, but they must not expect him to play the way I play.' Such were the thoughts of Keegan, still mulling over Hamburg's opening defeat and his chill reception there as he contributed his usual ghosted column to the *Daily Express* on the Thursday before Dalglish's league debut with Liverpool. But Keegan displayed both modesty and foresight in evaluating his replacement: 'Dalglish is a star player now, but if he settles in at Liverpool and knocks in a few goals he will be an even bigger name than he could imagine possible ... Kenny may prove a better player for Liverpool than I did.' The new hope in the red number seven strode out against Manchester United in the Charity Shield at Wembley, its surface repaired from the abuse it had received from Scotland's fans back in May. The Liverpool support chanted 'Dalglish!' The mantle had been passed.

PART II

7

Make It Anywhere

1977-78

'If you've got three Scots in your side, you've got a chance of winning something.'

Bill Shankly

Keegan opened his account in the Bundesliga on the season's fourth Saturday, scoring the second Hamburg goal in a 3-1 win over Kaiserslautern. A chipped cross from the right bypassed a dreamily ball-watching defence, but Keegan's header, if unimpeded, was a bullet. His momentum carried him right into the Kaiserslautern goal, where he leapt, clung to the netting and swung there, seeming like a man who was pleased, for sure, but also getting rid of some pent-up frustrations.

As he tried to find his feet in Germany, Keegan the superstar was aware he had placed himself at quite a disadvantage. The German language made a bar, for one, and he found German bureaucracy and form-filling – even the weekly shop – a perplexing experience. He and Jean and the dogs had escaped from the Plaza hotel but only so far as a rather soulless apartment. Still, as ever, Keegan pitched in with maximum enthusiasm, gleaning a handful of resonant German phrases from the team

talks given by bilingual globetrotter Rudi Gutendorf. In training Gutendorf's stress was on ball skills and shooting: a change
from the Liverpool Way, where Keegan had professed to feel
increasingly like a cog in machine-like set patterns of play. But
Hamburg's set-up posed Keegan a new sort of challenge, for
he was assigned a midfield role behind two strikers – no longer
being fed the ball as the scampering red-shirted forward man.

It soon became clear that Keegan wasn't seeing much of the
ball in any case. On 3 September Hamburg played their newly
promoted neighbours St Pauli, to whom they hadn't lost in 17
years. Defender Peter Nogly predicted Hamburg would walk
it eight-nil. But St Pauli kept things tight and counterattacked
smartly, scoring one and then another. Keegan had no doubt
now that he was being purposely denied the ball. The neglect he
faced on the pitch carried over into the changing room, where
his cheery greetings to teammates routinely went unanswered.
'I'm like a motherless child,' he lamented to Jean.

At Liverpool, too, Dalglish – by no means as approachable or
outgoing as Keegan – had to come to terms with the perforce
apartness of the new start. Until the right house was secured
for his family he would be put up at Liverpool's Holiday Inn,
the football club's preferred venue for this purpose. On paper
it didn't look the easiest domestic arrangement for Marina, still
just 23, and the two Dalglish infants, Kelly and Paul. But the
Inn was managed by a Scot, Jack Ferguson from Cumnock
(10 miles from Shankly's Glenbuck), and he and his wife were
old friends of the Harkins. Ferguson had been making special
accommodation arrangements for Liverpool since Shankly's day,
and regularly travelled with the team as a sort of major-domo
to assess hospitality and catering.

Dalglish would profess to find Liverpool 'a bit like Glasgow'.
Here, after all, were two football-daft places: port cities,

industrial hubs of empire, strongly influenced by Irish immigration. Glaswegians and Scousers shared a sure sense of themselves and their essential and enviable character, however much their environs were now marked by visible decline and deprivation. A Scouser could easily appreciate Glaswegian gallus (as in 'flash', nonchalant, full of oneself). Dalglish, though, was a different sort of Glaswegian: his the Scottishness of few words, focused intensity, and no little suspicion of strangers.

The Liverpool changing room Dalglish entered, if not cliquey, had a clear sense of the law as laid down by seasoned, mainly Scouse, senior pros. So Dalglish had to reckon with Scouse banter, where any verbal slip-ups ('ricks') were mercilessly jumped on, schoolyard-style. There was one fellow Scot, at least, in young defender Alan Hansen, newly arrived from Partick Thistle, whose method of managing the banter was to sit in a corner with his mouth shut. Dalglish was further bemused by the amount of careful haircare and grooming that went on among these rough-arses; and, as at Celtic, the team had a serious drinkers' rota, Jimmy Case playing the Dixie Deans role in trying to draft Dalglish, to predictable non-effect.

Dalglish fitted right in, nonetheless – because he could handle himself, off the park and on it, where he settled with stunning speed. Seven minutes into his league debut at Middlesbrough he strode onto a smart lay-off from Terry McDermott and slotted the ball home. On his first start at Anfield he scored again as Newcastle were despatched 2-0. Against West Brom, Steve Heighway's pace teed him up with a chance, and that made three goals in three. Then, away to Ipswich, came a strike that was inimitably him. Tommy Smith steamed forward and laid the ball off to Ray Kennedy, whereupon Dalglish flagged that he wanted it, controlled it when it came, then struck a carefully lofted curler all the way into the furthest right corner. Three weeks later, against Chelsea, came another prime piece of quick-wittedness. Meeting a long ball from Hansen, exchanging headers with a defender, Dalglish spotted the goalie marginally off his line and curled the ball round two blue shirts into the right of the net.

Phenomenal goals, then. But Dalglish's dream start had even more to it than that. The support could feel that he seemed to have figured out instantly where everybody else was on the park. Rather than seeking to react first and fastest – the classic hound-like Keegan manner – Dalglish looked always to read and anticipate what both his teammates and opponents might do. His tempo was new, but his new team took to it. In the dugout, Paisley was developing a growing crush on the player he had nabbed.

'We've got a passing team,' he had stressed post-purchase. Pass-and-move was possession football, triangles and double passes, the rhythm of looking for and helping out teammates, making oneself available above all. The mantra was: 'Give it, get it, go!' Dalglish did all of this as finely as any player one could name – though it surely helped that he was doing it with the battling Case, the big and skilful Kennedy, the tireless McDermott and the finessing Heighway. The sum of what Dalglish brought, though, was more even than Keegan had provided.

Dalglish had also brought with him a set of superstitions, as precise as everything else about his game, if nothing like as considered. Given all the rigours of his approach to football, superstition seemed the irrational outlet – the devil's share – of what Dalglish knew he couldn't control. And so he shaved his stubble in one direction only, undressed and donned his kit in an unvarying order, and relieved himself only in the right-hand lavatory of the two in Anfield's home changing room. To Ray Kennedy, these 'magic rituals' only added to the sense of interior apartness Dalglish gave off. Yet in some odd way they seemed to fit with the club's Shankly-instilled, quasi-religious confidence, the 'animal spirits' that maintained Liverpool FC's faith in its own exceptionality.

Still, no game of football could be directed by any one player on the park; and the defenders of England's top flight were not about to sit back and admire Dalglish as he zipped by. He was subjected to a newly punishing type of tackle. He was also – having got used to a deeper role for Celtic – now the focal point of Liverpool's attack. Toshack was not going to be his strike partner; instead, he was mainly paired with David Fairclough. Liverpool looked a lot less assured, though, if they failed to keep the ball on the deck and centred it high as if Toshack were still there.

Seven league wins from 11 put Liverpool in second, two points behind Brian Clough's emergent Nottingham Forest; but then three defeats dealt big blows, and they fell to sixth. Where inconsistency seemed to dog Liverpool, Forest were well organised, always behind the ball whenever they didn't have it, fast and effective in counterattack. By Christmas Liverpool had more or less conceded the league. Dalglish, who always took defeat badly, had at least the hope of Europe, where Liverpool got past Dynamo Dresden and into the last eight.

Scotland's World Cup qualification, meanwhile, came to the crux one Wednesday night in mid-October. At Anfield Scotland beat Wales to ensure a second successive passage to the finals, a deeply dodgy penalty being loaned a ring of respectability when Dalglish's smart angled header made it 2-0. In Luxembourg, England managed the same scoreline in a game more notable for the now familiar and serious crowd trouble both in the ground and outside. Italy, though, had only to win their own last qualifier, at home to Luxembourg in December, to proceed at England's expense. This minor business duly got done, inflicting upon Keegan the pain of missing out on a second consecutive World Cup.

With Hamburg's season a clear misfire, Peter Krohn stepped down as sporting director at the end of October. His managerial hire Rudi Gutendorf followed him within 24 hours. The new gaffer was Ozcan Arkoc, the club's Turkish-born assistant coach and former goalkeeper. The exodus of the men who had bought Keegan risked piling further ignominy on what was already looking like a misadventure of a move. A glimmer of salvation was at hand, however – for Krohn's replacement was a man after Keegan's own heart.

With his usual entrepreneurial zeal, Gunter Netzer had approached Hamburg with a business proposal to take over the publishing of the club programme. Instead, Netzer was offered the director's job by club president Paul Benthien. After an initial demurral, Netzer bit. Hamburg, despite its difficulties, was a big club and had a big star player in Keegan, with whose pains Netzer was unusually well placed to identify, since his own move to Real Madrid in 1973 – a counterweight to Barcelona's purchase of Johan Cruyff – had put him in a similar alienated predicament. Netzer and Keegan were kindred spirits in other respects, too. 'There are eleven businessmen on a pitch,' Netzer had pronounced of the modern game, 'each looking after his own interests.' He would not, in short, be treating Felix Magath's criticism of Keegan's outside interests as a reasonable complaint.

Netzer, though, could not effect any instant change of fortune. In early November, Anderlecht eliminated Hamburg from the Cup Winners' Cup, after which a two-legged European 'Super Cup' tie against Liverpool proposed a marker of sorts for where Keegan's team stood – in Europe, and as opposed to the team he had left to 'better himself'. Hamburg hosted the first leg, and got the first goal. Keegan looked purposeful, at one point embarking on an ambitious dribble only to lose the ball in a challenge by Kennedy, whereupon Dalglish sought to take it away and Keegan nearly cleaned him out. (The Scot glanced back at Keegan on the deck, as if to say he'd felt that.) Just past the hour Dalglish received a pass with his back to goal, turned, stayed on his feet despite a stiff challenge, then lofted the ball invitingly to the left post where Fairclough headed right through the keeper's hands. At the final whistle, Hamburg fans were notably restive, though both clubs had exhibited deficiencies to reflect upon.

For the return a fortnight later Hamburg were put up in the Liverpool Holiday Inn that Dalglish called home; and he was occupying his baby daughter's attention in the comfort of the lounge when Keegan approached to exchange a few pleasantries. Dalglish presented a picture that spoke well of family duties maintained alongside football. Keegan, three years into married life with Jean, was perhaps feeling broody. The friendly encounter with Dalglish turned out, at any rate, to be the nicer part of his day.

Inside Anfield Keegan was met with boos, while the Kop was dressed in 'King Kenny' banners; and on the pitch Dalglish was at the heart of everything. Heighway got the opener, then McDermott, moving inside from the right, helped himself to a hat-trick. Keegan, who hardly had a kick all night, also had to contend with chants of *'Keegan, Keegan, what's the score?'* and *'We all agree! Dalglish is better than Keegan!'* The game became stunningly open, the Hamburg defence increasingly hard to spot, and it was Dalglish who rounded off a 6-0 rout. Keegan was first to shake Dalglish's hand at the final whistle. But the beating had to smart. He could see things had changed: Dalglish wasn't running for flick-ons; his old team were relaying it sharpish from defence to attacking feet – usually Dalglish's. Liverpool had certainly adapted to his absence. The question, then: could Keegan adapt to Germany, against the rising odds? He would candidly admit that his first five months had been 'diabolical'. Still, there was a little further to go to hit bottom.

New Year's Day of 1978 brought Hamburg a friendly against their near-neighbours VfB Lubeck, and Keegan found defender Erhard Preuss niggling at him as if it were Leeds United he faced. He was flattened a couple of times, grew visibly ireful, and when the red mist descended Keegan got truly lost in it. He threw a left-hook at Preuss then a right-cross, and headed directly for the tunnel as the ref waved a card in his general direction. They were, Keegan would later say, 'the hardest punches I've ever thrown. My fists were powered by five months of frustration . . . I thought I had killed him.' The consequences were a big fine and a ban, plus Keegan having to return to Lubeck to make a personal apology to their fans. His consolation was a call from Shankly, ever the boxing fan, who extended compliments to Keegan on the quality of the blows he had landed; and so, did a fair bit to lift his former favourite's unusually flagging spirits.

The New Year saw Bob Paisley give his Liverpool side a belated Christmas present – and Dalglish found himself with interesting new company at the Holiday Inn – with the purchase of 24-year-old Graeme Souness, a son of Edinburgh who had once aspired to crack the big time at Bill Nicholson's Spurs only to grow homesick in London and wind up making his mark on Teesside with Jack Charlton's Middlesbrough. There was a flair to how Souness carried himself on and off the park, as Dalglish knew well. They had roomed together for Scotland in 1974, and Dalglish had felt that Souness' careful grooming routines were suspiciously effeminate. In fact, liking the look of himself was just one facet of Souness' formidable self-regard. Under Charlton, his chief reputation was for ferocious toughness.

On his first morning in the Anfield dressing room Souness sought a loan of Tommy Smith's hairdryer. 'Smidge' very deliberately blanked the new start, remarking to Phil Neal, 'Everyone's allowed to make one mistake.' Souness got the message: he would have to prove himself anew. Luckily for him, like Dalglish, Souness' talent was special. 'Most midfields are made up of a buzzer, a cruncher and a spreader,' Paisley enthused to the press. 'This boy is all three.' The 'spreading' was perhaps the flashiest element: Souness had a rare gift for abrupt switches of play from left to right through pinpoint flighted passes. In his third game, against Manchester United, a 3-1 win, he made just such a pass out to McDermott on the right flank, shouted for the ball back, then met it with a left-foot volley into the roof of Alex Stepney's net.

At the Holiday Inn Souness got to observe the Dalglish family rituals and travails with a bemused bachelor's eye. He grew accustomed to a knock on his door to find Dalglish on childcare duty, seeking a clean bathroom in which to change baby Kelly. Souness' own routines were far freer and leisure-oriented: partial to champagne, in his first fortnight he ran up a hotel bar tab of £200. Dalglish's banter was that Souness ought really to fetch him breakfast on the way up from the bar in the morning.

The banter that came Dalglish's way in the changing room was quite often to do with his status as Paisley's favourite: a cod-County Durham chorus of 'My Kenny, my Kenny' sometimes greeted him. Certainly, no one else enjoyed immunity. That win over Manchester United was bracketed by defeats; and when Paisley, after another poor showing, fulminated about 'playboys and Champagne Charlies', there was little doubt whom he had in mind. Souness would have to shape up, and by himself – for after eight months in the hotel the Dalglish family were finally ready to move into a home of their own in Southport.

The European Cup campaign remained the lodestar of Liverpool's season, for Dalglish as much as anyone. He was learning that European ties could be sterile chess games, often decided by patience and away goals. In March they got past Benfica. Against Borussia Moenchengladbach in the semis they slipped two behind in the tie but grabbed a vital late goal in Germany. Come the return Paisley deployed Ray Kennedy further forward, and Souness was formidable. Kennedy got the first in six minutes, Dalglish and Jimmy Case ensured the contest was over within the hour.

Keegan's suspension over the Lubeck ruckus meant that he couldn't return to first-team action with Hamburg until the beginning of March. And yet, strangely, the ban seemed to help his cause – for one, because Hamburg lost seven games in his absence (including a 6-1 thumping by Cologne) and were clearly much the worse without him. His return seemed a kind of fresh start, then, and the very first game back signalled a difference: they beat Eintracht Braunschweig 4-2. A week later Keegan scored in a 5-3 win at FC Saarbrucken. The season ended with a 6-2 thrashing by Moenchengladbach, and the record showed that Hamburg had lost as many as they had won. But if Keegan still didn't see enough of the ball for his own liking, his 12 goals and his hard-running graft had endeared him to a significant tranche on the terraces. Younger fans, in particular, coined for him the sort of nickname his stature had long suited: *Mächtig Maus*, 'Mighty Mouse'.

Life was assuming a normalcy. Keegan had, by application, begun to surpass Jean's A-level German. They had procured their first house in Germany, a plain but big £80,000 prefab bungalow on a *fertig* (finished) estate. There would soon be another move to a larger property. Most meaningfully of all, Jean was expecting their first child. The matter of whereabouts said child would be born remained moot.

On 10 May 1978 Liverpool defended the European Cup at Wembley versus Club Brugge of Belgium. It was a boring, cagey final, as they so often are. And then midway through the second half Liverpool knocked on the door of the Brugge area and Souness threaded a fine ball through to Dalglish, who had kept the line with the Brugge defence but now reacted with superb anticipation. It was a massive moment, but Dalglish was nerveless. He had previously noted how the opposing keeper, Jensen, dropped low and early to save from McDermott. Seeing

Jensen come out now, Dalglish decided in a flash, dummied a little such that Jensen dropped, then dinked the ball over the keeper and into the net. Momentum carried Dalglish in a run-and-jump over the Wembley hoardings, towards the Liverpool support, who rejoiced in the shared schoolboyish elation of their lately anointed hero popping up with a stroke of genius to win the cup.

There was Dalglish, then, on the telly, always scoring – a source of misery to the fans he had left behind at Celtic. If no sum could have kept Dalglish at the club, his lucrative sale had only left them with money they couldn't seem to spend. Celtic's 1977-78 was a disaster, for all that Jock Wallace's Rangers side hardly looked like world-beaters – Rangers still achieved their second domestic treble in three years. In May 1978 Jock Stein was kicked upstairs as club director with special responsibility for Celtic Pools, a job that had a derisory look to it given Stein's eminence. Dalglish, by his departure, was inevitably felt to be a factor in the big man's decline. Stein had favoured his former skipper Billy McNeill as successor, and Celtic duly lured McNeill south from Aberdeen where he had cut his teeth as a manager. To replace McNeill, Aberdeen hooked the outgoing St Mirren boss Alex Ferguson, who had taken his young side up to the Premiership, and had the look of a coming man – not short on steely self-belief, at any rate.

Back in that summer of 1967 when Dalglish had made peace with the idea of becoming a Celtic player, Ferguson had been snapped up by Dalglish's beloved Rangers for a Scottish record fee of £65,000. He was a forward, and had looked a natural goalscorer; but it didn't work out for Ferguson at Ibrox. In the 1969 Old Firm Scottish Cup final, Ferguson was blamed for the first of Celtic's four goals, on account of failing to pick up Billy McNeill. It would be Ferguson's last first-team appearance for Rangers; he was thereafter demoted to the second string, where Dalglish ran into him more regularly as a young pretender with Celtic's reserves. Ferguson had felt the sting of reproof from Rangers keenly, but he had collected himself, made a hard judgement on how he would henceforth make his living, and turned to management, progressing with impressive application. Ferguson had studied Stein closely and aspired to a version of the Big Man's complete control – rigour with regard to training, players' codes of conduct, and close study of the opposition. He also exuded an 'us against them' mentality in leading his sides into battle with the establishment forces of the Old Firm which he sought to dislodge from their perch in the Scottish game.

The air of a longer-term slump around Celtic, however, could not be denied. European glory was a thing of the past, the ground was falling into disrepair, the board's refusal to invest was unpopular. Celtic's success of the 1960s and 1970s had been built on player development: the 'Glasgow and District XI' that were the Lisbon Lions, and the 'Quality Street Gang'. Of those young stars, only Danny McGrain remained. Scottish football seemed to have become largely a finishing school for the English League.

And yet, the Scotland side that travelled to the World Cup in Argentina had quality right through it, however much of it drawn from English clubs, and hopes were not unfeasibly high for a good showing. The team got a grandiose send-off (shown on live TV) at a packed Hampden Park, the players piped and drummed onto an open-top bus to the airport. Manager Ally MacLeod was confident enough to leave at home Liverpool's Hansen and Aston Villa's Andy Gray. He had Souness, Macari, Hartford and Forest's Archie Gemmill at his disposal, though he was banking big on two relative veterans: Don Masson as playmaker, and Bruce Rioch as captain. Still, MacLeod was exuberant: 'You can mark down 25 June 1978,' he told reporters, 'as the day Scottish football conquers the world.'

MacLeod's mouth caused the diffident Dalglish some disquiet, and there was worse to come. The true slackness of

Scotland's preparations for the greatest of tournaments was to be sharply exposed. Their 'luxury' hotel in Alta Gracia had an oppressive, isolated feel, two players to each small room under stony-faced security, the 'Olympic-sized' swimming pool bone dry. The supposedly convenient nearby training facility had a rough playing surface, where Joe Jordan hurt his ankle, thus requiring the team to commute hastily to a pitch 20 miles away. It wasn't a happy or well-conditioned camp. Souness and Dalglish, rooming together, tried to keep their heads apart from the disarray.

Nobody in the camp had bothered greatly to research the first opponents, Peru. Nobody knew Peru routinely played two flying wingers, for a start. Forward Teofilo Cubillas was supposedly 'tubby', out of shape. And when Scotland took the lead – Dalglish and Hartford crafting a chance for Rioch, saved, but with Jordan at hand to capitalise on the keeper's spill – that wilful ignorance seemed no great shame. Then Peru levelled, a good move finished by Cueto. The Scotland dressing room at half-time was disputatious, full of frustration that these opponents were not being more easily put away. MacLeod gave no great leadership, and so vying factions formed on what to do next. In the second half Peru bossed the midfield and looked awfully dangerous at the edge of the area. On the hour, Masson had a penalty saved. Then Cubillas rocketed a shot past Alan Rough. Belatedly, Masson and Rioch gave way to Macari and Gemmill, only for Cubillas to hit a swerving free kick past Scotland's wall and Rough – and that was that. Scottish fans, sure they had been sold a pup, barracked and battered their team's bus as it bore the wounded players away, back to Alta Gracia.

Dalglish had been played deep and right-sided, behind Jordan. Possibly, teaming him alongside Andy Gray might have been more fruitful. But as Scotland came out for their second, must-win match against Iran, Gray was in a London TV studio, hopefully assessing Scotland's chances in a chair beside Kevin Keegan. Before a crowd of 12,000 in a 30,000-seater stadium, Scotland were tense and muted. Nothing went their way, fair enough, but 1-1 was the outcome. MacLeod, looking hunted and despairing throughout, was reduced to rehearsing his excuses for failure in advance of the final game against Holland.

And yet: a move to Mendoza brought a nicer hotel and a lusher training pitch. Late, too late, Souness was drafted into the starting XI. Scotland went behind to a penalty, and Dalglish had a strike rather unfairly ruled out. But then came a neat combination, Jordan heading down for Dalglish, in yards of space, to pivot and crash the ball into the roof. Souness then won a penalty of Scotland's own that Archie Gemmill converted. When Gemmill performed a stunning slalom through the Dutch defence to score a soloist's third for Scotland, they were on the cusp of a massively implausible triumph. Within minutes, though, Holland struck back: 3-2 it finished – glorious failure, early plane home, what might have been, *et cetera*.

If not, in the end, an utter disgrace, Scotland had been a dispiriting letdown. Dalglish was left to contemplate another world-stage disappointment. 'The catatonic displays of Dalglish have been a misery to his admirers,' wrote a head-shaking Hugh McIlvanney. He had given some grist to the standard Scottish antipathy towards 'Anglos' – to the ignorant idea that he played with greater conviction for club than country. It was more complex than that. But then, the Scottish support had been promised the world.

Another fan base for whom Dalglish cut a dubious figure was Celtic, made brazenly clear when Liverpool went up to Parkhead for Jock Stein's testimonial on 14 August 1978. (Stein was about to head south to manage Leeds United, where he lasted all of 44 days away from Scotland before accepting an offer to take over the national team from the spent figure of Ally MacLeod.) Dalglish knew by what he'd heard from the craic at Pat Harkins' pub that he was due for some stick. His Liverpool teammates thought that comical, given what he'd achieved in green and white. The match programme promised 'a smashing welcome home reception for Kenny'. But the game was indeed 90 minutes of dog's abuse for Dalglish. Running towards 'The Jungle' to retrieve the ball for a throw-in, he had a meat pie flung in his direction. Dalglish was learning, as Keegan had, just how hard it sometimes was to be a hero.

8

Force of Will

1978-80

In close season, with Hamburg brooding over its status as the 10th best team in West Germany, Keegan called a summit with Gunter Netzer, perhaps the one man at the club who understood him. He issued an ultimatum: either use me, or sell me. Netzer assured him that the team's new coach, Yugoslav disciplinarian Branko Zebec, had been hired to replace Ozcan Arkoc with precisely the objective of deploying Keegan properly.

It was clear that a small but obdurate anti-Keegan clique had been poisoning the Hamburg changing room. Zebec dismantled that. Though Felix Magath was judged indispensable, Arno Steffenhagen and Georg Volkert were out. The squad was strengthened, meanwhile, by astute picks from Germany's second division: 'Jimmy' Hartwig from TSV Munich 1860 and big Horst Hrubesch from Rot-Weiss Essen, a hard shooter also known as *Das Kopfball-Ungeheuer* ('The Header Beast'). Netzer and Zebec were hopeful that target man Hrubesch could prove another kind of Toshack for Keegan.

Zebec spoke German rather as Keegan did, not strictly grammatical but enough to be clear. He wore black shades that exuded *hauteur* (though rumour had it that they also masked his regular hangovers). Zebec was a rigid systems man, and

Hamburg were about to be schooled in a pressing game that required high fitness levels for constant harrying. The coach introduced a punishing twice-daily training regime, sending the team for extra sprinting. Keegan found it absurdly hard going even by his own rigorous standards, but he understood the virtue of what was being preached. Now living in Itzstedt, in the afternoons he would pound through the woods of nearby Kisdorf, flanked by his sheepdogs.

Even with the new arrangement, Keegan retained an unusual apartness. The spectators who came to watch Hamburg train were keen above all on *Mächtig Maus*, and he signed every scrap of paper as ever. But he would not routinely eat lunch with his teammates after training. He kept his distance, too, from German media, partly because of his exclusive British contracts, partly from suspicion of their sympathies, partly because he remained unsure of his German language abilities.

The side acquired a new shape: Rudolf Kargus in goal, behind a defence of Manfred Kaltz, Peter Nogly, Ivan Buljan and Peter Hidien; a midfield of Hartwig, Caspar Memering, Magath and Keegan; and up front, Hrubesch and Willi Reimann. Hamburg kicked off their season against the lately dominant Moenchengladbach and were 3–0 up in 20 minutes, though Keegan missed a penalty. They went on to thump champions Cologne, then put away Hertha Berlin, Schalke, Nurnberg and Fortuna Dusseldorf. Keegan had still to score his first of the season: the goals were coming from big Hrubesch, feeding on Kaltz's crosses from the right, and from Magath's prompting force in midfield. But it was progress, for sure. After a surprise defeat at Braunschweig, Hamburg thrashed Dortmund 5–0; Keegan got on the scoresheet and they sat second in the league behind Kaiserslautern. He got a brace in a 4–2 beating of Schalke. And in November he celebrated one of life's great moments as Jean gave birth to their firstborn child, a daughter they named Laura Jane.

Before the winter break Hamburg had to travel to the Olympic Stadium to take on Bayern Munich, still bolstered by the veterans Gerd Muller, Paul Breitner and Sepp Maier, but newly dangerous thanks to a sharp young striker, Karl-Heinz Rummenigge. It was Keegan, though, who swung the game in the 19th minute. Having made himself available with a blistering run across the back four, he took the ball with his back to goal, worked his way down to touch, then turned his defender inside out, motoring down the line and laying the ball off smartly to Caspar Memering, who tucked away a side-footer. One up, Hamburg defended valiantly in numbers to secure a crucial win. A week later Keegan bagged a hat-trick at home to Arminia Bielefeld, and Hamburg were just a point off the top. In a remarkable validation, Keegan's form was rewarded with the European Footballer of the Year prize for 1978 – proof, perhaps, that Europe had been second best at the Argentina World Cup, and redress, maybe, for his having been overlooked the year before after Liverpool's double. What was beyond doubt was that Keegan had turned his fortunes at Hamburg right around.

In England Liverpool were imperious, a 7-0 demolition of Tottenham setting a sort of benchmark, Terry McDermott's seventh epitomising Paisley's passing Liverpool much as Keegan's third in the 1974 FA Cup final had done for Shankly's team. The game's true immortals, though, were the sides that had won a hat-trick of European Cups – Real Madrid, Ajax and Bayern. Liverpool were about to embark on the quest for their third. The rivalry with Clough's Forest, however, was established and seething; and in late September the holders Liverpool were freakishly drawn against league champions Forest in the first round.

Emlyn Hughes had begun to look susceptible in Liverpool's defence; and at Forest's City Ground it was a Hughes error that helped Birtles to shoot the home side ahead. One-nil would have been a passable result on which to resume at Anfield; but Liverpool ditched everything they had learned in Europe about the need for patience, attacking Forest as if in a domestic cup tie, pressing furiously for an equaliser. Dalglish was at the heart of it, first selling Larry Lloyd an immaculate dummy to drive towards goal – yet as defender Kenny Burns neared, Dalglish made an uncharacteristic stab at power, and fired straight at Peter Shilton. In the second half he again showed his class, spinning Viv Anderson in the box and pulling the trigger on goal – but Shilton reacted to parry the ball over the bar. Liverpool were then undone by a typical Forest counterattack and a second goal. Following the Anfield return, another full-blooded effort but a goalless draw, Liverpool had been deposed.

With Hughes receding from the first XI and shortly on his way to Wolves, the captain's armband needed passing, and Dalglish accepted the mantle from Paisley for a while. Unlike at Celtic, though, these duties seemed not to suit him. Jock Stein had taken charge of Scotland and also made Dalglish captain; but he didn't want that job any more than the one at Liverpool, where Phil Thompson took over the role with local-boy pride.

After Christmas Liverpool would lose only two more league games en route to the title. They had the look of a great side, and their spine was Scottish – the 'Jocks', as they were jocularly known, the most influential figures. In defence, Hansen was a fulcrum, anticipating well and bringing the ball out, his lofty composure never betraying the angst he always felt pre-match. In midfield, Souness was maturing into the general of a quartet, holding the ball and holding off challenges, dictating a game's tempo, on top of those startling passes. And Dalglish, ever-present in the campaign, was top scorer with 21 goals, a popular winner of the Football Writers' Association Footballer of the Year award.

For all Liverpool's success, the club was not rolling in money: one of its finest seasons had ended with a profit of barely £70,000. In the summer break John Smith would lament 'the paucity of money in British football' and speak even of 'fighting for our existence'. The occasion for his remarks was

Liverpool's striking a deal for shirt advertising with Hitachi, worth £50,000, though such promotions had been frowned upon by the FA because of TV coverage. 'The days are gone,' Smith warned, 'when a club like ours could control their destiny on the money coming through the turnstiles. It is absolutely essential to generate income from other sources.'

For Dalglish, income outside the game remained relatively modest, mainly derived from his investments in licensed premises with Pat Harkins, though in a gesture down the path forged by Best and Keegan he agreed to put his name to a gentlemen's outfitters in Liverpool. Schmutter, though, was not to be a trade in which Dalglish prospered.

In 1978 Kevin Keegan earned around £250,000, only half of that from playing football. The rest was media work, endorsements and promotion, putting his name and face to a great range of comestibles, some of them quality products, some pure tat: Patrick boots and Pirelli slippers, Smith's Crisps and a Lyons Maid ice lolly, the Grundig 'Hit Boy' transistor radio and the 'Match of the Day' Electronic Soccer Action Game. For Christmas of 1979 he even prepared an illustrated book-length reflection on his England career – quite a conceit, with England not having made it to a major finals in a decade. But *Against the World* was a product of Keegan's cottage industry, a study of his wider success, in which the puzzling obstinacy of failure with the national team was just a hurdle yet to be cleared. In places the book read like a diary of his crazed professional schedule: catch-ups with his agent, 'talks with a film producer', 'a personal appearance at a Toy Fair', 'dinner with a sheikh who wanted to name a racehorse after me'.

His career as a recording artist was formally resurrected, too, the result of an introduction by Ivan Buljan to a couple of music producers who wanted to enlist Keegan in the recording of a

single, 'Head Over Heels in Love', written by Chris Norman
and Pete Spencer of the soft-pop English group Smokie. Keegan,
naturally, was up for it. He was offered his pick of royalties or
a one-off fee of £20,000, and in a rare commercial misstep he
settled for the latter. The record went on to sell 220,000 copies
in Germany and cracked the UK Top 30.

Come the end of the 1978-79 season Keegan's two-year
contract with Hamburg would be up. Real Madrid had kept an
eye on him, and Juventus remained interested. A less illustrious
but richer party popped up with a novel sort of offer. US soccer
side the Washington Diplomats were newly rolling in dough
having been acquired by a subsidiary of Gulf and Western, and
wished to buy success. They approached Keegan with a view
to his playing their summer season, a contract worth around
$250,000. Gunter Netzer waved it through, but Keegan realised
he would be a Diplomats player at the cut-off point for players to
be registered to play in the European Cup. In the nick of time he
withdrew, and Hamburg even compensated him for the payday
he had lost. The Diplomats had to settle for Johan Cruyff.

Keegan's special concern for the next year's European Cup
derived from his growing faith that Hamburg would be in the
draw. Sluggish at the start of 1979, they went unbeaten from
March into June. The fitness levels demanded by Zebec were
paying off. At the start of April they beat leaders Kaiserslautern
3-1, Keegan scoring, whereupon Kaiserslautern began to stut-
ter. Stuttgart sneaked to the top but Hamburg marched on, and
Keegan, linking up adroitly with Hrubesch and Magath, scored
11 in the last 12 games. It was decided on the penultimate match
day as Hamburg obtained an edgy draw with relegation candidates Arminia Bielefeld, but Kaiserslautern and Stuttgart lost.
Hamburg couldn't now be caught, and had their first Bundesliga
title for 19 years. They lost to Bayern Munich in a meaningless
final fixture (the chief incident of which was a crush among
spectators that saw a fence giving way and 71 people injured).
At a great celebration at Hamburg town hall Keegan got to hold

aloft the championship shield – a moment to savour, a massive accomplishment. He had made it to the summit, succeeded where so many Brits overseas had failed, and made himself a legend in the German game. He was 28 years old, and it was the last winner's medal of his career.

In late May, Keegan and Dalglish shook hands in Wembley's centre circle as opposing captains for the England–Scotland home international. For both men, international duty had been a source of pride tinged by disappointment: caps and goals aplenty, for sure, and Old Enemy contests had their lustre, but they were nothing next to the major tournaments at which Keegan had yet to appear and Dalglish had seemed off-colour. At Wembley Scotland got ahead with a goal from Ipswich's John Wark, before an equaliser on the stroke of half-time put England on top, Keegan going on to score the third in England's 3-1 win. Keegan's England fortunes were changing at last: new manager Ron Greenwood would steer the team through to the 1980 finals of the European Championships with seven wins from eight group matches, Keegan top scorer.

Stein's Scotland, however, were eliminated, beaten home and away by their group's winners, Belgium. Liverpool, too, had a poor start to 1979-80, beset by injuries, though one of the absentees, Ray Kennedy, simply felt that the team was 'idling in second gear'. Paisley pointed to a lack of cutting edge, exemplified by his usual favourite in the number seven shirt. 'The whole crux of this season so far has been the way Kenny has been playing,' Paisley tutted. 'He's not been at his best and could have had a few more goals.' It was a classic Liverpool kick up the arse. From the first week of October Liverpool didn't lose again until mid-January, going top in mid-November, beating their main rivals Manchester United on Boxing Day. They lost in the semis of both domestic cups, but retained the title with a

4-1 win at Aston Villa in the penultimate game of the season. Dalglish, again, played every league game and contributed 16 goals. Once again, the European Cup delivered a blow, as they lost in the first round to a consummate Dinamo Tbilisi side driven by their playmaker David Kipiani and the Russian national captain Aleksandre Chivadze. That result ruled out what could have been another Liverpool–Hamburg match-up in the last 16; but there Hamburg roared past Tbilisi, winning both legs, Keegan scoring in each. His side was in a rich vein of form, vying again for the Bundesliga title with Bayern Munich. His sizeable part in that form earned him the Ballon d'Or for the second successive year.

The moment had come, then, for Keegan to consider his next move. After the tortuous start, he was on the cusp of achieving everything Hamburg could have offered: a domestic/European double of Liverpudlian proportions. With a few more prime years in him as a player, he desired another challenge. Juventus were very keen, but Jean was uneasy about Rome from the view of security. (The 1978 kidnap and murder of the states-man Aldo Moro was still unnervingly sharp in the memory.) Peter Robinson had slipped a first-option clause into Keegan's deal back in 1977, and he and John Smith flew to Hamburg to take Keegan for dinner, where they ventured the thought that he might come back to Liverpool as player-coach, perhaps to replace Paisley in time. Keegan, flattered by the offer, nonethe-less had no special interest in a backroom role, and other than that aspect the proposal had nothing new to it. The vision of Keegan and Dalglish together in red, then, was not to be.

Keegan was, however, thinking seriously of England again, above all for family reasons, but also thanks to a cheeky punt in his direction ventured by Lawrie McMenemy, affable Geordie manager of Southampton, who called Keegan in Hamburg with a friendly enquiry about a special German variety of light fitting. McMenemy, in truth, was merely fishing for a way to sound Keegan out about moving to the Saints. They had won the FA

Cup in 1976, had been finishing decently in the league, and McMenemy was assembling a squad of young bucks and veterans who could still do a job: Mick Channon, Alan Ball, Dave Watson, Charlie George. McMenemy let Keegan know all this fascinating stuff in the hope that he might appreciate the special challenge of a 'smaller club'. In fact, for reasons McMenemy could only have half-guessed at, his offer ticked most of Keegan's boxes.

Keegan agreed to take a meeting in London at the loaned house of a Saints supporter; McMenemy's finance director Guy Askham also attended and brought a contract along just in case. To their amazement, Keegan signed it. McMenemy stayed on in London to watch Keegan run out for England at Wembley against Ireland, tickled by his private knowledge that the England captain was now a Southampton player. Keegan scored both goals, superbly, as England won 2-0. McMenemy continued to keep his £420,000 signing completely secret until the following week, when he invited press to a conference suite at the Potters Heron hotel in Romsey, on the enticement that they would get to meet someone with 'a big part in the club's future'. Into the suite strode Keegan, fresh off the plane, and well pleased by the matinee performance McMenemy had made of it all.

Back in Germany, three crushing wins put Hamburg top of the table above Bayern on goal difference; then in the European Cup quarter-finals they fought past Hajduk Split on away goals to set up a meeting with Real Madrid. The first leg at the Bernabeu took the air out of Hamburg's tyres, Real winning 2-0, Keegan effectively patrolled out of the game by Perez Garcia. In the Bundesliga, further deflated, Hamburg surrendered a two-goal lead against Dortmund to drop a point and let Bayern overtake them again.

For the return with Real at the Volksparkstadion, Hamburg were condemned to all-out attack; but they did so with stunning aplomb and a high tempo. Kaltz gave them an early lead from the spot after a lunging foul on Keegan by Perez Garcia, then Hrubesch squared the tie with a stooping header. As Hamburg didn't let up, so Real got a chance, and Laurie Cunningham scored what seemed a vital goal. But Kaltz replied for Hamburg, and on the stroke of half-time Keegan released Memering on the left to cross onto Hrubesch's head: 4–1, and for the first time Hamburg had the advantage. In the second half, Real were frustrated so effectively that midfielder Vicente del Bosque threw an exasperated punch at Keegan and got his marching orders, after which Memering sealed Hamburg's win. Gunter Netzer, in the manner for which he was admired, described the night as 'the funniest and best thing I've ever seen from HSV'.

After the euphoria, Hamburg let the league slip: a loss at Bayer Leverkusen while Bayern won at Stuttgart left them with too much to do. All of Keegan's chips, then, went on the European Cup final, his farewell to Hamburg just as the 1977 final had marked his leaving of Liverpool. The venue was the Bernabeu, the opposition Nottingham Forest, defending champions though minus their main goal threat, Trevor Francis. Hamburg had Hrubesch on the bench nursing an ankle knock, so Keegan was played further forward, but his side resumed the attacking manner of their semi-final success – only to run into the well-organised Forest and the staunch Peter Shilton in impassable form. John Robertson squeezed in a goal for Forest after 19 minutes, whereupon it was all Hamburg – Magath the chief threat going forward, Keegan gradually dropping deeper to chivvy and instigate attacks. But Forest, if the less attractive side, saw the game out and lifted the trophy: a loss that felt especially hateful to Keegan. Later he would rate it 'probably the biggest disappointment' of his career to that stage.

Their league title relinquished, Hamburg closed the season with a nothing win over Schalke, Keegan subbed at half-time. It was not the departure he had planned; rather, a pale sequel to the stage-managed bow at Southampton. Still, he was leaving Germany as the European Footballer of the Year, medals to his name, and the assurance that no other English player had done it half as well. Besides, in Keegan's portfolio of interests there remained a big prize to play for: the European Championships in Italy – remarkably, his first international tournament with England, and one for which his hopes were customarily high, despite the wearying season and a niggling fitness concern over his knee ligaments.

England's first game was in Turin against Belgium, conquerors of Scotland. Ray Wilkins gave England the lead their support expected, which lasted three minutes before Jan Ceulemens equalised. And then tussles were seen to break out behind the England goal, and Clemence felt his eyes water and his vision blur dramatically. The Italian police had fired tear gas, then pressed into the throng of the fighting crowd amid clouds of yellow smoke. Play was suspended, the players escorted from the pitch. The game never recovered its purpose and ended in a draw. 'We have done everything to create the right impression here,' fumed Ron Greenwood, 'then these bastards let you down.' The FA despaired of 'a few silly louts', 'not fans at all'. It was hard to say which group of so-called supporters had started the bother. What was clear was that for those who went to football in the hope of participating in exhilarating disorder, international finals were a big-stage version of the weekly awayday, a brainless Roman holiday at the expense of those who had come to play football or to watch it.

Three days later England played the host nation, though Turin's mayor had threatened to cancel the match. Despite a bristling police presence there were fights among fans before kick-off. In the game, Keegan was simply marked out of proceedings by Marco Tardelli, who also volleyed home what turned out to be the winner. At the last Keegan saw his overhead kick parried by Dino Zoff, but at the whistle England were out of the tournament.

The English FA optimistically made it known they would still be keen to host the 1984 European finals. UEFA exuded the feeling that those finals might be better off without England. The 1980 edition, for sure, had been marked by manifestations of what some called the 'English Disease'. Prime Minister Margaret Thatcher, in Venice for an EEC summit, had condemned England's support. One year into her government, with unemployment around the two million mark, the rate of inflation rising and the UK economy in recession, Thatcher had bigger problems than football. Still, a growing commentariat would take the view that her government was a major part of the problems besetting the English game.

Keegan had always stayed out of politics, wisely, for there was no gain in it for him. He had identified himself with his dad's views, and his dad had been Labour. Still, the England squad had attended a Downing Street reception before their departute to Italy, the majority of them very probably just as 'apathetic Tory' in their political preferences as the Spurs side studied by Hunter Davies 10 years earlier. Keegan and Emlyn Hughes posed alongside Thatcher for a photo in which they mimed the placing of smackers on each of her cheeks.

In public Keegan always made plain that he saw himself as a self-made man who had made his own luck by dint of effort. He would not disown his working-class upbringing; but nor would he apologise for aspiring to better. This, after all, was the man at the head of companies named Kevin Keegan Investments and Kevin Keegan Enterprises, with swingeing views on income tax. He was no class warrior; and nor, it seemed obvious, were the young men fighting at football matches, whose 'selfishness' appeared hardly less conspicuous than that of the most tough-minded Thatcherite. Aside from that similarity, one had to wonder – as the England manager railed against the 'bastards' and his players ran for cover while the punches flew – about the widening gulf between footballers and their purported fans.

9

The Top, and Staying There

1980-82

'A football club's soul is located in the dressing room. The spirit emanating from this room will touch everyone, colour every aspect of club life . . .'

Eamon Dunphy, *A Strange Kind of Glory* (1991)

At Hamburg, Keegan had cut the uncommon figure of businessman–player, all briefcase and boots, viewed askance by Magath among others. Back in England his commercial instincts caused no such complaint. The autumn of 1980 saw the launch of the 'Kevin Keegan Collection at Harry Fenton', a menswear range that ran from slacks and jumpers to three-piece pinstriped suits. Keegan modelled the clobber himself, naturally. To mark his return to the English game he even cut another pop single, a gentle croon over strummed acoustic guitar. 'Oh how I yearn to be home again in England,' Keegan sang. The sentiment was no doubt sincere, but this was arguably one tie-in product too many, and it failed to chart.

The Southampton changing room he had joined was one with plenty of old mates of his, in which his authority preceded him. And yet Lawrie McMenemy's squad also contained a core of hard-wearing younger lads, mainly local, dubbed 'The Hampshire Hogs' after a popular cricket club. There was a strange sort of rough-housing ethos going on at Southampton, and the European Footballer of the Year had to take this in his stride.

TV crews were attracted to Keegan in the standard manner, but 23,320 still packed into the Dell to see his Southampton debut against Manchester City. The Saints won that one, and four of their first five. But Keegan picked up a hamstring pull, which he then aggravated in the most pointless fashion, playing with a heavily strapped leg at a lucrative club friendly in Casablanca since the club required his presence to fulfil their promise to the sponsor. One can imagine what Shankly would have said to the idea. Kenny Dalglish would not have got on the plane.

At a club where any player carrying an injury was left to feel like it was a fault of their own that they ought to remedy fast – 'otherwise,' in Alan Hansen's view, 'you really were persona non grata' – Dalglish had stayed fit and racked up consecutive games like none before him. But at last, after 180 straight games, some unshakeable knee ligament bother forced him to miss his first Liverpool game through injury. This statistical testimony to his resilient place in the side was remarkable, not least for a player so routinely kicked. Dalglish could look out for himself but, still, Souness had taken to a certain special invigilation of Dalglish's treatment by opposition defenders.

Injury cost Keegan a few games for Southampton, also the start of England's World Cup qualifying campaign. But he was back in time for the visit of Liverpool to the Dell in late September. Souness put the visitors in front with a low right-footer, having had his path cleared expertly by Dalglish's timed run that dragged two defenders off the scent. But goals from Chris Nicholl and Phil Boyer got Southampton ahead at half-time. Phil Neal, having missed a second-half penalty, atoned in typical Liverpool fashion with a cross for David Fairclough

to level. Southampton sat third in the table, Liverpool fourth –
contenders both, but Keegan's new side more conspicuous, and
performing at the level he required.

Liverpool's progress in Europe saw them run into the first
Anglo-Scottish 'Battle of Britain' since Celtic's bouts with
Liverpool in 1966 and Leeds in 1970, as Paisley's team were
drawn against Scotland's champions. 'The moment we knew it
was Aberdeen,' Dalglish would remember, 'the mood around
the dressing room changed.'

Aberdeen were an emergent force under Alex Ferguson,
now 38 and making a very serious fist of management, having
fashioned an Aberdeen side of notable industry and flair that
boasted superb young Scottish players in Miller, McLeish,
McGhee, Strachan and Archibald. Thus, Dalglish felt his share
of Liverpool's anxiety as the banter came down from north of
the border, of Anfield's Anglos 'being sent homeward to think
again'.

Ferguson had learned a fair bit from Jock Stein, both in the
matter of letting players know who was boss, and in playing
on the nerves of rivals. After Stein had publicly conceded the
title to Ferguson's Rangers in 1968, the Gers had bowed to the
pressure of presumption and fallen to bits over the final games.
In the spring of 1980 Ferguson had run the same ruse on Celtic,
prior to Aberdeen beating them twice at Parkhead and going
on to pinch the trophy by a point. To match wits with mighty
Liverpool, though, was a big new test for Ferguson, who rated
the European draw as a 'nightmare'. He did his homework,
travelling to Anfield to study his opponents, and suffered an
introduction to Shankly that left him feeling both awestruck
and unmistakably twitted. ('So, you are down to have a look at
our great team,' Shankly told him. 'Aye, they all try that . . .')

For the first leg, Aberdeen's Pittodrie stadium was a bear

pit for the visitors; and yet within five minutes Dalglish
made a shrewd pass to David Johnson, who delivered a ball
for McDermott to finish past keeper Jim Leighton. One-nil
it stayed, and the balance of power sat with the Anglos. At
Anfield, Aberdeen got stuck in and McGhee missed an early
chance. But then Miller headed into his own net from a corner,
and a slick back-heel from Dalglish set Neal up for a second. The
second half was a red succession of attacks, Dalglish scoring a
rare header for number three, Hansen securing the triumph of
the Anglos with the fourth.

The spanking was sorely resented by Ferguson. He could
not wait to be gone from Anfield, and Gordon Strachan would
recall the gaffer demanding total solemnity from his players
on the coach home. But the Aberdeen lads had first to retrieve
their gear from their hotel, and there in the lobby was Graeme
Souness, in the company of women, suavely dressed for a bit of
a night, evidently content with his day's work. Ferguson would
not forget the mortification of this defeat nor the manner of it.
He had felt the knife go in, and was resolved to pay Liverpool
back some day.

One sunlit October Saturday at Manchester City's Maine Road,
Dalglish added one more to his gallery of goals that stunned
both opposition and onlookers by their speed of vision and execution. He turned this way and that before a strike with his left,
low and hard from 20 yards, which the keeper could only parry
into the net. Liverpool had made a spotty start to the season,
though Dalglish bagged a brace to beat Aston Villa. He would
manage a good few in the cups, too, as Liverpool marched
to the League Cup semi-final. But from late November right
through to the end of the season, Dalglish didn't score a single
league goal. In mid-December he had to submit to a troublesome ankle knock and missed a league game against Ipswich.

His replacement at number seven was one Ian Rush, making his first-team debut seven months after signing from Chester. It was a significant run-out for Rush, who was low on confidence, attracting suspicion among the senior squad that he wasn't up to it – someone who, according to David Johnson, 'just looked like an ordinary player', and not, therefore, a Liverpool player.

The Liverpool changing room was a tough environment where players were expected to show their mettle and merit their selection – no excuses, no passengers, any problems sorted in the player's own time. When Dalglish had joined, the untouchable figures in this den had been mainly Merseysiders; but now it was the 'Jocks' who were masters at Melwood and Anfield. Dalglish, 'King' to the support, was also 'Super' in the changing room; and if not such a dominant dog in the pack as Souness, he could still make newer teammates wary of a bark. Never averse to a nag at the ref, Dalglish was also tetchy with teammates if a pass hadn't come exactly when and where he'd wanted it. He was considered a moaner; but was always heeded, because he was so bloody good.

In the eyes of Craig Johnston, who signed for Liverpool in the spring of 1981, the Scottish triumvirate 'set the tone' at the club. 'They decided what was funny, what was acceptable, who played well, who played badly ... They understood how you had to behave if you were a group of men who wanted to win things.' South African-born goalkeeper Bruce Grobbelaar, who arrived at Anfield from Vancouver Whitecaps around the same time as Johnston, came to the same conclusion: 'Souness, Hansen and Dalglish were very harsh. They'd be your best friend if you were playing well and winning. But if you made a mistake, they never spoke to you.'

Ronnie Whelan – another new start circa 1981, bought two years earlier from Irish League side Home Farm – felt there was a 'raw and ruthless' edge to the dressing-room banter. It was hardly top-drawer repartee or lancing wit. Grobbelaar had witnessed some awful things having enlisted and fought in the

Rhodesian bush war, but any reference to same would occasion a Dalglish crack about his hailing from 'Shepherd's Bush'. Such was the price of peer group acceptance.

No player suffered quite so much in this line, though, as Ian Rush. Since he wore his hair a little slick, Dalglish and Hansen nicknamed him 'Omar'. Since he was partial to the post-punk music of Two Tone and The Human League, rather than the bland car-stereo sounds beloved of most footballers, he was rated weird. And since he wore skinny jeans with white socks rather than the golf-course-ready leisurewear of senior players, he was made to accept derision. 'Dalglish would always lead the banter,' Rush recalled, 'muttering some wisecrack like, "Been repairing the car, have you?" And that would start them all off.' ('All' the operative word, as Howard Gayle, the squad's solitary black player, noted: 'Everybody thought they were style icons, wearing the best gear and being quick about the tongue.') Understandably, then, in the manner of the new boy facing the bullies of the lower sixth, Rush initially 'hated' the Liverpool dressing room. 'He let the banter get to him,' Gayle observed, 'and nearly went down because of it.'

In later years Dalglish would have the grace to be contrite, up to a point. 'In today's politically correct times,' he wrote in his 2010 memoir, 'some people might consider that our behaviour was bullying but it wasn't. It was character-building, and this was how Liverpool forged a formidable collective spirit, holding us together in difficult times.' By that definition, character was built by sucking up abuse and learning to give it back, the best riposte being to deliver the goods on the pitch. There would be no relief for Rush until such time as he began to bang in the goals.

So much, then, for 'the soul' of Liverpool FC as embedded in the changing room. When it came to the training ground, what did the club do, really, that was so very different from any other top-flight club? There surely had to be an answer to explain their success; and Manchester United, for one, had a burning urge to know. Ron Atkinson, boss at Old Trafford since 1981, did his reconnaissance on Liverpool's methods and could see they weren't working to any textbooks other than the well-thumbed logbooks of past games kept in the 'Boot Room' where Paisley and senior staff had been meeting since 1973.

The gospel of pass-and-move made a defining difference, perhaps. As Ronnie Whelan soon learned at Melwood, 'They didn't like you running with the ball when you could pass it. They didn't really like you running with the ball, full stop.' Atkinson's United, encouraged by their most skilful players, had a go at emulating the style – only to lose heart in front of a home crowd that, on the whole, just hated to watch the ball going sideways. Defender Kevin Moran decided that Liverpool had taught their fans a degree of patience borne out by results. 'When we did it at Old Trafford,' Moran lamented, 'there were forty thousand shouting "Get on with it!"'

A seeming anomaly in the Anfield success story was what Jimmy Case would describe as 'something of a drinking culture at Liverpool in those days'. No one could seriously say that booze made a team better. Yet the Spurs double-winning side of 1961 had been famously thirsty, led by Jimmy Greaves and Dave Mackay; and no football club could hope to bar its players from the pub. The ratio that Liverpool FC drank in relation to how often it won, though, was noteworthy: one had to assume it was helpful to the fabled 'team spirit'. But in Ray Kennedy and Jimmy Case – fast friends but an often volatile combination – the drink was felt to be problematic. In March of 1980, with the team on a break in Wales after beating Everton at Goodison, Kennedy and Case had caused an inebriated incident in a hotel bar that led to police involvement, an admission of actual bodily harm, and fines of £150.

'Super', of course, rarely took a drink. He knew his limits, for one thing. ('One glass of champagne and he was rocking and rolling,' Souness recalled. 'You couldn't shut him up.') For another, he had learned his good career-extending, self-caring habits in the parish of Jock Stein. Dalglish's preferred tipple, if pushed, would be a Cinzano and lemonade – proof in itself of his utter imperviousness to homosocial peer-group pressure. He would not be changing anytime soon, unless he really needed to.

As Dalglish was enduring an exile from the scoresheet, Keegan had problems of his own in front of goal. When he notched Southampton's first in a 4-0 beating of Leicester over Christmas of 1980 it was his first since August. The team had goals in it regardless, chiefly from young Steve Moran, and its form remained relatively buoyant up to a defeat at Anfield on the final day of February. Southampton sat a respectable seventh; Liverpool went third; but they had a gap to close if they were to get at Ron Saunders' Aston Villa and the attractive Ipswich side built by their Durham-born boss, Bobby Robson.

As in 1974, as in 1978, Liverpool looked to the cups for solace. A Souness hat-trick helped them past CSKA Sofia to the semi-finals of the European Cup; and they won their first ever League Cup after a replay with West Ham, Dalglish sending them on their way with the deftest of volleys, executed at full stretch from the acutest of angles. Bayern Munich awaited in the last four of Europe. The Anfield leg was worryingly goal-less, though the clean sheet was a boon. In Munich, Dalglish was taken out of the game within minutes, his ankle ligaments damaged by a clattering tackle. It was Howard Gayle, previously anonymous to Bayern's coaches, who stepped in as sub to give a hugely industrious performance, while the diminutive Sammy Lee was stuck onto Paul Breitner and harried him out of the match. A 1-1 draw got Liverpool through to a final in Paris with Real Madrid. But for Dalglish, whose ankle had to be put in plaster, there was a serious question as to whether he would be fit to get on that pitch.

Keegan got properly back among the goals – a winner against Manchester United, a brace at Stoke. Southampton stayed in touch at the top without being quite in contention, unable to get points from the crunch games. They finished the season at Ipswich, who had conceded the title to Villa, and a 3-2 win saw them into sixth place. Liverpool were only one place better off, their worst finish in 10 years. They were short of goals, and Ian Rush had persuaded no one that he offered a solution.

Dalglish's main concern, shared by Liverpool, was his fitness or otherwise to compete in Paris, having been out injured since the Bayern game. Paisley made the wager that an hour or so of Dalglish would be better than nothing, and that was what Liverpool got. Short of pace, his running carefully reserved, Dalglish started playing very much back to goal, then a little deeper in the second half, looking in the main to release Terry McDermott. But Real stayed stubbornly locked up, and when Dalglish pushed up the best he could manage was a shot into the stratosphere. Suddenly, on 81 minutes, to everyone's stupefaction, defender Alan Kennedy galloped into the Real box to trap a throw-in with his chest, then wellied a shot into the top-right corner, sparking red-shirted pandemonium. With five minutes to go, at a point when a bit of frustrated argy-bargy with a marker might have seen him booked, Dalglish was withdrawn, Paisley with an eye on protecting what he held.

It was a triumph. And yet, the league form told another story, one that just wasn't good enough for Liverpool. Paisley, as Alan Kennedy recalled, told the players that 'the team needed freshening up, and he went out and did it'. Clemence, still England's goalkeeper but vying with Shilton, and conscious of Grobbelaar's claim, chose to up and leave for Spurs. The famous four-man midfield was dismantled. Case was moved on to Brighton, and Ray Kennedy would soon join Swansea where John Toshack was boss. Even Terry McDermott's number was up. Graeme Souness, the last man standing, would pronounce of all three players that, whatever their gifts, they 'overdid their leisure time' in the boozer.

Souness was going nowhere, his imperious toughness giving Liverpool fans the gratifying sense that he was one of them, the man you wanted in your corner. Local playwright Alan Bleasdale, who gave Souness a cameo as himself in the TV drama *Boys from the Blackstuff*, would compose a glowing foreword for Souness' first memoir in which he characterised the Scot as a defender of distinctly Scouse working-class virtues. 'Even if you're a nobody who cleans the boots,' Bleasdale argued, 'if he thinks you're getting picked on by someone ... "Charlie" will put them in their place ... And I'll tell you one thing, he only has to do it once.'

But Souness, an atypical Scot, was also an atypical Liverpool captain. His avowed personal style was a version of the high life: tastes for cold Sancerre, Cardin slacks and the Commodores on the stereo. It was not the style of the terraces, that much was clear. Souness was candid enough to wonder how 'the average punter at Anfield' was supposed to relate to him. The Toxteth ward of Liverpool, riven with tensions between the mainly black community and the police, erupted in riots in July 1981. But, whatever Alan Bleasdale believed, the travails of the city of Liverpool were hardly reflected in the manners of their majestic team.

Keegan – who had long ago bidden farewell to the life of the average working man – returned to international duty in late May for a must-win World Cup qualifier. England's campaign had been going poorly, tarnished by a troublesome 2-1 defeat away to Romania and a draw in the Wembley rematch. The prize he sought was a last chance to test himself at the highest level, missed in 1974 and 1978. Espana 1982 was looking like a long shot as he faced what was plainly the autumn of his playing career. George Best was widely felt to be the greatest player never to have competed at a World Cup. Keegan was desperate not to inherit that mantle from 'Bestie', after all the others of which he had been a willing recipient.

Running into Switzerland away was not great timing for Ron Greenwood's team right at the end of a demanding domestic season. Worse, the *Daily Mirror* queried the recovery powers of what they dubbed a 'Dad's Army' England team. On the night, England shipped two goals in the space of a minute; sections of their support took their now predictable offence, leading to punch-ups and injuries, and the bother wore on after England's eventual 2-1 defeat, with shops looted and pub windows shattered in Basel. Amid the equally familiar choruses of FIFA crying disgrace and England fans pleading innocence or else intolerable provocation, FA secretary Ted Croker began to think aloud about a ban on travelling support.

Greenwood felt an understandable urge to quit; but with England looking down the barrel of another qualifier a week later, away to group favourites Hungary, he was persuaded to soldier on for the time being. Trevor Brooking, Phil Neal, Phil Thompson and Terry McDermott were restored as starters for that game, with Keegan pushed further up in support of Ipswich striker Paul Mariner. Hungary edged the first half, but Brooking struck lucky in scoring from a mishit, and though Clemence gifted Hungary an equaliser, Keegan and Brooking combined for the latter to restore England's lead; then Keegan, brought down in the area, converted the penalty for England's third. England had wrenched qualification back into their own hands. For all that, Greenwood still wanted to be gone, but on the plane back to England Keegan and Brooking led a delegation of senior pros to talk him round.

Come 9 September 1981 Greenwood surely wished he had jumped sooner, as England fell to an infamous defeat in Norway. When Neal, Thompson and McDermott slunk back to the Liverpool dressing room that Friday they were subjected to

Souness blaring 'Y Viva Espana!' through a tape-player, since Scotland's qualification was all but settled. But there was one more twist, Switzerland proving to be England's saviours by obtaining a shock 2-1 win in Romania and then a goalless draw in the Berne rematch. England only had to draw their final home game with Hungary. In his programme notes captain Keegan promised to 'spill blood' in the cause, but ended the contest with a bloody lip, and having had his ankles chopped at all night by Sandor Sallai. Still, a scuffed goal by Mariner won it, ensuring England's return to the World Cup arena, and Keegan's debut there, at long last.

In a First Division now boasting the novelty of the game's first artificial pitches and three points for a win, 30-year-old Keegan adjusted to the onset of veteran status. At Southampton he had expected more 'name' signings to join him; but David Armstrong from Middlesbrough was McMenemy's only notable recruit. Form was patchy from the off, but Keegan scored with regularity, including one in a thrilling 4-3 comeback win against Ipswich.

Dalglish's league drought continued, however, as he failed to score in any of Liverpool's first nine League games. Finally, against Brighton, after 11 fruitless months, he got his head to a Sammy Lee corner and the keeper's parry couldn't keep it out. But that game ended in a draw, typifying Liverpool's poor start. At the end of November Keegan's Southampton came to Anfield sitting fifth in the league, Liverpool down in ninth. The game looked bound for a goalless finish when Keegan made a lovely first touch to release Steve Moran, who rounded Bruce Grobbelaar to score and secure Southampton's first win at Anfield for 21 years.

The following week league leaders Manchester United visited the Dell and found Southampton playing highly stylish one-touch stuff, getting at the opposition in a manner somehow sharpened by the tightness of the small ground. Keegan had a stunning volley chalked off, but went on to score a legitimate goal in a 3-2 win that put the Saints third. 'Games all seemed the same,' Keegan would recall of this purple patch. 'We got the ball, we attacked. It was like a pinball machine.' Over Christmas a Keegan double sunk Toshack's Swansea and they were second, a point behind Manchester City.

On Boxing Day, City had visited extraordinary chaos upon Liverpool at Anfield, after a 3-1 win in which Grobbelaar was blatantly at fault for two goals and the home side were booed back down the tunnel. Liverpool were to begin 1982 in 12th place. If Paisley was unhappy, his deputy Joe Fagan was incandescent, and asked the boss for some private time with 'the lads'. According to Phil Neal, Fagan proceeded to lambast each player in turn, sparing the 'Jocks' not a mite. ('Hansen, start heading the ball, Souness, you haven't won a tackle, Dalglish, you should have twice as many goals by now.') Paisley's part in the badly needed remedials was to remove the captain's armband from Phil Thompson and hand it to Souness. Kirkby-born Thompson took this very badly; yet the turnaround was immediate. Liverpool destroyed Swansea away in the FA Cup, then went on a run of form to the end of the season that would amount to 20 wins, three draws and just two defeats. In that run they retained the League Cup by beating Spurs, though CSKA Sofia put them out of Europe.

No small part of the revival was that the diffident Ian Rush, starting regularly alongside Dalglish, began to show his mettle, and the makings of a strike partnership. It was the inverse of Keegan's with Toshack: Dalglish lying deep, the younger and lankier man running onto his slide-rule passes. What Rush had suddenly developed was anticipation to go with pace, and there was extraordinary new assurance in his finishing. In the first week of February Liverpool murdered Ipswich 4-0 at Anfield, in their classic manner, fast and penetrative from the back, Dalglish running things. They were up to third.

On top, though, were Keegan's Southampton – the club's first ever taste of the league summit. 'Tip Top Saints!' cried the *Southern Evening Echo* after a Keegan winner at Middlesbrough put them there. Home wins over West Ham and Birmingham saw them open a four-point lead as February ended. And then they faltered: just a single win in eight. Steve Moran got injured, the defence got leaky, a couple of goals a game; and Keegan felt that McMenemy missed a moment to strengthen the side while its big chance lay before it. One day on the team bus Keegan, backed by other senior players, urged McMenemy to go and get Peter Shilton. Southampton, though, were not Liverpool, nor Hamburg. Their ambitions, as measured by their readiness to spend, did not match Keegan's.

They were still top at the end of March, but Liverpool had three games in hand and won the lot, a 1-0 midweek beating of Manchester United at Old Trafford completing the revival that Fagan's New Year rollicking had begun. When Southampton entertained Aston Villa the following Saturday they were miles adrift, and fell to a 3-0 defeat after which McMenemy accused Keegan of cutting a stationary figure in the middle of the pitch. Keegan took this badly. ('I felt I'd been accused of cheating. That stung me.') McMenemy probably knew it was the end of the affair. 'The one thing I had learned about him,' he would say of his marquee signing down the road, 'was his single-mindedness and ultra-sensitivity.' Southampton would finish seventh, still good enough to get into the UEFA Cup.

The season brought one more clash of Keegan and Dalglish: Southampton versus Liverpool at the Dell in late April. The newly infallible Rush put Liverpool ahead, sticking an immaculate volley onto a long ball. Then Keegan fashioned a chance for Channon, who shaped and smashed past Grobbelaar. Whelan clipped Liverpool back into the lead after a smart counter, but Keegan levelled again with a penalty. Channon nearly won it but for the width of a post. Then Rush, tussling by the right-side touch, winkled the ball out to the feet of Dalglish, who trapped, feigned, then turned and slid a pass across goal to Whelan, the finishing touch made academic.

Liverpool sealed their 13th championship, and Paisley pronounced himself proudest of this one above all, since there had been 'so much more to do'. Young Rush had 17 league goals, his former tormentor Dalglish 13. Keegan, though, had defied all doubters himself to score 26 times, his best-ever season's return, winning him the divisional Golden Boot. He was, moreover, PFA Player of the Year; and a father for the second time to newborn daughter Sarah. No question, then, that he would lead England to Spain and his first World Cup.

England's opening game was against France in Bilbao. Five days before, Keegan felt the sudden and excruciating flare of an old back injury that put him prostrate on his bed. In a career largely unmarred by bad luck, this was a cruel stroke. His perennial hotel roommate Trevor Brooking witnessed at close hand what Keegan was loath to let others see. Leaving his pal in the bath one morning while he went down to breakfast, Brooking returned an hour later to find Keegan still marooned in the tub, unable to hoist himself out. In Keegan's absence England began well with a 3-1 win, and won, indeed, all their group matches to proceed into a group of three with West Germany and the hosts, giving Keegan the lifeline of a chance to recover and get into the game.

Scotland's group offered a familiar set of variously sized hurdles: the mighty Brazil, the threatening Soviet Union, the supposed makeweights New Zealand. Jock Stein knew they would likely need more than one win. But the big man – though he no longer trained much – remained a big presence, and his squad was as strong as any Scotland had assembled: Liverpool's Jocks, Alex Ferguson's Aberdeen posse, Alan Brazil and John Wark of Robson's Ipswich, Dundee United's David Narey and Paul Sturrock.

Scotland sought to make short work of New Zealand in Malaga. Gordon Strachan was inspired, first making a probing run at the defence that set up Dalglish for the first, then laying on two for John Wark, hungry for goals from midfield. Three up after 35 minutes, Scotland then leaked two sloppy replies, repairing the scoreline only through John Robertson and Steve Archibald, for whom Dalglish had made way. Dalglish's replaceability proposed shades of 1974; and for the Brazil game Stein was unsentimental, opting to start with Archibald as lone striker. A screaming strike by Narey actually put Scotland ahead, only to antagonise their consummate opponents, who soon got into the flow of passing triangles, impish one-twos and audacious finishes. Scotland had planned on man-marking but found they just couldn't catch their men. It was 3-1 to Brazil when Dalglish got a belated run-out, and Falcao still found time for a fourth.

The USSR had beaten New Zealand and lost by fewer to Brazil, meaning Scotland had to beat them. The Russians boasted Aleksandre Chivadze and Ramaz Shengelia of Dinamo Tbilisi, former thorns in the side of Liverpool FC, and both men scored against Scotland, who managed a face-saving draw only at the death, courtesy of Souness. Dalglish watched from the bench, gloomily aware that his World Cup record would likely amount to plenty of chances, a couple of goals, but precious little impression on any of the three tournaments in which he had featured.

Still racked by back pain, Keegan did not even have that much to console himself with. He resorted to an epidural injection, but it brought no relief. In a last, desperate effort to get himself in the frame for selection he made an appointment to see a trusted specialist in West Germany, borrowed the England hotel receptionist's car, drove himself to the airport and caught a plane. Following his treatment Keegan declared himself fit;

but Ron Greenwood was not convinced. A goalless draw with the Germans left England needing to beat Spain, but Keegan was only on the bench. After Francis, Mariner and Woodcock had all missed chances Greenwood introduced Keegan. Late on he found a good position in the box as a smart passing move led to Bryan Robson floating an ideal ball for his head. Keegan, though, snatched at the chance, skewing the header well wide. The game ended goalless; and that, then, had been Keegan's one and only taste of the World Cup. 'No excuses, I should have scored,' he admitted afterwards. But England were out, Greenwood resigned, and Bobby Robson was confirmed as England manager almost immediately.

For a dispirited Keegan the prospect of Southampton's pre-season tour held no great savour. He had made a judgement about the club; and he never changed his mind. His mate Mick Channon was leaving. The funds would always be limited. He saw a crowd of youngsters and a club not going forward. For their part, Southampton could not have been unconcerned by Keegan's fitness issues, despite what he had accomplished in the previous season. If they couldn't quite achieve the big step up in the league, they were not going to fall apart without him.

McMenemy met with Keegan and would recall the player's message as 'If I am not allowed to leave I'll hang up my boots'. Resigned to losing his man, McMenemy found Keegan agreeable to going on Southampton's pre-season tour in return for the freedom to seek another club. Southampton received an enquiry from Manchester United regarding Keegan's availability, but that interest didn't last. Second Division London sides Chelsea and Charlton both tried their luck, to no avail; but the problem there was not so much one of reduced status as a clear lack of the certain stardust Keegan needed to have around all his endeavours.

The providers of that pizzazz proved, against the odds, to be Newcastle United, whose manager Arthur Cox had first contacted Keegan's agent Harry Swales – fishing, if you like – while he was still at Hamburg. As of 1982 the once-mighty Newcastle – three-time champions before the Great War, six-time cup winners though not since 1955 – were no great shakes, looking lamely settled in the Second Division. Cox had a few promising, raw youngsters, like Chris Waddle from Tow Law, ex-employee of a sausage-seasoning factory, taken on at Newcastle after trialling with Sunderland, who hadn't fancied him. In truth, Waddle's curious demeanour on the park – all drooping shoulders and hung head – gave the impression he didn't much fancy playing football. He had scored in Newcastle's last home game of 1981-82, a 4-2 win over Wrexham, but there weren't 10,000 people there to see it. Still, if Newcastle were struggling to draw crowds, so was every club in the tier above. Prices were not dear, but times were tough, and the English game wore a sullen air.

Newcastle, though, was the club Keegan's father Joe had supported, and he could see the drama in his going there now, to one of the heartlands of English football – a sort of homecoming, to a club with a history, a lineage of great players, a famous shirt, a tradition of passionate support, and obvious room for improvement. The question, customarily with Keegan, was the deal.

Cox, his chairman Stan Seymour and Newcastle's club secretary Russell Cushing travelled down to London to meet with Keegan at the Swallow hotel in Knightsbridge. A significant addition to their party was Alastair Wilson, managing director at the club's sponsor, Scottish & Newcastle Breweries. Keegan told Wilson that he would do nothing to advertise beer, but it was clear there were sporting activities bearing the brewery's brand to which Keegan could lend his endorsement and which would improve the terms Newcastle could offer. For all the sense of sporting romance around Keegan, he was harder-nosed than most. He agreed to sign for a fee of £100,000 and a weekly wage of £5,000, plus (a rider he was proud to have negotiated) a guaranteed 15 per cent of any excess on Newcastle's usual gate receipts.

On 20 August 1982 Newcastle – a city of one football club whose fortunes were, at times, all-consuming – was alive with a low-level buzz, centring on the Gosforth Park hotel five miles out of town, where it was hotly rumoured that Kevin Keegan had been sighted and was set to be unveiled as a Newcastle player. Fans had descended upon the hotel grounds, taking up residence on its grassy verges, looking through any window to see if the rumours were true. The Newcastle *Evening Chronicle* would confirm the story in their first edition: 'HERE HE IS!' Underneath Keegan's picture in the paper was the story of his granddad Frank and the Burns pit.

Keegan's patter to the gathered press had his usual passion: 'I needed a new challenge . . . nothing to do with money . . . my father was a Geordie.' It was showbusiness, for sure, but how seriously could one take Keegan's much-ballyhooed homecoming to his latest home, or the sincerity of the *Ich bin ein Geordie* routine? Newcastle city councilman Stuart Bell remarked that Keegan's financial package would be a cause of woe to the 'many unemployed people in this area', that they would have preferred cheaper match tickets and cheaper Scottish & Newcastle beer to a high-priced hero. But a great swathe of the support undeniably felt the thrill of this millionaire star, a man of humble origins and big ambitions, having chosen to don the shirt and come among them.

Keegan's first turn in black-and-white stripes came a week later at home against QPR, who had won 4-0 at St James' Park barely three months previously in front of 11,000 bored souls. Keegan's debut, though, was a sell-out. He ran out to a capacity 36,718 crowd, in a party mood under the sun. He was already in the money. Around the hour mark, defender John Craggs lofted a ball forward that Keegan nodded on to striker Imre

arless determination was already a Keegan hallmark at Scunthorpe United, shown
re as he battles against the Tranmere defence in the FA Cup at Goodison Park in
ovember 1970. In the crowd was someone who would change his life. (Getty Images)

egan is joined by his mentor Bill Shankly after signing for Liverpool for £32,500 in
ay 1971. (PA)

Having done his homework on Peter McCloy, Dalglish calmly slots the ball past the Rangers keeper in the Old Firm League Cup tie in August 1971 to get his career under way. (PA)

On the muddy Baseball Ground pitch in February 1972, it was Dalglish who starred in the England v Scotland Under-23 game, scoring both Scotland's goals, though Keegan made his debut in the fixture. (Getty Images)

November 1972, Keegan was celebrating his full England debut – and already the ss were marking him out from the rest as he began to build his 'brand'. (Getty Images)

finished the 1972-73 season by helping erpool to the league title, which was ost guaranteed by this goal against eds United on Easter Monday. (PA)

Celebrating with Emlyn Hughes a year later, after Liverpool became FA Cup champions, with Keegan having scored twice. (Getty Images)

Half-hidden between two Denmark defenders, Dalglish scores his first goal for Scotland in November 1972, helping his country on their way to the 1974 World Cup. (PA)

Dalglish in action against Zaire during the 1974 World Cup in West Germany. Sadly, his form during the tournament didn't quite live up to expectations. (Offside)

ove: Tempers flare in the Charity Shield as
egan and Billy Bremner are both sent off
er exchanging blows right in front of the
eree. (PA)

Right: England captain Keegan discusses a
point in training with manager Don Revie,
Mick Channon and Joe Royle ahead of a
World Cup qualifier in 1976. (PA)

low: Berti Vogts of Borussia
oenchengladbach brings down Keegan
concede a penalty in the 1977 European
ip final. After leaving Liverpool on a high,
egan was moving to Hamburg to seek his
rtune. (PA)

While manager Jock Stein hands round th champagne, Dalglish sticks to Coke as Cel celebrate winning th league title in April 1977. But Dalglish would soon join othe on the road south to England. (PA)

Dalglish left in no doubt about the level of expectation as he joins Liverpool in the summer of 1977, accompanied by not only manager Bob Paisley, but also the European Cup, the league trophy and the Charity Shield. (PA)

He didn't disappoint. as he helped Liverpo retain their Europear crown. (PA)

Keegan salutes the crowd during a pre-season friendly for Hamburg against Barcelona. (Offside)

Keegan and his wife and childhood sweetheart Jean in Germany in 1978. The Old English Sheepdogs appear very much in tune with the times. (Offside)

Keegan and Henry Cooper 'spar' together as part of their advertising campaign for Brut. Keegan's ability to merchandise himself was without equal among footballers of the time.

(Getty Images)

Above: The two captains in action together, as Keegan tackles Dalglish during the Home International against Scotland in May 1979. (Getty Images)

Right: Footballer chic, 1979. Dalglish with his wife Marina and their children Paul and Kelly. (Getty Images)

Below: The three self-styled 'Jocks', Graeme Souness, Alan Hansen and Dalglish celebrate winning the league title in 1983. (Getty Images)

Varadi, who nodded it right back. Then Keegan got it down from head to foot and foraged straight for goal. As QPR keeper Peter Hucker came out, Keegan adjusted himself, slotted the ball into the bottom-right corner, and ran for the Gallowgate End crowd, which roiled and rolled down to welcome him in – a mass of bodies just on the right side of perilous. Among them was a Gosforth schoolboy prospect named Alan Shearer, a Magpie fan like all the rest, suddenly able to believe, against the odds, that Newcastle United could be magic again. If few looking in could quite understand why Keegan had made his eccentric choice, these supporters were true believers.

10

Last Orders

1982-84

'I realise that one day it will end — when Liverpool decide that I'm not doing the job that they want from me. As a professional footballer I accept that. It's going to be a sad day, though . . .'

Kenny Dalglish, 1982

Keegan's second game for Newcastle was a midweek away win at Blackburn's Ewood Park: inevitably, a bit of a chore after the hubbub of his debut. Once the job was done Keegan let the Newcastle changing room know that he didn't fancy spending a whole season as the target of long balls lumped forward. Then a defeat at Bolton provided the first earthbound moment since his arrival. In time for a Tyne–Tees derby with Middlesbrough, Arthur Cox unveiled another veteran 'new' face: Mick Channon, who duly scored on his debut. Old stagers clearly could do a job in Division Two. But it was now a harder thing perforce to judge Kevin Keegan against the absolute highest standards — the standards he had always set himself.

This much was on the mind of new England boss Bobby Robson, who had come to see Keegan's Newcastle debut and readily joined the acclamation of it. Robson, however, was weighing his options ahead of a big Euro 84 qualifier against Denmark; and the widespread view that too many of Greenwood's team were on the wrong side of 30 was one he happened to share. It was near closing time, then, for Ray Clemence, Phil Thompson, Trevor Brooking and Terry McDermott. As for Keegan, Robson would observe that he was 'no longer getting in where it hurt to win big matches, preferring the role of playmaker and provider'.

There were issues beyond England's use for such a string-puller, or even Keegan's stamina for it. Robson had heard the story about Keegan's single-minded fight for fitness at the World Cup, and to him it signified something potentially 'disruptive' to a squad. Lawrie McMenemy also gave Robson a briefing, from which Robson gathered that Keegan 'liked to take over', which was quite something to ponder for a new boss.

If Robson did not mean to finish Keegan's international career after 10 years and 60 caps, he had failed to read the form book, or any of Keegan's various memoirs. On 14 September 1982 he named his first England squad, minus the now ex-captain Keegan, though he did not make a personal call to tell Keegan as much. Keegan was at Newcastle's Benwell training ground when a journalist told him he was dropped. His public response was swift: 'I'm finished with England. I'll never kick a ball for my country again.' His insistence was that the manners, above all, were all wrong. 'What upset me is the way I heard about it,' Keegan told TV cameras. 'I mean, a 10p phone call from the FA is not a lot to ask.'

Jack Charlton was among the vocal critics of Keegan's England retirement, rather as Bobby Moore had criticised the manner of his aggrieved walkout from Don Revie's squad in 1975. These England World Cup winners, undoubted admirers of Keegan as a player, felt still that he had let his emotions overtake him. On Tyneside, however, Keegan's choice was felt to be just champion, among a support that considered its region to be more than a little apart from the rest of the country

anyhow. Already Keegan was adding value to the neighbour-
hood, fulfilling his agreed obligations to Scottish & Newcastle,
attending fan forums and 'Blue Star Soccer Days' for schoolkids.
Newcastle fans now knew that they would have one hundred
per cent of Keegan's footballing attentions, for as long as he
stuck around.

On the pitch, though, Newcastle began to revert more to
type: no wins in five, losses to Shrewsbury and Barnsley. Mick
Channon was paid off, and Arthur Cox's next gambit was to
sign Terry McDermott from Liverpool. The worth of that move
was tested when Newcastle visited Rotherham, their player-
manager Keegan's and McDermott's old Liverpool captain,
Emlyn Hughes. McDermott began to earn his keep from the off
via some top-drawer link-ups, first playing a lovely through-ball
for Keegan to round the keeper and slot home from an acute
angle. McDermott then got clattered in the area and Keegan
scored the penalty. Varadi set up Keegan's hat-trick, and Keegan
managed a fourth before it finished 5-1. 'Bobby Robson,' the
Newcastle crowd crowed, 'are you watching on the box?'

Still, if class was permanent, form was temporary, for Newcastle then went and lost 4-1 to Fulham. In the changing
room afterwards, Keegan was narked: young Kenny Wharton
ventured that it had, at least, been a good game and Keegan,
by his own later admission, 'went for' Wharton, arguing that
he was accepting defeat far too readily. 'You Geordies are too
easily pleased,' Keegan snapped – involuntarily revealing that
Newcastle was his place, and Geordies his people, only up to a
point and no further.

Keegan found Newcastle's training regimen plenty stiff, for
Arthur Cox was as much a heavy disciplinary grinder as Branko
Zebec, though the Newcastle squad had fewer raw diamonds
to work with. One was Chris Waddle, but Waddle thought
Cox was 'like a schoolyard bully'. Conversely, Keegan and
McDermott, the seasoned pros, felt at liberty to pull Cox's leg
over his severity. A permanent resident of the Gosforth Park

hotel, Keegan presided over a sort of senior players' cabal there, with 'Terry Mac' and Dave McCreery, newly arrived from Manchester United. He ventured into Newcastle city centre only when he had to, for the city was a goldfish bowl and he drew crowds wherever he went.

One cost of Keegan's fame, though, was that Newcastle had become the big scalp in the Second Division; and already they had been scalped more than once. Early in November, Keegan suffered a detached retina from a testimonial match at Middlesbrough, and missed six league games, of which Newcastle won only one. At the close of the year the team sat 12th. Promotion seemed a faint hope now, and Cox was getting stick in the local press and radio. Keegan made it known that he considered his own position was linked to Cox's and any threat to the manager's employment would cause him to reconsider his own. A 4-0 win over Shrewsbury seemed to mend the mood. Newcastle started to match their rivals and duff up some of the lesser lights, until they lost to the bottom two clubs, Derby and Burnley. They finished fifth, three points shy of the promotion places.

Keegan ended the season with 21 goals and the credit of having put seven thousand onto Newcastle's average gate. It was, nonetheless, the most modest season he had enjoyed in football since leaving Scunthorpe. Contract or no contract, elements of the Newcastle support were not wholly convinced he would stick around for a second try. There was something in the tone of his voice, perhaps. He had assessed the Newcastle squad and found it wanting in key areas, among them his support up front. ('Varadi has scored twenty-one goals this season,' he complained to staff. 'I've set him up to score sixty. How many times has he set me up? None.') Arthur Cox knew the side needed firepower, and at one point told Keegan that he had half a mind to try for Kenny Dalglish. There was as yet no sign, though, that Dalglish should be plying his trade anywhere but at the top.

Bob Paisley had decided 1982-83 would be his final season as Liverpool manager. By Christmas Joe Fagan had agreed to succeed him, a careful, continuity-minded choice from the 'Boot Room', which the club kept under wraps until the season's work was done. Liverpool had a new sponsorship deal with Crown Paints, yet the club's income remained a pale reflection of how it dominated the English game. Others at the helm of lesser-achieving clubs had bigger ambitions, albeit with as much concern for lining their own pockets as for spending on the team. (In October 1983 Irving Scholar's Tottenham Hotspur would become the first English club to declare an intent to float on the stock market.)

Liverpool set off well, faltered in the autumn, but logged a further seven wins before Christmas, including a 5-0 humiliation of Everton at Goodison, defined by Glenn Keeley's sending-off for a hopeless attempt to drag Dalglish back by his shirt. Rush scored four in that game and was ascendant. David Hodgson had come from Middlesbrough and was paired with Rush, Dalglish withdrawing to midfield as creator of chances. Rush's timed runs onto Dalglish's passes had a clockwork precision. There was a growing appreciation of Dalglish as a 'continental' type of player, now that his veteran sophistication was being deployed to supply the tireless Rush. (By the end of the year he would finish second – a distant second, but up there nonetheless – to Michel Platini for the Ballon d'Or.) But, if a less frequent figure on the scoresheet, Dalglish could still remind people powerfully of his aptitude in that department, as in a cup tie with Stoke when a long effort from near enough the touchline brought his 300th professional goal.

In the European Cup Liverpool ran into 'unfancied' Widzew Lodz, first in Poland where Grobbelaar proved a good deal less impermeable than Lodz keeper Mlynarczyk, and Lodz won 2-0. A virus ruled Dalglish out of the return leg where Liverpool fatally shipped two away goals, and a late rally to win 3-2 was for naught but pride. Still, by mid-April and with six league games to play Liverpool led by a staggering 17 points, then staggered to the line with just a single point from those last half-dozen fixtures. The hard yakka, however, had all been done. Dalglish was voted Footballer of the Year by both the Football Writers' and Professional Footballers' Associations, a stunning double honour for a 32-year-old pro.

Part of the Liverpool Way was to move players on in order to serve the higher purpose. No one's time was forever. Yet any sense that it might be the moment for Liverpool to consider who would succeed Dalglish in the red number seven, just as he had followed Keegan, had a faintly sacrilegious air. Michael Robinson was a tidy young attacker bought from Brighton in the summer of 1983, but no Dalglish, by Robinson's own estimation. Dalglish remained a winner, a leader by example. Early in the new season at Arsenal he added a classic to his goal collection: a typically Liverpool passing attack in which all angles were covered, completed by a back-heel from Robinson to which Dalglish applied one of his graceful measured curlers. Still, whenever Liverpool went to market for a forward it was a reminder that the end had to come sometime – this, and the signal of Dalglish's training schedule, steadily reduced with the passing years and the toll on his body.

Paisley had moved on and Joe Fagan, no ingenu, was nonetheless having to learn fast what it meant to be in charge of Liverpool FC, how to pull the levers so as to get something done. The onus of Paisley's success was heavier even than Shankly's had been upon Paisley. 'The first couple of weeks were a bit rough,' Fagan would admit, 'because my mind was racing everywhere, yet I seemed to be doing nothing.' Fagan, moreover, had a dyspeptic side that, unlike his predecessor's, was not so very far from the surface: 'Joe could be vicious,' Ian Rush would remember, 'and he used to get far angrier than I ever saw Bob Paisley.'

In late November Liverpool struggled to a second draw with Fulham in the League Cup and Fagan confided to his diary that the team's fulcrum number seven had been too often caught in possession. 'Dalglish has lost his edge,' he wrote gloomily. Dalglish, as so often, responded in the next game, against Ipswich, with his 100th Liverpool goal, a fantastic cut-in and strike to the top corner. Fagan had been experimenting with a 4-3-3, but now he reverted to two men up front, and those two were Rush and Dalglish. It was Michael Robinson who dropped to the bench.

Newcastle had begun patchily, a loss to Middlesbrough in early September coming as a special blow. That month, though, the team was bolstered by a new signing, a local lad, albeit one who came in a roundabout way, already 23 years old. But Peter Beardsley had an air about him, the kind of player fit to wear a number seven shirt.

Son of a lorry driver, not much cop at school, the boy Beardsley was known to his peers as 'football-daft Peter' – and his footballing idol was Kenny Dalglish of Celtic. After a promising start at Wallsend Boys, always a hotbed of young players, Beardsley had struggled to kick on, knocked back by Gillingham, tied to the job centre and the giro to keep going. His looks were distinctive, and yet something about the bridge of his nose, the line of his jaw and his pudding-bowl barnet led the lads to dub him 'Quasimodo'.

'It was my dad who kept me going,' Beardsley would remember. '"Don't worry, golden feet, you'll make it," he always told me.' Beardsley certainly possessed considerable skill at beating defenders with a deceptive shimmy, feinting with one foot then skipping off the other way. But he had the right kind of resolve about him, too: Beardsley knew he was good, learned early how hard on the spirit the game could be, and seemed to log every slight he received with the intent of rebutting it further down the road.

Ex-Newcastle captain Bob Moncur took Beardsley for Carlisle, then Ron Atkinson recruited him to Manchester United for decent money. But it didn't happen for Beardsley at Old Trafford, either, and he had wound up in Canada with the Vancouver Whitecaps. It was from there that Arthur Cox recruited him to Newcastle, the team Beardsley supported and whose capture of Kevin Keegan had delighted him as much as any other fan. On his first day in training Beardsley was observed keenly by Keegan, who saw something distinctively continental – mercurial flair, not dogged graft – in the style of the new man. Keegan dubbed him 'Pedro', a nickname that stuck.

Beardsley was soon getting a start and making a difference, Cox playing him in a front three with Keegan and Waddle, the veteran linking with the two young men of promise. Keegan advised them not to look to him all the time, not to be awed. Still, Beardsley's vision fed Keegan with passes from which he scored freely. Newcastle climbed to second place, then had a sticky patch of three defeats in four, a clear problem being the shipping of 32 goals in their first 22 games. Cox then made another crucial signing from rivals QPR: defender Glenn Roeder, who confessed to having joined 'because of Kevin Keegan, to play with him'. Roeder tightened things up at the back, and promotion had a realistic look again. Then the draw for the third round of the FA Cup – the 'dream draw' – paired Keegan's Newcastle with Dalglish's Liverpool, who were top of the First Division again. For the many who had followed both careers through the years, this match-up had a compelling look: a preview of how both men might clash for one last time in the top flight.

The meeting wasn't to be. In midweek before the match Liverpool entertained Manchester United at Anfield, and early in the second half Dalglish jumped for a ball with Kevin

Moran, who was wearing a heavy support brace on his wrist. Moran raised his arm, the brace smacked Dalglish full in the face, and the impact was calamitous. If Moran had not intended injury, Dalglish had certainly been 'done'. The referee elected not to show a card, though Dalglish refused Moran's hand and an incensed Graeme Souness sought to have it out with the brawny Irishman. Dalglish 'tried to stay on', Craig Johnston remembered, 'but his face was a real mess. He was as white as a ghost and, obviously, he was told "No way".' Instead, escorted from the field, Dalglish gestured defiantly in the direction of baying United fans.

It emerged that Dalglish's cheekbone had been broken in four places, and he faced a lengthy lay-off. His injured physiognomy was an alarming sight, and on visiting him in hospital his bantering teammates blanched a bit, uncommonly stuck for words. Defender Mark Lawrenson, as Dalglish recalled, 'had to be taken to a side-room for a cup of tea'. Dalglish professed himself unbothered by the fuss or the hard knock, but the lay-up was a burning frustration, just as on each of the rare occasions he had been sidelined by injury.

In the first week of 1984 Newcastle came to Anfield, bringing 11,000 fans in hope rather than expectation. Liverpool were at their imposing best and ran out 4-0 winners, scarcely taxed at any stage. Such threat as Newcastle posed came from Waddle. Keegan, though, looked well off a First Division pace. When released on the right he was caught and dispossessed by Lawrenson with little bother, then stood for some moments, hands on hips, as if in disbelief. Whatever disappointment was felt by the travelling fans was immeasurably worse for Keegan. In the changing room afterwards, he sat silent and pensive, slow to get out of his mucky kit. The drubbing had shown him something that was personally very unpalatable.

Newcastle got back on the horse, beating Portsmouth 4-1 with two apiece from Keegan and Beardsley. But on 14 February, his 33rd birthday, Keegan announced he would retire from football at the end of the season. 'I've always said I wanted to quit at the top and I really feel I'm still there,' he declared, though there was a rationalising air to that argument. No one, though, could question the accuracy or finality of his supporting words: 'When I make a decision, whether others think it right or wrong, I stick to it.'

Keegan made plain he had no interest in management. Indeed, in valedictory interviews he exuded a certain wistful tone about falling standards and conditions in the English game – lamenting the lack of hunger in players, the crazy transfer fees, the dominance of big clubs that got first pick. Keegan had worked hard for every penny, no doubt; but he had always made sure he was paid the best attainable rate in a game he knew as dog-eat-dog. Still, one of the game's greats was heading for the door: a player, moreover, who had changed the game, by the expense of prodigious energies that had set him up for life as he had always intended. If football had been, by Keegan's admission, just a part of his wider business endeavours, it had been a huge part from which all other fortune had flowed, not least the fame and adulation that had given his name its value. As a relatively young retiree, leaving football behind, how on earth was this perpetual motion man going to fill his hours?

Dalglish stewed, waiting for his face to heal, itching to return to the fray and what he knew best while more than a dozen games went by without him. In Europe, Liverpool were well immersed in a traditional campaign, grafting and grinding out results over two legs with guile and application. John Wark came in from Ipswich, bringing the promise of midfield goals, and was quickly schooled in the Liverpool Way at Melwood. ('We pass and move it nice and short here,' Bugsy Moran would hector him. 'Don't ever stand there admiring what you've just fucking done.')

Liverpool also eked their way to a League Cup final after a replay with Walsall, the second meet-up at Fellows Park marked by an unsettling incident after Liverpool's second goal when the traditional surge of spectators behind the goal caused a section of the wall to collapse. Supporters cascaded down upon one another, with inevitable injuries, and there was chaos as fans ran onto the pitch, whether angry or panicked or simply exuberant at having escaped the crush. The game was restarted and finished, but the accident had the look of one that had been waiting to happen. Terraces were badly crowded, and the sea of bodies could take an alarming aspect once the game got busy – hostage to the push and the shove and the surge, the back of the crowd possessing no collective mind about what happened at the front. All these things were part of match day, there but for the grace of God.

Dalglish was just about repaired for the European Cup quarter-finals against Benfica, running alone onto the Anfield pitch for the second half of the first leg to a huge expression of love from the crowd. In late March came the League Cup final against Everton, the first such all-Merseyside contest, which Liverpool won in a replay with a goal from Souness. The team's captain, however, had already decided to be on his way. Newly married to Danielle Wilson, divorcee daughter of a multimillionaire businessman, Souness had certainly bettered himself by his Liverpool experience but had decided (rather in the manner of Keegan) that there were now better terms and challenges on offer elsewhere. Sampdoria of Italy were in for him, and he and his new wife were house-hunting in Genoa.

Dalglish, though, was going nowhere. Whatever the financial appeal of overseas football, he must have known his reticent manners would make him a difficult fit in a foreign changing room. (This was a man noted by Scotland teammates for his remarkable adeptness, wherever in the world he travelled, at getting someone to make for him the Caledonian delicacy of a lorne sausage in a white roll.)

The unusual air of permanence around Dalglish at Liverpool became more concrete at the end of March 1984 when he
had the pleasure of being offered another four-year contract
at the club. Chairman Smith and Secretary Robinson very
definitely wanted Dalglish around longer. In the hot seat, Joe
Fagan may have entertained a different view. In mid-April
Liverpool stumbled to an away defeat by Stoke and Fagan
wrote of Dalglish as being at his 'worst in years, bored, out
of touch'.

But Liverpool had done enough to clinch a third successive
league title. It was Souness, above all, who powered them
through an aggressively contended European semi-final against
Dinamo Bucharest, thus to a final against Roma – in Rome,
of all places. As in 1981 Dalglish was not fully at the races, still
dubiously match-fit, visibly oppressed by the Roman heat. He
had one of his frustrated flare-ups with Roma captain Agostino
Di Bartolomei, and as the game went to extra time he was
withdrawn for Craig Johnston, so being spared participation
in a penalty shoot-out. As in 1981, Liverpool's hugely unlikely
hero was Alan Kennedy, who now scored the decisive kick. The
glory of Liverpool's fourth European Cup was felt not at all by
Roma ultras, who rained stones upon the Liverpool support as
they left the stadium.

Joe Fagan had presided over a treble of trophies in his first
season. He capped it with the purchase of 21-year-old Luton
striker Paul Walsh, already a 20-goals-a-season man. Walsh
would later contend that Fagan had recruited him 'to replace an
ageing Kenny'. The Liverpool Way was that you made way, in
the end. But Fagan did not have *carte blanche* at Liverpool, and
the two-decade Liverpool success story had shown that no one's
longevity – not on the pitch or in the dugout or office – could
be taken entirely for granted.

Keegan, preparing to take his bow at Newcastle, anointed publicly the man he thought best fit to fill his number seven shirt.
'Of all the players I've seen over the last five years,' Keegan told
a TV reporter, 'I think he is more like probably I was at his age
than any player I've ever met.' He was speaking of Beardsley,
with whom he had led Newcastle's promotion push. A nine-
game unbeaten run took Newcastle to third, though defeat to
second-placed Sheffield Wednesday made plain that the real
fight was to fend off Manchester City in fourth. Just when the
fortunes seemed set, Newcastle contrived to lose at home to
bottom club Cambridge.

On 5 May 1984 St James' Park saw the day's biggest attendance anywhere in the Football League, for the visit of Derby.
Waddle crossed for Keegan who dived in, like old times, where
angels feared to tread; but a defender came in so hard at the same
moment that Keegan sustained a black eye while scoring. Still,
Beardsley dribbled deftly through some lead-footed defenders
for Newcastle's second, and the eventual 4-0 scoreline assured
promotion. Keegan had delivered, just in time to ride into the
sunset. As a now ex-employee, he nonetheless considered himself
entitled to advise heavily on Newcastle's possible future. 'Now is
the time to go into debt because they have got a great chance,' he
told a Tyne Tees documentary crew. 'With three good signings,
this club could not only go into the First Division and hold its
own, it could challenge everyone bar Liverpool and Man United.'

Keegan's final fling in black and white was a post-season
friendly against Liverpool on a chilly May midweek evening
on Tyneside. The crowd was entertained by a Royal Marines
marching band and the perimeter tour of a new minibus to
ferry disadvantaged kids to games – Keegan's gift. An amiable
2-2 draw was played out, after which fireworks accompanied
Keegan's lap of honour and he was dogged around by a gaggle
of ball boys in tight-fitting Co-op tracksuits, members of the
County Schools team invited to the occasion – among them
Alan Shearer from Gosforth. Keegan hugged a substantive

proportion of the 36,000 spectators, bowed and genuflected to the Gallowgate End, then exited the pitch from the centre circle, still in his muddy kit, by way of a ride from a white helicopter. Both to Keegan and to the fans, the gesture, the theatre, the level of gratitude seemed entirely appropriate. After a bash at the Gosforth Park hotel Keegan and family were ferried to Newcastle airport and a flight down south.

The warm and fuzzy feeling on Tyneside lasted a week, then Arthur Cox handed in his resignation. He had been offered a new contract he thought derisory, and his wish list of 'three good signings' – Kevin Sheedy, Steve Bruce, Mark Hateley – had been dismissed. 'I felt the board did not appreciate what has been done,' Cox told the *Chronicle*, 'and were not talking to me in the proper manner.' Cox repaired to Derby County, and Newcastle recruited Jack Charlton, who accepted the club's limited transfer budget and the gulf where ambition might have been.

For Keegan the rest seemed to be silence as far as football was concerned. Following a world tour of summer exhibition games, he retired to a new family home in Marbella and to the golf course at Las Brisas, where he found a playing partner in his old England boss Don Revie. Keegan had developed full-blown obsessions with the single-figure handicap and the maddening sports science of how to swing a golf club. A few bits of property development, inevitably, caught his eye and kindled his commercial instincts. When his old Scunthorpe manager Ron Ashman visited the family in Spain, he found Keegan contented by comfort, sunshine and cold wine, with no obvious remorse at having put football behind him. And there, for more than six years, Keegan would stay.

A special retirement issue of *Shoot!* magazine hailed 'King Kev' for having been 'a jewel in a fairly tarnished soccer crown', lighting up 'an era in which football passed through a critical period of its history'. Even from such a cheery publication as *Shoot!*, there was no avoiding the perception of a game at a low ebb, which was about to sink to somewhere a great deal more dire.

11

'The English Disease'

A Diagnosis

'We have got to recognise that football has come to attract the type of person who have (sic) engaged in a kind of tribal territorial warfare on football grounds . . . They are not interested in football, not interested in football . . .'

Margaret Thatcher, August 1985

'Personally, my quality of life improved under [Mrs Thatcher's] governance . . . But I could also see that for most working-class people, she didn't do a lot of good things.'

Bruce Grobbelaar, 2015

You could surely say – surveying the condition of English football in the light of 1984's close season – that for some time very many ordinary fans had been suffering for the transgressions of a relative few, a minority for whom wrongness was right up their street: those for whom match day was not about watching football but, rather, making raids on the territory and person of rival supporters. It had come to be called 'The English Disease', though it surely wasn't peculiar to England. But it was a huge problem in England, no doubt about it, and had been so all through the 1970s.

Very few clubs could honestly count themselves immune; though sociologist and Liverpool fan John Williams of Leicester University would try to argue retrospectively that 'in general Liverpool fans were not really interested in violence, although they could look after themselves. The idea of being a "scally" was to be above the kind of pointless destruction which neanderthals like Leeds or Chelsea or England fans went in for. That is why Liverpool fans were never organised into firms; there were just small bunches of mates who stood together at the match or in the pub.'

But no close reader of the individual in society could really suppose that Liverpool's support was some homogeneous entity. Liverpool had its share of supporters with a solid interest in 'pointless destruction'. One such, by his own admirably candid admission, was ex-player Howard Gayle. 'I was a hooligan,' Gayle told the writer Simon Hughes. 'It was the culture. When teams came to Anfield, there was always us waiting for them and it was the same when we went away. It was accepted. Skinheads and hooliganism was part and parcel of football. I gave out a fair share of digs and I took one or two as well.'

In 1999 Liverpool supporter Alan Edge would publish a vivid memoir, *Faith of Our Fathers*, recording the changing complexion of his tribe from when he began going to games in the 1960s, the era when Liverpool's Kop impressed itself on cultural memory as a big vibrant all-singing force. From the late 1960s, though, Edge became miserably conscious of 'the bastards who tried to ruin it for everyone else', a 'mob of sub-humans', 'with their shaved heads and braces and half-mast jeans and big boots'. As of the mid-1970s onwards, Edge could see that a new style-oriented bunch had emerged at Anfield, very snotty about the rightness of their match-day clobber. (Quite a fuss was made about training shoes, and jumpers.) But in Edge's eyes the 'more casual looking firms' were still 'mindless callous bastards'.

Edge's testimony points in retrospect to why grounds were also becoming gradually less populated, growing numbers of traditional match-goers having found other things to do with their leisure time at weekends. The spectre of thuggish behaviour, inside the ground or around it or on the way there, meant that the stadia had menace around them: the routine police presence certainly wasn't there for nothing.

Since the 1970s many clubs had fenced in their terracing to prevent fans going onto the pitch. Such fences may have been a primitive solution, but they were hardly a security-state imposition. In a 1985 FA Cup tie between Burton Albion and Leicester, the Burton keeper was poleaxed by a block of wood hurled from the crowd. At Coventry's Highfield Road, Manchester City fans rioted and ripped out seats. Millwall fans went up to Luton for an FA Cup tie but really for a ruck – seats were ripped out, missiles hurled, a police sergeant struck on the head with a concrete block, all this followed by a rampage through Luton. The second leg of the League Cup semi-final between Chelsea and Sunderland saw serious fighting. Luton contemplated the banning of away fans, Chelsea the electrification of fences.

Meanwhile, an awful lot of football grounds were creeping towards outmodedness if not outright decrepitude, and the clubs were not going to spend the money necessary to renovate them. Evidently, they felt that the fans who still loyally showed up wouldn't stand for paying extra through the gates to fund infrastructure improvements. Consequently, facilities at football were generally unpleasant, and increasingly unsafe. The main stand at Bradford's Valley Parade ground was due for reconstruction when, on 11 May 1985, its old wooden structure caught fire, leading to an inferno and the deaths of 56 fans. It was the worst tragedy suffered in British football since Ibrox in 1971 and posed colossal questions about safety standards.

On the same day as the Bradford City fire, Leeds United came to Birmingham's St Andrew's, and rival supporters clashed in the stadium, leading to the collapse of a wall that caused the death of schoolboy Ian Hambridge who had been attending his first live match. Whether the fault was structural or the wall was pushed over by unusual force was never quite determined: the local council blamed the football club, the club blamed the police. The big question, so pressing as to numb the understanding, was why anyone should die at a football match.

Appointed to report on the St Andrew's riot, Judge Popplewell would conclude that alcohol was a substantial contributor to the violence. He recommended that closed circuit television be introduced into grounds, to combat the perception that thugs were shielded by large crowds, free to behave violently with a good chance of escaping detection and arrest. By the spring of 1985 this near-weekly brutishness was too big a problem for government to ignore, and Margaret Thatcher met with the FA, with CCTV on the agenda, plus the government's own favoured policy, an identity-card scheme for all those attending matches.

Sociology had been taking an understandable interest in football for a while; and the left-wing caste of the discipline inclined its scholars to ask if football violence didn't, in fact, have something to do with the government and its policies. Unemployment in the UK reached 12 per cent by January 1985, and joblessness was often cited as a contributing factor in 'hooliganism' – the idea of fans cutting up rougher in reaction to the desperation of no job and low prospects, the erosion of those norms, if you like.

To express deep unhappiness with how Britain was being governed was, for sure, the regular habit of large numbers of Britons. But to argue that crowds of young men causing grief around football matches were presenting some kind of inarticulate but razor-edged demonstration to the authorities by battering one another was to make quite a leap. While being out of work very possibly loomed large in the lives of some of the men who fought at football, the research of academic Eric

Dunning indicated that most of those arrested by police for offences in this line had jobs – albeit very often in unskilled manual occupations (barmen and bouncers, porters and ware-housemen). At the more skilled end you had factory workers and building labourers, bricklayers and carpenters. They were clearly fighting, however, for nothing but the frisson of it, which left sociologists at risk of seeking to ventriloquise, albeit eloquently, for a load of annoying louts.

If a case against Thatcherism as the cause of men behaving disgracefully could not quite be made to stand up, then the reactions of Tory government ministers to football violence could be more fruitfully characterised as blinkered, unsympathetic, and open to criticism for inadequacy given the threats to public order that had become the custom of the English weekend. Still, it was no easy thing to propose viable solutions, put a price on them and decide who would pay. A great many worrisome factors had got the authorities more focused on the heaviest tools for preventing crowd trouble, rather than what should be done and what monies spent in order to ensure the safety of spectators.

12

The Stakes of the Game

1984-85

'Whenever as a group of players we get together, we never, ever mention Heysel. Ever. It's as though deep down we do feel partly responsible for what happened.'

Mark Lawrenson

Kenny Dalglish's private rituals of self-tending were thoroughly endorsed by Liverpool FC come the autumn of 1984. His training was all done on one day, his customary rest periods expanding through the week, and even when he trained he was spared the quick sprints and the hard turns. His rare gifts were being nursed, meted out. John Wark, his Scotland teammate and now roommate for Liverpool's travels, had to respect the etiquette of Dalglish's customary afternoon kip. That meant a few solid hours of silence, Wark required 'to draw the curtains like I was an apprentice', lights off, and no telly, under the threat of a cross word. Still, for all these rigours, the season saw Dalglish having to sit and watch more than he had bargained for.

Liverpool were not at full strength in any case. Ian Rush, hurt in pre-season, needed a cartilage operation. Joe Fagan had replaced Souness with, in effect, two men: Jan Molby from Ajax and Kevin MacDonald from Leicester. But the bedding-in was slow. Liverpool slumped to a yield of just three points from a run of seven games. Come October, they sat second bottom. There would be no assault on the title. When Liverpool met Spurs in mid-October Dalglish was, for the first time in his Liverpool career, dropped from the first team. He had to read about it first in the papers, the cause of a Keegan-like ruction with Fagan. Liverpool lost the game and Fagan would express contrition for a bad call. Still, dropping the King had been a very Liverpool stroke: it let the whole squad know that nobody was above the cut.

It seemed a time for unfortunate firsts, though, as Dalglish then suffered the first sending-off of his playing career against Benfica in the last 16 of the European Cup at an absurdly sodden Estadio da Luz. Benfica full-back Minervino Pietra went through him, and he responded angrily, raising a hand, though he pleaded self-defence. But Dalglish was off, and landed with a three-match ban. Was the bell suddenly tolling on Dalglish's playing career as it had done for Keegan? As so often before, within a week Dalglish answered back on the pitch, albeit in Scotland colours, with a left-foot curler that sealed a win over Spain in a World Cup qualifier. In the New Year Honours List he was awarded an MBE for 'services to football'. One just had a sense, though, that Dalglish the player might be contending for his last medals.

The league was gone, but Liverpool brushed aside Austria Vienna and Panathinaikos to reach another European Cup final where they would meet the daunting Juventus of Michel Platini, Marco Tardelli and Zbigniew Boniek. The venue, the Heysel stadium in Brussels, seemed an unintelligent selection by UEFA – nestled in a leafy suburban district, rated as a 'dump' and visibly dilapidated. The entire southern end of the stadium was allocated to Juventus fans. The terrace behind the opposite goal was divided into three sections (X, Y, Z), with X and Y reserved for Liverpool fans. Tickets for section Z were to be sold only to Belgian residents, supposedly a 'neutral' area. But they would find their way to Italian supporters, making Z a *de facto* 'Juventus' section, albeit one of largely expatriate Italians and their children. Section Z was separated from the English in Y only by the kind of wire mesh that might barely suffice to section off municipal tennis courts. That people who went to football bent on starting aggro would revel in the disorder seemed likely. Among the Anfield administration there was unease. Peter Robinson made written objections to UEFA and to the Belgian FA.

Meanwhile, Liverpool's FA Cup run ended in the semis with a replay loss to Manchester United, but more striking than the settling of the longtime rivalry on the pitch was the thuggery that accompanied the first tie at Goodison Park: two fans stabbed outside the ground, a flare fired at United fans within, United winger Jesper Olsen struck by a missile near the corner flag.

Joe Fagan informed John Smith and Peter Robinson that he wished to quit as Liverpool boss. The conveyor belt of Boot Room succession could no longer be seamless, as questions of age and aptitude now weighed heavily. Ronnie Moran was the most senior coach, but his gifts did not seem like those of a gaffer. Roy Evans, only 36, looked to be not yet the finished article. The next tier was the playing staff; and skipper Phil Neal was known to fancy the job. But the man John Smith fancied was Dalglish: a man with no experience in this line or, indeed, any obvious inclination, who had never even relished the captain's armband – a leadership duty much less onerous than the boss's job. English football, moreover, had not brought forth many promising models in the way of player-managers: no one had done both jobs in the top flight before.

The subtler concern about Dalglish's suitability was a more intricate question of temperament. Dalglish's old Celtic captain Billy McNeill was among the sceptics, wondering if a man he considered so 'insular' and who set 'such high standards and goals for himself' could really adapt to the outward-going ebullience of management. After all, a lot of robust-looking football men had come to find management an obsessive, haunting business: that crushing responsibility for the club's fortunes, for the welfare of players, above all for results, and accounting for them before assembled media. The dugout was going to be an odd place for Dalglish, totally at odds with his usual preparation, simply not his natural perch from which to influence or seek to direct a game of football.

The case for Dalglish was shorter and more to do with faith, or superstition, if one preferred. He had a proud, fiercely focused record of football success, and was devoted to the game to the exclusion of everything else in life apart from his family. He possessed a sound football intelligence and a presence that set a standard. Would he prove sufficiently hardened for the tough stuff of decision-making and player-management? Graeme Souness had testified to the usefully daunting quality of Dalglish's presence. ('People are a bit frightened of him. He growls at them, he makes them jump.') As for credentials – Bill Shankly had never bothered with any coaching badges. And there remained something golden about Dalglish, the degree to which he summoned and exemplified the passion associated with Liverpool, and commanded the support's affections.

As Liverpool made ready to leave for Brussels, Smith and Robinson called on Dalglish at home, and the deal was discussed. They had guessed correctly that Dalglish would see the job as his best opportunity to extend the success he had been bred to, within an environment he understood. Bob Paisley was added to the deal: a consultancy role on a two-year contract. Dalglish accepted Liverpool's offer, and the board were informed, though a public announcement was held back until after the Juventus match. Dalglish had to keep schtum in Brussels, then, though he wound up confiding in his good friend Hansen.

Come the bright sunlit morning of the match, Joe Fagan – cheerily, if doubtless wistful – told his players, 'After tonight you can call me Joe.' They had reason to expect the club would appoint wisely, and they had a massive match to look forward to. It was Europe's premier spectacle between two of its greatest names, and the venue UEFA had chosen for the game was a death trap, a mortuary in waiting.

The atmosphere in the city on a hot afternoon had been reasonably affable, inevitably fuelled by strong Belgian beer, but manageable – nothing so out of order in the relations between rival fans. But there were, without doubt, roving elements who were on edge and jumped-up. A 'minority' in a sell-out crowd of 58,000 was all it took: the hard core with an interest in causing trouble, plus others aspiring or easily swayed – enough for people to get hurt.

Once the two clans converged on the stadium, a bristling pre-match tension began to build. There was a rowdy crush at the ground's sole turnstile, and ticket inspections were derisory. Still, at various points around the outer concrete masonry of the ground ticketless fans had a go at kicking out hatch-sized gaps in order to crawl in.

As the Liverpool team bus approached Heysel the players were puzzled by their first look at the tired, aged aspect of the place. Inside, Heysel had the roaring feel of a big and dominant Juve crowd. Liverpool's allotted section Y was soon full up, but through the meagre wire barriers, past attending gendarmerie, the Liverpool contingent could see that the neutral section Z had plenty of space and a good few Juventus colours. Some began to agitate, starting with the police.

Around 6.30pm the players came out onto the running track round the pitch for a look at the surface and a feel of the atmosphere. What was most noticeable in the air were stones being thrown between hostile fans. The ground was crumbling, rubble lying loose around the terraces, fist-sized missile material.

Hostilities broke out between section Y and section Z. Who can say how it started? The Liverpool support appeared most active in pelting Z with beer cans and stones. Soon the wire fence was rent with tears and police could not hold a line. Then the antagonising turned to attack – Liverpool fans surged through the holes, some brandishing bottles and lengths of rigid plastic pipe stolen from an unlocked hut. Some would later maintain it was self-defence, or reacting to provocation, or seeing some of their own getting hurt. The trouble is that even years later the images would still look an awful lot like an away contingent 'taking the end', making a charge from which the Italians fled.

With no escape at the top of the stand, they clustered to the bottom corner of their section, there to be trapped between the low side wall and a lower wall facing the pitch. The chaotic and panic-stricken flight from the aggressors quickly became a dreadful crush. People stumbled, fell and were trampled, asphyxiated, a crush, an unbearable weight of bodies, pressed against the wall. At 7.30pm the wall gave way.

In their cramped changing room directly beneath section Z the Liverpool players were kitted out and booted up, getting mentally ready, psyching themselves up. Suddenly through open windows they heard a loud bang, remembered by Ian Rush as 'like that of cannon firing' – then a noise like 'distant thunder', soon followed by a din of human voices in desperation.

Outside the catastrophe was clear – many people, mostly Italians, were dead, crushed or asphyxiated beneath the weight of hundreds. Among the deceased were many more injured, trapped alongside friends and relatives with the life already forced from them. Some scrabbled clear, to stagger, dazedly, away from the disaster. Emergency medical services amounted to a single doctor and Red Cross volunteers. They, and the understrength gendarmerie, were simply overwhelmed by the size of the calamity.

Some Liverpool players left their changing room to try to establish what was going on. Alan Kennedy, not in the team, was an appointed sentinel. Bruce Grobbelaar had a look out. Craig Johnston, too, came in and out with updates. Kenny Dalglish would always maintain he was aware of 'an incident', indeed a 'serious one', but not of its severity, as he was apart from the others, getting attention on the treatment table.

Outside, refugees from section Z fled to the other end of the crowd where Juve's ultras were confused and incensed. The news of the calamity spread, and Juventus crossed the ground, round the track or over the pitch, to confront section Y. Police had to keep Liverpool fans penned and to drive Juventus fans back.

Kick-off was delayed, of course. The Liverpool team had been told to stay indoors. Joe Fagan had seen the carnage, was distressed and didn't want the players to see for themselves, but some had got the idea. Others, such as Dalglish, remained in their own zone, with the particular capacity of players (in the words of Roy Evans) to 'just keep themselves to themselves and kind of switch off to external things'. A UEFA represent-ative, looking haunted, came in to confirm there had been 'trouble'.

The Juventus team, meanwhile, had seen their changing room overrun by upset and enraged fans, had been out into the stadium to see for themselves, and felt the terrible sense of mayhem. There were 38 people confirmed dead, more than 500 injured (a 39th victim died in hospital). The idea that a football match could be seriously contested now seemed a ghastly one. And yet a hastily convened but long and scarcely coherent meet-ing of the authorities was ducking the decision, no one wanting to be responsible. Finally, the head of gendarmerie ventured that the game should go ahead – better to distract the crowd than have to disperse it into the night. UEFA gave the nod to that view. The two teams did as they were told.

The match that began at 9.41pm was a stiff, grim charade, won by a highly debatable penalty that the referee seemed only too happy to award in the cause of getting a result in normal time. Juventus had never won the European Cup and wanted it desperately. Arguably, the dreadful events of the evening had gripped the players with a desire to accomplish something in honour of the people they knew to have died. This European Cup, though, was irredeemably tarnished goods.

Come the morning the Liverpool FC party could not get out of Brussels fast enough but, still, their coach was surrounded by Italian protesters and the players berated through the glass, Dalglish acutely conscious of the fury in the faces pressed against the windows. The coach was granted special permission to go onto the tarmac at Brussels airport so as to taxi right up to the aeroplane's steps. On disembarking at Speke, Joe Fagan was an anguished figure, insupportable in his upset. Around Liverpool people struggled to know what to think amid the enormity of the awfulness. 'As players,' Mark Lawrenson would later reflect, 'for whatever reason, we all felt guilty.'

John Smith announced that Liverpool would withdraw from European competition, but the FA went one step futher, banning all English clubs from Europe for a year. UEFA then declared an indefinite ban of its own. Police proceedings were afoot, a process that would end with the conviction of 14 Liverpool supporters for involuntary manslaughter. The failure of policing and the dilapidation of the stadium, irreducible elements in the disaster, had been clear to see. English football faced daunting questions. What was to be done to stop this happening again? The UEFA ban, meanwhile, meant a serious loss of revenue for the English game. Where was the money to come from to address the declining physical condition of English grounds, and compensate for the hole in funds made by the ban?

Margaret Thatcher had no interest in football but could see the public order issue and the game's dysfunction as a business. In an interview with Piccadilly Radio she stated her intent to see football 'restored to its former place in our national life, and for families to feel that they can go along there . . . and have a marvellous day out'. The first proposition was a tall order. The second reflected no previous reality anyone could remember.

On 3 June 1985 Thatcher made a statement in the House of Commons regarding Heysel, expressing 'the sense of outrage and shame at the behaviour of some of our citizens' and stressing what she believed would be 'effective measures to combat violence' – a clampdown on match-day drinking, enhanced police powers, CCTV and fan membership schemes. In reply, Labour leader Neil Kinnock referred to a previous appeal of his for 'action to identify and deal with the causes of these afflictions and the breakdown of behaviour in society'. Other Labour members sang similar hymns. 'Something has gone wrong in this country,' the former home secretary Merlyn Rees opined, 'and the Right Honourable Lady as prime minister must give some thought as to what it is.' Jack Ashley MP argued 'that the despair and disaffection of so many young people in Great Britain today is the breeding ground for the mindless and appalling aggression that we saw in Brussels'; and that the prime minister had to 'face the fact that aggressive economic and social policies exacerbate the problem'. Kinnock wound round to saying that while he and his party certainly wanted 'the thugs caught and punished', what was needed was a 'thorough investigation' to establish 'not only those who commit the crimes but why they commit such crimes'. Thatcher, however, batted Kinnock's proposal aside. An investigation of that sort, she responded, 'could go on for years and find as many answers as there are people on such an inquiry. There is violence in human nature. There are only three ways of trying to deal with it – persuasion, prevention or punishment. We shall try to operate all three.'

Whatever the scale of challenge prior to Heysel, managing Liverpool FC now had the look of a poisoned chalice being put to the lips of Dalglish. Among the players, defender Jim Beglin would remember 'a lot of satisfaction' at the news of Dalglish's appointment. ('We all thought they couldn't get anybody better.') But any manager is, in Ian St John's words, 'carrying the can for the whole club'. As of 30 May 1985, when Dalglish's appointment was announced to the media at Anfield, that can was an extraordinary load to carry.

There was no point in trying to make effervescent PR out of the day, which would, in any case, have been about a million miles from Dalglish's natural instincts. John Smith told the gathered press that Liverpool had found a man with 'an old head on young shoulders'. Dalglish quickly served notice of the degree to which he would be taking the commentariat seriously. 'You know nothing about football and I know nothing about journalism,' he told Ian Hargraves of the *Liverpool Echo*, 'so we should get on well.'

Liverpool could only have been relieved by Dalglish's readiness to shoulder the burden of the club's injured reputation and to take arms against the weight of accusation over Heysel. Dalglish, when he was ready to speak at length some years later, would express the feeling that Liverpool FC had been 'unfairly vilified from many quarters'. He would refer to UEFA's failings in the selection of Heysel, to the provocations of Roma fans in 1984 and Juventus fans on the night, to the good repute of

Liverpool's support and their possible infiltration at Heysel by fifth columnists from other clubs. In other words, for someone whose chief claim was to have been oblivious to so much on the night, Dalglish eventually would have much to say about who might have done what and why in the moment. As of May 1985, however, his role seemed clear: to be the defender and standard-bearer of Liverpool Football Club, through thick and thin – a distinguished position, but a tall order.

13

After the Fall

1985-89

'I had just one fall-out with [Kenny] ... I left him out of an Under-23 match once ... He didn't like that.'

Tommy Docherty

'There were players who didn't like Kenny, for the same reason I didn't like him in December '85: they weren't in the team.'

Ronnie Whelan, *Walk On* (2011)

When Dalglish addressed the Liverpool squad as boss on the first morning of pre-season he faced a wrenching change – an end to old, dependable pleasures. Operationally, training was just as anyone could remember – the Liverpool Way. The players warmed up, then the cones got planted and it was hard-fought five-a-side under the gaze of Bugsy Moran and Roy Evans.

But the man who had been 'King', 'Super' and 'Dog's Bollocks' of the dressing room was now 'Boss' or 'Gaffer', to be addressed as such; and where previously Dalglish had made his feelings known to teammates by baiting wisecracks or a cold shoulder, now he would have to do a fair bit of patient

explanation as to what was on his mind. He remained on
Liverpool's books as a player, formidably so. But playing was no
longer his chief function at the club. Football being Dalglish's
life, and being one of the lads so integral to that, he had to feel
the loneliness of his new perch.

The difficult fusion he was being called on to achieve, in the
view of defender Gary Gillespie, was that of 'being your mate
and being your boss at the same time ... it was tricky sometimes because you didn't know if he was talking to you as a
mate or a boss.' However one might rate the quality of repartee
in Liverpool's changing room, it was the soul of the club, and
Dalglish was now left out of it. Whenever he entered, whatever
fun and games had been going on ceased abruptly. Who would
act that way with a mate? 'I miss the banter, Al,' Dalglish would
tell his pal Hansen, plaintively.

Still, as Souness had anticipated, Dalglish did not stint
from the duty of growling at people when he had to. Lest
it be imagined that those well-established players who were
Dalglish's neighbours in upscale Southport had some sort of
immunity, the gaffer thoroughly rebuked Mark Lawrenson for
late attendance after a spot of summer coaching in Dublin. A
thornier issue was Phil Neal, aggrieved that he had not been
preferred for the job having believed that Liverpool had inti-
mated some such role for him. Neal pointedly wouldn't call
Dalglish 'Boss', leading to some sharp exchanges. And after
Neal made his disappointment known to the press, Dalglish
summoned him and delivered the news that Hansen would be
captain henceforth. Hansen was a pal, of course, but Dalglish,
the man of magic rituals, also believed that his mate was a lucky
general. For Neal it was the end of the road, and he accepted an
approach from Bolton to play and manage there, Steve Nicol
filling his boots on the right.

This squad of players had, of course, just been through the
trauma of Heysel together. Some had seen more on that night
than they could stomach: Bruce Grobbelaar had contemplated

quitting the game and had to be talked round. Liverpool's season opener against Arsenal was their first competitive game since, and the team felt an uncanny tension. TV cameras were absent, the BBC and FA having missed the deadline to agree the monies of their usual broadcast deal. Before kick-off there was a short service in memory of Heysel's victims, albeit hampered by a faltering PA system.

But Liverpool soon enough got on top and stayed there, winning 2-0, Jan Molby at last looking influential. Shortly, Dalglish would bring in as his first big signing ex-Evertonian Steve McMahon, whose battling qualities, allied to Molby's vision and passing, suggested that Souness might at last have been adequately replaced, albeit by two men.

Dalglish had 'Old Bob' upstairs, had inherited Paisley's secretary Sheila, and Tom Saunders shared the office. The Boot Room remained the Boot Room, though Dalglish, unlike his predecessors, would not be dropping in for a bottle of Guinness. Dalglish made clear that his players could relax in their preferred fashion in their own time so long as they approached match day with a rigour akin to his own. As to the names on the team sheet, Dalglish would keep his selection close to his chest until shortly before kick-off. If that kept the players a little on edge, it also ensured that no one felt at liberty to coast through training.

Certain players, such as the versatile Ronnie Whelan, had to get used to being shifted around positionally. Others began to feel unfavoured. Paul Walsh, signed by Fagan as Dalglish's putative successor, challenged the gaffer's decision to leave him out at Oxford, and earned a detention in the form of extra training. Dalglish was not picking himself in the side routinely – he would play only eight times before March, preferring to pair Rush with Walsh, who bagged 18 goals in 25 games. Still, Walsh was unsettled and suspicious. What Dalglish was capable of could still set a daunting example. Away to the champions Everton in late September he scored from an outrageous distance inside 20 seconds: the ball laid back to him,

Dalglish – near-balletic in his poise – leaning back to strike a curler that evaded the keeper. Liverpool were 3-0 up by half-time, but Everton got two back and then Dalglish – from the sublime to the gobsmacking – missed two absolute sitters near the end, so condemning himself to a load of stick in the changing room from which he defended himself. ('He said the first ball in was bouncing,' Molby remembered, 'and the second one was behind him. Phil Neal took the flak for that . . .')

Despite the absence of telly, not resolved until the New Year, attendances were at their lowest since 1922. But a lot of fans were missing out on a lively season. It was Manchester United, 19 seasons without a league title, who came out flying with 10 straight wins, while West Ham were in contention thanks to the goals of Frank McAvennie and Tony Cottee; likewise Chelsea, armed with Kerry Dixon and David Speedie. But when Liverpool visited Old Trafford in mid-October they looked the better side, after which a run saw them reduce United's lead from nine points to two. United's wheels then came off: a kindly fixture list had flattered them a bit, then their talismanic captain Bryan Robson was toppled by injury. Still, Liverpool's own form through the New Year was patchy, just 14 points from 12 games. Hansen told Dalglish it was the worst Liverpool side he'd played in.

In early February Liverpool were unlucky not to beat United at Anfield, but the grim story of the day concerned attacks by thugs on the United team, first as their bus approached Anfield, then outside the entrance as the players climbed out. CS gas was sprayed, and some spectators, including children, got the worst of it. Paul Walsh's campaign ended that afternoon when he ruptured ankle ligaments after a clash with Kevin Moran.

Seemingly poised to profit from others' misfortunes were Everton, who had hugely strengthened their side with the cheerily predatory striker Gary Lineker. In late February they rolled over Liverpool at Anfield – Grobbelaar at fault for the first, Lineker putting the seal on it – to move eight points clear of their rivals. The first great test of the Dalglish era was here. What managerial magic did he have to conjure with now?

There was his well-tested will to win. 'Kenny was a winner and he wasn't going to accept anything less from any of his players,' defender Jim Beglin recalled. But then a winning mentality is not necessarily transferable to players who have no previous experience of it. The unique element Dalglish had to offer was the possibility of leading by example. He restored his own name to the starting XI, and Liverpool didn't lose another game.

First they thumped QPR 4-1. 'Kenny really made them play,' lamented Rangers boss Jim Smith. Then he was the provider in a 6-0 crushing of Oxford, turning and passing with all his old accomplishment. It was Everton's turn to crack, drawing games they needed to win, losing at Oxford while Liverpool took care of Leicester. Dalglish's team now needed to beat Chelsea at Stamford Bridge on the final weekend to be sure of the title. Twenty-four minutes in, a rasp at goal by Whelan was blocked, but he headed the rebound firmly, helped along by Beglin to Dalglish, who chested and volleyed into the right corner, bringing joy unconstrained among the red contingent. The script, as if thieved without shame from *Roy of the Rovers*, decreed this goal should be the winner: the veteran player-manager scoring to scoop the league in his first season. Only the addition of the FA Cup to make a double could strain credulity further.

One week later Liverpool faced Everton in the final at a heaving and expectant Wembley. It was goalless in the first half when Dalglish took a sharp pass from Molby, only for his control, so rarely, to fail him. Peter Reid, gifted the ball, played a long, weighted pass over Lawrenson for Lineker to chase, and at the second try Lineker bundled it home past Grobbelaar. Advantage Everton; and Dalglish got niggly near half-time, a bit of aggravation with Kevin Sheedy after a move broke down, leaving him lucky to evade a caution. In the changing room Dalglish apologised for his fault over the goal and tried to rouse his team with some strong words, softly spoken, about the need to seize the moment.

On the restart, though, Liverpool were hardly better, Grobbelaar haranguing his defence, Lineker sniffing for another long ball. It was Hansen who put his stamp on proceedings, reinstating composure and Liverpool's usual passing approach. Suddenly, from Whelan to Molby to Rush, it was 1-1. Five minutes later, Molby to Johnston: 2-1. And with six minutes left: Molby to Whelan to Rush, game over. A year after their lowest ebb, Liverpool were once again bathed in success, English football's object of envy, most vitally and painfully for Evertonians. Pressed for comment by reporters in the usual futile manner, Dalglish deflected all praise he received towards the team, the club, the support. And yet the charm around his aura had never seemed so radiant. It was as if all his many superstitions stood vindicated at once.

'He's 35 now,' Alex Ferguson noted of Dalglish, 'but he is all class and presence.' It was another World Cup summer, that one remarkable and ritual form of disappointment for Dalglish; and in the Scotland camp it was now Ferguson whom Dalglish called 'Gaffer'. Jock Stein had been in poor shape for some time and on 10 September 1985, amid the tremendous stress of the final moments of the team's qualifying decider with Wales, he had suffered a fatal heart attack.

Scotland were to play in the Mexico World Cup's customary 'group of death' with West Germany, Uruguay and Denmark. Dalglish had made it to the summit of 100 international caps, and Ferguson expressed every confidence about the prospects for Dalglish's contribution to the World Cup effort, making room for him in the squad though there was none for David Speedie or Steve Archibald. At the same time, Ferguson decided he had no place for Alan Hansen. Dalglish called Ferguson and registered a dissenting view. Dalglish would withdraw himself from the squad the day before the flight to Mexico, citing the severity of a knee injury sustained towards the end of Liverpool's season. Speedie was now unavailable, having booked his holidays, and Ferguson fumed. Though Dalglish had spoken up for his pal Hansen, he would always insist there was no snub.

Scotland's performance in Mexico was a failure less valiant than usual, one point and bottom of the group. It was Graeme Souness' turn to feel the Dalglish-like ignominy of being dropped for the last game, but Souness had other duties, having followed his old roommate into playing and managing, at Glasgow Rangers, reinvigorated by US-based owner Lawrence Marlborough and chief executive David Holmes. Alex Ferguson was also ready for a new challenge. It would come in November when Ron Atkinson got the axe at Manchester United, and Ferguson took his place, inheriting a side that some saw as hardly more than a good cup team with a drinking problem.

The Liverpool Way was to take success as the reason to rebuild: a side that won one league could never expect to retain it. Liverpool's double winners were a functional team, with the spine of Hansen, Whelan and Rush, and the player-manager who could still conjure moments of game-changing magic. But Liverpool had not signed a true star since Dalglish himself, in 1977, and now he was on the verge of retirement. The club, though, were more than usually strapped for funds having exiled themselves from the rewards of European competition. And so, over the summer, Dalglish accepted a bid of £3.2 million from Juventus for Ian Rush, the move to take effect 12 months later so as to preserve the balance of the Old Lady's quota of foreign players. It was a hard call to let Rush go, but typically Liverpool, the money right for all sides, allowing Dalglish some leeway to rebuild.

He paid Sunderland a quarter of a million for full-back Barry Venison, and got a bargain in Irish left back Steve Staunton, spotted at Dundalk. Perhaps the most notable personnel changes, though, were behind the scenes. Tom Saunders retired as youth development officer, and Steve Heighway took over. Backroom sackings had been scarcely known at the club since Shankly's arrival but Dalglish now dispensed with the services of the venerable chief scout Geoff Twentyman and reserve team coach Chris Lawler. Phil Thompson took over Lawler's position and another ex-club captain, Ron Yeats, replaced Twentyman – albeit with no prior scouting experience. But then Dalglish had never managed before winning the double. Bob Paisley's consultancy role, meanwhile, had become redundant, a case of one too many cooks in the kitchen. Paisley, still a keen observer in the stands, would sometimes head down to Dalglish's dugout to offer a pointer. He was, according to Roy Evans, 'told to fuck off on more than one occasion' – a simple matter-of-fact in the heat of a sporting encounter. Dalglish was showing himself to be his own man, ready to be judged for it.

However, 1986-87 was to be a cursed season for Liverpool. Kevin MacDonald and Jim Beglin suffered broken legs, Steve Nicol missed half of it through injury, Paul Walsh never played and was soon off to Tottenham. Ferguson's Manchester United, who had themselves begun poorly, came to Anfield on Boxing Day, and Dalglish started himself alongside Rush. But Ferguson outmanoeuvred him in midfield and United scored a fluent winning goal. By the turn of the year Liverpool were third, trailing Arsenal by nine points, tossed out of the FA Cup on Luton's artificial surface at Kenilworth Road.

Under some pressure, Dalglish needed to spend, to pay the money that star players, transformative flair players, demanded. He had his wish list, and at the top were two such stellar performers, Watford's John Barnes and Newcastle's Peter Beardsley. Barnes was a superior athlete, a force going forward, virtuoso in his dribbling and crossing and conning of defenders, and a scorer of amazing goals. Whether crossing or shooting, when Barnes struck the ball he really unleashed it. But London or Italy were the places where Barnes saw himself. He was a smart man, and not convinced that a city so backward in the matter of racial tolerance as Liverpool would cope with him.

Beardsley, since emerging from the patronage of Keegan at Newcastle, had become as beloved of England boss Bobby Robson ('my little gem') as Dalglish had been by Paisley – playing, too, in a Dalglish-like hole between midfield and attack. He was a figure in whom Dalglish could see a little of himself – a team fulcrum, of service to any mobile striker. And Beardsley would assuredly be available: Newcastle United was still run as a selling club and, despite the ardour of its support, the proper ambitions of its best players could not be denied.

Also on Dalglish's list were John Aldridge and Ray Houghton of Oxford United. The Scouser Aldridge was swiftly procured, but Houghton would take until October. Deals for Barnes and Beardsley, though, were going to be more protracted. Liverpool won nine of the first 11 league games of 1987 and by mid-March they had crept ahead of Everton. But they fell to three league defeats in a row, also losing the League Cup final to Arsenal, in the midst of which run Lawrenson ruptured an Achilles tendon against Wimbledon. Everton ran out as champions comfortably, by nine points. It was an empty-handed season at Liverpool, and that meant cold, hard reflection and the imperative to change. For Liverpool's final, meaningless home game against Watford, Dalglish chose himself in the starting line-up. He would never do so again.

It was time for Liverpool to outspend their rivals, because they could. Alex Ferguson also coveted Barnes and Beardsley, but he was thwarted, at considerable cost. And after Arsenal had wearied of waiting for Barnes to make up his mind, Liverpool were left in prime spot to hand Watford a cheque for £900,000. At long last, then, Barnes swanned into Liverpool, to be bemused by the meat-and-potatoes training regime of Melwood. Equally surprising to him was that Dalglish remained such an active, competitive figure in the small-sided games; but, as one maestro to another, Barnes was respectful of Dalglish's obvious gifts. Within weeks Beardsley was prised from Newcastle for a new British record fee of £1.9 million, and Dalglish handed him the number seven shirt – finally buying Liverpool a true replacement for himself in the shape of 'Pedro', previously Kevin Keegan's successor in black and white.

'In all my time here,' Alan Hansen would opine, 'we've had no one with the something extra-special except the boss. Now we've got two of them.' On paper, perhaps, the set-up looked like 4-4-2 but on the pitch it was more like 4-2-3-1 – Whelan and Steve McMahon doing the crunching, then Barnes and Houghton either side of Beardsley, who roamed behind Aldridge. Nine minutes into the new season at Arsenal, Beardsley played Barnes in down the left and his cross was headed in by Aldridge. They stuffed Coventry, then put four past Newcastle, Derby, Portsmouth and QPR.

Barnes was immediately at ease, though Beardsley seemed a little overshadowed, not quite fitting in – with his teetotalism, his thick Hexham accent, his earnest trying aspect. 'He'd collect the bibs, cones and balls after training had finished,' Barnes recalled, remembering 'a few snide remarks' from the lads and a feeling that Beardsley was 'sucking up to the manager'. But then, Dalglish had been Beardsley's boyhood hero.

Barnes had his own special share of acclimatising problems. Upon his signing, racist graffiti had appeared on the walls outside Anfield, and the club had received abusive letters. When Liverpool met Everton away in the League Cup, sections of the crowd made moronic 'monkey' noises and chucked bananas onto the pitch. The clubs were due to meet again in the league four days later, and Everton's chairman appealed to their fans to show decency. Beardsley scored in that game, a belter into the roof en route to a 2-0 win, and he was hugged by pitch-invading fans as if he had finally arrived. But the foul receptions given to Barnes wouldn't go away. He showed his class to such backward elements when Liverpool went to Goodison in the FA Cup, casually back-heeling one of those bananas off the playing surface.

Liverpool's familiar adversaries could not prevent the team's march, though Everton did stop them from surpassing Leeds' 1974 record of 29 league games unbeaten. Brian Clough's Forest were well back in the rear view, beaten 2-1 in the FA Cup semi-final at Hillsborough after having been annihilated at Anfield 5-0. But Manchester United rescued a draw at Anfield and in a post-match interview Alex Ferguson complained bitterly of match officials being daunted by the volume of Liverpool's support. Dalglish, passing down the same corridor and carrying his two-month-old daughter Lauren, told the press to ignore Ferguson's gripe, indicating the baby: 'You'll get more sense out of her.' Just banter, of course. Ferguson, though, had turned United round, and it sharpened a little needle between the two managers from west Glasgow. Liverpool romped to the title by nine points from Ferguson's work-in-progress side, but on the day Dalglish was certainly finding United hard to beat. No such threat seemed to be presented by Bobby Gould's Wimbledon team in the FA Cup final, where Liverpool were expected to secure Dalglish's second double. But Wimbledon were a bull-ishly determined bunch on the day, who knocked Liverpool off their stride, grabbed a set-piece goal, and made it to the finish line. It was a historic chance missed, if a failure only in light of the vaulting standards Dalglish had set.

In the overall rating of Dalglish's 1988-vintage Liverpool, plenty of informed viewers offered superlatives to spare. Tom Finney – one of the greats of the postwar English game over 15 years of service to Preston and England – hailed the 5-0 drubbing of Forest as 'the greatest exhibition of football' he had ever witnessed. This was Dalglish's team now; he had built it, no question. Money, though, had talked: all the top clubs had coveted Barnes and Beardsley but Liverpool had offered the best packages, thus recruiting the English game's two most gifted players to the team that had finished second the previous season. How extraordinary was that team's subsequent dominance, in a league now three seasons removed from European competition? How exceptional to beat Clough's declining Forest 5-0 so handsomely then lose to Wimbledon in a cup final? Posterity would have to judge Dalglish's side against such opposition, rather than, say, Arrigo Sacchi's AC Milan of Gullit, Van Basten, Maldini and Donadoni, consummate *Scudetto* winners who stood poised to put their own lock upon the European Cup for a season or two.

At Juventus Ian Rush had hardly failed – rather, he had been forced to scrap in a new sort of game, denied his obvious preference for playing on the shoulder of the last defender. If seven goals over a season were a meagre return by his standards, he was still the team's top scorer. But Dalglish had kept in touch with his former strike partner, and could see it wasn't wholly working. Two days before Liverpool's rematch with Wimbledon in the Charity Shield, they brought home the prodigal son, Rush returning to Liverpool for £2.7 million. Dalglish mustered one of his mildly more dextrous gags, about Italy having been 'like a foreign country' to Rush; and, like old times, Rush endured the banter.

In October, though, Liverpool lost Jan Molby's services for a while. Molby, carrying four driving convictions, had climbed into his BMW one evening with drink on board, and on being pursued by police had chosen to put his foot down. Caught, he was sentenced to 90 days in jail, of which he served six weeks, unsure of whether Liverpool would welcome him back. He came out having lost a few stone, and was fined two weeks' wages. John Smith and Peter Robinson had qualms but Dalglish, the fiercely loyal defender of players he rated as first-teamers, made plain Molby's importance to the team.

In the league Liverpool were contenders, but inconsistent, losing at home to second-bottom Newcastle, then again a week later to the scarcely more fancied Luton. The team really catching the eye were George Graham's Arsenal, chock-full of young talent largely developed within the club: Tony Adams, Paul Merson, Paul Davis, David Rocastle, Michael Thomas. In December Liverpool drew with Arsenal, then drew the Merseyside derby, holding their own but making no progress. Sitting fifth, they lost at Old Trafford on New Year's Day. Dalglish locked his team in the changing room and played war, a resort to the remonstrative style of Fagan back in 1982.

Rush and Aldridge began to combine profitably, Molby's return proved influential, and results improved. But Dalglish began to look to set up more defensively than the quick, one-touch attacking style that had got neutrals swooning the previous season. Beardsley was brilliant, for sure, especially when Liverpool were on song; but in the teeth of adversity he wasn't a player who niggled, he didn't exude that unbeatable quality. Dalglish's plan to beat a physical Millwall in the FA Cup – successful, as it happened – involved leaving Beardsley on the bench. But Beardsley got benched more and more, even at Newcastle; and football-daft Peter was immeasurably 'gutted' when he wasn't being picked.

To seasoned observers, Liverpool appeared to be taking a familiar roundabout route to steaming towards the title. But Arsenal's lead was imperious. George Graham, too, left out creative players when he had to. His Arsenal was a tight side built on a hard midfield four protecting a solid back four, and every player was switched on, leaving no gaps, keeping a good shape when possession was lost, getting in front and seeing games out. Still, Liverpool hit on a run, nine straight wins through March and early April, and Arsenal finally began to falter. In the meantime, Liverpool proceeded to an FA Cup semi-final, against Nottingham Forest at Sheffield Wednesday's Hillsborough stadium. It was mid-April, and Liverpool Football Club was exactly where it liked to be. 'We loved that time of year,' Ronnie Whelan would write. 'The dressing room was always buzzing . . . the weather turning, the spring full of promise and summer in the air.'

14

Hillsborough

1989

*'Perhaps it is understandable that policemen go to football matches
these days with their thoughts concentrated on keeping hostile mobs
at bay rather than on supervising the safety of a mass audience.
But that predisposition carries the seeds of deadly consequences.'*

Hugh McIlvanney, 1989

*'. . . [M]y aim was to bring the people close to the club and the
team and for them to be accepted as a part of it. The effect was that
wives brought their late husband's ashes to Anfield and scattered
them on the pitch after saying a little prayer. That's how close the
people have come to this club. When they wanted to scatter the
ashes of their loved one, who wanted to be part of the club when
they were dead, I said to them: "In you come, you're welcome."'*

Bill Shankly

Saturday, 15 April, and the Liverpool XI ran out onto the
Hillsborough pitch around 2.50pm, ready for action. They were
warmed up, the changing-room team talk behind them: these
were professionals wholly focused on a huge game. Dalglish
headed for the visitors' dugout. Though the day was seasonally

warm he was clad in his armour, a big down-filled coat sponsored by the white-goods maker Candy. Through the players' eyes it all looked as if the day's vitally important main business was afoot. But outside Hillsborough was a roiling mass of mayhem, incapable police on horseback, frustrated Liverpool supporters waving tickets. And inside, beyond the white line, behind what was to be the Liverpool goal, people's lives were in the direst danger, their terrible plight deepening from second to second.

Just as at their previous Hillsborough semi-final the year before, Liverpool supporters – though the larger contingent – had been allotted the smaller Leppings Lane end of the ground: a terrace split into five fenced pens with a 10ft steel fence at the front. A gesture to where fans had travelled from, it was nevertheless a blinkered decision in light of a history of worrisome crowd congestion at that end, such as a 1981 Spurs–Wolves semi-final at which Spurs fans had clambered over the fencing to escape a crush.

From around 2pm the Leppings Lane centre pens (numbered 3 and 4) were filling up. That the ground had an aged, ramshackle feel; that breathing space would be at a premium – these uncomfortable facts were wearily familiar to many Liverpool fans. It would likely be a packed enclosure in an old ground on a big match day. Adrian Tempany was one among the faithful in Leppings Lane: to his eyes, 'the pitch was the colour of a ripening lime, and the sun was flickering over the hills around the city.'

By 2.30 things were shifting, alarmingly. Plenty of fans had got to Leppings Lane in good time but the admission system, the inadequate turnstiles and inadequate stewardship of numbers once inside were piling up terrible trouble. The pressure of bodies was dangerous outside, but immeasurably worse inside.

Pens 3 and 4 were overfull, and there was no respite: fans were asked over the PA system to 'move forward' and 'spread out', a hopeless request. Delaying the 3pm kick-off was a sensible idea that the police considered but chose not to proceed with. Instead, the police froze and lost such grip as they had on the situation. Meanwhile, in the tunnel that led to the terracing, people were turned away from the shockingly congested central pens, yet not diverted to the two nearly empty 'wings'.

On the outside South Yorkshire Police Chief Superintendent David Duckenfield elected to relieve the pressure there by ordering a side gate to be opened. Police horses withdrew, fans rushed forward and were waved towards the tunnel, towards the mounting claustral crisis already made by over-congestion. And in short order there were rising levels of panic, pain, fainting, intolerable suffering. Two minutes before 3pm, with the teams on the pitch, people were desperate to get out of the central pens, grasping hands that pulled them up to the standing tier above. Some onlookers, unaware of the gravity of what was unfolding, misunderstood this as typical Scouse behaviour.

The whistle that brought kick-off also meant another surge into the centre pens, making the plight at the front intolerable. Police refused desperate entreaties to open the gates. They were on guard against the wrong enemy entirely, and so did everything wrongly.

The football-loving British public were watching on the BBC, and the game was continuing like some upended toy turning its wheels, the players with their horizons fixed, as more and more people scrambled over the fence. Two supporters approached Alan Hansen in distress: 'There are people dying back there, Al.' At 3.05 a Beardsley strike from a Liverpool corner hit the crossbar, causing fans to rush forward again. Officers still believed they were witnessing a pitch invasion. Years later Dalglish would volunteer that his 'immediate reaction had been that there was crowd trouble in the Leppings Lane, that Forest fans had got in there to cause hassle'.

At last, too late, an assessment approaching the gravity of the situation was made, ambulance staff alerted, police realising a game of football was no longer tenable. An officer ran onto the pitch to instruct referee Ray Lewis, and the teams were escorted back to the changing rooms, there to await further instruction and try to get their heads around the chaos – much like the Forest support at the other end. But as people were lifted or hauled from the terracing onto the pitch – makeshift stretchers made from hoardings, failed resuscitation on the turf, distressed and desperate and furious people – the scale of the disaster became clear by increments.

Dalglish was the one man in motion while his players were kept sequestered, and everything he was hearing from roaming fans was dreadful. ('Kenny, there are people dying out there.') He went directly to see his wife and daughter Kelly in the directors' box. There was a personally piercing matter to consider: his 11-year-old son Paul had travelled to the game in a group that would surely have entered via Leppings Lane in order to find their places. Needing urgently to locate Paul, Dalglish ventured back to the pitch, crossed the white line, and was confronted anew by havoc. 'I saw what seemed like a war-zone,' he would remember. The damage was huge, the response clearly flailing in places, the sense of death growing thick. It was a dwarfed, helpless place to be for Dalglish. He had duties both to his team and to the support, and a role to play, too, for the authorities; but he surely had to deal with a tightening sense of terror over what might have befallen his son.

And then he was delivered, and his 'heart leapt' to see a steward escorting Paul across the pitch towards him. The boy's coach had arrived at the ground on time, he had been fine. They embraced silently, he took Paul to Marina, and turned back to face the losses of others.

A major incident was belatedly declared, fire engines and more ambulances arrived at the ground, Tannoy announcements called for fans to clear the pitch. The dressing rooms backed onto a car park, and the Liverpool players could hear the sirens. Those who had been at Heysel – Grobbelaar, Hansen, Nicol, Whelan – doubtless felt the rising dread especially. Dalglish was asked to speak from the DJ booth, to request that the crowd stay calm and in their seats, to assist police and first aid. Then he returned to the dressing room: 'Get changed lads, we're leaving. There's been fatalities.'

The match was formally abandoned and the disaster began to acquire definition, beginning with reports of eight dead, these emanating from the gym to the side of the stadium which had become a makeshift mortuary. Soon the toll was dozens; the local hospitals were filling up. It was when the players, washed and changed, met up with their distressed wives that what Dalglish had seen became plain to everybody. They boarded their coach back to Liverpool, Dalglish sat numbly with his wife, everyone lost in thought for a journey of silence, visibly unscathed but heavily marked.

By the end of the evening 82 people were known to be dead – the toll would rise to 96. The failure of management on the day had been so vast as to numb the senses, but a proper account of decisions and events had to be established without delay. At 3.15pm when the secretary of Sheffield Wednesday and the FA's Graham Kelly had gone to the police control box to ask for information, Duckenfield had told them, wrongly, that a gate had been forced open, followed by an in-rush of Liverpool supporters. Placing blame on supposedly 'drunken, ticketless Liverpool fans' was a story instantly formed that looked as if it could be made to stand up. Senior South Yorkshire police, facing mistakes too monstrous for remorse, were quickly concocting a doctored narrative from which they might emerge without blame.

That English football was again steeped in misery, that people had gone to a match and not come home, made the Sunday

morning of 16 April a grey and terrible giant for the city of
Liverpool, an unbearable dawn for the many bereaved. In the
evening, a requiem mass at the Metropolitan Cathedral was
attended by thousands. A Liverpool FC banner hung by the
altar, and became a memorial spot where tributes were laid.
Bruce Grobbelaar read the scriptural lesson. A boy chorister
sang 'You'll Never Walk Alone'. From the morning on, though,
many Liverpudlians went as if by instinct to the Shankly Gates
at Anfield, seeking some form of communion. Peter Robinson
instructed the ground staff to open the stadium to the public,
and people filed in as mourners.

On Monday morning Dalglish contacted his players, and
Marina their wives. They were all in turmoil and, to some
degree, awaiting instruction. Some players would testify to
unfathomable feelings of guilt – that people had died having
come to see them play football. Dalglish, nevertheless, had come
to a decision, swiftly, about what was the right thing to do in the
circumstances, abetted by the manner in which the football club
was responding more generally.The Liverpool team returned to
Sheffield by coach to visit the Northern general hospital where
victims were being cared for. The sight of 14-year-old Lee Nicol
on life support, visibly unmarked yet near death, was profoundly
distressing; and the players had only attended his bedside for a
few minutes before he was pronounced dead. Hansen wept. 'I
tried to say something to comfort the mother,' he would recall,
'but I almost felt that she was comforting me.' Nothing in life
had prepared a group of footballers to respond to such levels of
unanswerable pain. But Dalglish had decided that they all had
to be present, among the fans, and to bear witness.

Wednesday 19 April saw a disgraceful front page of the *Sun*
newspaper, the worst possible carrion-picking of human tragedy, in which the Liverpool supporters at Hillsborough were

branded drunken hooligans, 'animals', accused of urinating on dead bodies, pinching wallets, obstructing police. It was a risible fiction based on police sources, splashed by editor Kelvin MacKenzie. Belatedly sensing the wrongness of what he had done, MacKenzie contacted Dalglish to try to 'resolve' the matter, but was firmly rebuffed, since he lacked the decency even to withdraw the allegations. But the tabloid reporting led to Dalglish visiting HMP Walton at the governor's request, since the inmates had been greatly agitated by what they had read.

Dalglish was inviting extraordinary stresses upon himself with regard to Liverpool's mourning. In maintaining that this was part of his job and of no consequence next to the anguish of the bereaved, he was speaking the truth, to a degree; but this was not to say that he could or should be capable of shouldering such a weight of emotion. Dalglish was a man of serious disposition, mentally and physically tough. He knew how to observe courtesies like a well-brought-up professional. But off the football pitch he had near-religiously kept his horizons low and his interests narrow, his sphere of concern limited to his family. The astute football writer Kevin McCarra would characterise Dalglish as 'much too watchful and wary to come across as a man of the people in any role except that of star footballer'. How on earth was this football man to cope with such tides of feeling coming at him continually?

As Liverpool began burying its dead, Dalglish and Marina were steadfast attendees – as many as four funerals in one day. All the players attended ceremonies likewise. Beardsley, who did this duty once, found that he 'just couldn't cope', that 'it was completely soul-destroying'. Hansen would speak of the exquisite difficulty of 'knowing what to say to the families and friends of the deceased'. The answer, inevitably, was to discuss football: a mixed blessing for the players, since the families proved adept at 'wry remarks about their lost loved ones' obsession with Liverpool' – a conversational boon, but a reminder of how their lives had ended in the act of following the football club. John Barnes would acknowledge both the sense of guilt and its irrationality: 'I wasn't sure how they would react because had that been my loved one, I wouldn't want to go and meet footballers or the football team, or ever watch football again.'

Returning to Anfield one day, Dalglish saw that the Kop was covered with tributes, and flowers had been spread across the pitch towards the halfway line. To the press he described it as 'the saddest and most beautiful sight I have ever seen'. This was a striking eloquence, deeply felt. Inspecting the Kop, Dalglish had been hit forcibly by the meticulous, faithful placing of tributes at the spots where those who died had stood for years – that ritual of communal match-going into which he had been inducted by his father at Ibrox. 'The sense of absence,' he would write of these small personal tokens that now signified the dead, 'could not have been more pronounced.'

In his memoirs Dalglish would refer to this realisation with a powerful, chastened sense of self-reproach: 'I should have known that about the Kop before Hillsborough … I realised that in all my years as manager and player I had miscalculated the importance of the club to the people. It was a mistake. I never fully appreciated the part we played in their lives.' Now Dalglish went onto the Kop every day; occasionally with his daughter Kelly, who had the child's formative experience of seeing her father visibly upset for the first time.

The players' lounge at Anfield became the congregational point for the bereaved families to gather and, alongside the clergymen and psychiatric professionals, the players' wives were marshalled by Marina Dalglish to offer cups of tea and an attentive, listening presence. Dalglish himself ensured that all squad members and senior staff took their turns in the room, even if only for football talk. 'There was huge pressure not to put a foot wrong and upset anyone,' Kelly Dalglish would remember. Her father set the standard. John Aldridge would say of the famously recessive Dalglish that he 'proved himself to be a good listener to those who had something to get off their chests'.

And yet his eldest daughter would recall it as a 'heartbreaking' thing to see how 'strained' and 'wrung out' her parents looked at the day's end. Dalglish was offered the services of a counsellor for himself. He made plain that was not for him: 'I wouldn't dream of opening up to her, a stranger, about a matter so intensely private.' His wife joked that the psychiatric professional would last 'a couple of minutes' with her client before running out of the room to seek help for herself. But the humour masked a truth. Since the idea of unburdening in this way was anathema to him, he would be taking the pain into himself, saying nothing, pressing on. Dalglish was no ordinary introvert but an introvert nonetheless, internalising his stresses, risking a fracture.

Was it the right thing for Liverpool to return to business and play out what remained of the season? Dalglish had to consider a great weight of evidence. He received copious letters, many from the bereaved, expressing a variety of views on the wisdom and appropriateness of replaying the aborted semi-final. His daughter would recall him speaking to her in despairing, newly indecisive tones: 'What do I do?'

As the force of grieving demonstrated, football was integral to Liverpool. If all the weekly hopes and stressing pinned on getting a result had been made to look a petty thing by the lost lives, that could only be temporary for a football-loving city in which life had to go on, football included. For Liverpool FC to resume their competitions, though, would add a new and unique stress: to succeed, on behalf of the dead and their families. This was a huge burden to put on top of the onus that a striver and winner such as Dalglish had already elected for himself.

John Smith's line was that 'an overwhelming majority of people in Liverpool' wanted the team to carry on contesting the FA Cup. A fortnight after the disaster the squad resumed training, and the Forest replay was scheduled for 7 May. A charity match with Celtic raised £300,000 for the bereaved families, then on 3 May Liverpool restarted their league campaign away to Everton, with a minute's silence, uncommon solemnity, and a great deal of decency and natural piety shown. A banner held aloft in the travelling supporters' section extended appreciation to the blue side of the city: 'The Kop thanks you. We never walked alone.' As with Alex Ferguson sending a delegation of Manchester United support to pay their respects at Anfield, it was a show of solidarity within the game and its constituents.

The team got back to what it knew how to do, beating Forest in the cup, jockeying with Arsenal in the league. Dalglish looked cautious again, paying Wimbledon the outsized respect of three central defenders and Hansen as sweeper, having to resort to bringing Rush on to salvage a 2-1 win. But Arsenal lost at home to Derby that day and the title was in Liverpool's hands. In searing heat on 20 May, they beat Everton 3-2 in a Merseyside derby in the FA Cup final. Then they played their game in hand, West Ham at home, and won it. On 26 May Arsenal came to Anfield. Liverpool had 76 points, Arsenal 73. Liverpool's goal difference was 65-26 (plus 39), Arsenal's 71-36 (plus 35). A two-goal win for Arsenal would swing it on the basis of goals scored, which seemed highly improbable and so, perhaps inevitably, that was how it turned out – though it took until stoppage time, with Liverpool 45 seconds from the title, for Michael Thomas to win it for the Arsenal by 2-0. Dalglish had set the team up cautiously, they had played nervously – as if a 0-1 defeat was a desirable and manageable outcome – and they had paid the price.

'Dalglish just stands there,' said ITV's Brian Moore over

pictures that, indeed, showed Dalglish apparently frozen by the hard fate of it. It was cruel but, yet again, it was only football. On that, Bill Shankly would surely have had to agree. In the changing room, Bugsy Moran came in and put runners-up medals on the table, a different colour but the same message to the squad: So much for that, see you in a month for pre-season.

But business as usual – the business of Anfield as it had been for most of a couple of decades – was no longer possible. Kelly Dalglish would recall that her mother was strongly advised by a psychiatric professional 'to keep an eye on Dad', that it might be 'at least a year before he'd react to what happened, but that he would react. The counsellor was right.'

15

Keeping It Together

1989-91

'A lot of people in the past – and even now – think I had a problem with Kenny. I didn't. Obviously I wanted to be in the team, but I never had a problem with him . . .'

Peter Beardsley, interviewed for Liverpoolfc.tv, 2009

'When you have to make a hard decision . . . it makes it easier if you think that your family's well-being is depending on it.'

Kenny Dalglish, quoted by Alan Hansen

You could pay £4 to stand on Liverpool's Kop, a price fit for most pockets, on the August afternoon when the 1989-90 season kicked off. Time was about to be served, though, on that particular tariff. On the Monday after the disaster at Hillsborough the government had appointed a Lord Justice of Appeal, Gosforth-born Peter Taylor, to chair an inquiry into what had caused the calamity and what could be done to prevent a repeat. A Newcastle United supporter, Taylor had interesting opinions – most especially that, whatever the trough it was in, football still commanded 'massive public support and interest' and that this support had been badly served for years. Concerning the loss of life on 15 April 1989, he deduced that the main cause was a failure of command among senior police officers. But Taylor would also suggest a class-divided sport, writing of 'old grounds, poor facilities, hooliganism, excessive drinking and poor leadership' – in other words, the odour of rot, of rubbish piled up and people pissing anywhere, of police attention imposed on troublemakers and true fans alike, and of the long dereliction of duty by clubs with regard to structural renovation.

Where Taylor failed to oblige the government was in his resistance to the idea of an identity-card scheme for fans. Rather, his chief action point, the real eye-catcher, was the recommendation that standing terraces and fencing be scrapped, and British stadia convert to all-seater facilities, beginning with the heavily supported clubs of the top two divisions. At a time when even the big clubs were feeling the decline of their traditional revenue streams, this proposed an awful lot of expensive civil engineering. 'Finances for ground improvement must be raised by the clubs themselves,' Taylor concluded sternly. Yet he offered a couple of fundraising hints for the footing of the bill, advising the FA 'to extract the highest possible price for TV rights' and suggesting that clubs might 'well wish to charge somewhat more for seats than for standing'.

The fans, then, were going to have to take a big hit of the cost for cleaning up football. But at the same time the top clubs had reason to expect they were on the cusp of becoming a lot more flush. In 1988 British Satellite Broadcasting (BSB) had looked to get in the game of rights to broadcast football, their intervention paving the way for ITV to finally outbid the BBC in a four-year deal worth £44 million. In an auction situation, there was a new intrigue as to what might be the 'highest possible price for TV rights'. The chairmen of the biggest clubs were like-minded on their common interest in splitting from the Football League to capitalise on what the highest bidder would pay. There was new money on its way into football: that much was on the wind.

Dalglish had Liverpool on song again, all the support could hope for. Early in the season they humiliated Crystal Palace 9-0, John Aldridge scoring in his final game in red, for he had been deemed surplus to requirements and was off to Real Sociedad. John Barnes stepped up to centre forward and scored freely on his way to the Golden Boot. Beardsley, though, was feeling neglected: Marseilles had come for him in the summer, Dalglish had indicated he could leave, but he had stuck. Unbeaten in seven months save for the Arsenal title decider in May, Liverpool had a mini-slump before Christmas that drew them into a cluster of contenders alongside Arsenal, Aston Villa and Chelsea. But by the end of March they were back on top, if only on goal difference from Villa. As for Alex Ferguson's United, he had gambled on a clear-out of players and spending that had reached £13 million, including fat fees for Mark Hughes, rescued from Barcelona, Gary Pallister from Middlesbrough, Paul Ince from West Ham. But what this outlay delivered was United's third bottom-half finish in four seasons, and they still looked to be at least two key players short of a title push.

Dalglish took on loan a bustling Israeli striker named Ronny Rosenthal from Standard Liege and Rosenthal delivered a barrage of important goals that helped to carry them clear. The team's Achilles heel was set-pieces: Crystal Palace obtained a meaningful revenge in the FA Cup semi-final, a 4-3 win that left Dalglish incensed about the four goals shipped. The result helped Manchester United towards a clinching of the trophy that possibly saved Alex Ferguson's job, as his team would scrap to a 1-0 over Palace in a replayed final.

Liverpool were champions before the end of April; and on the first day of May, a ceremonial win over Derby in the bag,

39-year-old Dalglish, wearing 14 on his back, jogged onto the pitch as sub for Jan Molby, a small sentimental ritual marking the end of his playing days. Now he was the Manager of the Year. Privately, he wondered if this was the pinnacle of his work. He had initially told his wife he could see five years bossing Liverpool; and that milestone now approached. His views on the future had a complexity around them.

The club had a new chairman in Noel White, John Smith, overseer of the Paisley era, having moved on. Before Dalglish went on his summer holiday he discussed a new contract with White and Peter Robinson, intimating that he felt the need of 'a break' from executive decision-making. Robinson's view was that he just needed a proper close-season holiday. Dalglish further stated that he would favour shares in the football club rather than a fatter wage if he signed a new deal. Robinson told him this was not possible. If not the sort of condescension shown to Jock Stein in the end at Celtic, it did evince that curiously backward insistence on business as usual when nothing at Liverpool was very usual anymore, other than the garnering of silverware. Dalglish fought off his doubts and kept going, thrown the bone of a testimonial against Real Sociedad at Anfield in mid-August.

Liverpool won their first eight matches of 1990-91, including an imperious 4-0 over Manchester United in September with a Beardsley hat-trick. Come the start of December they ran into a wall against Arsenal, a game that seemed to summarise certain prevailing ills. Dalglish's tailoring of the side to the opposition quite frequently meant an extra defender: now he sent out a team featuring six defenders in all. The 3-0 loss was a game Beardsley had expected to play, though Beardsley wanted to play every game, no doubt. He was 'devastated at being left out'. Knowing every such decision left Beardsley so unhappy, Dalglish quite possibly felt a problem deepening. The issue was kicked down the road awhile when Beardsley tore ankle ligaments in the next game against Sheffield United, sidelining him for six weeks. But it was hard to say that Liverpool looked a better team without Beardsley.

Dalglish's Liverpool, league leaders still, had not become a mediocre side based on one bad beating. But by a little and a little, some lustre or aura had receded from the team. It was related to the broader standard of the top flight in the absence of European competition, but also to the spread of quality in the squad. Ronny Rosenthal had earned a permanent deal but didn't look like a Liverpool striker in the long term. Glenn Hysen had looked a class act for one season, but how many more? Steve Heighway was at work with young homegrown talent, but the results had yet to come onstream. Under Ron Yeats the quality of recruitment had paled. After a summer's buying rated as substandard, Liverpool opted mid-season for the unimpressive Jimmy Carter and David Speedie, nearly 31, one of the last British footballers to have worked in a coalmine. Still, Speedie scored on his debut at Old Trafford then twice in the Merseyside derby, a win that gave Liverpool a three-point lead on Arsenal. It was no one's idea of a crisis.

Yet the pundits jabbed at Liverpool and Dalglish appeared notably raw. He had to put up, moreover, with being characterised as not merely reserved but sulky, miserable, boring. This was to speak only of the outer shell of a character in football's weekly soap opera, the ceaseless churn of which had long since moved on from the events of April 1989, though Dalglish himself found that he could not.

'His personality seemed to change,' Kelly Dalglish would later recall. 'He became snappy and awkward and different from the dad we'd known.' Gary Gillespie remembered having a meal in a Chinese restaurant with Dalglish and Hansen, the two old comrades descending into an argument that seemed stunningly fierce to a table who had never seen the like. 'Kenny would fall out with his shadow at times,' Gillespie observed, 'but never with Alan Hansen.' Marina Dalglish, always in charge domestically, was also at a loss. 'I know that she found my dad very difficult to live with during that time,' her eldest daughter remembered.

'I was a mess,' the man of disciplined habits would admit. Dalglish knew enough to remonstrate with himself, without knowing how to turn off this new and unwelcome current of behaviour. Nobody as controlled as Dalglish suddenly becomes a 'problem drinker'; and yet the drink taken to relax, in the hope of dissolving certain obstinate inner stresses, had got a foothold in him. His sleep was disturbed, he was prone to headaches. In December 1990 he developed a persistent rash for which the club doctor administered antihistamine, leaving him drowsy by nightfall. The rash was shingles, commonly brought on in a grown man by stress. Dalglish was paying a price for all the unmanageable tensions he had invited into his person since Hillsborough. The ineluctable business of managing a top club – match day, its build-up, the drive for the result – aggravated everything. 'In the past,' he reflected, 'I would make the decision, usually more right than wrong, and move on without thinking. Now I agonised over everything.'

In Marbella with his family, Kevin Keegan turned 40, a major moment in a man's life. It's possible that the approach of that big number had begun to stir him from the expatriate life. He had shown no interest in football management – in anything, really, to do with football. For him, life was a dip in the pool, a little tennis, a little business, al fresco lunches and the company at pro-celebrity golf games where, however keenly he competed, he was celebrity rather than pro. Years of unadulterated golf, though, will grind a man down: the special mania of the game, its innumerable minor details, the incremental diminution of handicap. To devote himself so fully to becoming a type Norman Mailer once characterised as 'one of those boring golfers who work for years to improve their swing and never stop talking about it' could hardly be enough for Keegan's spirits, his competitive instincts and his sense of himself as 'an entrepreneurial sort of person'.

Keegan had paid attention to the new generation of arena entertainments, laser-tag contests based on infrared signalling in a designed environment. Rather than kids shooting laser guns at each other, what if they kicked footballs? The idea brought plenty of challenges to do with hardware and embedded software, how to make things talk to each other, how to design a visual environment adequate to capture a young person's overstimulated imagination. He took steps to patent his 'Soccer Circus' concept, but it was not a business that was going to push on from Marbella. His daughters were nearing secondary school age, and he and his wife had a feeling they should have their education in England. His mother's health was a concern. By the back end of 1990 it was settled, and he house-hunted in Romsey, Hampshire.

In early April 1991 Keegan packed up a Range Rover and left Marbella to drive through Spain and across France to Calais, then to Dover and towards Romsey. With 80 miles still to do, he pulled off the M25 into a car park for a nap, only to be woken by the smashing of the driver's window with a baseball bat. He was beaten and robbed by a gang of four youths, but managed to drive out of the car park and flag down assistance, whereupon he was taken to East Surrey hospital and stitched up. In years to come the ascent of the internet allowed various anonymous followers of football to speculate that Keegan had brought about his own debacle, since the incident had occurred when he was, by his own admission, 'on my own in a lover's lane'. But irrespective of what Keegan branded as these 'disgusting theories', his assailants were eventually arrested, three of them convicted and given custodial sentences. For the moment, however, it was scarcely a happy return for Keegan. 'Oh to be home again in England,' as the old song went.

On 20 February 1991 Liverpool FC prepared for an FA Cup replay with Everton, following a goalless draw at Anfield. By the afternoon of the game Dalglish was fairly sure that his instincts over the last summer had been right, that he needed to step down from his job. His mind was just not fully on the game.

The game played that night was certainly an amusement for neutrals. Beardsley was back in the starting XI, with his customary urge to prove a point. Twice he put Liverpool ahead, first with a fine half-volley, then an unstoppable swerver from 25 yards. But both times Everton pegged them back. Rush restored Liverpool's lead only for a third Everton equaliser from Cottee. A right-foot curler by Barnes seemed surely to settle it. Dalglish's first thought was to shut up shop, stick Jan Molby back to sweeper: 'I could see what needed to be done and what would happen if I didn't. I didn't act on it.' Within the space of that indecision Cottee grabbed Everton's fourth equaliser.

'Kenny was quiet afterwards,' Ray Houghton remembered, 'but he was quite often quiet.' Dalglish told the press it had been a classic cup tie, but he was going through the motions. If his mind was to have been swayed, Liverpool's haphazard showing and the draining result had not done the trick. He went home to Southport and told Marina he was done.

The following morning he suffered through 20 minutes of his regular monthly meeting with White and Robinson, before letting go of the news that was roiling in him. His employers reacted naturally – stunned, alarmed, trying to put out the fire by suggesting a sabbatical. Dalglish knew there could be no seat-warmer at Liverpool while they chased the league and cup. An emergency board meeting turned out to have no purpose other than to accept the resignation, though they prevailed on Dalglish to attend a press conference the next day. This was when Dalglish – briefly choked – broke the news to his players, who were expecting nothing but the usual day's work at Melwood. After he left the room, Hansen, possibly less stunned than most, elected to do the Liverpool thing and address the issue with banter, acting like he was to be the new boss and things would be different now: double training, no more Kentucky Fried for John Barnes, no more nipping into the Crown pub for Steve Nicol.

At the press conference Dalglish was a low, stricken figure, his words underlining that this was not a resignation related to bad results or boardroom shenanigans: 'It is just me as an individual who had a problem and the best way to solve that problem was to take this action.' Back home he had still to explain to his children why the world they had always known had now been turned upside down. The sweetener he could now offer them was the promise of family holidays never previously feasible – a skiing trip, long coveted by Marina but never an option in his playing days, and then the grand prize of Disney World Florida.

As bad a day as it was for Dalglish, the club, the players and the support, Liverpool had been through more grievous things. Clearly Hillsborough had left its mark, and Liverpool FC still had about it the rawness of a damaged environment, of people who had suffered through something together. Dalglish was just the most conspicuous example of that tendency. 'He completely fooled me and Roy,' Bugsy Moran told an ITV reporter. The possible consequences for the football club's fortunes were clear enough – but this was Liverpool, which had regenerated itself before, and surely could again.

Since Shankly's departure the managers had come from within, even Dalglish promoted from the playing staff. There was no obvious successor of that sort after Hansen ruled himself out. Phil Thompson bossed Liverpool's reserves and Steve Heighway the youth team, yet neither had demonstrated the desire to manage. As for the Boot Room, while Moran was to take temporary charge of first-team affairs, he was a coach, not a gaffer. Roy Evans was not felt to be ready. The strongest cases seemed to come from ex-Liverpool legends who had already proven themselves in other top jobs. John Toshack had lately left Real Madrid. But Peter Robinson looked hard at Rangers, closing in on their fourth Scottish title in five years, and made a call to the man who had driven that success: Graeme Souness.

An air of boldness and assurance surrounded Souness as player-manager, and it was more than results, or strokes such as the signing of ex-Celtic striker Mo Johnston. The club had been years ahead of the curve in converting Ibrox to an all-seated stadium as a consequence of the disaster of 1971. The costs of that work seemed as nothing next to the success under Souness. Rangers had innovated in corporate hospitality with its Thornton Suite, and wore the logo of McEwan's beer from a deal with Scottish & Newcastle. The influential figure behind the scenes was commercial director Freddie Fletcher, appointed by Lawrence Marlborough from within the John Lawrence group. While football clubs struggled to see past the takings at the turnstiles, Fletcher had spoken of a 'commercial model in which gate money amounts to only thirty per cent of our annual income'. After Souness joined the Rangers board in 1988, he persuaded his businessman friend David Murray to buy Marlborough's controlling interest in the club for £6 million. Undoubtedly, then, Souness embodied drive, graft, ambition and success. Yet there remained things about him – an individualism, a clear regard for the Thatcher government, that Champagne Charlie fondness for conspicuous consumption of the finer things – that sat less easily with how Liverpool felt about itself.

Souness himself felt a powerful pull back to Liverpool. In Moran's care, the team's results had faltered, and other candidates had fallen away. After Souness reopened communications with Robinson in late March things moved at speed. When Souness took soundings from Tom Saunders, the former youth-team coach told him that 'the challenge was greater than anyone on the outside recognised'. Robinson was candid about the big problems Souness would inherit: the jadedness of the squad, its star qualities extending barely further than John Barnes. He warned, too, of Manchester United's growing potential. Ferguson's team were heading for an unremarkable sixth place in the league, but the squad was growing stronger: Lee Sharpe, Andrei Kanchelskis, Denis Irwin, a Welsh youngster named Ryan Giggs. They had a European Cup Winners' Cup final to contest in Rotterdam with Barcelona.

On 16 April 1991 Liverpool appointed Souness. Dalglish was with his family in Orlando, Florida, and was informed by telephone of the club's decision. Already feeling the benefit of resting up, and still very much a Liverpool man, Dalglish felt 'a twinge of regret' at his old teammate's succession. Like Keegan, he was newly 40. Unlike Keegan, he had made no vow to exit the game. No one would have thought it odd if he had stayed away, after what he had been through. But Dalglish knew he would have been ready to contemplate a return to Liverpool, had they asked.

Souness, meanwhile, pronounced the squad his friend had left him with to be unfit for purpose: 'The ability wasn't there and the attitude was bad.' Souness rightly rated himself a leader and a man with a passion for Liverpool. As gaffer he was going to demand that the players followed an example set formidably by him. And he began the reconstruction of the squad that Robinson and others had thought needful. David Moores, scion of the Littlewoods pools and shopping empire family, was about to become club chairman and would back Souness at length. Out would go Beardsley and Gillespie, and the latter-day Dalglish signings Hysen, Carter and Speedie.

Souness was, on the face of it, a kind of continuity choice; and his remodelling of the side had precedents in Shankly, Paisley and indeed Dalglish. But the test of a good manager was how the thing got done. 'Kenny knows how to treat people,' Speedie would say. 'When Kenny speaks to you, he gives you advice, you listen. When Graeme Souness speaks to you, and gives you advice, you don't listen.' Bigger changes were afoot in football, though, which made every decision count double. Liverpool were in danger of missing a trick, coming too late to exploit the 20-year eminence they had enjoyed in the English game – the era of Keegan and Dalglish.

A Premier League was in the works, you could smell it. The First Division clubs had long plotted to break away from the Football League. Now they had their sights focused by the prospect of the next TV rights deal, up for renewal in 1992. The Football League knew it had to run on a unity ticket. But the bigger clubs concentrated zealously on their own interests and eminence, opening private lines to the broadcasters and the FA.

Rupert Murdoch had got into the business of satellite TV in 1989, in a somewhat jerry-built, piratical manner that had a ropy look to it amid the traditional high-toned scene of British broadcasting. But Murdoch had stayed tenaciously in the game, taking advantage of his in with government and the pulpit of his newspapers. In 1990 he was thought to have remortgaged his New York penthouse to save Sky from bankruptcy, and then managed a merger with BSB. Now Murdoch's British Sky Broadcasting was known to be hungry. Exclusive rights to live football coverage seemed a big bait to entice a serious subscription base.

With a new elite being shaped, an awful lot of ambitious people and interests wanted a piece of that pie. And with a brand-new top flight poised to decouple from the lower three divisions, it was clubs vying near the top of Division Two who felt the most pressing need to elbow a way aboard that departing train.

Blackburn Rovers had felt the pain of Division Two play-off defeats in 1989 and 1990. Then 1991 brought a deeper disappointment as the team fell to 19th place. One of the great old names of the English game, Rovers' last silverware had been the FA Cup of 1928, and their Ewood Park stadium was in an advanced state of decrepitude. Yet they remained a team with a travelling support, and in 1991 that support had reason to dream – for among their number was a man who shared sincerely in the seemingly outworn romance of Blackburn's blue-and-white halved shirts; and who was ready, moreover, to put millions of pounds into that passion.

In 1987 Rovers chairman Bill Fox, also president of the Football League, had faced a gaping problem as one of the grandstands at Ewood was visibly keeling back towards the River Darwen that ran behind it. Fox could not obtain any local council funding for the plainly needed renovation. He did, however, have a good friend – a former schoolmate – in one of the club's directors, Jack Walker, a considerable figure in the steel business who was willing to donate the cost of materials needed. The Walker Steel Stand duly arose, a staging point in Blackburn's history: for Jack Walker had long hankered after renewed big-time success for his beloved Rovers, and now decided to bankroll that dream from his tax-exiled perch in St Helier, Jersey.

Jack and his brother Fred had inherited their sheet metal business from their father in 1951, built it steadily over decades, and then the 1984 purchase of GKN Steelstock made Walker the UK's largest steel stockholder. As of 1987 Walker was discreetly funding Rovers, first so that they could afford transfer fees and fat wages to nab Steve Archibald from Barcelona, then Osvaldo Ardiles from Spurs. Agents began to sniff that Blackburn were in business and ready to pay more for players than their gate receipts alone could have allowed. A former vacuum cleaner salesman named Paul Stretford was getting very proactive in the football agenting game, his wife friendly with the wives of various Manchester United players. Stretford arranged for Frank Stapleton and Kevin Moran to join Blackburn, adding a few of Blackburn's existing players – Colin Hendry, Scott Sellars, David May – to his books for representation.

In January 1991, mere months after selling his company to British Steel for £360 million, Jack Walker's Jersey trust acquired a 52 per cent shareholding in Rovers. He was in the open now, and the Premier League was the target. This was a bind for his old friend Bill Fox, who in his Football League capacity loathed the very idea of what a Premiership would mean for the organisation. But as a Blackburn man Fox knew that Rovers just had to get on that train, and Walker's millions offered the best chance of success. Walker was not, after all, the only high-net-worth individual in England who had newfound aspirations to football glory.

Newcastle United had stumbled to an 11th-place finish in Division Two in May 1991, but like Blackburn they had been going backwards since a play-off loss in 1990 – at the semi-final stage and, cruelly, to their Wearside rivals Sunderland. In February 1991, manager Jim Smith was ousted for Ossie Ardiles who, deprived of transfer funds, was building a team of fledgling local talent – 'Ossie's Babes', such as teenagers Lee Clark, Steve Watson and Steve Howey. In the years since Kevin Keegan had checked out of the Gosforth Park hotel, average crowds had receded back down to 15,000. But Newcastle had the benefit of a vice-president who believed, akin to Jack Walker, that his club needed to be at the top table when Premier League service commenced.

John Hall, an ex-NCB surveyor from Ashington, Northumberland, had amassed great personal wealth from property development, his *pièce de résistance* the raising of £1 million to buy a plot on an ash dump on the outskirts of Gateshead where – as an avowed fan of American shopping malls he had seen on Florida holidays – his Cameron Hall Developments built the largest such complex in Europe. In 1987 the Gateshead MetroCentre was sold to the Church Commissioners for £272 million, and Hall's share enabled him to acquire the country estate at Wynyard Park in Durham, family seat of the Anglo-Irish Marquesses of Londonderry. That a pitman's son should acquire the grand property of a former 'Lord of Coal' was as much self-made symbolism as any chronicler could wish for.

Like any rich man Hall began to receive a lot of suggestions as to things he might usefully do with his money. One that commanded his attention came from the Newcastle Supporters Association (NSA), a group formed in 1976 by a man called Malcolm Dix, in despair at how Newcastle United was being run (its board led by Tyneside solicitor Gordon McKeag, who made the telling blunder of referring to the football club as 'part of the family silver'). Hall, Thatcherite in his instincts, saw Newcastle United as a stagnating business, starved of investment, lacking proper ambition.

Dix and Hall formed the 'Magpie Group', enlisting a number of local businessmen who were willing to pledge fair old wedges of money to the cause of taking control of the club. By 1988 Hall was bankrolling the tracking-down and buying-up of shares, his pitch that a new share issue would 'democratise' the club, raise new money to refurbish the ground and enable a player policy of recruitment rather than sell-offs. The Newcastle board resisted, so bidding up the share price to £1,000 each. Towards the end of the 1989-90 season peace broke out, with Cameron Hall Developments now the biggest single shareholder, Hall installed on the board. But that autumn the share issue was an undersubscribed flop, the team's supporters insufficiently enthused, and a chastened Hall left the board to be nominal vice-president. McKeag was replaced by George Forbes, and Hall's son Douglas took his dad's board seat.

Alastair Wilson of Scottish & Newcastle, a friend to Hall's ambitions, rated Freddie Fletcher for his work at Rangers, though Fletcher had quit the club after the David Murray take-over of 1988. Wilson now asked Fletcher to Newcastle to meet the Magpie Group businessmen, and Fletcher was struck by Hall:

'He was a kind of North-East Nationalist. It wasn't so much that he wanted to own the football club, he didn't, but he was desperate for success in any form for his region of the country.' Fletcher's association with Newcastle also enabled another link, for come the summer of 1991 he was talking to Kevin Keegan, savvy as ever, who knew of Fletcher's association with Ibrox and had got interested, in his entrepreneurial way, in the commercial potential of the Taylor Report's stipulation for mass conversion to all-seater stadia. By hook or by crook, Keegan looked to have set himself on getting back into the football business.

Kenny Dalglish – decently rested, equilibrium restored, a football man above all – was open to offers once more. The first considerable one he received came from Olympique de Marseille president Bernard Tapie, hustler extraordinaire and owner of the adidas brand. In 1986 Tapie had bought Marseille cheaply, declaring that he would make the club great again; and he had done so, recruiting players keenly and expensively (among them Chris Waddle), courting the press, generally burnishing his image. On one local-born talent in particular, he lavished a French record fee: Eric Cantona, a volcanic young man known for tearing off his shirt, rucking with teammates and insulting the French national coach.

After the 1990 World Cup, Tapie had lured the victorious coach Franz Beckenbauer as technical director, though Marseille's incumbent manager Gerard Gili had just led the side to the Ligue 1 title and didn't fancy being monkey to Beckenbauer's organ-grinder. Gili went to Bordeaux in pique. Beckenbauer assumed the dugout, but was not much liked, didn't speak French, and lost four of his first five games. Raymond Goethals was installed as coach, Beckenbauer back upstairs. They won the league again in 1991 and lost the European Cup final to Red Star Belgrade on penalties.

Dalglish met Tapie in Switzerland, and was invited to the French Cup final against Monaco on 8 June. The deal on offer was lucrative. There would be a home in Provence, and plentiful opportunities for good golf, the game having got Dalglish in its grip as it had claimed Keegan. But when Dalglish saw the cut that would be taken from the deal by its agent-intermediary, he lost interest. As with Keegan's misgivings over the efforts of agents to muscle in on his big move in 1977, Dalglish clearly felt that there should be only so many parties to a deal, receiving no more and no less than what they were worth.

In June 1991 the English FA unveiled their 'Blueprint for the Future of Football', putting forward the idea of a Super League of 18 clubs to be 'governed by a committee of the FA'. Bowing to the idea of a breakaway league, the FA wished to ensure they would be in charge of it and that it would be driven by a concern for the good of the national game rather than 'commercial considerations'. The top clubs had no faith or interest in the FA running anything, and simply carried on making their own arrangements. On 14 June 1991, 16 First Division clubs signed a document indicating their intent to join the newly named 'Premier League'. The lower tiers, the rump of the Football League, would just have to take the crumbs from the table. (Earlier that same week, Manchester United had floated on the stock exchange, immediately making £6 million for majority shareholder Martin Edwards.) The Premier League became official on 23 September 1991. Arguably its first and biggest task was to dispose of the TV rights to broadcast the new top flight's matches from 1992 to 1997.

ITV had bid big and won the last time round. Rupert Murdoch's BSkyB was the new contender – unusually, in that Sky was leaking money, around £1.5 million per week as of September 1991. But Murdoch believed live football could be the 'battering ram' he needed for his investment in pay-television to take flight at last, on the back of a proper customer base. ITV fought hard to retain their rights, but BSkyB joined forces with the BBC for their counterbid, the BBC's part being to revive the *Match of the Day* highlights package, while BSkyB would have a monopoly of all live Premier League matches, beginning with the 1992–93 season. Murdoch was willing, in the end, to make an offer worth £304 million, enough to blow ITV out of the water, just as he had been urged by Alan Sugar, chairman of Spurs and the maker of BSkyB's satellite dishes.

It was clear, then, where the new money led. Any properly ambitious club would need to be in the Premier League; and those outside of it had to think quickly about how to make the step up. Investing in proven talent seemed a compelling idea, for all that would cost. This mindset was, quite suddenly and dramatically, to improve the sort of offers liable to come the way of legendary professionals available to start work immediately.

PART III

16

Sleeping Giants

1991-94

'People tend not to turn down Kenny Dalglish.'

Kevin Moran, 1992

'If you walk in the dressing-room and Kevin Keegan or Kenny Dalglish is standing there, everybody is in awe ... The pair of them could wind you up and get you running through a brick wall ... Mentally, [Kenny] still plays every game, and he loves to show that he can still do it. Kevin is just the same.'

Barry Venison, 1993

Blackburn Rovers set about the 1991-92 season with renewed hope on top of Jack Walker's pile of capital. After three league games they had a solitary point, and the last of those three, a home loss to Ipswich, saw fans visibly and vocally hacked off. In the first week of September Rovers showed the door to manager Don Mackay, and their perennial pawky coach Tony Parkes stepped in as caretaker. No one, though, imagined that the height of Jack Walker's ambitions for a permanent appointee would be realised in Parkes.

Kenny Dalglish was in Monaco for a charity match when Bill Fox reached him on the phone. Dalglish agreed to let Fox come visit in Southport, whereupon a handsome deal was laid before him: a fat three-year contract with Rovers, highly remunerative personal terms, and the promise of substantial transfer funds. Negotiations, nevertheless, stretched out over a month. Dalglish insisted on the hiring of Ray Harford as his assistant: an unglamorous choice but someone he rated as a proper footballing brain. In the end the package proved sufficient to prise Dalglish away from his lingering attachment to Anfield. (Indeed, it would cost Blackburn a fair whack in compensation to Liverpool.) He signed, and on a sunny October Saturday the appointment was made public as Dalglish sat to watch his new side take on and beat Plymouth Argyle.

The Candy bench coat of red, white and grey was in the past. Dalglish now affected loose-cut Italian tailoring and a fawn cashmere coat. Packing his boots and commuting from Southport, he would climb out of his car on Nuttall Street, a high unemployment area of heavily weathered housing stock and visible deprivation. The sense of a well-heeled near-regal visitor was palpable; and yet Dalglish brought with him such stuff as dreams are made on. The fans knew that serious money was being spent, a major project was afoot. The terraces of Nuttall and Kidder Streets were marked for compulsory purchase, as Walker planned to make Ewood Park a £20 million all-seater venue. New training facilities were envisaged, too, at a site in Brockhall seven miles north of town. In the meantime, though, the new gaffer had to put up with a bit of make-do-and-mend.

The squad would go through their paces at Pleasington playing fields, a public park with no changing rooms. Dalglish was initially asked if he would prefer to train 'on the sand pitch or the grass pitch?' While grass was clearly preferable, every such session would require a careful, fretful inspection of the turf for lurking dog dirt. Dalglish had to resort to a spanner set to screw together temporary goalposts – shades of his boyhood in

Milton. Pleasington, moreover, was by the town crematorium, and a certain decorum had to be observed on occasions. Players coming by car had to make way as hearses went by; and out on the grass they had to be mindful not to boot any loose balls too close to parties of mourners.

If Dalglish was bemused by the amateurish air of disuse around Blackburn's operations, he didn't make a fuss. He was visibly chipper to be back around football and footballers. The actual coaching regimen, led by Harford, was simple: games of eight against eight, practice of shooting and set-pieces. Dalglish brought his boots for a reason, and joined in the small-sided games, a moaner and a stickler as ever. 'He was still the business,' observed forward Simon Garner. 'It was just we could never finish until his team had won.' These young pros were in awe of him, all he represented and now meant to Blackburn. They were desperate to impress, not to incur a sceptical wince from King Kenny.

Arte et Labore was the motto of the club: both skill and graft were certainly needed if Blackburn were to get out of the second tier. Dalglish could call on Anfield discard David Speedie up front, and at the centre of defence he had a captain in Kevin Moran (any grudge from their grisly clash in 1984 long buried). As at Liverpool Dalglish kept his pick of the team to himself, and no one would know if they were among the elect until 2pm on match day. Simon Garner, having scored twice in the Plymouth game, was dropped for the next, which Blackburn lost, 2-1 at Swindon.

Still, Dalglish's first five games in charge would yield four wins; but he didn't believe he could storm the summit of the league with the players he had at his disposal. He began recruiting with some pricy homegrown signings. Brawny, flaxen Scottish defender Colin Hendry returned to Rovers from Manchester City for £700,000; Alan Wright joined from Blackpool for half a million. Following a second defeat on the road at Southend, he and Harford decided on a long-ball game for their next away fixture, at Charlton, a game Rovers won 2-0. Dalglish then landed a couple of starrier signings. Striker Mike Newell, whom Don Mackay had long pursued in vain, was now persuaded to leave Everton by the Dalglish aura and £1.1 million. Then Aston Villa's skilled and England-capped veteran Gordon Cowans came for £200,000. The Southend loss was followed by a run of 16 games that yielded 11 wins and just a single defeat. Blackburn topped the league for Christmas, and the bookies ceased to take bets on their promotion.

By November of 1991 Newcastle United's season had the look of smoking ruins. Ossie Ardiles' young team – mad-keen but poorly organised and feckless – were dead last in Division Two. Ardiles was playing these kids largely because the club just couldn't afford new players, sitting £6 million in debt. It was all rather as though Kevin Keegan had never landed on Tyneside with his boots back in the sunlight of August 1982.

And yet, as 1991 dwindled, Keegan – ever open to a business proposition – was letting himself be lured into the orbit of various opportunities that had arisen around Newcastle's centenary year; albeit a celebration that had an increasingly doleful look. Ardiles, nobody's fool, clearly intuited that Keegan's interest was more than merely social.

On 23 November 1991 Keegan travelled to St James' to attend the launch of a fat tome entitled *United: The First 100 Years*. He watched United draw 0-0 with Blackburn, his professional opinion that Dalglish's team looked 'a cut above, a lot classier'. In truth, Newcastle had the better chances and might have won the game save for some ill-assured finishing. But it was Rovers who were on the up, and the example set by Dalglish and Walker had a look about it that Keegan likely thought compelling. The set-up that John Hall was overseeing at Newcastle was a much more rickety work-in-progress.

w signing Keegan helped Southampton get off to a flying start in the 1980-81 season, a hamstring injury soon knocked him out of his stride. (Getty Images)

Trevor Brooking and Keegan, England's two great hopes for the 1982 World Cup, finally get ready to make their late entrance to the tournament, but can't help overcome Spain, so their World Cup careers lasted only minutes. (Getty Images)

An instant hit. Keegan scores on his debut for Newcastle United at St James' Park in August 1982, and a special relationship is born. (Getty Images)

In the aftermath of Heysel, stepping up to become player-manager of Liverpool was no small challenge, but Dalglish took to the role with ease, winning the Double in his first season, 1985–86. (Getty Images)

Then came Hillsborough, where Dalglish witnessed suffering that should never have happened at a football match. (PA)

Afterwards, he felt the pressure mount and decided to resign in February 1991. Director Sir John Smith sits alongside him at the press conference to announce his departure. (PA)

Keegan's arrival at Newcastle in February 1992 created a huge sense of excitement that better times were ahead. (PA)

Labour leader Tony Blair and Keegan in perfect sync in a heading contest in October 1995. (PA)

Keegan looks across to see a celebrating Alex Ferguson, after Manchester United had beaten the Magpies 1-0 and shifted the momentum in the 1995-96 title race. Within a year he would resign as manager. (PA)

Dalglish returned to management at second division Blackburn Rovers, his first taste of football below the top level, and secured promotion to the new Premier League via a Wembley play-off. (PA)

Three years later in 1995, and helped by massive investment from Jack Walker, Dalgli (joined by Tony Parkes and Ray Harford) won the title again. (Getty Images)

er eight months away from the game, Keegan returned to football at Fulham,
cially as chief operating officer with Ray Wilkins as head coach, but soon took charge
manager himself. (Getty Images)

egan celebrates with Alan Shearer after
gland's 1-0 victory over Germany in
ro 2000 – it was the first time England
beaten their old rivals in a major
rnament since 1966. (Getty Images)

Almost four months later, and a defeat at
Wembley against Germany led to Keegan
leaving the pitch with a tear in his eye
as he decided to resign from the role as
England boss. (Getty Images)

Dalglish followed Keegan into the manager's seat at Newcastle in January 1997. Despi[te] his previous success with Alan Shearer at Blackburn, the two endured tougher times b[y] the Tyne. (Getty Images)

In 1999, Dalglish returned to his first club, Celtic, with John Barnes as head coach, bu[t] the arrangement was shortlived. (PA)

ck in club management, Keegan again revived spirits with his ew team Manchester City, but a succession of signings of players who had passed their peak, such Robbie Fowler, saw him decide step away from management for good. (Getty Images)

egan, Terry McDermott Arthur Cox were briefly nited at Newcastle United, the return of the Geordie ssiah was not a happy one. ty Images)

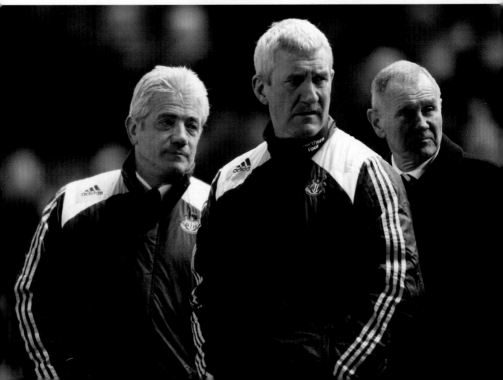

Kenny Dalglish's support of his talented but troubl[ed] striker Luis Suarez would end up costing him dear after he returned t[o] Liverpool as mana[ger] in 2011. (Getty Images)

Keegan and Dalglish together at Anfield in April 2016, for the 27th anniversary of Hillsborough. (Getty Images)

The King – on the day it was announced the Centenary Stand at Anfield would be renamed in his honour, May 2017. (Getty Images)

In December 1991, Hall treated himself and the wife to a round-the-world tour with Thomas Cook, and was at leisure in Repulse Bay, Hong Kong, when his son Douglas reached him to report that Barclays would be pulling the plug on Newcastle's current account unless Hall deposited £645,000 forthwith. The club had rashly bought striker David Kelly from Leicester for a quarter of a million: a move their overdraft terms didn't permit. Hall swallowed hard and transferred the funds; but he was grimly determined to get his money back, and with bells on. On returning to the UK he moved to take over Newcastle United, muscling out the old board, using his Wynyard estate as security, becoming club chairman, employing his son and bringing in Tyneside businessman Freddy Shepherd as vice-chairman. Drawing on Scottish & Newcastle connections, Hall also formally engaged Freddie Fletcher as a consultant. To run the football side of things, though, a proper football man would be needed.

Bad-to-worse results tolled the bell for Ardiles: a 4-0 thumping at Southend on New Year's Day, then a 4-3 home reverse to Charlton having led 3-0. Hall, knowing not so much about football, continued to back Ardiles. But his son and the two Freddies took a different view. Following a nearly fogbound 5-2 loss at Oxford, Fletcher told Alastair Wilson, trusted by Keegan, to get onto his pal.

The following Monday, 3 February 1992, a meeting took place in London between Keegan, John and Douglas Hall, Fletcher and Shepherd. Keegan sensed Hall was uneasy, for understandable reasons. He sought assurance there would be money for players; Hall offered £1 million straight away, and a further million if truly necessary. Keegan refused the proposed three-year contract, signing instead on a consultancy basis until the end of the season: £60,000 for three months' work plus the same again if he kept Newcastle up. That Wednesday morning at 7.30am Freddie Fletcher drove to Ardiles' house and sacked him. The visitors' centre of the Tyne Brewery was then the site for another press conference heralding Kevin Keegan's return to English football. Keegan would admit he could barely name a current player in Division Two, much less at his own club. What he brought was the unique passion he felt for Newcastle. It was to be an experiment, a leap of faith, a long shot. If it failed, there was a clear limit to how far Keegan could be made to carry the can.

Re-establishing headquarters at his old haunt of the Gosforth Park hotel, Keegan put in a call to Terry McDermott, who had kept himself busy since retirement in 1987 with opportunities in the catering trade, chiefly a burger van at Aintree racecourse. Keegan now advised Terry Mac that there could be a handy three-month assignment for him on Tyneside. McDermott wavered. He was staying in shape by training early doors at Melwood before Souness' Liverpool squad showed up; and there had been intimations from Souness of a possible role at Liverpool come the season's end. Keegan, moreover, would require him to lay off the lagers. But some savour of the escapade, of saddling up again alongside the Lone Ranger, must have got to McDermott; and he got on the road up to NE1.

The new management duo convened the squad for hellos and five-a-sides at Newcastle's Benwell training facilities. Keegan, though, was deeply dismayed by the state of the place – the curling carpets, the historical grime of the communal bath, the solitary relic-like 'multi-gym'. Laundry service was being skimped on; a proportion of black-and-white strips had turned dishwater-grey. This was just not Newcastle United as Keegan saw it. The gaffer, confident he was in credit with the board, convinced them to spend £6,000 to refurbish and fumigate – new paint, new tiles, new bath. It was a chunk of change for a club staring at relegation, but a big part of Keegan's thinking about what constituted professional, properly motivational behaviour.

He also had ideas for economies: the heroically portly striker

Mick Quinn was on too much money. It was clear to him, moreover, that the squad was so-so, forward Gavin Peacock arguably the one bit of class. (Keegan and McDermott kidded each other they were the standouts in the five-a-sides and ought, really, to be the first names on the team sheet.) But if Keegan's renown preceded him to Benwell, he was dealing with younger players who had been blooded and brought along by Ardiles. Keegan saw far too much truculence in one such, 19-year-old Lee Clark, a builder's son from the deprived ward of Walker in Newcastle's East End. An England Schoolboys captain, Clark had admired Keegan as a Newcastle player, but it was Ardiles who had given him his chance in black and white. Keegan rated Clark as combustible: he was on the bench and not favoured thereafter.

For Keegan's first game, Newcastle's home crowd near doubled. His arrival to the dugout was acclaimed on all sides; and Bristol City were ideal victims on the day. David Kelly scored early in the second half, and Keegan punched the air. When Liam O'Brien added a second Keegan raced onto the pitch. Kelly swept in a third, and Keegan and McDermott clutched one another giddily. Three points, and the great escape was afoot. The prize if Newcastle could stick around in the second tier was very evident. The Premier League was now formally constituted, and that was where Newcastle needed to be.

This was Jack Walker's burden of expectation on Dalglish, who had never known a promotion battle of any sort. Walker continued to use his wealth to improve Blackburn's odds. Rated midfielder Tim Sherwood dropped a division to sign from Norwich for half a million pounds. Many rival fans cavilled, cried foul. It was an easy thing for Blackburn to cry envy in return. What fan of what club would not have loved to have a fan like Jack Walker at hand? Keegan's second assignment with Newcastle was at Ewood Park. There they were, Keegan and Dalglish, the two great footballing heroes of their day, now sitting tensely in Second Division dugouts, engrossed and yet nearly helpless on the wrong side of the white line. 'It's not Keegan versus Dalglish, is it?' Keegan instructed a reporter overeager to hype the contest. 'You go and ask Kenny if he can influence the result when three o'clock goes.' It was in fact David Speedie's influence that was decisive, his hat-trick for Rovers securing their 18th win of the season, and they were clear at the top by seven points.

But despite the bookies having lost interest, Blackburn were to be knocked off their perch. Mike Newell sustained a broken leg in the Newcastle game, and what followed for the team was a horrendous return of one win from 12 games, including six straight defeats in March/April, one of these to Newcastle's relegation rivals Port Vale. Rovers dived down a tightly packed table, to seventh, outside the play-off places.

Dalglish, having looked so comfortable in his new skin, began to evince the strain as Rovers' season appeared to capsize. He was newly voluble in the dugout, and forced to account for himself to the press. Yes, second-tier pitches were heavy, a cultivated passing game didn't always work. But knocking the ball into the channels could seem a profitless pursuit for Blackburn, too. Who would chase those long balls anyway? Further to Newell's broken leg, Speedie had pulled his hamstring.

Dalglish retained his cool, like one who evidently hated to admit to upset while noting and harbouring anything said against him. But there was no little *schadenfreude* going around about the mess that moneybags Blackburn had got themselves into. Dalglish defended his players to the media, and looked to encourage them in training. There was, perhaps, a certain problem in the headcount of his burgeoning squad: was he sure what was his best team? Arguably he suffered from too many options. Still, he bought again, Roy Wegerle from QPR for £1.1 million, and Duncan Shearer from Swindon for £700,000, so drawing the teeth of a promotion rival.

Rovers managed draws with Tranmere and Sunderland, beat Millwall at Ewood and, sitting seventh, knew that if they were to squeak into the play-offs they needed to win again on the last day of the season, away to relegation-threatened Plymouth, now managed by Peter Shilton and assisted by John McGovern – two stalwarts of Brian Clough's Nottingham Forest side that had frustrated Dalglish repeatedly as a Liverpool player circa 1978. With regard to bad omens, any neutral would surely have hoped for Dalglish's sake that he was not a superstitious sort of a fellow.

Newcastle won their third league game under Keegan against Cambridge, but relations between Keegan and John Hall had sunk into the cellar. Keegan had made a few fast, cheap recruitments to the playing squad but there was a niggle over the permanent signing of defender Brian Kilcline – on loan from Oldham – priced at £250,000. It dawned on Keegan that Hall's pledge of funds at their first London meeting had been a cheque Hall wrote with his mouth, intended to force the hands of fellow Newcastle directors. But those directors, asked for their views, were disinclined to cough up. Keegan, as was his long-attested standard procedure, reacted to what he considered a slight by deciding to walk out, albeit not at once.

He was resolved to quit on the Friday night of 13 March before playing Swindon. McDermott, with no little skill, persuaded him to at least see out the match. Newcastle won 3-1 and moved to 18th, five points clear of the drop. But afterwards Keegan went straight home to Romsey. 'It's not like it said in the brochure,' was the stray remark the pressmen picked up on. The news reached Wynyard, and John Hall, seeing the size of the hole he was in, had his wife Mae write a cheque for Kilcline, drawing on funds that he convinced Barclays to leave alone. But Hall had been offended by Keegan's flightiness and it took the persuasions of Mae to make him call Keegan at home and attempt the rebuilding of bridges. Keegan believed that he had made his point, and a truce was agreed.

Newcastle drew at Grimsby then won the all-important derby against Sunderland. Happy days on Tyneside. Then came five defeats on the trot, including a 6-2 mauling at Molineux and a 4-1 at Derby. On 25 April 1992 Newcastle entertained Portsmouth and with five minutes left, playing a draw, they were in the relegation spots, with only promotion hopefuls Leicester still to visit. Keeper Tommy Wright threw the ball from the Leazes End goal out to Ray Ranson, who hoisted a long, angled pass to David Kelly, who flicked on to Micky Quinn. Quinn somehow hooked the ball back to Kelly, and Kelly rammed the ball into the net mid-left. Ecstatic Newcastle fans were now sure that Keegan had brought magic powers with him. It was nothing tactical or technical – just what the players described as 'positivity'.

On the season's last day Newcastle went to Leicester and fought with admirable conviction. Peacock gave them a lead that lasted until the final minute, Leicester's equaliser sparking a pitch invasion. Keegan paced the touchline, wincing. The referee got the game restarted and Newcastle grabbed a winner. Cue pitch invasion, part two. As it turned out, a draw would have sufficed. Keegan's deal was done, mission accomplished, though the script suggested he would surely continue. 'We certainly want to stay,' McDermott told TV reporters. 'If anyone can bring them good days back to Newcastle it's the boss.'

Keegan was duly made an offer, one that he considered derisory, much like what Arthur Cox had considered beneath his dignity back in 1984. So, once again put on the spot, John Hall decided to go all in, and Keegan agreed to an improved three-year contract. Previously, Keegan had paid McDermott from his own pocket but now McDermott, too, was on staff. Cameron Hall Developments moved to hoover up all remaining shares in Newcastle United. However tentative and tetchy had been the beginnings, Keegan and Hall, just like King Kev and Terry Mac, were a double act from here.

On that afternoon of 2 May when Keegan accomplished his mission at Leicester, Dalglish's Blackburn were at Plymouth, making things marginally less hard for themselves despite losing a soft early goal. Peter Shilton was not at the height of his powers, and Speedie scored twice in quick succession right at the end of the first half, completing a hat-trick midway through the second. Blackburn's play-off semi-final pitted them against Derby, the first leg at Ewood, where Derby scored two fine goals in the first 15 minutes. The good fortune of a bobbling free kick from Scott Sellars brought Rovers into the game round the half-hour; then just before half-time Newell fashioned a shooting chance for himself and buried it. In the second half Rovers took command, Derby got rattled, and Speedie picked off a couple of chances to secure a 4-2 win. In the return, Derby led until a valiant headed equaliser from Kevin Moran, but they got back in front with 16 minutes to go, bombarding Blackburn's nerves and rattling their crossbar before the final whistle brought its towering relief to Dalglish and Walker.

The experience of Wembley on play-off final day, 25 May 1992, was a 'different feeling' for Dalglish. On the turf where he had scored a European Cup winner and secured a double as player-manager, his team now had to get past Leicester to claim on Jack Walker's big wager. On a blazing hot day, Dalglish elected to stay on the sidelines in a tee-shirt and trackie bottoms, sanctioning Tony Parkes to don the suit and tie and lead the team out on the turf. Newell's first-half penalty gave Blackburn the advantage, but then he missed a second as if to ensure that agony would be extended right to the end of normal time. Upon that whistle, though, Blackburn had secured their ticket to the inaugural season of the Premier League. For Dalglish above all the alternative had been truly unthinkable – Walker would not go broke backing Blackburn, but for Dalglish it would have been an unprecedented failure in a golden career.

Tim Sherwood, too, had taken a risk in dropping a division to join the Blackburn project; and as he recalled, 'Kenny used to say to me all the time, "You show me a good loser and I'll show you a loser."'

Blackburn were a top-flight team again but did not have a top-flight first XI. An irreducible part of what Walker was paying Dalglish was for the boss's perceived ability to lure players of big promise to Ewood Park, to make them feel special, to have them buy into the great project. In July 1992 Dalglish paid Middlesbrough £1.2 million to secure the crossing prowess of Stuart Ripley, and a key part of the pitch was Dalglish's confiding to Ripley, subject to contract, the name of the fellow he would be crossing to.

Alan Shearer, 21-year-old Newcastle-born striker for Southampton, was a centre forward so 'classic' in his skill set that he might have been tooled in a factory and delivered box-fresh in a number nine shirt. That summer, every club in England that reckoned itself was interested in him; Souness at Liverpool and Ferguson at Manchester United were hungry for his signature. Dalglish had to ensure Shearer shunned Anfield and Old Trafford and came instead to Nuttall Street, BB2. A product of Wallsend Boys, Shearer had grown up following Kevin Keegan's every move; now he was making his own name with a purposeful, slightly pursed air that Dalglish quite possibly recognised from the bathroom mirror.

Dalglish met Shearer at Haydock Park's Thistle hotel, assuring him that he would be playing exactly where he wanted to play and receiving service. While the men talked the game, Marina Dalglish went to work on Shearer's wife Lainya, seven months pregnant with the couple's first child. Southampton and Blackburn agreed a fee of £3.3 million. Shearer promised Dalglish an answer within four days. Manchester United made their pitch, too, and Shearer was willing to hear them out. They didn't quite have the money to hand, though, whereas Shearer had no doubts about Walker's ability to pay. He said yes to Dalglish. (David Speedie went the other way to Southampton.) It was a signing that blared out Blackburn's ambition: they intended to challenge.

John Hall was not Jack Walker – not in respect of his net worth, or with regard to the extent of devotion to the football club whose interests he controlled. It had cost Hall some years and around £3 million of his own money to buy Newcastle. Still, with that job done, the big decisions were his, and Keegan lobbied him strongly, having found his voice and assurance after the seat-of-the-pants escapology of the previous season. The club swiftly acquired the air of a driven going-places business in the image of its manager. 'We are saying out loud we will be in the Premier League,' Keegan declared, 'that nothing will be bigger than this club.'

He persuaded Hall that the club's debt had to be attacked aggressively: '[I]f you ever want to get your money back, and turn the club around, we have got to speculate first.' Hall decided that he would guarantee loans, as well as lending the club his own money with interest. Keegan began to add players: John Beresford from Portsmouth, Paul Bracewell from Sunderland, Barry Venison from Liverpool. 'I came only because of Kevin and his enthusiasm and ambition,' Venison told the press. 'I wouldn't have come if I hadn't thought that the club was about to take off.'

A month into the new season Robert Lee would come from Charlton for £700,000. 'Painting pictures for people' was Keegan's gift, as it was Dalglish's: it seemed that so long as he could get face to face with a player then he could persuade them to buy into his uplifting vision of where Newcastle could go. Middlesbrough were after Lee, too, and the player himself, newly a father, was chary of moving too far out of London. But Keegan straight-facedly assured him Tyneside was closer to the big smoke than Teesside. 'I only went up there to talk,'

Lee would recall, 'but he said he already had a press conference arranged. He had such charisma I'd have signed anything. A week later me, my wife and baby were being driven around Newcastle by Kevin Keegan looking at places to live.'

Benwell having been judged unsatisfactory in spite of its six-grand makeover, Newcastle now took their training on Durham University's well-tended football pitches. It was that old Liverpool Way: warm-ups and stretches then competitive small-sided games. The gaffer joined in gamely, making himself a pick in the five-a-sides, taking his turn in finishing practice. Terry McDermott, naturally, had a go as well. 'We can still compete at a fair level,' Keegan insisted to a visiting sportswriter. If anyone wrote McDermott's job description it might have included the terms 'provider of banter', 'court jester', 'social secretary' or 'intelligence gatherer'. For sure he was Keegan's confidant and admirer, and a part of the uplift round the club.

Derek Fazackerley was the organiser of Newcastle's sessions, the ringmaster in the Bugsy Moran/Ray Harford role. Keegan's interests in training were focused on the attacking players, such as Gavin Peacock. He wasn't wildly interested in systems. Where he sought some sophistication was in enlisting a proper exercise physiotherapist and a running coach: he wanted his team to be the fittest team. Another wheeze: a public footpath ran by the Durham pitches, and Keegan elected to make all Newcastle training sessions open to onlookers. Soon the supporters were turning up in their hundreds.

Barry Venison could see what Keegan was up to – it was much like what Dalglish was up to at Blackburn, and had been up to at Liverpool, like Fagan and Paisley and Shankly before him. But man of few words Dalglish was more in the mould of 'Old Bob', the loquacious Keegan closer to Shanks. Keegan hadn't taken any coaching badges but he had taken no end of a lesson from the boss who made him. 'The greatest thing I took from Shanks to Newcastle,' Keegan would say, 'was the belief that a football club is for the fans.'

For Graeme Souness things had only gone backward, a grim tes-
tament to how a hallowed and redoubtable player could abruptly
draw scorn and reproof. On 9 May 1992 he had been in the
dugout for Liverpool's FA Cup final victory over Sunderland,
but looking unwell and troubled, as well he might. For all his
formidable fitness, heart disease ran in his family and he had
recently undergone a triple bypass operation. Determined to
sail through it, he sold the story of his treatment to the *Sun*,
reviled on Merseyside since Hillsborough. A subsequent story
plus photo ran in the *Sun* on 15 April 1992, the third anniversary of the disaster. In later years he would hold up his hands,
and in the language of the Liverpool dressing room – 'I made
one almighty rick.' Was it his fault? It was clear he just hadn't
thought, that he was not on that shared wavelength with the
support that Dalglish had occupied easily.

Souness tried the stiff broom in methods – a new training
regimen, a European diet – but had made no friends, and his
manner was a big factor. He had moved people on sharpish, but
arguably the wrong people, and too soon. His incomings were
not so great either. While he recovered, his side had spiked
Manchester United's title aspirations with a 2–0 win at Anfield
that handed the prize to Leeds, a team driven by the turbulent
Eric Cantona, whom Dalglish might have managed at Marseille
had Bernard Tapie's deal been made sweeter. Souness had been
offered an option on Cantona when Liverpool met Auxerre in
Europe and Michel Platini spoke to him highly of this prospect,
'a problem boy but a proper player'. Souness didn't fancy any
additional problems.

The curtains drew apart on the Premier League in August 1992.
Had anything really changed? Fans were expected to sign up

to subscription packages, the prize being football all through the week on telly, though from this point on the broadcaster would be saying to the clubs what time kick-off would be. BSkyB's billboards proclaimed it 'A Whole New Ball Game', the broadcaster having spent big on a TV advert scored to the big, booming, stadium punch of Simple Minds' 'Alive and Kicking', awash with taut bare torsos in locker rooms – associating the game with handsome, grinning, well-turned-out athletes. But above all BSkyB were selling drama and it needed to be compelling.

On the opening weekend Dalglish took Blackburn south to Crystal Palace, and Rovers were trailing 2-1 when a long ball from defence was headed down by Mike Newell to Alan Shearer, who chested it and walloped it from 25 yards out, a wager on catching Palace keeper Nigel Martyn by surprise. Indeed the ball cleared Martyn's reach by a glorious arc, and Shearer's Blackburn account was open. A few minutes later he won a chase for another long ball, foraged in from the left flank, saw his spot beyond Martyn and curled the ball to the bottom-right corner. A late Palace equaliser took the cream off Rovers' bun, but Dalglish had shown how well he had spent Walker's money; and the new league had one new star, for sure.

Next, Arsenal came to Ewood Park, the north London sophisticates sampling the ground's pawky, pie-eating feel, the 1960s hits over the PA. Stuart Ripley looked just as creative as Dalglish had hoped. Shearer, on his home debut, dispossessed the hapless Jimmy Carter, dumping him on his backside, then left Tony Adams in his wake to score a partially deflected winner. With 11 points from five, Blackburn topped the league, and vied with Norwich at the top all through September. When Norwich came to Ewood, Blackburn pasted them 7-1, the pick of the goals from Shearer as he ran solo to the edge of the opposition box then checked to execute a stunning scooped finish over the keeper. It was Dalglish-like, and Shearer had scored 14 in 14.

Whatever sums Walker had spent, Manchester United remained the moneybags club of the league by sheer gross outlay, and Ferguson had still to bag a league title. United were unbeaten in their first 11 fixtures but five successive draws had left them looking a tad toothless: they seemed, still, to miss a 30-goals-a-season striker. That was Shearer, clearly, but Dalglish had him and Ferguson didn't. He *did* have a formidable new keeper in the Dane Peter Schmeichel, whom even Shearer couldn't get past when the teams met at Ewood, though Blackburn went top again. Ferguson then at last secured the sort of attacking match-winner his team had sought by raiding Leeds, remarkably, for Eric Cantona, and at a knockdown rate. Some thought Ferguson would struggle to manage him. But United won eight and drew two of his first 10 games for them.

In mid-December Dalglish took Blackburn to Anfield, a game inevitably touted as a sentimental journey. Asked by reporters if he had changed, his assent was deadpanned: 'I didn't wear this suit the last time I was here.' It was a gesture to the newly relaxed Dalglish as much as to his Armani-style threads. Anfield had its biggest crowd of the season, and the fans received the King warmly, while making a point to chant the name of Souness louder. Dalglish let the photographers get their shots and acknowledged Anfield before disappearing into the dugout. Liverpool were not at full strength but Barnes was the driving force; they got in front, and then, despite a superb Shearer equaliser on the turn, they got a winner. 'Kenny, Kenny, what's the score?' rang round Anfield, a taste for Dalglish of how Keegan must have felt on his forlorn return with SV Hamburg some 16 years previously.

Then on Boxing Day against Leeds, Shearer attempted a volley with his body not properly settled, and felt an adverse effect in his right knee. He soldiered on, though bowed out of the next game away to Ipswich, but was sure nonetheless that he was carrying a knock that would fade in a week. Dalglish put him out in a League Cup tie against Cambridge United in the first week of

1993. But it proved a struggle and afterwards he learned at last that he had damaged cruciate ligaments and would be sidelined for maybe six months, maybe a year. Certainly, it was the end of his season; and, at least for the immediate future, of Blackburn's higher ambitions. For Dalglish it was a test of the more philosophical outlook he had seemed to be trying out of late.

On the February day before Keegan turned 42 he was booked to take Newcastle and 4,800 buoyant fans to Ewood Park for the fifth round of the FA Cup. Newcastle were seven points clear at the top of Division One, looking like top class, ready to measure themselves against the side sitting fourth in the Premiership – for all that Blackburn minus Shearer were on a run of three losses. (Dalglish was about to go shopping again, signing an attacker in Kevin Gallacher from Coventry for £1.5 million, and a couple of good-value defenders, the Norwegian Henning Berg from Lillestrom and Graeme Le Saux from Chelsea.) Keegan versus Dalglish, then – except that Keegan was poleaxed by a heavy cold on the day and didn't travel. The game was settled by Roy Wegerle in Blackburn's favour, but aleady it seemed clear that this meeting would be reprised the following league season.

Newcastle had simply torn into the First Division programme and won their first 11 games, romping clear of all rivals. A hiccup of three defeats in a week upset the merriment somewhat, but after a battling win over Birmingham the team was flying again, to the joy of their support. Of this success, Barry Venison observed that its 'brand-new' quality for a fan base that had seen little to cheer in 20 years meant 'the fans appreciate it a bit more than they did on Merseyside'. If not quite sacrilege on a par with Keegan's querying of the support he had left behind back in 1977, it suggested Keegan wasn't alone in thinking Liverpool had got complacent.

Keegan now had a side recognisably his own, one in which he expected reciprocity of regard. Between him and Mick Quinn there was mutual distrust, and Quinn was moved on to Coventry. Having felt himself underrated by the new gaffer, Quinn had made some critical comments that got into print, and so ran into an aspect of Keegan's make-up that seemed ever-green. Recent signing John Beresford had figured it quickly, having heard words to that effect from others: 'As most people know, once you upset Keegan it's often difficult to get back on his good side.'

In the sizeable berth left by Quinn, both David Kelly and Gavin Peacock were still doing the business for goals; Keegan, however, had his eye on what the next division up would demand, much as Dalglish had set his heart on Shearer. Come March he made enquiries about Andy Cole of Bristol City. Reaching the player directly by phone, Keegan absent-mindedly addressed him as 'Adrian'. This, as it transpired, was quite some rick to have made with the player.

As a youth, Cole had done time at George Graham's Arsenal, but Graham had been vexed by what he saw as an excess of self-assurance in the player. Cole, for his part, felt denied of the chance he really deserved at Highbury, and once Bristol came and got him for £500,000 he scored 20 goals in 41 games. Cole was lean and quick, durable in a challenge; and the stats showed he was a finisher. The personality that rubbed Graham so much up the wrong way was still visible, though. Cole did seem laconic, rather a loner, not much of a trainer, inclined to make his mind up about people. He didn't much care for Keegan's 'Adrian' slip, for starters, and so took his time to head north for a meeting with the supposed great man in Newcastle.

The deal was done, though, for £1.75 million. Cole would be the first 'black lad' (in local parlance) to wear Newcastle's famous number nine shirt. There had been black players in black and white before, but demographically Tyneside remained more or less the whitest place in England. Cole, though, had the air of one who wouldn't brook any disrespect. He scored on his home debut, and managed 12 more in 11 starts. At the same time, Keegan bought midfielder Scott Sellars from Leeds, a deal overseen by the busy agent Paul Stretford. Sellars advised Cole that Stretford was a good man to have in your corner, and Cole, too, became a Stretford client – as in short order did Rob Lee, Robbie Elliott, Lee Clark and Steve Watson.

As April dawned with trophies to be won, Liverpool came to Blackburn with neither of them in the running. Graeme Souness had fewer excuses than Dalglish for why this was so. Liverpool sat scarcely above the relegation places, and Souness' unpopularity with the team was painfully clear. He still had the backing of chairman David Moores, but the sands were running for him. When the ex-Liverpool forward David Hodgson moved into management at Darlington he would seek and receive two pieces of advice from his old teammate Dalglish: be lucky, and don't ask the players to do the things you could do. Souness might have profited by the same.

At Ewood, Peter Robinson ran into Dalglish and made charming insinuations about his 'coming back to Liverpool'. There was no substance there, but Dalglish could not deny that his interest was piqued by such talk. His Blackburn then thumped Souness' 'old' Liverpool 4-1, and Souness fumed and argued with senior players in a dressing room that he had patently lost. A few weeks later Blackburn finished fourth in the league, tucked close to Aston Villa and Norwich if a full 13 points behind champions Manchester United. Liverpool managed sixth, though only 10 points above the bottom three. In years to come Ferguson would state that 'knocking Liverpool right off their fucking perch' was the light of ambition by which he had steered. With United now installed on said perch, he was going to be loath to cede it. Leeds and Arsenal had slipped back considerably. Dalglish's Blackburn looked the most likely challengers.

Newcastle secured their entry to the Premiership and the Division One title with a win at Grimsby, and left knowing they wouldn't be meeting Grimsby again for the foreseeable. Then, at home to Oxford, Newcastle were poor in the first half and Keegan, miffed, walked out on the game early, leaving McDermott in charge. His team were familiar now with these fits of flightiness. Keeper Tommy Wright – who had lost his first-team place to Pavel Srnicek – was respectful of Keegan as a motivator, but felt the boss could lose heart rather easily at times: 'His attitude was "We're better than the rest" which can give you confidence but he didn't take defeats well and back at training he'd mope around in a huff with Terry McDermott having to tell him: "Come on, gaffer, the lads want you to join in."' Once again, Newcastle's season ended against Leicester, and they were six goals up at half-time when, as Beresford remembered, 'Keegan did his usual joke of saying, "Well, that was pretty crap", but for some in the dressing room that didn't go down too well . . . one or two felt he should also have been there with the players when things weren't going so well.'

Keegan was back on the upswing, though. In his match programme notes he wrote, 'Look out Fergie, we're after your title.' A banner at the game proclaimed him 'God on the Tyne'. When Keegan hailed a mass of fans gathered outside St James' Park he could have been forgiven for imagining himself the head of an imperial cult. He told them they were better even than Liverpool's European Cup crowd, proof positive that he had gone native.

Gavin Peacock and David Kelly were moved on, and Keegan was trusted to do good business. In a one-to-one in his office with Andy Cole, he told his thoroughbred goalscorer, 'I'm going to sign a player just for you.' Keegan was talking about Peter Beardsley, whom he envisaged as bringing versatility in attack as well as the head of a seasoned pro for the top division. In John Hall's eyes, however, a 32-year-old veteran was not a promising investment at a seven-figure fee. With matters at stalemate Keegan took himself off to Spain, and discordant silence reigned for a bit. Keegan was beholden to no one, independently wealthy, ever ready to walk if he didn't get his way. But Hall, even wealthier, liked to call the shots, too. In the end it was the chairman who blinked and the deal was done to bring Beardsley home. Keegan was elated, saying of the new arrival that 'anything could happen. It's a case of lighting the blue touch paper and standing back.' After Newcastle enjoyed a good pre-season there was indeed a violent reaction, only the opposite of the sort that Keegan hoped for – Beardsley's cheekbone was broken by Neil 'Razor' Ruddock, and he would be out for six weeks.

To the media Keegan remained upbeat about his hopes for the season. 'I see the top three in the league as a realistic target,' he asserted. He was clear-eyed, though, about the two teams he couldn't see his way past – Ferguson's Manchester United ('They could dominate English football for ten years') and Dalglish's Blackburn ('because if anyone good becomes available they can buy them').

Since Manchester United were top dogs, however, Dalglish could not expect always to get his first pick in the transfer market. He wanted Nottingham Forest's fierce young Irish midfielder Roy Keane; and Keane, impressed as anyone by the force of Dalglish's presence and the scale of Jack Walker's ambitions, agreed terms and money before heading home to Cork for the weekend. That Sunday, though, Ferguson reached Keane by telephone and made a case for his joining the champions – one that persuaded the player, alongside a commitment to break the English transfer record for his services. Keane was big enough to call Dalglish and admit he had changed his mind. This time he was treated to less of Dalglish's famous cool, more of the sharp tongue. Saying no to Kenny Dalglish remained a big deal. Instead, Dalglish bought defensive midfield 'cruncher' David Batty from Leeds. Goalkeeper Tim Flowers from Southampton was a significant capture, Souness, again, missing out, Walker's money trumping any of the players Souness offered in part-exchange.

At the same time Dalglish was having to show some finesse in the care of his record signing, the recuperating Shearer, who, while glad of the enforced time spent with his little daughter, had grown weary of hanging round teammates as an emblematic crock. Shearer burned to return to action. Dalglish was cautious as the season began, confining him to the bench until late September, and there was a slight disagreement between the two. At least Blackburn got away usefully, notching three wins in four even without their talismanic number nine. Newcastle opened with two defeats but then drew at Old Trafford and beat Everton. As August ended it was Keegan versus Dalglish *redux* at St James' Park. Andy Cole, on the cusp of offside, ghosted in behind Blackburn's back four to put Newcastle in front from close range. Dalglish called for Shearer. With 15 minutes left Sherwood released the returning hero who put a slide-rule finish past Pavel Srnicek with the outside of his right boot, and Blackburn were properly back in business.

As much as both Keegan and Dalglish still loved to pull on the boots and strike the ball, each was feeling the hand of time on his shoulder vis-à-vis their persistent participation in small-sided training games. Dalglish, dumped on his backside by Mark Atkins in one such session at Blackburn, could not hide his displeasure, but the team were only doing as they should. Keegan had looked pleased as punch to don a black-and-white shirt and skipper a Newcastle XI in a pre-season benefit at Annfield Plain commemorating the 1909 West Stanley pit disaster. But in training he, too, was put onto his posterior, by Lee Clark, and Barry Venison let the gaffer know he shouldn't be mixing it with the pros anymore. From then on Keegan would sideline himself, a withdrawal that must have hit him hard, if not quite as firmly as he'd been hit by young Clark.

That Keegan could not pretend to be one of the lads was obvious from the man-management issues that confronted him routinely. During a loss at Southampton he substituted Clark and the player kicked out at the magic sponge bucket while storming down the touchline. The team were then supposed to bond at a Quasar laser game in Bournemouth but Venison, Steve Howey and Alex Mathie decided they fancied the pub instead. Keegan rumbled them and was incensed, issuing fines, stripping Venison of the captaincy, having to be talked down from yet stronger measures.

The following week brought a League Cup tie at Wimbledon, and the team were training in London, Keegan expecting vigour and vim. Andy Cole was more dilatory – tired from the weekend's game, if relieved to be in London rather than Crook, County Durham, which he reluctantly called home. Cole was finding Tyneside too much of a goldfish bowl, the avidity of Newcastle fans a bit oppressive. Thinking Cole more than usually slack on the training pitch, Keegan proposed that he was as well to 'fuck off in then'. Cole did just that, clearly keen that Keegan understand him, then took a cab to his girlfriend's place in London. He missed the Wimbledon game and only returned to the camp back in Newcastle for Friday training, where the rift was patched up, though the temperamental issues were glaring.

But Cole went back to work. An understrength Liverpool visited in late November and Newcastle shot holes in their defence, Cole marauding to a hat-trick within half an hour, serviced by Lee, Beardsley and Sellars. Keegan rated it the best football played in his tenure at the club. Yet a week later at Arsenal, Newcastle were undone by two set-piece goals, a marker of lapses on the training ground, however much motivating was going on. Whatever the talent going forward, Newcastle lacked a proper organiser at the back. In a couple of meetings with QPR, Cole had found his man-marking by centre-back Darren Peacock to be fairly effective, and so in March 1994 Keegan bought Peacock from QPR. Peacock had been accustomed to hours on the training ground consecrated to defending. He soon understood that in a Keegan team he would have to do most of that hard thinking on his own.

In the first flush of 1994 Manchester United, formidably consistent, led the league by 16 points. But come mid-February Blackburn had put together a run of 11 wins out of 12, the stray result a creditable draw at Old Trafford. Blackburn were a team of likely lads now, bonded together, and Dalglish was doing his utmost to hunt Ferguson's United down. While Ewood Park was being redeveloped for the benefit of Blackburn's new and improved following, visiting teams were required to convene in temporary dressing rooms two hundred yards from the pitch, thence to be conveyed by minibus to the turf. It was a useful way to make visitors uncomfortable from the off. When Blackburn beat Leeds with a last-minute bullet of a header from Shearer they were 13 points behind United, but with two games in hand and Ferguson's team still to visit Ewood.

First, though, were Keegan's Newcastle, fourth, but coming off three successive league defeats plus an exit from the cup. Blackburn were not fluent or assured, and Steve Howey kept Shearer shackled, but Keegan's team, with Cole out injured, couldn't create much either. Fittingly, it was won by a close-range conversion by defender David May. Now there were seven points in it. Abruptly, Blackburn were hobbled by a loss to Arsenal. Beating Liverpool while United lost to Chelsea revived their hopes, but a defeat by Wimbledon gave them too much to do. Still, there was a proper edge when United visited Ewood at the start of April, and Shearer settled the game, first with a perfectly measured header then with a run-on and smash past Peter Schmeichel. Dalglish, regal in his soft-shouldered cashmere, was visibly delighted. Ferguson, looking boiled and bothered in an Umbro bench coat, had a bit to chew over. 'We battered them that day,' Jason Wilcox would remember, 'and from that day we knew we had them.' In the end Blackburn would finish eight points short of United, but it was their best league finish for almost 80 years.

Newcastle, having not seen the top four since 1950-51, were closing in on third, and mid-April saw Keegan's first return to Anfield as Newcastle boss. His team felt a bit of apprehension in the normally assured gaffer. It was the five-year anniversary of Hillsborough, and wreaths were laid on the Anfield pitch. The Kop, moreover, was scheduled for demolition, with all-seater reconstruction set to start in a fortnight. If Liverpool's support were roused by the occasion it didn't appear to much motivate their team, now managed by Boot Room alumnus Roy Evans since Graeme Souness' departure. Liverpool were poor; Lee put Newcastle ahead inside three minutes and Cole finished it off. The travelling fans made the ground resound to 'Keegan!', and their hero substituted Venison and Beardsley late on so that Anfield could show its appreciation. As the whistle neared, the Kop was awash with raised flags and scarves, and resounding to 'You'll Never Walk Alone'. Keegan stepped from the dugout to applaud.

In the summer he bought Paul Kitson from Derby, Marc Hottiger from FC Sion and Philippe Albert from Anderlecht, having admired the Belgian in the World Cup. Albert was yet another in thrall to the legend of Keegan from boyhood. ('I was one of his fans.') Keegan bought Albert to carry the ball out from defence, rove forward as Barry Venison never could. Keegan was now installed in a house in the grounds of Wynyard Hall, sending racehorses to the stables in Lambourn owned by his old mate Mick Channon. The players' car park at Maiden Castle was offering a fine spread of Porsches and BMWs. There was conspicuous wealth around Newcastle United, no question. In May 1994 John Hall threw a press conference in Monte Carlo to declare the next stage in the club's business development. Some £40 million would be needed, and Hall expected much of this sum to come from the fans, a season ticket bond scheme. For £500 'investment' fans got dibs on a season ticket for 10 years and complimentary home cup tie tickets for three years, and their name on 'your own personal seat'. The club offered a loan scheme, at 19 per cent interest. In total, 9,500 Newcastle fans bought in.

Dalglish's handsome three-year contract with Blackburn was just about up, yet he was notably chary about signing a new one, and Rovers were on edge with the suspicion that he might be off. Over the close season he received another overture from Peter Robinson about 'coming back' to Liverpool. The old bond had been revived in another respect: Dalglish's son Paul was now at Anfield with the youth side. Dalglish curtailed his summer holiday, flew home and drove to David Moores' house to meet the chairman, Robinson and Tom Saunders. Robinson, though, had changed his tune – swayed, perhaps, by what was right with regard to Roy Evans. Dalglish was deeply irked. He had been ready to jack in the Blackburn project: now he confirmed to the Rovers board that he'd have one more throw at realising Jack Walker's dream.

The team would need defensive reinforcement, for they lost David May to Manchester United, agent Paul Stretford doing the deal. The leonine Colin Hendry, at least, was coming back from injury. But Rovers also lost the services of the veteran

Kevin Moran to retirement. Dalglish offered Moran the job of reserves manager, but the Irishman, astute and business-savvy, had a fancy for something more remunerative. Stretford was an old friend of his and was getting together with the former Danish international Jesper Olsen and ex-Ajax player Soren Lerby to form a sports management firm he would name Proactive. In 1994 football agenting was an awfully good business to look to get into. Premiership players had become a lot wealthier than their predecessors, and in greater numbers. While Keegan had been a rare player in his day to be paid big money, there were just many more now in need of advice about how best to bank, manage and spend their screws.

As for Blackburn's attack, with Shearer restored and in good fettle it did seem that one more piece was needed. Dalglish had encouraged Rovers towards a fairly direct form of football. For sure, the team looked to pass it around when conditions permitted; but getting it up to Shearer fast made an awful lot of sense when their target man had such presence and exploited his muscle just as fully as Dalglish had made use of his famous backside. Shearer's preference, though, was to have a battling companion up front with him, to divert the ball his way, since he didn't tend to waste too many knockdowns. Mike Newell had offered a valid option but Dalglish decided it was time to go back to market.

Chris Sutton, a tall, rangy East Anglian who had begun his career at centre-half, had played a fine season up front for Norwich, and Arsenal were interested in him. But Sutton liked the look of Blackburn's project, and fancied the idea of a strike partnership with Shearer. Blackburn blew Arsenal and everyone else away by paying £5 million for Sutton and pledging him £10,000 a week. It was stunningly inflationary, but Dalglish was sure he had his man, a player who was respectful of the responsibility that came with saying yes to him. In Sutton's eyes Dalglish was 'a strong character, someone, when I signed, I wanted to please'.

17

'That's Bottle Out There!'

1994-95

When Keegan and Dalglish next met on a touchline, in early October of 1994 at St James' Park, it was Newcastle who led the Premier League. Rovers had set off purposefully, Shearer securing an opening-day point at Southampton, Sutton getting off the mark in a 3-0 cruise past Leicester. Sutton even displayed his prowess as an emergency centre-half to secure Blackburn a goalless point at Highbury – this between thumpings of Coventry and Everton. But the team's first league loss of the season came, as if by karma, at Sutton's old side, Norwich – the start of a mini-stutter in form.

Newcastle, though, went unbeaten for weeks, and also sallied forth into the UEFA Cup, a pair of five-goal thumpings handed out to Antwerp home and away offering a model of the manager's attacking ethos. Meanwhile, Dalglish's team fell out of Europe at the first hurdle, losing at home to Norwegian part-timers Trelleborgs and looking in the process to be awfully dependent on a nullified Shearer. Still, if Newcastle had shown how to win in style the Keegan way, they had not learned the Paisley-era Liverpool lesson of progress in Europe: Athletic Bilbao did for them in round two, by the classic European *coup de grâce* of away goals.

When Blackburn and Newcastle clashed in the league Rovers edged in front after Jason Wilcox was toppled by Srnicek and Shearer converted the penalty. Two minutes from time, though, Newcastle managed a harum-scarum equaliser, Hendry contriving to flick on a Scott Sellars corner that fell to Steve Howey, whose shot was cleared off the line by Wilcox only to cannon back into the net off Tim Flowers.

Blackburn had enjoyed the better of the contest and it was they who kicked on, beating Liverpool 3-2, before Manchester United came to Ewood in late October, a game that had become the standard clash of the top flight's top two – an elite that had included Liverpool for nearly as long as Dalglish had been playing the game, but from which Liverpool had been firmly supplanted by the old Govan rivals, Dalglish and Ferguson. Rovers led the game until a refereeing error saw Henning Berg sent off for a fair challenge, and Cantona levelling from the spot. Though Hendry managed to restore Rovers' lead the 10 men leaked three late goals, and the team seethed, Dalglish left to choke in the manner once lamented by Ferguson.

Blackburn got off the canvas, however, rebounding with a 2-0 win over Nottingham Forest that began a run of seven straight league victories. Manchester United's European commitments stretched their squad, probably contributing to successive away losses at Leeds, Ipswich and Sheffield Wednesday. In November Blackburn leaped back over them to the top spot.

Dalglish's team was well-knit on the park but not especially close when away from it. These were handsomely remunerated pros who made their homes across the north-west region. If there were no changing-room or training-ground cliques, there were barely even social partnerships. In private, Dalglish knew that Chris Sutton was a more complicated figure than the forceful big man he seemed, prone to self-doubt. Dalglish saw, too, that his newer signing had 'a wee sort of an issue with Shearer', a certain awkwardness at having supplanted Shearer's friend

Mike Newell in the side – an awkwardness unlikely to be dispelled by the fiercely focused Shearer, whose reticence was just as forbidding as Dalglish's had seemed to new starts at Anfield. At any rate, Shearer and Sutton were delivering goals, and the headline writers liked the sound of 'SAS'. A strike partnership it was, then, albeit comprising two not wholly complementary elements.

The promise of Newcastle's season drained away again, exemplified by the waning enthusiasm of the team's valuable number nine. Andy Cole's goals had won him huge appreciation among the Newcastle support, who simply hadn't seen such prodigious finishing since Malcolm Macdonald wore the shirt. But Cole himself had bigger ambitions, part-fostered by the agent on whom teammate Scott Sellars had sold him – Paul Stretford.

When Cole was absent from Newcastle's training one day early in 1995 his teammates assumed he was off on another of his furloughs to London. In fact, he had gone to Salford, and was about to become a lodger at Stretford's place. Keegan agreed to sell Cole to Alex Ferguson for £7 million including exchange of the Belfast-born winger Keith Gillespie. Keegan told reporters that Gillespie was a cracking deal, a key element in his greater project for Newcastle. But that project would need a big centre forward for Gillespie to cross to, and while Keegan had his eye on QPR's formidable Les Ferdinand there was no deal in the offing. Ferguson, meanwhile, had gone in and grabbed a rival's key man just as easily as he had procured Cantona from Leeds two years previously.

A substantial pocket of Newcastle fans, stunned by the news that they were losing Cole's goals, made their way directly to St James'. From within the offices, Keegan saw through the window that the horde was on its way, and he sensed their mood. Douglas Hall suggested a retreat. Keegan, instead, proposed a group discussion – an idea much resisted by Newcastle's security detail. Keegan, undeterred, went down to the steps of the Milburn Stand to face his critics, believing perhaps that he had roused them many times and had the power also to pacify.

He could not hope to satisfy the fans as to why Cole was off; what he had to offer was the assurance that they should trust his judgement. 'When I came here a year and a bit ago,' he asserted, 'our biggest rival was Southend United, now it's Man United.' He met some unrest. But, still, a big proportion of the faithful, having had their misgivings addressed, were ready to believe. 'I''ve got to be allowed to manage,' he insisted. 'If you think I'm making a mess of things then chant for me to go.' There was a blitheness that also contained another element: Keegan simply didn't fear for his job, in light of who he was and what he had done for Newcastle.

Cole and Gillespie were ruled out of selection against their old clubs when Newcastle and Manchester United drew 1-1 in mid-January. A week later Manchester United and Blackburn resumed rivalries at Old Trafford, a game contested keenly but settled by Cantona. Advantage United – but within a week the balance swung again. Ferguson's team travelled to Crystal Palace, where Cantona got himself dismissed for kicking out at an opposing defender and then, leaving the pitch to barracking and taunting from the Palace support, reacted by launching himself kung-fu style at one tormentor beyond the hoardings. United suspended him from the first team for the rest of the season. The inevitable disciplinary proceedings meant that Cantona would not pull on a red shirt again in United's campaign, and the supply lines available to Andy Cole now looked majorly diminished. Cantona's short fuse was looking like great good fortune to Dalglish and Blackburn.

Rovers were never going to sway the begrudgers who claimed they had bought their seat at football's top table. The playing squad was of a size that even when certain pricier buys were out with injuries – David Batty, Kevin Gallacher, Paul Warhurst – they were not massively missed. There was, however, a second-order criticism of Blackburn's success – namely, that they played an ugly kind of football. The backline marshalled by Hendry was admirably solid; Atkins and Sherwood were a fine pair of holding midfielders; Ripley and Wilcox foraged down the flanks, and up front was the heft of battering front men in Sutton and Shearer. It was 4-4-2, fairly direct, typically British, and it produced goals and results.

Playing Everton on April Fool's Day 1995, Blackburn's performance served to define them in the eyes of many neutrals. Sutton and Shearer each converted simple chances within five minutes, and Everton appeared done for; yet they rallied and fought, and began to dominate, winning corner after corner then pulling a goal back. Tim Flowers had to make a desperate parry that rebounded off the post and back into his hands. Hendry stuck out a leg to deny a certain goal. But Blackburn survived and succeeded in slowing the pace, running down the clock, Shearer assiduously working the referee. Everton's support hated it, of course. But, call it what you like – taking your chances, grinding it out, winning ugly – it kept Blackburn on course for the title.

Then they wobbled – a 2-3 home loss to Manchester City, a 2-0 defeat at West Ham. The unease of a side with no experience of clinching silverware was suddenly palpable. Manchester United, meanwhile, were just about getting the results they needed, and Ferguson – having once psyched Celtic out of a title race – decided to muse to pressmen about the fate of Devon Loch, the racehorse who led the 1956 Grand National before pulling up on the home straight. He wondered if Blackburn had sufficient 'bottle' to win it. Dalglish, close-lipped by nature, capable of storing stresses in pockets all round his person, gave no sign that he minded Fergie's goads.

But Blackburn absolutely had to get past Newcastle at home in their penultimate game of the season, knowing that a win would put them five points ahead with one game to play, albeit at Anfield. Keegan's team battered them before Shearer powered home a header from a Le Saux cross. Newcastle, undaunted, came forward in waves and Flowers summoned half a dozen vital stops, from shots by Beardsley and Lee and a close-range effort from John Beresford that required a stretch. Little wonder, then, that when the Blackburn keeper was pulled in front of Sky TV's cameras post-match the adrenaline told in his voice. 'Don't talk to me about bottling it,' Flowers shouted, 'cos that's bottle out there!' The point was made: United would have to win both their last two and hope Blackburn couldn't beat Liverpool.

Two nights later Southampton came to Old Trafford, Dalglish and his players following events as closely as they dared. When the visitors took the lead the Blackburn squad dared to dream the title could be theirs without kicking another ball. Then clownish Southampton defending gifted an equaliser to Cole, who proceeded to win United a very late, very soft and successfully converted penalty. It was down to the final day, then: Sunday 14 May, Rovers knowing that if United won at West Ham then they, with an inferior goal difference, would need all three points, too. Chris Sutton would admit to feeling 'mentally and physically exhausted from the build-up', of having never known 'nervousness or adrenaline like it'.

On Sky TV's part, the pile-up of possible dramatic outcomes was everything they could have wanted for the fortune they had sunk into the Premier League product. They offered their subscribers simultaneous coverage of the two big games. On the day Dalglish took his place in the Anfield away dugout fully conscious that a monitor with Sky's pictures from Upton Park was close to hand in the tunnel. Kevin Gallacher and Mark Atkins had not made the subs' bench: Atkins recalled Dalglish advising them to go and get drunk: 'You can't be expected to have to be put through this sober.' Some Manchester United

fans, for sure, feared that Liverpool might show some favourit-
ism to their returning King Kenny; and some Liverpool fans did
indeed turn up clad in the blue-and-white halves of Blackburn,
just for the jape. When Shearer put Blackburn ahead on 20
minutes there was some cheering among the home support,
which didn't sit well with everyone. But then for Dalglish and
Blackburn's fans came the immeasurable gift of news that West
Ham had gone one up.

Whereupon a previously diffident Liverpool began themselves
to impress, and the swing of the pendulum gave Rovers a thump,
as John Barnes equalised. The fans were keeping them aware of
events at Upton Park, and Tim Flowers heard more than most:
'Someone from the crowd shouted out that Man United had
equalised,' he recalled. 'I just thought, well they're 1-1, they're
Man United, they're absolutely bound to get a bloody winner
in the 93rd or 94th minute. There's no way they won't nick it.'

In short order the West Ham goal was being besieged – Cole
getting chance after chance, Ludo Miklosko saving somehow.
A draw for Blackburn just didn't seem sufficient as the minutes
dwindled down. Then Jamie Redknapp busted a free kick
into the Blackburn net, and for Dalglish and Blackburn the
sudden inconceivable loss of the game appeared to symbolise
an inevitable loss of the title. Within those same awful seconds,
the whistle went at Upton Park, where United simply hadn't
managed to force a winner – and Dalglish was bearhugging
his benchmates, grinning that grin, living the dream of every
schoolboy once again, and at Anfield of all places.

Blackburn had got to the mountaintop and no one could
now take that away. Kevin Gallacher, having been at liberty
to start his drinking early, ventured to ask Dalglish about the
plan for the big celebratory do: 'Kenny said there were no plans.
We thought he was taking the mick but he was deadly serious.'
The players prevailed on Jack Walker's son, Howard, who had
a booking at his dad's favourite old haunt, Bistro French in
Preston. Rovers nabbed the function room, and made so merry

that they joined the downstairs where a Drifters tribute act was working its way through 'Under the Boardwalk' and 'You're More Than a Number in My Little Red Book'. If there was an element of bathos to the big night out – hardly the high-rolling expected of young Premiership hotshots – it seemed nonetheless typical of Blackburn's benefactor.

'Kenny celebrated too,' Gallacher recalled, 'but he had been pretty laid-back about the whole thing on the run-in.' Dalglish had now followed Tom Watson, Herbert Chapman and Brian Clough in the feat of managing two different clubs to league titles – immortal, in that way. Alex Ferguson, bested, sent Dalglish his congratulations and cheerily vowed revenge. Unquestionably the pressure of outrunning United had been intense, the final act a sort of torture. And yet the sense of mission accomplished also seemed to signal Dalglish's detachment from the Blackburn project.

He had removed himself by some distance from that Liverpool ethos expressed by Emlyn Hughes: the never-satisfied standard that what you did after winning the big pot was to go right out and win it again. 'I did not crave another trophy,' Dalglish would later admit. 'Europe was not an attraction.' He had indicated to Blackburn that after one more year he would be done, and he was as good as his word, stepping down as manager in favour of Ray Harford and taking a nominal kick upstairs to 'director of football'.

In a further close-season sign that Blackburn's great experiment was over, Blackburn under Harford ceased its investment in top players. 'We were linked with plenty,' Shearer remembered, 'but we didn't get anyone in. Ray said he wanted to give everyone a chance to go on and try and win it again, which you can't do. You have got to sign top-class players when you are at your strongest.' The handful of buys Blackburn did make were not liable to inspire fear at Old Trafford: Lars Bohinen from Forest, Billy McKinlay from Dundee United, Graham Fenton from Aston Villa.

Ambition had drained from the club. Harford was certainly liked by the squad but, as the 'good cop' side of the partnership with Dalglish, he lacked the King's aura that had driven the title-winning pool of players. 'Ray was our friend,' as Jason Wilcox put it. 'He had gone from being our friend to our boss. Kenny was never our friend, he was our boss.' This was not a well-starred arrangement. Over the next season Dalglish would exude an air of focusing his ambitions on his golfing handicap *à la* Keegan; and Blackburn's challenge at the top evaporated like breath off a blade.

The 1994-95 finale had put the seal on the revival of English football. Ticket prices, though elevated, were within reason. Players' wages were handsome, yes, but not absurd. Clubs were carrying more debt, but debt that seemed manageable. Despite the flotations of Spurs and Manchester United, the City remained to be convinced that there was a great deal to be made out of football – it was hard to see how one could glean sufficient revenues from the fans.

The last day's drama had, moreover, served as a terrific advert for the Premiership as home entertainment. Sky, naturally, hankered after a sequel. Manchester United were surely likely to rally and come out wanting their title back. Gripped by the uneasy sensation that his job was on the line, but customarily ready to make big decisions, Ferguson now dismantled the side that had won the double in 1994, and blooded a number of younger players nurtured within the club's ranks. Mark Hughes, Paul Ince and Andrei Kanchelskis were out. Paul Scholes, Nicky Butt, David Beckham, Gary Neville – all contracted since 1993, all just out of their teens – moved into first-team consideration. Ferguson had given his team the rigour and the ruthless drive to recreate success – and he would have Cantona back, too. But if Blackburn fell away as authentic rivals there was, after all, another side chockful of quality homegrown players, managed by one of the game's iconic winners – another sleeping northern giant, revived by big spending.

As Dalglish, in effect, concluded his business at Blackburn, Keegan sallied into the transfer market for the players he felt he needed in order to snatch their title away. In June the long-coveted Les Ferdinand came from QPR, a thoroughbred replacement for Cole. As Ferdinand recalled, Keegan told him 'he was building a team to fight for the title, and he wanted to make sure I knew what wearing the number nine shirt meant to the people'. Defender Warren Barton signed on from Wimbledon for £4 million, keeper Shaka Hislop came from Reading. They were joined by the prodigiously two-footed and high-cheekboned David Ginola from Paris Saint-Germain, a runway model in his spare time, and a hothouse talent who was assured by Keegan that his gift would be prized and well tended on the Barrack Road.

When the *Guardian*'s Richard Williams had visited Maiden Castle in September 1994, Keegan had gestured vigorously to the value of the money invested in his team and his club – but also the imperative to achieve a defined outcome with it: 'I always tell the players, "You've built this stadium – not Sir John Hall, not me. Because by your performance on the pitch you've given people the confidence to come and buy executive boxes, to buy bonds, to buy Platinum Club memberships . . ." And I've said to them, "If you want to be remembered as a really good side, you've got to win something."' The pressure was on the players now, but on Keegan, too – he had spent all that money. It would all be fine when Newcastle ended seven lean decades and won the league, for the first time since 1927. But not until then.

18

Nemesis

1995-97

'What I loved playing under Keegan and Dalglish was that we could do what we wanted during the week, as long as we produced on the Saturday ... Just as long as you go out, beat that team, then go on to the next week and do it again ... Keegan and Dalglish, they just told you to go out and play ...'

David Batty

'At a football club, there's a Holy Trinity – the players, the manager and the supporters. Directors don't come into it. They are only there to sign the cheques, not to make them out. We'll do that – they just sign them.'

Bill Shankly

In November of 1971 West Ham came to Anfield, and Shankly entered the home changing room directly from having given the visitors his customary sharp-eyed welcome. He drew Keegan aside and spoke in head-shaking terms ('Jesus, son ...') of the shambling, sleep-deprived figure Bobby Moore had cut, how Keegan would surely destroy him on the park. Liverpool went out and won – after which Shankly drew Keegan aside again,

and shook his head over the towering stature of Moore's performance. This was quintessential Shankly, the sort of canny man
management that had made a huge impression on the player.

As the 1995-96 season came round, Keegan's fourth full
campaign as Newcastle boss, there remained a sense that the
question against which he tested his judgement as a manager,
in any situation, was: *What would Shanks do?* – above all, in his
desire for a bond with the support, and with the vigour that he
put into fostering self-belief in his players. As John Beresford
said of Keegan's motivational manners, 'He'd get the [opposi-
tion] team sheet off the ref, walk into the dressing room, look at
it for a bit and go, "Jesus, if we're not 2-0 up after five minutes
against this lot, there's something wrong." Then he'd screw it
up and throw it in the bin.'

Jim Crawford, a young Irish forward recruited by Keegan
from Bohemians, quickly cottoned on to this style in training:
'You'd be jogging around the place and you might stop to do
a stretch and Keegan would say, "Look, we're the best squad
in this country. Look at all these people coming out to see you
train. Why? Because you're the best." He'd turn to Ginola and
he'd say, "Fans are paying so much money to watch you play."'
Arguably, Newcastle were over-motivated. Arguably, too, they
were under-drilled.

But the new season saw Newcastle on the upswing in some
style, their free-flowing and attacking proficiencies hugely
abetted by the addition of David Ginola to whip balls into the
area, and of Les Ferdinand to hammer at them with boot or
head ('Zebedee' became Ferdinand's nickname in point of his
prowess at jumping high for the header). Just off Ferdinand
through the middle was the still-ingenious Beardsley, and Keith
Gillespie was out right doing the thing Keegan had professedly
got him in for.

Manchester United's season had got under way a good deal
less surefootedly, as Ferguson's refashioned side – boasting
Scholes, the Neville brothers, Butt and Beckham from the

bench – took a first-day beating, 3-1, at Aston Villa. 'He needs to buy players,' pronounced Alan Hansen on *Match of the Day*, the ex-Liverpool defender now installed in the TV pundit's chair. 'You can't win anything with kids.' And yet, kids and all, they won their next five, including a 2-1 win at Ewood Park against a listless Blackburn, and would go 10 weeks unbeaten.

Newcastle, though, got to Christmas with 14 wins, three draws and just two defeats. Manchester United were without a win in five when they welcomed Keegan's team to a frozen Old Trafford, but Andy Cole and Roy Keane scored in a 2-0 win. Ferguson's team, though, lost at Tottenham on New Year's Day then drew at home with Villa, while Newcastle were back reeling off the victories; and on 20 January 1996, a 2-1 beating of Bolton put Newcastle 12 points clear at the top. It wasn't meant to be so easy. Dalglish's Blackburn hadn't managed to catch Manchester United from such a disadvantage in 1994. But Newcastle's attacking style just kept yielding three-point returns. The way Keegan had got them playing had hoovered up a great reserve of goodwill and admiration among fans without a dog in this particular title fight: his team were now dubbed 'The Entertainers'. 'Keegan never told us to take the ball into the corner if we were 2-1 up,' Rob Lee recalled. 'We were told to try to get a third goal, then a fourth.'

Pragmatically, Newcastle could probably have used another defender to help with the grinding-out of results whenever things, inevitably, got a bit tighter and tenser at the sharp end of the season. Defence, though, was just not Keegan's priority. Alan Hansen, in his pundit's role and now versed in the 'to be fair' manners of the ex-pro, would note that without that open style of play Newcastle 'might not have got to the top of the table in the first place'. Instead, they were top by some distance, and the title was Keegan's to lose. Lose it he surely did.

In March of 1972 Malcolm Allison's Manchester City, leading the First Division title race by four points, had forked out a club-record fee for QPR's maestro Rodney Marsh, hoping this was the stroke to make the damn thing certain. In the 20-20 hindsight of most onlookers, Marsh actually proved to be a spanner in the works of a functional set-up, disturbing the team's formation. (Marsh, over time, candidly agreed: 'I have to hold my hands up – I cost Manchester City the 1972 league championship.')

The Marsh example was being widely debated not long after Newcastle acquired Colombian forward Faustino Asprilla from Parma for close to £7 million in February of 1996. It was not a luxury purchase. Ginola had missed a few games with injury, so there was room in the side. A private plane brought this rare bird of a player, clad in a fine fur coat from the Milanese designer Byblos, to a snow-blown Tyneside. The next day Newcastle played at Middlesbrough. Asprilla was supposed to be spectating from the warmth of the bench, and he had enjoyed a little wine with his lunch. But Newcastle went one down, and Keegan threw Asprilla into the action for Gillespie in the second half. He transformed the game, first with a Cruyff-like turn on the left followed by a cross for Steve Watson to head home; after which he set up Ferdinand for the winner. It was a very cavalier, very Keegan kind of a debut.

Gillespie, though, came to feel he had been fully displaced from the side, depriving Ferdinand of the crosses he preferred; while Asprilla playing off Ferdinand pushed Beardsley too far right. To be fair, Beardsley was never so one-track. Away to West Ham Asprilla actually started in place of an injured Rob Lee, and Keegan lined up with five defenders. Asprilla hit a post, as did Peacock, and a couple of decent penalty shouts went unrewarded. Ferdinand missed a great chance with Newcastle 1-0 down. But West Ham bagged a second and that was that. Newcastle then went to struggling Manchester City, rearmed with Ginola, but needed three equalisers to take away a point.

Asprilla scored one and made one, but threw an elbow at City defender Keith Curle; and it was clear his misleadingly languid, suddenly flaring style of play had an analogue in his temper.

It was also clear about Asprilla that he lacked the savour for anything much going on after Newcastle lost possession. This was not a weakness he had introduced to Keegan's team. Its defensive unit was not sorted; hard shifts were not being put in. Keegan knew as much to realise that a little erring on the side of caution could still see Newcastle home in comfort. On the last day of February, emulating Dalglish, he procured David Batty from Blackburn as a midfield cruncher for £3.75 million, describing him as the 'last piece in the jigsaw'. Batty came just in time for the vital visit of Manchester United to St James' Park on 4 March.

Newcastle's first-half performance was near-faultless: Lee and Batty bossed things in front of a flat back four; Asprilla got around and was full of good touches. Ferdinand, if anyone, was at fault for a couple of spurned chances. But Newcastle ran into Peter Schmeichel on a peerless day, as stalwart as Tim Flowers had been in thwarting them back in May 1995. Six minutes into the second half, Andy Cole evaded Albert, passed to his left and Phil Neville hoisted a cross to the far post that Beresford could not intercept. Eric Cantona watched the ball, volleyed it into the ground, and the bounce took it past Srnicek. It was a counterattacking goal, and it decided the game. 'If they want to know who is the best team in the country,' Keegan ventured afterwards, 'they only have to look at the tape of the first half.' But you haven't hammered anyone 0-0, certainly not after 45 minutes. Newcastle's lead was down to a point, with a game in hand.

Newcastle rebounded by thrashing West Ham, but a 2-0 defeat at Arsenal put them right back on edge, since Manchester United were cranking out the victories. (They were to win 13 of their last 15.) The first Arsenal goal was lost to not marking up at a corner, the second came from Warren Barton gifting possession. Asprilla blithely walked out of Keegan's changing-room post-mortem, hopping on the back of a motorbike ride that he had prearranged. Manchester United went top on goal difference, then got past Tottenham, and uncatchable Newcastle were suddenly playing catch-up.

They travelled to Anfield to meet Roy Evans' exciting but unfinished Liverpool side, third in the league, loaded with the threat of goals in young local hero Robbie Fowler and the pricily acquired but moodily unsettled Stan Collymore. 'The one thing we said before the game,' Ferdinand recalled, 'was "Let's keep it tight".' And yet there was no black-and-white marker on Fowler as he met Collymore's fine cross to give Liverpool the lead. Asprilla, though, found the response, beating Neil Ruddock – not the stiffest test – and picking out Ferdinand who did well to shape and crash a leveller high into the net. Then came a lovely flowing Newcastle move from the back, Ferdinand feeding Ginola who side-footed home smartly.

Shortly thereafter, Liverpool right back Jason McAteer decided he had sod-all chance of catching Ginola in forward motion, but better odds of pushing forward himself, since Ginola showed no signs of tracking back to help out John Beresford. It was McAteer who supplied Steve McManaman to pierce a backpedalling Newcastle defence with a pass from which Fowler made it 2–2. Asprilla once more stepped forward to get Newcastle out of the hole, Lee releasing him to achieve a delicate dink with the outside of his boot. Could Keegan's team now show its mettle, keep it tight, shut the game down?

They could do nothing of the sort. Collymore slammed in a shot across goal to level. In stoppage time Newcastle had five men back and, still, there was no one near Collymore when John Barnes picked him out and Liverpool had their winner. Sky's cameras found Keegan slumped over the advertising boards. It was ideal soap opera stuff for Sky, a game with all the right dramatic elements, which the broadcaster would celebrate as a 'classic' contest. But as was now clear even to those neutrals who liked to cast an approving eye over the attacking verve of Keegan's team, it was a contest for second place. (Three days later Liverpool proved the true state of their title credentials by losing at relegation-threatened Coventry.) A year before at Anfield Dalglish had clinched the title with Blackburn; but it was Anfield where Keegan and Newcastle saw it slip away.

David Batty would say of the team Keegan built that it 'was the best I played in'; but, unlike Dalglish's Rovers, this team proved unable to stay in front down the final straight. A late brace by Beardsley got Newcastle past QPR but a loss at Blackburn two days later served the *coup de grâce*. Keegan deployed Lee on the wing and Newcastle looked narrow. It was goalless with 20 minutes to go when Keegan swapped Asprilla for Gillespie, and Ray Harford sent on a young Geordie, Graham Fenton, for Mike Newell. Gillespie had a hand in setting up Batty to shoot Newcastle in front, and it remained like so with four minutes left. Then a Shearer shot was blocked and fell to Fenton who bundled it in off Shaka Hislop's knee. Still Newcastle strove for a winner, only to concede instead: route-one stuff; Shearer collecting to release Fenton who squeezed the ball home. Afterwards Keegan looked truly crestfallen, insisting the cause was not yet lost, surely knowing better. 'The final chapter has not been written ... I would like us to finish runners-up if we can't win it. This club has not finished runners-up for a long time.'

Still, if Ferguson's team were very much in the box seat there were no medals on the table yet, and their gaffer was by no means sitting calmly above the fray, paring his nails. Manchester United were well beaten at Southampton, not helped by a fit of Dalglish-like superstition from Ferguson who sent his team out for the second half changed into their away strip. They then made hard work of beating a Leeds side reduced to 10 men, after which Ferguson resorted to the sort of goading that had left no visible mark on the reticent Dalglish, but which seemed to inflame the combustible Keegan. ('At the time,' Terry

McDermott would tell it, Keegan 'didn't really like Ferguson'.)
Master of the us–against–them motivational style, knowing that
Leeds were Newcastle's next opponents, Ferguson claimed vic-
timhood. 'You think for some of these teams it's more important
to get a result against Manchester United and stop them winning the league than anything else,' he observed. 'Of course,
when it comes to Newcastle, you wait and see the difference.' It
was a gratuitous suggestion, mere devilment, though Ferguson
could quite possibly convince himself such imagined iniquities
were real.

Newcastle eked out a win over Leeds with a header from
Gillespie. They were three points behind, two games left apiece.
Sky was covering every game in the run-in and it was a toler-
ably satisfied Keegan who left the Newcastle changing room
to do his duty before Sky cameras over a relay to studio pre-
senters Richard Keys and Andy Gray. Keegan set forth cheerily
enough. But soon there was a reference to 'slanderous' remarks
by Ferguson – and Keegan was not having this marked down to
banter. He had never liked the sound of an accusation of players
going soft, taking it easy – he had not let Shanks get away with
it, much less Lawrie McMenemy, least of all Ferguson whom
he hadn't played for and didn't much care for. Thus Keegan
spilled his vessels live on TV, louder than he had intended on
account of wearing heavy headphones for studio relay, jabbing
a finger for unneeded emphasis: 'I've kept really quiet, but I'll
tell you something – he went down in my estimation when he
said that . . . I'll tell you, you can tell him now if you're watching it, we're still fighting for this title, and he's got to go to
Middlesbrough and get something, and . . . and . . . I'll tell you,
honestly, I will love it if we beat them. Love it.'

It was quite a show. McDermott, having watched the broadcast in some incredulity, reached Keegan on the phone. 'Ah,
sod him,' said Keegan, still seething with regard to his nemesis
at Old Trafford. Were Newcastle's players galvanised by the
boss's free-flowing emotions? According to David Ginola, the

psychological change in Keegan was an alarming sight: 'We saw Keegan change . . . he was fighting with [Ferguson].' Newcastle had to win their last two games at a canter to have the slightest chance. They won neither.

Keegan could not have envisaged the extent to which his public image, into which he had put so much graft and applied so much polish, would come to be defined by that flailing and profitless outburst against Ferguson. No golden goals for Liverpool or England or Hamburg, no pop records or TV ads or *Superstars* heroics would be recalled with such relish in the coming internet age as '*I will love it if we beat them*'. And yet, for seasoned Keegan-watchers it was nothing so unusual: the resurgence of the heart-on-his-sleeve 'emotional lad', as observed in sympathy by Bob Paisley, and vindictively by Johnny Giles. Here, too, was a version of the driven hater of 'cheating' and its taints, who butted heads with Shankly and McMenemy and Hamburg teammates over this principle. But to those same students of his career it was a reminder, too, that Keegan's top-drawer medals were things of the past: none since Hamburg's title win in 1979, while their European Cup final loss to Forest in 1980 had perhaps been supplanted as his bitterest career disappointment. Having failed – or, rather, not succeeded – Keegan would have to regroup and refit his side, as Ferguson had done the previous summer, and try, try again.

'Had we done it,' Keegan insisted 10 years after the event, 'we may have changed the thinking of some very dour people who almost indoctrinate that you have to work from the back.' Perhaps he had the likes of Dalglish's Blackburn side in mind but was too polite to say. Still, with regard to their respective mid-1990s duels with Ferguson, history would record that Dalglish succeeded and Keegan failed, by a gnat's whisker at either side, and yet the whisker was effectively as wide as a chasm. Keegan would carry on stubbornly insisting it was worth it to have lost against Liverpool for the spirit in which the game had been played: Geordie fans, he claimed, wanted entertainment above all, more even than winning. But it didn't sound plausible. Keegan, such a driven winner as a player, seemed to be locating himself in a contented losing party of one.

In late August Dalglish quit the role of Blackburn's director of football, by mutual consent, for the relationship had clearly run its course. Keegan, though, agreed to press on at Newcastle, the club ditching an implausible 10-year contract agreed in 1994 and replacing it with a more sensible two-year deal. Keegan had transformed the club's fortunes and the club knew his worth to them, even while cultivating a set of commercial interests that didn't truly coincide with those of their charismatic boss.

Newcastle's business plans were driven by John Hall and Freddie Fletcher, a born maximiser of revenues. The football club had grown quickly, its turnover vaulting, despite that nagging absence of silverware. For Hall, who had already announced the ill-fated creation of a 'Newcastle sporting club' to comprise football, rugby, ice hockey and basketball teams, St James' Park was self-evidently too small and what was wanted was a new 55,000-seater stadium next door on Leazes Park, the old ground making an ideal roofed arena for other games.

These ambitions were no longer bizarre. The City was now convinced of football's growth potential. Pension funds and insurance companies were buying shares in listed clubs. The European Championships of 1996 saw England reach the semi-finals, tantalisingly close to success, Alan Shearer claiming the Golden Boot. Clubs had proven revenue streams not just from the gates but from Sky, replica shirts and sponsorship. The UEFA Champions League was the big dream pot. The owners and directors could smell what it would mean to them, based on the Tottenham Hotspur model of forming a 'holding' plc, so as to bypass the FA's rules restraining personal money-making.

Leeds United was bought by the Caspian media group and

floated on the stock exchange. A clutch of clubs declared their intent to float, including Aston Villa, Chelsea and Newcastle. Newcastle's balance sheet and cash flow could not compare to Manchester United's until they properly became a power in the land – title winners, if not double winners. Keegan had spent £60 million on players. How much more speculation to accumulate could he be permitted? Flotation would mean being properly business-like. The prospectus for investors would describe the club's business as 'selling viewing rights to football matches' and managing 'high quality revenue streams'. Newcastle would have to be managed in a way the City understood. Arguably, the fun part of Keegan's ride since February of 1992 was over.

Keegan may also have sensed, rather dolefully, that his best chance of winning the title had gone begging, for all the reserves of optimism and purpose on which he could draw. Since leaving Hamburg he had made a habit of walking out on situations where his own expectations weren't being met. Still, he prepared for another season at Newcastle. When his players got on a plane for a tour in Thailand, he stayed behind for a bit of business. David Batty had not, in fact, proved the final piece in the jigsaw; the purchase of Alan Shearer from Blackburn, returning the local-born hero to the ground where he had grown up idolising Keegan, was a present meant to put a smile back on Keegan's face, albeit at a price of £15 million which Jack Walker insisted on having in one upfront instalment. Newcastle didn't flinch, and went cap in hand to a friendly lender.

The not noticeably sentimental Shearer had serious talks with Manchester United, too; but a meeting with Keegan in Cheshire sorted out the decisive matters. Shearer would get £25,000 a week, and Les Ferdinand would receive a fait accompli to surrender the number nine shirt, in line with Shearer's private aspirations and the club's projected replica shirt sales. Shearer was duly unveiled at St James', before 16,000 fans who reasoned that, surely, the *pièce de résistance* had to be close now, with Keegan's inspiring leadership and Shearer's goals in the bank.

In fact, Newcastle got off to a poor start, stuffed in the Charity Shield by a gloating Manchester United, then garnering just three points from nine. If the majority of observers had decided that the Achilles heel of the previous season's side lay in defence, Keegan was not obviously of the same mind. Facing Halmstads of Sweden in the opener of their UEFA Cup campaign he played 2-3-5, with a forward line of Asprilla, Shearer, Ferdinand, Beardsley and Ginola. 'The only thing that was missing,' Keegan enthused, 'was a goalkeeper with a woolly jersey and a flat cap.' Putting five goals past Ferguson's Manchester United delighted the faithful, and Asprilla's maverick brilliance kept them progressing in Europe. But regular match days saw more off-colour stuff.

Mark Lawrenson was asked by Keegan to have a look at the team in action and to work with the defenders in training. Lawrenson saw that for all the 'great pride' Keegan had in the team he had assembled, he understood 'that if they were going to win the league, he would have to change the style'. Lawrenson set himself to ensuring Albert and Peacock stayed in position. There was a slightly more intractable problem in an observable tension between Ginola and Shearer. Newcastle's new number nine was not greatly interested in Ginola's love of beating a marker, more in the quality of balls he got to his feet and head.

To oversee its flotation, Newcastle drafted in a banker named Mark Corbidge from NatWest Markets. Keegan, though, didn't care for the plan Corbidge had been hired to realise. The board were in line to make pretty good coin. Keegan would get a million-pound bonus three months after flotation – £600,000 after the hated tax. But Freddie Fletcher could expect £750,000, and Mark Corbidge £300,000 for his year's work. Keegan knew his own worth but, as ever, had his views on the worth of others, too. Whatever the directors knew about football, whatever Keegan thought to their opinions, he would feel henceforth that they were more concerned about banking their wedge than the good of the team. After all Keegan had invested of himself in Newcastle, the status he had been awarded on Tyneside, he wanted to stand with the people. He had given his blessing to the selling of 10-year named seat packages to season ticket holders, and those deals were going to be undone.

Worse, the club was pressing Keegan to offload players in order to offset that grandiose one-off hit of the Shearer purchase. £6 million was the magic number Newcastle had in mind to recoup by Christmas, and Les Ferdinand was £6 million-worth of striker: the possibility of selling him was put on the table and stayed there. But Keegan could not have relished the idea of going before the Newcastle fans with a rerun of the Andy Cole situation, one where he had, at least, been able to adduce footballing reasons for the sale. Keegan sold Chris Holland and Darren Huckerby for a bit under £2 million, but that would not get the job done.

Around this time a local schoolteacher and writer called Jonathan Tulloch made Keegan's acquaintance through some discussions about making a charity record; and he was witness to Keegan's reservations about Newcastle's direction of travel. 'He was referring to the directors as "them up there" ... Freddie Fletcher came in and was spitting feathers. You could see the friction ...' Fletcher, one of his advocates back in 1992, was no longer onside. Keegan's record was one of not dallying if things were not to his satisfaction. He could, clearly, get by on his own resources, and another managerial role could be his easily enough. His irrepressibility was gone; he seemed heavy-hearted, looking for the exit.

On the pitch Newcastle were in retreat. Seven games without a win culminated in defeat at Blackburn on Boxing Day, after which Keegan sat down with Fletcher, Freddy Shepherd, Douglas Hall and Corbidge. The club was in a delicate spot: if they agreed that Keegan was on his way they would be obligated to say as much to potential investors in the flotation prospectus, not a move that would project stability or inspire confidence. Keegan expressed readiness to stay until the end of the season. But then news of that arrangement leaked into the papers: the worst scenario all round.

Keegan's team, perhaps realising it was time to win one for the gaffer, returned to form with bells on, destroying Spurs 7-1 and Leeds 3-0, then fighting for a draw at Charlton in the cup. But it seemed Keegan was there only in body – the spirit was gone. On Tuesday, 7 January 1997 the club's senior executives reconvened at Wynyard Hall, joined now by Newcastle's lawyer, and gave Keegan an ultimatum, to either sign a new two-year contract or leave forthwith. Keegan chose to go, and papers had already been drafted for his signature.

The news reached the team at training the following morning. 'I am a bit reluctant to use the analogy,' Mark Lawrenson would remember, 'but it was like someone close had died. I think Peter Beardsley did say that.' For Newcastle fans this was a heart-in-the-boots moment to rank with Liverpool's loss of Shankly in 1974, or of Dalglish in 1991. They could not know the full thorny story – only that the man who had, for a second time, saved and revitalised the club was leaving again, this time amid clouds of ill will.

Who could possibly replace 'King Kev'? In fact, Freddie Fletcher had got on to Bobby Robson in Barcelona directly – John Hall having received a solid tip from a sportswriter friend that Robson's wife Elsie hankered for a return to England; that Robson, moreover, might be on the verge of an unwanted kick upstairs at the Nou Camp, so as to accommodate Louis van Gaal as team manager. Fletcher, Shepherd, Hall and Corbidge flew

out to Barcelona and found Robson amenable to their presentation. But by the time they were back at Newcastle airport
Robson had changed his mind, deciding (incorrectly, in the
event) that Barcelona would probably stick by him. One proven
winner was off the table, then. Where else could Newcastle find
a man with silverware adorning every stage of his CV, and an
aura of football brilliance remotely comparable to Keegan's?
On a moment's reflection, the obvious answer was 'Southport'.

Just before Christmas of 1996 Kenny Dalglish had accepted an
appointment as 'business development manager' for Rangers
chairman David Murray's public relations company, Carnegie
Sports International. This was only to formalise a function
Dalglish had been performing ad hoc, running the rule over
possible recruitments for Rangers from Europe. But the printer
ink hardly dried on that deal, for come 14 January 1997 Dalglish
was manager of Newcastle United, on a three-and-a-half-year
contract carefully crafted with an eye to the share price at which
the club would float in a few months' time.

The second coming of a Dalglish-for-Keegan exchange
made a feast for any backward-looking sportswriters who had
seen both men play: the solemn passing-on of the red number
seven shirt was now transmuted into a black-and-white branded
bench coat. Who among them could resist the sport of wondering whether Dalglish might, once again, go to a place where
Keegan had done great things and achieve something just a little
greater himself? Twenty years on it had a pleasing symmetry,
and a wager that most wise heads concerned for the fortunes of
Newcastle felt worthy of approval: a promising diversion of the
funds needed to buy success in the direction of a man who had
lately overseen that very accomplishment at Blackburn.

Keegan broke his silence to the *Mirror* on 7 February, three
weeks into Dalglish's tenure, indicating that he wholly approved

of the choice of his successor: 'They are in the safest possible hands ... if anybody can lead that team to the top Kenny Dalglish is the man ... If he brings a trophy to St James' Park he will experience a public reaction and celebration the likes of which he has never seen, even at Liverpool and Blackburn ... He replaced me once before, remember ...'

But the seeming symmetry was just an illusion. True, one esteemed footballing man was warm-heartedly endorsing another for a job. But the job, somehow, had gotten to be about an awful lot more than just football. Over 20 years, the game had changed beyond recognition, the stakes were different, and making a success of management, as both men had learned, was a far harder set of yards to make than achieving glory with boots on.

19

Succession Problems

1997-98

'Such is the complexity of [Dalglish] that he will not inspire the idolatry usually reserved for someone of his status.'

Ian Archer

'I have no axe to grind with Dalglish over his part in [Newcastle's] history. I know he wasn't very popular with supporters . . .'

Lee Clark

Dalglish re-entered the circus of football's top flight on 15 January 1997, for Newcastle's third-round cup replay against Charlton – the most immediate bit of business left unfinished by Keegan. In a smart long coat as per his signature style at Blackburn, he was a vocal, gesturing presence from the dugout. Newcastle got in front, Beardsley flicking on for Lee Clark to finish; but Charlton levelled from a free kick. It was 10 minutes into extra time, under sheets of rain, when Shearer curled a free kick of his own to the top left, then raced for the touch-line. Terry McDermott hugged a grinning Dalglish, to whom Shearer's propensity for comic-book match-winning was such a familiar sight. 'It's nice to be back,' he told reporters. 'It's better than working.' It was a newly pawky public Dalglish, then, gesturing to his love of the game but sounding a notable change of tone from the fervid, Shankly-esque, 110-per-cent manners of his predecessor.

Not everyone at St James' Park was pleased to meet the new gaffer. Come the weekend Newcastle were at Southampton, now managed by Graeme Souness. Dalglish put Ginola on the bench, possibly having come to a familiar judgement on the application levels of flair players. Ginola's response was to look determinedly uninterested during the gaffer's team talk. He had been dear to Keegan, and to a significant section of Newcastle fans (despite having fancied a glamour move in 1996 when Robson's Barcelona had come knocking). In the game Newcastle looked home and dry at 2-0 with minutes remaining, then shipped two goals, the leveller a hair-tearing long-ranger from Matt Le Tissier. A week later Dalglish lined up notably defensively at home to Nottingham Forest in the cup: an offside trap was played, and effectively sprung. And yet, still, two goals from Ian Woan knocked Newcastle out, and Dalglish advised the press that his team just weren't getting any luck.

A week later his team were 3-1 down at home to Leicester with 14 minutes left on the clock, when a foul on Ginola earned a free kick that Shearer blasted home through the wall. Within minutes Shearer had levelled and then completed his hat-trick, and the comeback, in front of the Gallowgate End. It had been a near-single-handed solution to what had looked a dire predicament for Dalglish.'There's nothing more you can say about Shearer,' Dalglish offered. 'Not with my education, anyway.' Again, the pawky humour was conspicuous: 'I have a better understanding now,' he quipped, 'why Kevin Keegan's hair was going grey.'

But Newcastle were exhibiting worrying signs of a dependency on Shearer as pronounced as that of Dalglish's Blackburn side. Bad news, then, when after a win at Middlesbrough it was apparent that a groin strain would sideline Shearer for a while. Dalglish then endured his first league loss at home – Southampton again, and Le Tissier, volleying in from 18 yards out. In Shearer's absence, Asprilla's mazy ways looked merely profligate. Upon the final whistle St James' Park was raining boos. 'It was a good time to be playing them,' Souness offered, almost apologetically.

Worse, Ferdinand had twanged his hamstring and upon Newcastle's return to UEFA Cup action, a quarter-final against Monaco, they were also minus a crocked Shearer, a suspended Asprilla, and Beardsley, concussed by a stray shot in training. Monaco won 1-0, so crushing the tie, which they would finish off with a 3-0 win a fortnight later at theirs.

Dalglish was not making friends widely outside the players he already knew and trusted. He had drafted in Blackburn's former youth coach Alan Irvine, and was making the squad bust a gut in training – inimical to Asprilla for one, Ginola for another, the latter making public his well-telegraphed dissatisfactions via a written transfer request which Dalglish acknowleged to the press with remarkable laconicism. ('The handwriting was beautiful.') Dalglish also frowned on the preferred social round of the squad's young Geordie stars, Lee Clark, Steve Watson and Robbie Elliott.

In this unsettled atmosphere Dalglish took Newcastle to Anfield, where he had yet to win as a visiting coach, and where Keegan and his team had cut such tragic figures a year before. Set up in a would-be smothering 4-5-1, Asprilla the lone attacker, Newcastle were murdered in the first half, quickly 3-0 down, their dense lines looking leaden and pierced at will by an effervescent Liverpool attack. Steve McManaman (wearing number seven) scored one and made one, whereupon the track-suited Dalglish suffered the indignity of a disgusted fan flinging a replica shirt at him. Ginola and Ferdinand were pushed on only for the latter to hobble off again 10 minutes later. And yet Newcastle clawed back: first Gillespie getting lucky with a speculative shot, then Ginola setting up Asprilla for a consummate lob, then pure route one and Liverpool disarray allowing Barton to poke an equaliser. This being Newcastle, however, predictable as rain, Liverpool nicked the win in time added on, thanks to a Fowler header. All good sport for Sky TV, but by no means was it great football.

Newcastle still had the lineaments of Keegan's side. As it became clearer that Dalglish had other ideas, the question arose: what sort of team did Dalglish care to build? No one was much the wiser when he sold Paul Kitson to West Ham and spent the takings on young Bradford right-winger Des Hamilton. What seemed clear was that Dalglish would be selling as much as he bought, pound for pound. Newcastle's pre-flotation Keegan-era bounty was spent. When the club was at last quoted publicly in April 1997 the proceeds were earmarked for debt servicing, payments owed on players already bought, and a youth academy. (The need to bring players through had been sharpened since Keegan had disbanded Newcastle's reserves side to preserve the St James' playing surface, a decision Dalglish reversed.)

The flotation valued Newcastle at close to £180 million. Early trading in the 40 million shares was not fierce, but Sir John Hall and his wife, son and daughter emerged with a 57 per cent stake valued at £102 million. From here on Hall would no longer be personally in the hole for Newcastle's finances, and he and his son and Freddy Shepherd would draw six-figure salaries. Newcastle United was fairly big business, yet still had no silverware to show, nor any immediate prospect of it. The flotation had been a wager made on Keegan-era exuberance, a bubble that had deflated somewhat. The worrisome thought for Newcastle was: what if, despite the hiring of proven winner Dalglish, the team no longer performed?

To the relief of everyone on and around the Barrack Road, Newcastle suddenly began to behave in the hard-to-beat manner of a Dalglish side and didn't lose any of their last 10 league fixtures, the money game being a 1-0 win at Arsenal. Manchester United were champions again, but Newcastle held them to a goalless draw at Old Trafford, and on the final day they beat Forest 5-0 to jump into second place by a feat of goal difference. New UEFA rules allowed runners-up into the Champions League; and thus Newcastle – having at no point truly challenged for top spot – had a seat at Europe's new top table. It had shades of the seat-of-the-pants manner by which Dalglish had managed Blackburn out of Division Two, and Newcastle had reason to hope they had found a lucky general with a knack for grinding out results at the pointed end of a season.

With a European challenge to stock up for, Dalglish paid £2 million for Dane Jon Dahl Tomasson, leading scorer at Heerenveen and a hotly pursued talent, whom he envisaged as an attacking midfield presence behind Shearer. More pell-mell close-season business followed. Keeper Shay Given appeared a good buy from Blackburn, and Alessandro Pistone, arriving for £4.3 million from Internazionale, appeared to be quality goods. The veteran Stuart Pearce came free from Forest, as did little-known forward Temuri Ketsbaia from AEK Athens.

It was the carefully matched set of outgoings, though, that raised hackles among Newcastle's support. Ginola was on his way to Tottenham, and Les Ferdinand also opened talks with the north London side, a long forestalled collision with the reality of Newcastle's debts. Beardsley also had permission to speak with Bolton, after Dalglish advised him that his first-team chances would be limited. Dalglish advised Lee Clark, too, that he was valued but could not expect to start ahead of Rob Lee and David Batty. The strong-willed Clark felt he was being rated as 'the local lad who wouldn't moan or sulk because I was just happy to be playing for my home-town club'. Kevin

Keegan would not have settled for that, and Clark made a previously unthinkable move to Sunderland. Robbie Elliott, another proven local talent, could not be assured of first-team football either, and signed for Bolton.

Whatever the rationales, Newcastle fans could smell plc-oriented decisions, Dalglish doing the plc's bidding, realising value on assets. Would he have let such players go, they asked, without pressure to balance the books – pressure at which Keegan had balked? There was also the heavy hand of an agent at play, Paul Stretford having overseen the deals that brought in Pistone and Tomasson and saw the back of Beardsley, Clark and Elliott. Clearly, six months into the job Dalglish was constructing a team in his own image; but the Newcastle support had seen so much that they liked in Keegan's, albeit at huge expense and for no tangible reward.

Still, in pre-season Shearer and Tomasson looked promising together, even as Ferdinand went down to London to sign for Spurs. On the afternoon of 26 July Newcastle were seeing out a pre-season friendly with Chelsea at Goodison Parkwhen Shearer overextended himself for a ball from Albert, slipped badly, and did not get up. In a meaningless contest the £15 million man had broken his ankle and snapped ligaments. Dalglish and Fletcher, ashen, got on the phone to Ferdinand with desperate entreaties for his return – but the cards had been dealt. With a two-legged European qualifier against Croatia Zagreb just a fortnight away, Dalglish had to go shopping for strikers, on a budget. Calling a couple of numbers he knew well, he took John Barnes on a free from Liverpool and a slightly hobbled Ian Rush on a free from Leeds. To have dismantled Keegan's side was one strike against Dalglish. To have restocked with vintage figures, veteran Anfield comrades – however limited the options – was quite another.

Newcastle began their league season at home to Sheffield Wednesday with all their new signings on the park but an edginess all around the ground. Tomasson, put clean through on goal, ran half the ground only to shoot tamely into the keeper's sprawled legs. It fell to Asprilla, in his voluminous shirt, to do the business, twice, in a 2-1 win. John Beresford, of all people, got a brace that enabled Newcastle to head to Zagreb with a 2-1 lead. The heat of a Croatian summer had Dalglish sporting shorts in the dugout, and two late Zagreb goals sent the tie into extra time, but the unsung Ketsbaia grabbed a 119th-minute goal to see Newcastle through.

The reward was an illustrious group: Barcelona, Dynamo Kiev, PSV Eindhoven. But Newcastle seemed to be running on fumes, exacerbated when Pearce and Pistone got injured, and they lost at home to a workaday Wimbledon side the weekend before Barcelona arrived on Tyneside. Their Dutch coach Louis van Gaal was not particularly concerned on the basis of the scouting reports prepared by Gerard van der Lem. Newcastle looked short on threat and van Gaal advised his left back Sergi that Keith Gillespie was single-footed and *cojo* (lame). Still, Gillespie on the wing and Asprilla alone in the channels was the sum of what Dalglish could send out to go at Barcelona. The game began at pell-mell pace, before Asprilla was upended and won a penalty that he converted. Then Gillespie, full of vim, skinned his man and crossed for Asprilla to leap, hang and head a second. Three minutes after the break Gillespie again left Sergi in the dust and fed Asprilla: 3-0.

In the last quarter of the match Newcastle gave away space and Barcelona rampaged into it. Shay Given, admirable in goal, could not stop Luis Enrique's header with 17 minutes left, but made two saves from Rivaldo before struggling with a corner from which Luis Figo fired Barcelona's second. Newcastle, somehow, made it to the whistle. It was a low ebb for van Gaal's faith in the dossiers of van der Lem. (Jose Mourinho, hitherto stuck in a translator's role at Barcelona, would now stake his claim as the chief marker of cards on upcoming opponents.) But the plaudits belonged to Dalglish, pleased as punch with the scalp and the winning start, his best European night since

Liverpool's beating of Roma in 1984. Asprilla had excelled. Alas for Dalglish, those three goals were the last the Colombian would score for Newcastle.

This time around, Keegan did not stay out of football for long – though it was not the cut-and-thrust of the professional game that revived his energies post-Newcastle; rather, his restless sense of himself as an 'entrepreneurial sort of a person' for whom football success offered a portfolio of business possibilities. As such Keegan, nothing if not persistent, had returned to a scheme he'd come up with in the late stages of his Marbella sojourn: the indoor football leisure activity he called Soccer Circus. Keegan went calling for high-net-worth individuals who might take a punt on his idea, and secured a meeting with Mohamed Al-Fayed, Egyptian-born owner of Harrods. Al-Fayed thought Soccer Circus was all well and good but had in mind a bigger sort of investment in Keegan's skills.

Al-Fayed had caught the fever of the times and bought Fulham FC and its Craven Cottage stadium, with plans for redevelopment and investment contingent on improving results. The team, revived by manager Micky Adams, had risen from 23rd in the Third Division to promotion. But Al-Fayed felt a bigger leap forward was needed, with a new man. He offered Keegan the job of chief operating officer at Fulham, plus a manager working under him. He would get £750,000 plus incentives and share options, and a guaranteed transfer kitty.

Keegan saw all too well what Al-Fayed had in mind. It was a job description – a mission to build and to buy success, with a five-year plan and a stack of money – that was tailored for no one in football other than himself or Kenny Dalglish. He had not seen a league as low as England's third tier since his Scunthorpe days, but Keegan was no snob and knew what spending money could achieve. He took the bait and set about the new venture with his customary gusto. His former England teammate Ray Wilkins, coaching at Crystal Palace, came in as manager, and Keegan arranged for Arthur Cox to be engaged as his personal number two. Since his daughters were settled at schools in the north-east he commuted from Wynyard like a top executive, based at Harrods in Knightsbridge, dropping in and out of Craven Cottage. The football club was being run rather like a department of Harrods, with a young MD, Neil Rodford, seconded from the store.

The raptures that had attended Keegan's arrivals on Tyneside were notably absent when his Fulham era began with a trip to Wigan, and Keegan's heart could not have soared in finding himself in the cramped changing facilities of Springfield Park. Fulham's travelling support, moreover, showed a visible loyalty to Adams, only three or four hundred making the trip, their view of Keegan at least free of the taint brought by Wilkins, alumnus of Chelsea and QPR. The media, however, turned out solidly, since Keegan always spelled column inches.

Wilkins, though, was ostensibly in charge of playing matters. Within four or five months Fulham, spending above their station, would recruit £10 million-worth of talent: Paul Peschisolido, Ian Selley, Paul Trollope, Chris Coleman, Maik Taylor, Rufus Brevett, Alan Neilson. Fulham climbed the table – credit to Wilkins, and yet Keegan and Cox were powerful figures near at hand, seen to be invigilating the project, whether or not that impression was intended.

Dalglish's Newcastle squad had grown weirdly thin, by ill fortune on top of austerity measures. Keegan's free-spending had inured the fans, who clearly wanted Dalglish to resist the financial constraints. But he had consented to them, and in consequence he had nothing like the strength in depth he'd had at Blackburn, nor was the team remotely comparable to those Liverpool sides of 11 men (Dalglish among them) good enough to work everything out for themselves. Dalglish had also needed time to build a Blackburn team, but quicker fixes were demanded at Newcastle.

Come October they resumed their European campaign against Dynamo Kiev, and two lucky second-half shots gave them an away draw; but Asprilla tore a stomach muscle to complete the depletion of the side's recently enviable, now forlorn threat going forward. Ian Rush could no longer function as a centre forward, so the increasingly angst-ridden and goal-shy Tomasson was made to venture up front. And yet, Newcastle for a while seemed to play as though one or other of Shearer or Asprilla were there, the ball being worked quickly from back to front for Gillespie to cross to some phantom centre forward with a leap like a salmon. The line-up began to look defensive, but not in a way that inspired confidence. Away to PSV in the next crucial European game Dalglish was reduced to starting Rush. They lost in Holland and lost the home return and that, effectively, was that – sealed by defeat in Barcelona after which Dalglish's players failed to acknowledge the travelling support. Dalglish did not like coming second, even to Barcelona, but he was having to adjust to uncomfortable realities.

His differences with Asprilla, plain as those with Ginola, meant that the Colombian was soon to be on his way back to Milan to re-sign for Parma. His son Paul, after fruitless apprenticeships at Celtic and Liverpool, signed for Newcastle in November 1997 but was not an obvious top-flight prospect.

Meanwhile, plans for a new stadium, unsurprisingly opposed by the council, ran aground and Newcastle resolved instead to refurbish St James' Park. Yet the fixation on the size of the ground had a delusive look about it when the team's top-flight challenge appeared to be waning. Suspicion remained that Dalglish had not yet taken ownership of Newcastle's condition, that he did not feel himself fully beholden. Yet his 'nice to be back' ease of a year ago had certainly vanished.

'Kenny,' John Barnes would observe, 'has never got over not being a player anymore.' Dalglish was still mucking in with five-a-sides at Newcastle's training ground and, for sure, still looked good with the ball at his feet, passing precisely, placing his shots, advising players on the astute use of the gluteus maximus when turning. Stuart Pearce, though, thought he looked somewhat adrift leading the training and coaching himself, shorn of Ray Harford as organisational foil. Five-a-sides were good sport, but Newcastle appeared to need more focus on things that were repeatedly going awry.

From 1 December into mid-January they lost six games, Andy Cole netting the now-obligatory winner for Manchester United, and relegation became a rear-view-mirror concern. In the first week of 1998, Newcastle scraped past Everton in the FA Cup on a muddy park, Dalglish redeemed by Barnes and Rush combining for the goal as if stirred by old Merseyside rivalry. The cup was a bigger shot at salvation, and Newcastle were in the hat for the fourth round.

Their surprise opponents turned out to be non-league Stevenage, whose barely 7,000-capacity Broadhall Way stadium had not been inadequate to host Birmingham in the previous season. Dalglish greeted the draw with some wary remarks about safety criteria that under normal circumstances – coming from a veteran of Ibrox, Heysel and Hillsborough – would have seemed reasonable to most neutral onlookers. But the air of disarray around Newcastle encouraged more cynical readings – not least after Newcastle sent a delegation to Stevenage and made clear their preference for a switch to St James' Park. Stevenage's manager and chairman affected a tremendous show of pique and accused Newcastle of running scared.

The FA ruled in favour of Stevenage, who rubbed their hands and erected a temporary stand, the cost of which was a mere bagatelle in light of the windfall due to them from Sky's decision to televise the tie. The *Sun*, too, jumped in with glee, taking advertising at Broadhall Way and offering free plastic hats to the locals. Dalglish, never much good at public relations, had suffered a particularly acute defeat in a PR war, and he and Newcastle were cast as pantomime villains. Winless in eight, they would host Bolton Wanderers for a mid-January league game a week before the trip to Stevenage. More than ever, they were in need of their wounded local hero.

When at Blackburn, back in the great Shearer injury crisis of 1993, Dalglish had taken inordinate care in the nursing of his record signing back to match fitness, ignoring the player's own testy declarations of readiness, wanting to be sure his chief asset was ready to go and free from the risk of breakdown. Newcastle's peril in early 1998, however, allowed no such time to spare: the £15 million man had to be recalled to service, the strange six months of his absence meaning that Britain's most expensive footballer returned to a side under threat of relegation.

On the day Bolton, marshalled by Peter Beardsley, looked the better team. Still, Barnes put Newcastle in front, only for Nathan Blake to equalise. With 18 minutes to go Shearer rose from the subs' bench and got stripped and ready, visor-eyed, his familiar force field raised. In stoppage time he headed a ball across the Bolton goal and Ketsbaia rammed home a winner, subsequently kicking out at the advertising hoardings in a show of vented frustration that said rather too much of the siege mentality now shrouding Dalglish's Newcastle.

They stumbled onwards to Stevenage where Shearer – subjected to vigorous verbal sledging from the home defence, who must have felt it was still Christmas – responded by heading Newcastle into the lead from a Gillespie cross. Stevenage, though, grabbed a headed goal of their own. It finished 1-1 and afterwards Stevenage defender Mark Smith told reporters he'd had Shearer 'in his pocket'. Shearer waited, grimly, for the return at St James', and did Stevenage with two strikes, though the first was later shown to have never crossed the line. Stevenage, then, claimed a sort of moral victory, while Newcastle's shrunken morale seemed hardly improved. The prize, though, was a draw against Tranmere and 10 days later Shearer got them through that one, too. Barnsley would be next, so keeping a dream alive.

Shearer's restoration, vital to Dalglish, spelled the end at Newcastle for the luckless Tomasson, swiftly despatched to Feyenoord. But Dalglish's renown for knowing a good player when he saw one seemed at risk. Gary Speed came from Everton for £5.5 million and went straight into the side at home to West Ham, but Newcastle lost. Tomasson's replacement was Andreas Andersson, signed from AC Milan for £3 million. Andersson wore an Alice band, which was one big strike against him with the Geordie support for starters. In time, Terry McDermott would characterise the tall, swishy-haired Swede as 'the one who done for' Dalglish.

Dalglish still had Shearer to lean on but the number nine was increasingly being seen as an egregious leaner upon others. Shearer, possibly conscious of the weight put on his shoulders in the midst of his fight back to form, was now routinely accused of throwing his weight into opposition defences. George Graham, now managing Leeds, described Shearer's challenges at corners as 'almost like assault'. Dalglish then took his squad to Dublin for a bonding exercise that occasioned a solid Sunday afternoon's drinking at the fashionable Café en Seine, during which Keith Gillespie, pickled in booze, invited Shearer outside. On the street Shearer decked Gillespie in full view of passing shoppers, so entailing a ride to Meath hospital and the closing of Gillespie's cut head with staples.

In the cup quarter-final against Barnsley their defender Adie Moses was sent off for a pair of fouls that Shearer had very astutely invited on himself; and yet manager Danny Wilson expressed the increasingly popular view ('I don't know how Shearer gets away with some of the things he does') that Shearer was the one out of order. 'It strikes me,' Dalglish retorted, 'that a lot of people have derived a great deal of joy from our misfortune. But if going to Dublin has helped us get through this tie, then we'll go back again before the semi-final.' It was fighting talk, typical of Dalglish in backing a player for looking after himself. Dalglish more generally continued to support his players in public – though Rob Lee would observe that he 'probably had every reason to slag off a few of the lads he signed because there were a few who let him down quite badly'. But this was hardly an instance of defending the indefensible. For Dalglish the fun of that sort of quandary was all to come.

For anyone familiar with the special problems of family-run businesses, the issue of succession was known to be problematic. Case studies showed a certain propensity for businesses to diminish when passed from father to son, particularly if eldest sons were preferred by rote rather than ability, talent perhaps skipping a generation – the father, even, having to retain a kind of power behind the throne as an emergency remedy for incompetence. There was evidence of problems such as these in the case of Cameron Hall Developments and Newcastle United plc.

That Barnsley cup game was a big day for Newcastle's loyal support; but also for chairman Freddy Shepherd and vice-chairman Douglas Hall, who had a big night out all planned to boot. The duo enjoyed a good drink before the game and after, then flew by private plane to Marbella for a meeting they had agreed to grant to an envoy from a would-be Saudi Arabian investor in Spanish football, who professed to seek guidance from the top-drawer executives of the publicly owned Newcastle United. The meeting venue was the swanky Marbella Club hotel but, since Shepherd's and Hall's host, trailing his full House of Saud regalia and trappings, was evidently a man of the world, the party went on to the MiLady Palace knocking shop and the Crescendo lap-dancing bar.

It was high-rolling, stag-do behaviour from an indulged scion and an overaged fun-lover, and would have been to no one's great surprise, had the ostensible Saudi envoy not, in fact, been the *News of the World*'s renowned investigations editor, Mazher Mahmood. His stock-in-trade was this kind of costumed sting operation – though he relied, naturally, on the credulity of his victims before a calculated display of wealth and exoticism.

The newspaper got two Sundays' worth of material to splash from the unguarded comments of Shepherd and Hall. In the lubricious world of paid female attention, the pair seemed to exult in sexual confidence. ('Newcastle girls are all dogs, England is full of them,' Shepherd opined, indicating his fondness for 'a lesbian show with handcuffs'.) And yet something seething inside these men, awash with booze, seemed to want to come out. They knew themselves to be big men, for sure, but not as big as they ought to be, frustrated by assorted other unworthies. Alan Shearer they derided as 'boring' ('We call him Mary Poppins'). Kevin Keegan, bizarrely, was dismissed as 'Shirley Temple', scorned for having spent £60 million and 'won nothing'. Manchester United, who had won a fair bit lately, were mocked for having signed Andy Cole while the forward needed surgery, though one doubted that Alex Ferguson harboured any regrets. There was nothing more risible to Shepherd and Hall, though, than Newcastle's support, whom the pair mocked for buying cheap overpriced replica shirts and for identifying, as they saw it, with the booze-and-bookies lifestyle of Keith Gillespie.

While the *News of the World* was laying out part two of these indiscretions, Shepherd and Hall insisted they would not be shifted from their senior jobs. Newcastle lost at home to Crystal Palace, and a hundred or so fans protested outside. Newcastle's team of non-executive directors indicated they would walk if Shepherd and Hall didn't go first. Finally, on 23 March, the two brothel creepers were off. Newcastle's share price, which had never soared, sustained another big hit.

Newcastle were four points off the relegation places, with seven of their last nine matches away. They lost at Southampton and drew at Wimbledon. The only possible solace was the cup, and when a Shearer goal got them past Sheffield United they were in their first FA Cup final since the 1974 loss to the Liverpool of Shankly and Keegan. Dalglish was careful to salute the support – 'they deserve better than some of the stuff we've been serving up' – but undid any good work in that direction with friendly words for Shepherd and Hall. Did Dalglish go along with it out of loyalty to his employers, needing a friend while his team struggled? The fans didn't want to hear it, certainly. But Newcastle's 2-1 home win over Barnsley on Easter Monday sent their opponents down, which meant one less spot for Newcastle to occupy. Then came a 1-1 at Old Trafford, when even Andersson scored.

When Saturday came round, though, Newcastle lost at Tottenham and remained in hot water. There was no love lost in Ginola's claim that Shearer set out to foul him; but Spurs boss Christian Gross accused Shearer of breaking Ramon Vega's nose. During a subsequent midweek draw with Leicester, Shearer and Neil Lennon had some argy-bargy whereupon the two fell by the touchline. The officials weren't looking closely but TV cameras were and Shearer, after wrenching his left foot free, looked for all the world as though he had directed a boot at Lennon's head. Shearer's visible frustration, perhaps compounded by the fallen status of the club he had chosen with heart over head, was seriously sullying his own image. Dalglish had plenty of issues of his own over which to brood. In early May, Newcastle secured Premiership safety with a 3-1 win over Chelsea, but this was the least Dalglish could have done in the post. He was utterly unused to relegation battles, to not having his football views respected and backed, and had come a long way in football just to be judged as a pale shadow of Kevin Keegan.

The glimmer of hope lay in the fact that a Newcastle boss only had to win six matches to be a club legend, so long as those games fell consecutively in the same cup competition. And so, at the end of a dismal season, Dalglish had a long shot at redemption.

As of March 1998 Keegan had another trusted sidekick on hand at Fulham – company, too, for his commute from Wynyard Hall – in taking Peter Beardsley on loan from Bolton. Keegan fixed him up with an Al-Fayed flat opposite Harrods, and they shared an East Coast Main Line train journey to put in their week's shift down south. There remained a somewhat leisurely, part-timer's feel to Keegan's presence at the Fulham project, like a retired executive doing voluntary work in the public sector.

The job, though, remained a serious one based on heavy investment of private funds: Mohamed Al-Fayed had spent big, made his team a target, and good results – indeed, an elevator-like progression to the Premier League – were expected, to ensure the dignity of the proprietor's aspirations. As Blackburn had in 1992, Fulham finished sixth and scraped into the play-offs. Grimsby would be their first hurdle. But in advance of that showdown came confirmation that Keegan and Wilkins had not seen eye to eye over the seven months of the latter's employment. 'He didn't want any input from me,' Keegan would say later, 'so it came to an impasse.' Since the power lay with Keegan, he sacked his friend and assumed control of all playing matters.

Before kick-off against Grimsby, Keegan told his players that 'there were plenty of people just waiting for all this to go wrong'. Beardsley led the way and put Fulham ahead from the spot, but then all went awry. Paul Moody was sent off, Beardsley did his hamstring, Grimsby levelled and probably should have won it. But they won the second leg anyway against a weakened Fulham depleted further by Peschisolido getting his marching orders. For Keegan another testing season lay ahead. How much did he want it? Enough to stick around?

The FA Cup final came around – Newcastle's first in 24 years, their day in the sun, and yet the team did not seem very glad of it, knocking around the turf pre-match dressed in sombre black suits. Against the champions Arsenal, they were Wimbledon-like underdogs, whereas their opponents had a swagger to them. Arsenal's French manager Arsene Wenger had been 'Arsene Who?' on his arrival in the English game in 1996 – lightly mocked at first for his gangling, academic demeanour and his curious stint managing Japan's Nagoya Grampus Eight. Wenger had become, however, a game-changing figure: a proper rival to Alex Ferguson and the first non-British coach to succeed in England, having brought with him a notable finessing sense of a football brain. He had got Arsenal players off the beer, onto good diets and scientific training habits – something Souness had tried and failed to instil at Liverpool. He had inherited a solid defence as a basis for 4-4-2, but had cannily imported foreign flair to the mix, having known where to look in France for midfielders Patrick Vieira and Emmanuel Petit, and teen-aged striker Nicolas Anelka. In Wenger's first full season he had found a title-winning formula; now his team looked hungry for a double. And what did Newcastle United do on big days, anyway, other than lose?

In preparing his side Dalglish had become preoccupied by the pace of Arsenal's Dutch winger Marc Overmars down the left. Perplexingly, he chose to deploy the left-footed Alessandro Pistone as right-back cover. Overmars only needed 22 minutes to put Arsenal ahead and, though their support urged attack, Newcastle had no means to surge forward. There were efforts to snatch a goal: Shearer hitting a post, Speed denied, too. But a second Arsenal goal from Anelka killed the game. Charged with negativity by the press, Dalglish would not hear of it. But Freddie Fletcher was heard to describe Newcastle's season as 'disastrous', and Dalglish didn't like that one bit either. He appeared beleaguered and untrusted as never before in football. The idea of any football club dispensing with the services of Kenny Dalglish was extraordinary, but stranger things had been happening in football for a while. Freddy Shepherd and Douglas Hall, for instance, engineering their return to the Newcastle board based on the size of their shareholdings, three other directors resigning in a futile protest.

Since he hadn't been told otherwise, Dalglish planned for another campaign, weighing the idea of bringing in Ray Harford to assist him. Indeed, Newcastle backed Dalglish to the tune of £14 million in the transfer market. French international Stephane Guivarc'h was acquired for £3.5 million, Peruvian winger Nolberto Solano from Boca Juniors for £2.5 million, midfielder Dietmar Hamann from Bayern Munich for £5.5 million. Outgoings were expected, in the usual way, but in late July Newcastle agreed to sell Keith Gillespie to Middlesbrough for £3.5 million. Dalglish, however, made plain that he hadn't given his approval to any such deal. ('There's a way to do things, and it's wrong if I haven't spoken to the player.') Freddie Fletcher and Dalglish were known to be at loggerheads.

For the first game of the new season at home to Charlton, Dalglish put defender Nikos Dabizas in central midfield, Lee and Speed on the flanks, Andersson allegedly supporting Shearer. This was Dalglish's team; it was full of proper players, but it had no width and little penetration. Even after Charlton had a man sent off inside the first half-hour Newcastle couldn't go on to score, and they were booed off the park. The following weekend they bagged a respectable draw at Chelsea, with the rare sighting of an Andersson goal from a route-one punt and a Shearer flick-on.

Come midweek Dalglish was in Southport, fitting in 18 holes of golf, preparing for the visit to Newcastle of Liverpool. On Thursday morning he was in his car heading north-east when Freddy Shepherd reached him – whereupon he turned back. By evening, though, he had made it to Durham, and was taking questions from reporters in the incongruous setting of the back bar of a pub. 'It seems to be the time for exam results,' he remarked, 'and I appear not to have done very well.' Dalglish was ready to own up to shortcomings ('Of course I've made mistakes') but could not confirm the club's story that he had resigned, because he had not. There was going to be war.

Newcastle's appointment of ex-Chelsea boss Ruud Gullit put £7 million on the value of Newcastle shares directly; but, as with the Keegan pantomime, the whole production had a shaky look. Dalglish would lodge an £8 million claim for unfair dismissal, settling eventually out of court for £300,000. His standing with the Newcastle support had reached a stunning nadir. Within months the act of going to watch his son play in a reserve match at Rotherham saw him get stick off a waiting gaggle of fans – small-time stuff from a small minority. The main point was that, for the first time in a gilded career, Dalglish had left a team's support bitterly disappointed; and, instead of choosing the manner of his departure, he had been given the boot.

Football managers are fated to take stick – if not outright ridicule – and the modern game had multiplied the means by which that stick could be applied: from BBC Radio's *606* phone-in and Sky TV's grim gallery of ex-player pundits, to the braying array of fan-run websites and bulletin boards. There was a kind of indignity in seeing men such as Keegan and Dalglish, supreme players in their day, subjected to such slings and arrows. But unless the team achieved success – and football permitted only a narrow elite – there was no hiding place. The longer such men lingered at the highest level, the greater the chance they would be caught out, a layer of varnish stripped from their reputations, victims of reversals they might rather have avoided.

Football was such a tough game in which to get a bit of fair credit. On the opening day of the Scottish season, Celtic chairman Fergus McCann was booed as he took the field, and this after Celtic had bested Rangers to win the Scottish title the previous May, the club's first in 10 years. McCann was a Celtic fan and had begun to rival Rangers' organisational success. The tarnish was that manager Wim Jansen resigned days after the title win. McCann, elderly, bespectacled and button-eyed, didn't cut a figure like David Murray, and was careful about spending, something to which Jansen had gestured in frustration. Josef Venglos was now in charge. Celtic, as was now the way in football, made their first call on Jansen's departure to the London Stock Exchange.

McCann had first approached Celtic's intransigent board in 1989, only to be rebuffed and then rebuffed again. But within a few years Celtic were being left far behind by free-spending Rangers. Then came the Taylor Report, and the requirement for a new all-seater stadium. Celtic was run the old way: break even and avoid debt. There were no cash reserves, just a Bank of Scotland overdraft, and the bank, observing Liam Brady's spending to the limits of Celtic's £5 million overdraft, decided to call time unless £1 million was lodged in Celtic's account. In stepped McCann, able to inject enough finance to satisfy the bank, keep Celtic in business, and take over the running of the club, becoming managing director and ousting the old board. It was akin to John Hall's takeover at Newcastle. Lou Macari was the Ardiles figure sacked within months of McCann's arrival. (He went for his next loan to the Co-op Bank in Manchester.)

McCann had overseen flotation in early 1995, oversubscribed and raising £21 million that helped to redevelop Celtic Park and revive season ticket sales. McCann had stabilised the club, but to some supporters he was just a dry-as-dust moneyman. He had committed to a five-year plan but he made no bones about wanting his money back, plus profit. Now he made clear he would be selling his 51 per cent majority shareholding and heading back to Canada (to where he had emigrated in his youth and made his fortune selling golfing holidays). His intention was to sell to existing shareholders and season ticket holders.

But in November 1998, Dalglish attempted a board takeover of the club where he was first a hero, joined by Simple Minds singer Jim Kerr and Ayrshire businessman Jim McAvoy, the linkage to the consortium's major backing. McCann as majority shareholder rejected this approach and a public war of words ensued, over the heads of Celtic fans who had never learned to love McCann and liked, at least, the noises Dalglish was making about buying players. But by December 1998 that sortie was going nowhere. Still, something about the game was summoning Dalglish back into the fray. Newcastle hadn't knocked it out of him. Since there was no vacancy at Liverpool, why not Celtic?

Properly installed in the dugout at Fulham, Keegan did the business, helped inordinately by Al-Fayed's approval of yet more spending. Fulham's attack-minded summer spend brought nippy wingers John Salako and Gus Uhlenbeek to supply a forward line newly bolstered by German striker Dirk Lehmann. By Christmas Fulham had 50 points on the board, and the project was motoring. Peter Beardsley, inevitably still wanting to play every week, made one last sensible move in order to do so at Hartlepool.

It was at Newcastle, though, where Beardsley was granted a remarkable testimonial game in late January 1999. Celtic would provide the opposition – Beardsley's boyhood team, all because of Kenny Dalglish, though as his career had turned out he had ended up much the closer to Kevin Keegan. Still, Beardsley's Newcastle XI – in which Andy Cole and Alan Shearer would combine with Chris Waddle and Paul Gascoigne – had room on the bench for both Keegan and Dalglish, even though the latter was still in legal dispute with his ex-employers at St James' Park.

In the event Dalglish jogged on after 67 minutes to replace John Barnes, and enjoyed a notably warmer reception from the visiting Celtic fans. But when Gascoigne left the field 10 minutes later and Keegan bustled over the white line in the number seven shirt, the huge ovation told that this was the guest star the fans had come to see. Chants of 'Walking in a Keegan Wonderland' persisted to the end, though Dalglish looked the tidier of the two in the game, squeezing a shot narrowly by the post before, in the dying seconds, releasing Shearer to be tumbled in the box for a spot kick that Beardsley scored at the second attempt. A nostalgic night for legends, then; Beardsley went back to Hartlepool, Keegan to a rather bigger game for Fulham at home against Northampton. But another project had come across Keegan's sights, and Craven Cottage was about to be made to look a lot like the minor leagues, too.

20

Gambling

1999-2000

'We used to ask the people who worked with him, "What is it with Kevin? Why doesn't he do more tactical work?" And they just shrugged and said that was him . . .'

Robbie Fowler

'Kevin was that sort of character, once he made a decision, he wasn't going to go back on his word . . .'

Ray Parlour, *The Romford Pelé* (2016)

In order to qualify for the European Championship in 2000 the English national side, managed by Glenn Hoddle, had to get out of a none-too-threatening group in which they joined Sweden, Bulgaria, Luxembourg and Poland. Consummate when a player, Hoddle had got England playing with a certain style, and was unlucky to see them exit the 1998 World Cup on penalties. But they fell to an ominous loss in Stockholm, ground out a dull draw in Sofia, and only got past Luxembourg with minimum assurance. Hoddle was suspected of certain high-handed, alienating manners with his squad; and his evangelical

Christianity inclined him to some risible beliefs about reincarnation about which he pontificated to the *Times*, so hanging himself in the court of public opinion where few accepted, as Hoddle seemed to, that people with disabilities were paying for the sins of past lives.

With Hoddle gone, England's next qualifier, against Poland, made a deadline by which time a new man had to be installed. If this man was to be English, as was the standard requirement, then there wasn't really a name above Keegan's. The squad had their views, but first among these was the captain, Shearer, who championed Keegan's cause with his usual plainness. The FA made a call, and Keegan welcomed them to Wynyard Hall to have the conversation, approved by Mohamed Al-Fayed, who must have known he was losing a manager but liked to offer evidence of his love for his adoptive country which still denied him a British passport.

Why would any sensible manager already well set up at a good club leave it behind to manage England, a job with the aura of a gilded coffin for reputations? Bob Paisley had never cared to go anywhere near it. Brian Clough might have fancied it on the proviso he could do as he liked, but that was not part of the spec. Clearly the best England could have wished for was Keegan's old nemesis Alex Ferguson; but he, like Paisley, considered it mission impossible. Manchester United, moreover, were on the brink of collecting a treble of trophies – Premiership, FA Cup and Champions League. Ferguson had made his team the standard-bearers of the new English game, after all the formative years and the long pursuit of Dalglish's Liverpool.

Ferguson knew that the scrutiny and the pressure to deliver, irrespective of time and resource, were incomparably high. Glaringly obvious, too, on a football level, was the difference from club management in terms of the sporadic number of games one got, and the loose ties with players from assorted sides. Keegan understood all of this perfectly well from his days as a player – nonetheless he gave no sign of being anything but powerfully pulled to the job, doubtless swayed by the idea abroad in the press that he was the 'people's choice'. He could believe in the idea of a rapport with the fans – that was what Shanks would have done.

In terms of the contractual nitty-gritty Keegan, already committed to one football team but ever the soul of industry, ventured the daring notion that, for four games only, he might run England alongside his Fulham duties. The FA were so set on him now that they agreed, and he was appointed by mid-February of 1999. At a press conference he went out and began earning his money with a show of confidence and exuberance, pledging that while he was in charge the players would sing 'God Save the Queen' with a passion. His tenure began at Wembley with the visit of Poland. After 10 minutes Andy Cole and Shearer linked for Scholes to poke past the keeper, then David Beckham crossed elegantly for Scholes to head a second. Poland struck right back, the England defence looking not exactly zealous. But when Shearer again serviced Scholes it was 3-1 to the England, and the world was right-side up.

By April Fulham had clinched the Division Two championship in some style, en route to a tally of 101 points. Keegan took England to Hungary for a friendly game and looked to be enjoying himself. A week later, while a guest on ITV's *The Sports Show*, he could not stop himself from revealing that the FA wanted him on a full-time basis, and the fullness of his heart on the matter spelled bad news for Fulham. 'Having had it for two games, my heart tells me to take it and if the Fulham fans do not understand that then I have to say, "I'm sorry, but that is the way I feel." I can't be more honest than that.'

Around Craven Cottage the chagrin couldn't quite be concealed. A lot of money had gone into Keegan's contract, into buying players, into the five-year plan. A section of the support rated him a Judas, and though he remained nominally in the job he made himself scarce during the season's finale. On 14 May he became England boss without strings.

In Scotland Celtic trailed home second to Rangers, who secured a domestic treble. Josef Venglos walked, and the Celtic board convened in Dublin to decide on a successor. Fergus McCann, mentally already on his way back to Canada, indicated he had no wish to dictate the choice. His successor as chief executive was Allan MacDonald, a former British Aerospace executive and a good golfing pal of Kenny Dalglish.

Among the board, still, there was a bit of ambivalence. Dalglish was a Celtic legend but a legend elsewhere, as well, and the world knew of his link to Rangers. Newcastle had taken a bit of the shine off his record, too. Non-executive director Brian Quinn, a leading economist and a Glaswegian to boot, was asked to spend an evening with Dalglish, just two 'Glasgow people' together, and to give his sense of Dalglish's intentions to the board. 'I have to tell you,' Quinn duly reported, 'that after four hours I don't know any more about Kenny Dalglish than I did before.' MacDonald would later say that he believed Marina Dalglish's wish to resettle in Scotland was a big part of her husband's thinking. Once Dalglish accepted the deal, he put in an offer on a smart villa in Newton Mearns, where they had moved as newlyweds 25 years previously.

In the second week of June 1999 Dalglish was appointed director of football operations at Parkhead, on a seven-year contract worth around £4 million. Dalglish seemed to do his utmost to make the prodigal's return look like a sensible piece of business, free of excess sentiment. 'I suppose it is like coming home,' he remarked. Asked if he was really making a long-term commitment to Celtic, he replied, 'That depends how long you live.'

His equivocation was, arguably, part of the package as agreed, since coming with him to Parkhead as head coach was John Barnes, from whom he was seemingly inseparable. Dalglish advised the press that Barnes would take training,

pick the team, set the tactics and decide incomings and outgoings; whereas Dalglish would be 'responsible for appointments
at the club, for the soccer academy, the training ground, and
the future development'. Dalglish's confidence about Barnes,
previously untested in coaching, was founded on a familiar
example, namely himself: 'It's a natural progression for John as
he is a magnificent footballer ... Bob Paisley gave me my first
stab at management and you have to start somewhere.' The
evidence Dalglish adduced was that he had liked what he'd
seen at Newcastle when Barnes took the reserves for a couple
of sessions. There was a suspicion that Dalglish offered a sort of
backstop should the rookie Barnes run into trouble. 'At times,'
Dalglish offered, 'we'll have to do each other's jobs to an extent.'

Dalglish's scorn for the sportswriting profession was alive
and well. 'You don't know if he is going to be good or bad and
neither do I,' he responded to one questioner, with perhaps
more candour than was wise. 'But I think I have a wee bit more
information than most people. And most people will have to
sit there and trust my judgement.' Asked if Celtic were gambling on Barnes, Dalglish tried out the hark-at-that levity that
had become his stock-in-trade: 'It's a gamble getting up in the
morning, isn't it?' But by any measure Celtic had taken a wager
on this so-called 'dream team'.

Barnes, for his part, seemed to be assured by Dalglish's faith
in him and in the sincerity of his mentor's plans to get busy with
Celtic's youth academy, plus the occasional muddying of his boots
in five-a-sides. Dalglish found a job for Terry McDermott, too, in
and around the training ground. And so Barnes began to spend
Celtic's money, boldly, on the players he felt he needed: teenager Stiliyan Petrov from CSKA Sofia for £1 million, defender
Olivier Tebily for £1.2 million from Sheffield United, midfielder
Eyal Berkovic from West Ham for £5.75 million.

England's Euro 2000 qualifying campaign resumed with a frustrating 0-0 at home to Sweden, Scholes getting sent off and Shearer spurning the game's best chance. Suddenly, it seemed that second place in the group and a two-legged play-off against fellow runners-up was the best Keegan's team could hope for – confirmed a week later by their 1-1 draw in Bulgaria. A familiar sense of English underachievement was adhering to the Keegan reign, and with his having been in the chair for not quite six months.

On the face of it Keegan had his pick of a gilded generation of young players. In the main, though, they came from Manchester United, Arsenal and Spurs; and leaving aside Shearer – whose place in the side was subject to mounting criticism from the support and in the press – Keegan wasn't close to any of his 20-something picks, most of whom had not been raised to automatically revere a Liverpool and Newcastle legend. Sequestered at the team hotel, the younger bucks were also perplexed by Keegan's convivial card-school style. To Arsenal midfielder Ray Parlour, it felt like 'going to Las Vegas with him for the week. It was all gambling, card schools, sports, race nights . . . He was a lovely man, a great laugh although tactically we were never going to win with him . . .' Even Liverpool's Robbie Fowler was Scouse-caustic in his assessment of Keegan's personal qualities, describing him as 'a bit of a biff when it came to dealing with us. He'd hang around the pool room at the team hotel and try to strike up a conversation, chatting away, but it was like having your maiden aunt there when you're a kid, long awkward silences punctuated by embarrassed chit-chat as you desperately tried to edge away . . .'

Parlour's recognisable concern about tactical naivety, though, was the one the pundits were paying attention to. The English 4-4-2 had always tended to a front duo of big man/quick man, creator/finisher, but no such line-up now seemed to do the business for England. They put six past Luxembourg at Wembley like they were supposed to, but then came another goalless draw, in Warsaw, leaving their play-off hopes in Sweden's hands. The

Swedes came good, beating Poland 2-0, but there were shades of the World Cup qualifiers of 1982, England and Keegan being helped out of a hole they deserved to have gone down. Ron Greenwood's 'Dad's Army' had its analogues in Shearer, Ince, Adams, Wise. In another gesture to the past, their play-off opponents were Scotland. Scholes scored a characteristic brace to earn England a first-leg victory at Hampden, yet four days later at Wembley it was all Scotland, England failing to muster one shot on target, David Seaman restricting their defeat to a non-fatal 1-0. The reward was a place in a finals group containing Germany, Portugal and Romania.

In February 2000 Shearer announced that the upcoming finals would be the last time he would make himself available for England selection. Some thought this an honourable bow to both the gravity of time and to critical opinion. Shearer's detractors accused him of blackmailing his way to a big send-off he oughtn't to be guaranteed – some falling-off for the former hero who had fired Dalglish's Blackburn to the title and England to the semi-finals of Euro 96. Signing for Keegan's Newcastle rather than Manchester United had seemed to diminish Shearer in the eyes of every fan outside NE1. But just as his single-minded pursuit of personal standards, and the surliness that came with that, put Shearer in the mould of Dalglish, Keegan, too, saw qualities in the big number nine that he believed he could trust right down to the bitter end.

At Celtic, John Barnes was also feeling what it meant to lose the backing of a big and vocal fan base. His pricey Celtic team did not get the important results they were supposed to, losing home and away to Olympique Lyonnais in Europe, where injury further deprived them of Henrik Larsson for the season – a blow comparable to Dalglish's losses of Shearer in 1993 and 1997. Celtic then came away from Barnes' first Old Firm game with a 4-2 defeat at Ibrox, where the scoreline rather hid the degree to which Celtic came a distant second.

Better form in December saw Barnes chosen as Scotland's manager of the month, but Celtic was a plc that needed a steady flow of good news, and the picture for institutional investors was looking peaky. Celtic threw away a two-goal lead to lose at home to Hearts, marooning them 10 points behind Rangers. Then in the cup, hosting the part-time plumbers and joiners of Second Division Inverness Caledonian Thistle, they floundered incomprehensibly. Trailing 2-1 at half-time, coach Eric Black suggested pointedly to Mark Viduka that perhaps he didn't care for the cold night air? Viduka, massively piqued, refused to play the second half, which brought nothing but a soft penalty for 'Caley'. Head coach Barnes had presided over unacceptable failure, and it was felt that the experienced director of football operations had failed to offer sufficient guidance to the novice appointment. (As Brian Quinn, now club chairman, would pronounce, 'Kenny did not deliver.')

Dalglish, in La Manga scouting for talent at the Nordic nations cup tournament, got an early flight home for an emergency summit with Barnes and Allan MacDonald, who asked Dalglish to assume the manager's seat. Barnes was offered a chastening demotion that he didn't fancy, and so at teatime it was announced his and Eric Black's contracts were terminated. Terry McDermott, whose usual amanuensis role had looked a lost cause at Parkhead, left by mutual consent.

There was a fair degree of belief that Dalglish could clear up the mess Celtic had gone into, if his heart was in it, but it was on that latter point that doubts persisted. Dalglish signalled that Barnes would, in time, be replaced properly though not by him: 'I am taking over until such time as we find a replacement and it will be done as soon as it possibly can be.' Dalglish also made clear – icily, and uncharacteristically – that he felt Celtic's players had been 'most responsible for results' and had let down his friend. ('Players can gain you results but can also get you the sack.') In short, Dalglish gave off a tired, grudging sense of once more feeling Rocinante's ribs between his heels as he took the reins and raised his shield. What had been a pleasant, familiar office job with occasional kickabouts now promised to be a whole lot more taxing.

Dalglish's first few results were fine, but then Celtic lost to Hibs at Easter Road and at home to Rangers. They lifted the League Cup, defeating Aberdeen 2-0 in the final; but then beating Aberdeen in style had been well within Barnes' reach, whereas Dalglish was setting Celtic up, as per his late manner, in a defensive way that was almost caricaturable, with extra defenders deployed in midfield positions. Still, the support felt the benefit of green-and-white stripes on a bit of silver. But the press and pundits had not been silenced after a generally poor year for Celtic. The club's answer, on the Friday before another Rangers game, was to shift a scheduled press conference to Bairds Bar, a poky haven of Hoops supporters near the Holy Ground, its walls dressed in Celtic paraphernalia and portraits of legends, Dalglish among them. In his modern-day gaffer incarnation Dalglish cut an incongruously smart figure among the usual Bairds clientele. 'I feel pretty comfortable,' announced one of the game's famous teetotallers, adding pointedly, 'I don't know about anybody else.' The atmosphere was as lively as a clannish pub full of confirmed drinkers tends to be, and if the express objective was to get closer to the fans, the corollary was that the press could feel a certain intimidation carried along on fumes of booze.

Dalglish returned to Bairds the following week, somewhat chastened by a 4-0 beating by Rangers, ready to concede that Celtic's points tally, running at 15 short of their rivals, was not 'as much as we'd like'. But when asked if Henrik Larsson's injury was the moment things had 'started going wrong for Celtic', he was snappish: 'Who says it's gone wrong? I don't remember winning any trophies last year.' As for the one that Dalglish had overseen, it would be for the Celtic board to judge if that represented an adequate return.

England warmed up for Euro 2000 against Brazil, Ukraine and Malta, with Keegan clearly unsettled over how his team should line up when it actually counted: 4-4-2, or three at the back with two wing backs, as he had fancied in his latter days at Newcastle? Shearer favoured 4-4-2 with Beckham supplying him from the right, and that was how it would be. But then who would play on the left? The conservative option of Chelsea's Dennis Wise, or the propulsion of Steve McManaman, now of Real Madrid? And who else up front? Liverpool's Michael Owen had the biggest claim, but didn't seem the obvious partner for Shearer; nor was Owen much keen on Keegan's vision for him. Owen didn't want to be playing with his back to goal or holding it up as Keegan was urging. He wanted to be the poacher sitting on the last defender's shoulder, scampering onto balls. There continued to be significant differences between Keegan and his younger stars.

Still, against Portugal the young guns came out firing and in three minutes England led, Beckham given time to cross, Scholes boldly and correctly choosing top right. On the quarter-hour, Owen found Beckham who ran and delivered, Scholes shrewdly luring defenders off McManaman, who slammed the ball into the roof. Portugal, however, didn't buckle. Soon, England's back four malfunctioned, warily dropping deep while Portugal, set up loosely in 4-2-3-1, over-ran the opposition midfield not just with numbers but with movement. Figo sped through the middle, unchecked, lashed a shot past Seaman and retrieved the ball impatiently, as if to say enough was enough. Nine minutes from half-time, Rui Costa was allowed to cross, and Joao Pinto made Sol Campbell look leaden with an adroitly angled diving header. At half-time Keegan made no change to plug the hole through which Figo and Rui Costa had rampaged. Just before the hour, Costa again surged at England and made a lancing pass to Nuno Gomes, given space by Tony Adams, and ideally placed to beat Seaman. It was a lumpen, typically English and ominous end to an evening that had begun with such verve.

Next up was Germany, and it rather looked a case of whether or not England would be eliminated before their support caused them to be expelled by UEFA, after the usual travelling reprobates in England colours were arrested for rucks in Brussels and Charleroi in the run-up to the game. But now Keegan went conservative, bringing Wise in for McManaman. A dull game got some flavour when Beckham swung a free kick across the box that cleared Owen, passed Scholes, and even had time to bounce on its way to Shearer, who placed his header perfectly. Keegan then replaced Owen with his Liverpool teammate Steven Gerrard to stiffen the midfield; Shearer ran down the clock, Ince kicked the ball away; Keown gave a classic English show of stalwartness. It was rather reminiscent of Shearer's Blackburn scrapping for points at Everton in their championship-winning season. In this case, England had just won one game, against a truly poor German side. Still, Keegan now knew a draw with Romania would get England out of the group, their prize a quarter-final with Italy at the King Baudouin stadium, formerly known as Heysel.

The problem, as versus Portugal, was that England were again facing a technically superior side that passed, moved and broke with a rapidity Keegan's team couldn't replicate. Romania deservedly took the lead, but the warhorses Shearer, Ince and Keown rallied well, Shearer levelling from the spot. Then Owen, disobeying Keegan's orders and roaming in his preferred fashion, put England ahead in first-half stoppage time, finishing from a narrow angle. Early in the second half, however, Romania equalised, capitalising on a keeper error. Owen's goal did not save him from being substituted as England again defended deep, scrapping desperately for the finish line. They were all but there when Philip Neville misjudged a tackle and Romania got to nick it with a final-minute penalty. In retrospect it seemed obvious that a Keegan side would never manage to see out a crunch game, as much as the gaffer had committed himself to trying. But Keegan vowed to see out his deal with England, and to soldier on to the World Cup qualifiers.

Dalglish had done his utmost to play down the romance of a return to Celtic, and the fans had taken the hint, things having not turned out so rosy. He was approaching his new day job with gritted teeth, and the supporters were unmoved by his pains on their behalf. They wanted a new manager appointed just as he did, but didn't appear to feel that Dalglish should hang around the office once that appointment was made. When Celtic finally secured the services of Martin O'Neill they knew they had hired a serious football man. They no longer needed two. On 28 June Allan MacDonald called his friend Dalglish to advise him that the board were terminating his contract. The *Telegraph* got wind and reached Dalglish on the phone, finding him to be 'clearly emotional'. ('To be honest with you,' he admitted, 'I'm just a wee bit empty at the moment.') To have been sacked by Celtic was a blow to the heart, but while Dalglish could not conceal that this had hit hard, he clearly intended to take legal advice, having turned down a settlement he considered inadequate to what his severed contract entitled him.

So now it was Celtic whom Dalglish took to court, seeking just under £1 million. In mid-December 2000 he would settle for £600,000 after a five-minute hearing in Edinburgh's Court of Session. The divorce had been done by the book, then. Yet as at Newcastle – only more poignantly at Celtic, where he had worn the colours with such distinction – supporters came away dismayed by what Dalglish had cost them in relation to where he had taken the team. No longer scooping the big trophies, Dalglish's managerial signature seemed to be all about sorting out big pay-offs.

The scrutiny that management brought down on a man's head was never more troubling to Keegan than in the England job, and immeasurably more so in late September 2000 when his mother Doris suffered a stroke at her home in Armthorpe and died in hospital, aged 76. England were just over a week away from a first World Cup qualifier against Germany at Wembley, a farewell to the old stadium as it was readied for rebuilding. It was a low time for the bereaved and emotive Keegan to have to account for football decisions within the restrictive England set-up – least of all his tactical choices. With Gerrard unavailable for selection in midfield, it leaked to the press that Keegan had decided to push defender Gareth Southgate further forward as a container on Germany's Mehmet Scholl. And no one else seemed to like that idea, except the Germans.

Match day was a cold early autumn drizzler, the opposite of an occasion, and England were clad in their heritage-industry costume of red shirts and white shorts, but the gesture looked forlorn. They played nervously and lumberingly, without confidence or fight. A low free kick from Hamann took a disarming bounce and beat Seaman, and this half-baked strike was enough to win it, Keegan failing to produce any game-turning changes at half-time or thereafter. The crowd had long since resorted to juvenile World War II chants, and after the whistle jeers came cascading down the old stadium's rafters – the jeers of a support to whom Keegan had believed he was responding when he took the job 18 months previously. It was all a bitter part of the job, as his predecessors knew well. It was not, however, to Keegan's taste. Typically, he made his mind up quickly.

Entering the dressing room he told Arthur Cox, 'That's it.' Cox suggested he step back a moment. Tony Adams, earwigging the news, also jumped in to urge that Keegan have a proper think. David Beckham got a bit tearful. It was a little reminiscent of the delegation Keegan had formed to talk Ron

Greenwood around in 1981 – also because England had another qualifier in Helsinki in four days' time. But – rather like when he had quit England as a player, affronted by Bobby Robson – Keegan's brooding thoughts appeared to have collected as much around the issue of his own dignity as the team's. The FA's big-wigs descended on the dressing room, first to hear the problem, then to adjourn with Keegan to the toilets where they hoped to find the privacy to talk him round – a hopeless errand. Finally, almost an hour after the end of the game, Keegan faced the media as he had planned, and made his confession: 'I'm not the man for the job. I've not been quite good enough.'

The apparent candour worked for some, not for others. When Keegan spoke of being 'true to himself', of being 'a man who knows when the time's right', of not wishing to 'outstay my welcome', the self-interest seemed clear. Once again, he was saying that he was finished – 'I look forward to a life outside of football . . . I just feel that for Kevin Keegan there is nothing more in football I want to do.' He packed up his things and he and his wife drove back to Wynyard Hall. But Keegan hadn't convinced everyone. While all political careers end in failure, the football hero nearly always gets a better option on deciding the manner in which he will bow out. Keegan had to expect one more chance, at least.

PART IV

21

The Cost of Everything

2001-07

'Not only is Kevin Keegan right up there with the Arsene Wengers and Alex Fergusons in terms of Premiership managers, but he is also . . . au fait with the world of business and finance and the last thing he wants to do is take this club down a road we cannot afford.'

John Wardle, chairman of Manchester City, March 2003

'The teams we are trying to compete with are spending big money and if we are really going to compete with them I don't think anyone is naive enough to believe you can do it without spending.'

Kevin Keegan, manager of Manchester City,
March 2003

Come the season of 2001-02 English football was fat with money, Sky having handed the Premiership £1.6 billion for TV rights. Flotations had hugely enriched a great many big shareholders, at least those who had cashed in quick. The City, however, had reverted to its default scepticism about where the serious money in the game was to be had. No club could hope to see its shares keenly traded unless they were achieving at the stellar level of Manchester United. Newcastle were a glaring example of such a letdown. But so were Manchester City.

Amid the gold-rush mood of the mid-1990s, City had been the laboratory of an experiment by one of their former greats on the field: midfielder Francis Lee, who wore a flashy Keegan-like coat of the player-entrepreneur, having prospered outside of the game by way of a stables behind his Cheshire home and a business making toilet rolls. In 1994 Lee and a cohort of local businessmen bought their way into a majority shareholding at City with an eye on flotation, for which purpose Lee recruited to the board David Bernstein, an experienced accountant and director at the Pentland Group business that had done nicely by their investment in Reebok.

The fans had bought into Lee's outgoing optimism: 'Forward with Franny' was the slogan plastered over his leadership. But he burned up much of the goodwill by sacking a well-liked manager in Brian Horton and installing his old England teammate Alan Ball. City's 1995–96 season was shambolic, exacerbated by the costs of converting Maine Road to an all-seater offer. Yet fortune shone on them come November, when Manchester won the beauty contest to host the 2002 Commonwealth Games, meaning that the city was going to need a big new stadium with repurposing value, for which the National Lottery would largely foot the bill. At a meeting of Premiership chairmen Lee ran into John Hall, who had learned a few things about real estate and councils in his time. 'You've landed lucky, haven't you?' said Hall to Lee. What was to be named the Millennium Stadium would be built in Eastlands, one of Manchester's poorest precincts; but so long as Manchester City were willing to up sticks then that stadium would be theirs.

City, though, were going to need a Premiership team to run out in their premier-quality ground. They were relegated in 1996, thus having to cope with the new facts of football life: lost TV income, and big wages on top of big debts. Alan Ball quit, and his successor Steve Coppell lasted only four weeks before succumbing to the stresses of the job. David Bernstein had to raise £11 million with a rights issue so that Lee could hire Frank Clark and give him a transfer kitty. But in that act City acquired new major shareholders: John Wardle and David Makin, founders of the JD Sports high-street chain, plus furniture businessman Stephen Boler. These wealthy men were big City fans and had plans of their own for the club, in which Francis Lee would figure less. The new moneymen brought another ex-player onto the board, ex-City winger Dennis Tueart, who had done well in the travel business and who now took over the daily running of the club from Lee. Frank Clark failed to lift the team, and Joe Royle came in with just seven matches to keep City in Division One, a forlorn task. Lee resigned as chairman and Bernstein stepped up, Tueart becoming director of football.

Joe Royle was backed, Makin and Wardle underwriting the club's losses and borrowings, and Royle achieved successive promotions only for City to slip one division back again in May 2001. But the City of Manchester stadium was well under way, and the club just needed to get synchronised. Dennis Tueart felt Royle had taken the team as far as it could go, and went to work recruiting his former England teammate, Kevin Keegan.

What was it about newly wealthy cash-to-burn Manchester City that made it so attractive to Keegan? The conditions were amenable, of course. With Bernstein the power on the board, there would be money for Keegan's contract, money for new players, money to get Arthur Cox and Derek Fazackerley in – it was all good weather for Keegan's ever-changing mood. He could perhaps envisage a second try at the Newcastle experiment: the chance to win things this time, and so diminish the legacy of non-achievement on Tyneside and with England. 'I'm not going to put a date on it,' he announced upon being confirmed as City boss, 'but we have to be looking to win the league.' That grand project would need to begin with promotion, but he was starting out with a better group of players – the likes of Paulo Wanchope, Shaun Wright-Phillips, Ali Benarbia – than he'd inherited at Newcastle or at Fulham. City fans were initially wary of the England debacle on Keegan's CV, but his club record stood up.

And Keegan soon had City playing a kind of football that the support could appreciate, after the toiling quality of Joe Royle's teams. They blew away oppositions to win the division on 99 points, scoring 108 goals. Keegan was then given licence to construct a Premiership side, though in doing so City were looking kindly on a poor first season of dealmaking in which, for instance, Keegan had blown £5.5 million getting Jon Macken from Preston. (In June 2002 he took Matias Vuoso for £3.5 million from Independiente, though Vuoso never played a single game.) Other big buys looked at least like money spent on proven ability – defender Sylvain Distin, keeper Peter Schmeichel, Nicolas Anelka from Paris Saint-Germain for £13 million. It was just that for every such competent buy there was a relative misfire: Vuoso, Tyrone Loran, Karim Kerkar, Kevin Ellegaard. Though fans could be forgiven for feeling that the easiest money in football was that earned by the Premiership's many mediocre squad-filling players, it was the agents enabling such deals who were taking the most extravagant liberties.

When Kenny Dalglish returned at last to a job in football after the Celtic debacle, he was on the other side of the game, one that had got a lot busier under the new dispensations of the Premiership. He became Football Operations Director for Proactive Sports Group, the super-agency set up by Paul Stretford, successfully floated in May 2001 and a remarkably attractive investment opportunity for top football managers who had dealt with Stretford on his way up.

Neil Rodford, Keegan's MD at Fulham, had left the club in 1999 to serve as business development manager for the Keegan

Partnership. But in January 2001 Rodford had joined Proactive in time for the flotation that valued the company at £30 million. Kevin Moran, now Proactive's finance director, had a 9 per cent stake of the business valued at £2.26 million. Dalglish had a 3.7 per cent stake and that was near enough a million quid right there. Kevin Keegan, too, had shares in Proactive.

In 2002 Keegan bought Danish defender Mikkel Bischoff for City, the club paying AB Copenhagen £750,000 but a further £350,000 to Proactive, this constituting a percentage of the player's projected earnings over a five-year contract. Proactive director Karsten Aabrink was on AB Copenhagen's side of the deal. In 2005 Aabrink would tell a Danish court he had been unaware City had asked the UK branch of Proactive to negotiate the move. But documents shown to the court indicated that Proactive may have acted on behalf of both main parties in the deal, which if true would have been to contravene FIFA regulations. Keegan, obviously, had made no personal benefit by it other than as a minority shareholder in Proactive. What couldn't be countered was the sense of an inflationary trend stoked by agents, of which a lot of managers had bought a piece.

Paul Stretford had got his start in football by persuading established players such as Andy Cole that he could improve their contracts. Very quickly, though, it had become clear that fledgling talents – unproven youths with the world potentially at their feet – were the greater objects of desire for agents. In the summer of 2002, 16-year-old Wayne Rooney – from Croxteth in Liverpool, his father 'Big Wayne' an occasional labourer, his mother Jeanette a school dinner lady and cleaner – was just such an object. Rooney had been scouted and snapped up aged nine as an early starter in the Walton and Kirkdale junior league. Not entirely 'football daft' – he would tell pals he wanted to be a boxer, and he was certainly built along such lines – Rooney loved the ball, and could make it do his bidding. Everton took him straight away, on £80 a week, and would have started him in the Premier League aged 15 had the FA allowed it. But it was only a matter of time.

Carefully watched over by Everton boss David Moyes, Rooney was first represented by an agent named Peter McIntosh on a contract meant to run from December 2000 until December 2002. But McIntosh's client roster had a slightly faded look, and by the time Rooney was ready to sign professional terms with Everton Paul Stretford had got involved and met with Big Wayne and Jeanette. Subsequently, Kenny Dalglish, it was later alleged in court, made a call to Big Wayne to speak well of what Proactive could offer. By July 2002 Rooney was a Proactive client. Two months into the new season Rooney was thrown into a Premier League game versus Arsenal, unbeaten in 30 matches, and scored an absolute pearler. A fortnight later he announced he wouldn't be putting pen to paper with Everton until a matter between McIntosh and Stretford was resolved. On the face of it, Rooney had been poached, though Stretford would claim to have represented Rooney fully only as of December 2002 after Rooney's deal with Peter McIntosh had run. But McIntosh, together with his associates Dave Lockwood and John Hyland, wanted compensation, and a high-stakes game of private meetings ensued, to which both sides brought progressively heavier teams along for the purpose of persuasion.

Keegan's Manchester City made a hit-and-miss return to the Premier League, but a lot was forgiven by the support come November when they beat Manchester United in style. It was only the kind of result the club needed to be shooting for, though, with their debts running at around £27 million. Keegan had spent £46 million on players in two years – more than any other Premiership side bar Manchester United. He remained a confirmed fan of John Hall and Mohamed Al-Fayed, his view of finance not so far from that of the typical disgruntled phone-in fan: spend all your money you can on players, whether or not it's money you've got. Keegan's avowed master plan was to spend what it would take to build City into a top-six side, so tapping the revenues of playing in Europe. But for all the outlays, that side was not yet built.

David Bernstein felt that City needed a dose of prudence, and borrowed £30 million from Bear Stearns on the promise of future gate receipts, that sum solely to service the debt. He also promoted a frugal finance director, Alistair Mackintosh, to become joint managing director, a move that underscored the sense of rival camps at City, since John Wardle seemed minded to back Keegan's plan of speculating to accumulate. A section of City fans, though, were wary that Wardle would prove indulgent, given Keegan's middling results. The team's fortunes had been up and down, and there was a fear they might emulate Leeds, whose chairman had borrowed £60 million to finance ambitions akin to Keegan's – a plan perilously holed by unexpected failure to qualify for the Champions League, leading to the fire sale of talents such as Robbie Keane, Rio Ferdinand and Lee Bowyer.

In late 2002 Keegan fancied a capture of his own from Leeds, the ex-Liverpool forward Robbie Fowler, a phenomenal scorer though lately injured and clearly not at his peak. Keegan visited Fowler in Liverpool and spent several hours enthusing him with a big-picture vision of City's ambitions. 'You've got to hand it to him,' Fowler would say, 'he talks a damn good game.' Keegan also managed to drop a stunningly misjudged gag in a radio interview, about how the trip to Liverpool had carried the risk of 'getting my tyres nicked and my wheels gone' – a reminder of remarks made in the memoir he wrote on leaving Liverpool back in 1977. This sparked a lot of incensed traffic on the Merseyside phone-ins, and the *Sun* sent reporters to City's Carrington training ground dressed in the black curly Scouser wigs popularised by Harry Enfield.

Bernstein's wary instinct was to make the fee for any Fowler deal contingent on appearances, which wasn't what Leeds fancied at first – but it was what they settled for. Keegan, though, made public his dislike of that sort of manoeuvre. The discord was clear, Keegan believing Wardle should take over the final say on transfers from Bernstein. Remarkably, it was Bernstein who walked. In public he referred to 'a divergence of views on fundamental strategic issues, particularly concerning finance and management structure'. In private he warned Keegan that the need to address the club's wage bill was pressing. In any case City malfunctioned on the pitch, a run of one point from 12 seeing them to slip to 12th place, out of the running for Europe. They were to be redeemed, however, when England finished top of the UEFA Fair Play table, allowing a spot in the UEFA Cup for the highest-finishing clubs in the national Fair Play rankings. That was City – some kind of karmic reward, perhaps, in light of Keegan's famous scorn for cheats. As a managerial achievement it had even less lustre than Dalglish's Cup Winners' Cup qualification achieved with Newcastle in 1998. But, like flukey goals, they all counted – the issue was whether or not you kicked on.

What sort of a person was 'fit and proper' to be the owner of an English football club? Observers had been pondering this question with ever greater perplexity in the Premiership era, since wealthy individuals seeking entry to the game could emerge from a variety of backgrounds, bearing bags of money or promises of same. It wasn't so very strange for a club director or major shareholder to have an insolvency somewhere in his business past: these things happen in business, especially in the pool from which directors were usually drawn. Fraud, however, had to be considered a real problem, likewise the growing threat of clubs being shackled to the uncertain solvency of major shareholders, so enhancing the risk of administrators being summoned. The FA established a finance advisory committee, chaired by the formidable economist Kate Barker, which agreed that a bar on directorship should apply on any person with an unspent criminal conviction involving dishonesty, or who had led a football club into administration twice. This was all very sensible if a bit thin, seeming still to accept there was an awful lot of money that would have no smell whatever its provenance.

The committee would have had nothing to say had its proscriptions been in place in June of 2003 when Chelsea FC was acquired by a trim and sphinxlike Russian billionaire, Roman Abramovich, who had begun his business career in plastic toys, advanced into oil trading, then quite abruptly become richer than a Renaissance prince by dint of his dealings in the post-Soviet world of former state assets farmed out to supportive parties in the golden circle around then-premier Boris Yeltsin. In 1997 Abramovich had taken over the big oil company Sibneft for a bargain price, then trousered the profits of a merger with Yukos. As of 2003 Abramovich had his oil and minerals empire, a big stake in Russian aluminium and had just cashed out on the Aeroflot airline. Thus he had something in his pocket to spend and – with the ex-KGB man Vladimir Putin now holding sway over all Russia – seemed to want a good reason to spend more time in western Europe. Whatever his feeling for football, Abramovich had resolved to buy a good-sized football club, and debt-ridden Chelsea were certainly buyable. It just took a swift meeting with owner Ken Bates at London's Dorchester hotel, whereupon Abramovich effectively waved a hand to pay £140 million and vaporise the club's hitherto frightening debt. Within two months, he had spent a further £111 million on new players.

The case of Abramovich was a feast for journalists naturally drawn to tales of Russia's devouring vastness and the menace of strangers bearing gifts. But for the owners, directors and fans of underperforming Premiership clubs a wholly other sort of fevered dreaming was now being fostered – the fantasy of purchase by a foreign potentate with big dreams of his own for reflected glory in the Premier League, and a share in that league's global brand.

Liverpool FC had never made much out of its dominance of the seventies and eighties, the hallowed years of Keegan and Dalglish. Now the club was jostling rather at the edge of the high-stakes game, trying to figure out how to muscle back in – a galling predicament given its reputation and pride in doing things a certain way. Chairman David Moores had compared himself to Jack Walker: a fan-benefactor, doing everything for love. But after 10 years of Premiership action Liverpool still hadn't won the pot. Moores did not approve of the idea of borrowing against the club in order to spend, but that was now the all-pervasive way of things. Moores came to the view that he should cash out, and that some other party should sully their hands in the world of deficit spending. As of 2003, Liverpool FC was looking for a buyer.

On 20 March 2003, Marina Dalglish, not yet 50, had to break the news to her husband that a routine mammogram had revealed her to be suffering from breast cancer. She would require chemotherapy. The couple put on their bravest faces, attending a Liverpool–Celtic game in the UEFA Cup that same night. It appeared, at least, that the cancer had been caught in time, was not of the galloping variety, and could be fought. A week later she was in treatment. She would undergo a double mastectomy at Aintree University hospital followed by chemotherapy at Clatterbridge Cancer Centre in Birkenhead. On the other side of the ordeal, Mrs Dalglish was the definition of sanguine: 'It's better to have no hair than no life.' 'We got on with things,' Kenny Dalglish would say. 'That's how Marina and I were brought up.'

In the close season of 2003 Manchester City could look forward to moving into the new stadium the council had built. Kevin Keegan's acquisitions policy, however, looked to have been coloured decisively by the example of Robbie Fowler and consisted mainly of picking up professionals more than a shade past their best. David Seaman, really, was near the end. Steve McManaman came on a free transfer but big wages. Claudio Reyna and Trevor Sinclair were soon injured. City's fortuitous passage into the UEFA Cup didn't go too far: Polish side Groclin put them out in the second round. They went from 9 November to 21 February without a league win. Nicolas Anelka was not loved, Fowler rated a waste of money. Spending had passed £51 million, debts around £50 million, and the club was in the relegation shake-up again.

City mustered an away win at Bolton, their first Premiership success in 15 games, then inflicted a remarkable 4-1 defeat on Manchester United, capped by Shaun Wright-Phillips, the main bright spot in the team's season. A 1-0 win over Newcastle in early May more or less assured their Premiership survival, and they limped in 16th. But Keegan picked his moment to declare he would not be looking to extend his contract past the summer of 2006. Many people at the club saw him straight away as a lame duck, first-teamers feeling at liberty to question his authority. Fowler, who had reason to be grateful to Keegan, would note nonetheless that the gaffer had begun 'losing a lot of respect from a lot of the players because he didn't talk to them' and appeared 'as if he was just winging everything'.

Keegan's chief grievance was a familiar one: that the club had shrunk from investing in new players at what he thought to be propitious moments. City, though, had come to its own settled view about Keegan's increasingly phantom presence around the club, his levels of tactical acumen and commitment to the job. It would not spend more to keep Keegan kicking on. Manchester City had the look about it that the England side had not – namely, of seeming to be Keegan's last job in football.

Paul Stretford's Proactive had swelled to the tune of 271 players on its books, to whom it offered a 'holistic' service – managing their money, arranging legal advice and representation, ensuring their palatial homes were regularly hoovered. It had made its name; but in April 2004 Neil Rodford indicated Proactive would shortly change that name to Formation Group, an indication perhaps that the business was feeling a need to shed some skin.

Proactive's brightest star Wayne Rooney had continued on his irresistible way: his first professional deal at 17 worth £13,000 a week, graduation to the England team and a starring role at Euro 2004, the sale of his life story to the *News of the World* and the *Sun*. With a certain inevitability, some messier parts of his private affairs then got splashed about in the *Sunday Mirror*. His eventful summer ended with Stretford negotiating his transfer to Manchester United for £27 million, a deal that earned Proactive £1.5 million.

There was trouble coming down the line, dating from the disputed manner in which Stretford had assumed charge of Rooney's representation, and the desire for compensation on the part of Peter McIntosh and his associates Dave Lockwood and John Hyland, leading to increasingly volatile meetings attended by large and sometimes livid individuals. As a consequence of one such, at the Lord Daresbury hotel in Warrington in June 2003, Stretford complained to the police, and three men – Hyland, and brothers Anthony and Christopher Bacon – were charged with making unwarranted demands with menaces on Stretford.

On the same day that Rooney announced himself in United colours with a Champions League hat-trick against Fenerbahce, the trial of Hyland, Bacon and Bacon opened in Warrington. On 11 October 2004, the prosecution's case collapsed. Stretford, its main witness, had attested under oath that Proactive had signed only an 'image rights' agreement with Rooney in July 2002, so not infringing on McIntosh's arrangement with the player. But the prosecuting QC now advised the judge that Stretford was an unreliable witness, and Rooney's deal with Proactive had indeed been full player representation. It was an admission that Proactive had poached Rooney, and it put Stretford in multiple violation of the FA code of conduct.

In court it was suggested that Rooney had inclined to Proactive in part because of Dalglish's advice to Rooney's parents. The court also heard it said that Dalglish had, as John Hyland's barrister Lord Carlile phrased it, 'a wide range of contacts among dishonest people'. The newspapers were all over this disparagement – though they struggled to name many of Dalglish's 'dishonest' contacts, other than, tellingly, the disgraced solicitor Kevin Dooley. Dalglish had refused to give a statement to police or to testify in court, and so one could only imagine what Lord Carlile meant. But, football being a sport in which its star players were recruited from working-class milieus within which some certain very bad characters thrive, it was natural to suppose that some such bad characters would get to mix and shake hands with sportsmen who made their livings in more conventional ways.

Kevin Keegan was in charge of a Premiership team staffed with quality players, blessed with devoted support and a state-of-the-art stadium. But there was a flat air of underperformance around Manchester City, a dearth of confidence and a surfeit of dissent in the side, underlined by a bad start to 2004–05 of four points from 15, capped by a home defeat to a 10-man Everton. Keegan was plainly out of sorts, and had the look of Dalglish at

Newcastle and at Celtic – a man not truly engaged in the vital business of the team. Stuart Pearce was widely seen as an obvious successor. The next game was against bottom club Crystal Palace, and two Anelka goals gave City their first away win in more than six months. 'I've been buried alive from what I've heard,' Keegan defiantly told the press, 'but I've got a stay of execution.' He retold the tale of Shankly tipping him to play for England and added a gloss. ('I said, "I know I will. That's the kind of person I am."')

Anelka wanted away, though, and come the New Year a £7 million transfer to Fenerbahce went through. In early March a home loss to Bolton left City 12th, and Keegan's remarks gave the sense that he had little to say of City's stagnation except that it was all a great big shame: 'We've got a history of not building on good situations,' he declared. 'We could have jumped into the European shake-up, again we couldn't make that leap.' Days later Keegan left the club, by mutual agreement, with immediate effect. Pearce duly took charge, got the team playing again and very nearly into Europe.

As for the Premiership title: ever since Keegan's Newcastle blew up in 1996 it had been destined only for Old Trafford or Highbury, the Ferguson–Wenger rivalry dominating the game, symbolised by the Vesuvian clashes of Patrick Vieira and Roy Keane on the pitch and the managers' frosty avoidance of one another off it. Their respective styles were bound to jar – Wenger wishing his team to win a certain way, in style, and expecting plenty of possession; Ferguson eager to wreck that composure, have his side break in, induce mistakes and capitalise with rapid counterattacks. In 2004–05, though, at the high pitch of this feud, a new contender cruised past both men.

Roman Abramovich, new owner of Chelsea, had sought to install a big winner as boss – a mastermind who might repay the Russian's millions with instant success. Jose Mario dos Santos Mourinho Felix had made himself a big name in football by bossing unfashionable Porto to the Champions League in 2004, dumping out Ferguson's United on the way. Mourinho had no form as a player but was a finical student of the game, a compulsive compiler of dossiers in his first significant role at Barcelona under Louis van Gaal. His talents were exceptional and he knew it: 'I'm European champion,' he announced at his first Chelsea press conference, as if he'd literally scored all of Porto's goals in the final. 'I think I'm a special one.'

Mourinho's singular presence posed a fresh rejoinder to a certain vintage of English supporter who evidently preferred to believe that the gaffer's job is, above all, to pick 11 good players and wind them up in the old-fashioned way. For such fans, 4-4-2 seemed to be nature's way: 'two up top', one little, one large; two wingers, two midfield battlers; and a hard back four. This had certainly worked for the mighty Liverpool of Shankly and Paisley. Alex Ferguson, too, had resorted pretty frequently to 4-4-2, as one might if one's midfield four was Beckham-Keane-Scholes-Giggs. Even the alleged sophisticate Arsene Wenger set Arsenal up rather similarly. The ascent of Mourinho, though, put 4-4-2 in a box for a while. His favoured formation was about midfield superiority: a 4-3-3 set-up that could even look like 4-1-2-3, but gave Chelsea the advantage of an influential extra man – Claude Makelele – in the middle of the park.

Sportswriter Jonathan Wilson, author of the widely admired history of tactics, *Inverting the Pyramid*, would lament a continued English unwillingness to see that formation is not secondary in football but, rather, 'the only thing that's important'. Keegan, for all his success in the game, seemed a byword for such intransigence. 'Everyone knows the way we play,' he had said blithely while England boss. 'We like to get down the wings and get in crosses for our front men, and as long as I'm in charge I hope we always will.' He appeared simply uninterested in any kind of harder thinking about the game. Thus at the low ebb of his time at Manchester City – as Oliver Kay of *The Times* reported in April of 2004 – Keegan's poorly performing squad had demanded that the gaffer take them for extra training, and additional 'work on set-pieces and on the team shape', elements the players felt to have 'been undermined by a laissez-faire attitude'. In the new era of Mourinho such an attitude seemed slipshod at best; and, at worst, antediluvian.

The site of Keegan's lingering ambitions shifted to Soccer Circus, the long-standing business wheeze of his own devising that he envisaged as 'the world's first interactive football attraction', and 'the next generation of the leisure centre'. On paper it was a perfectly fun proposition for youngsters who fancied a game that involved smashing a football around for electronic points. Like a PlayStation challenge brought to life, Soccer Circus would have its 'Training Academy' test of skill, its simulated match-day 'Powerplay' with pretend roar and floodlight glare, and personalised player video and statistics to boot. But research, development and delivery had eaten up years and money, and Keegan was personally in the hole for a fair bit of it, having found private investment not easy to come by. One party that did get involved was the devolved Scottish government, which awarded Keegan's company £250,000 from its Regional Selective Assistance grant that made possible the first Soccer Circus site, to be hosted in the hangar-like Xscape facility within a vast regenerated retail park complex in Braehead, Govan – Dalglish's old patch, and Alex Ferguson's. If not perhaps the dream location, it meant that Soccer Circus was up and running and selling tickets in Glasgow as of September 2006.

Keegan plunged into his business with both feet, not just owner but host, donning a green-and-yellow branded shirt for visibility, buzzing about, giving tips to the kids and signing footballs, serving drinks to the corporate types at the licensed facility he had, perhaps inevitably, named 'Shankly's Bar'. Shankly's face was one of many painted on the wall of the place, too, part of a Scottish Greats mural that also had room for Dalglish. He had his staff on hand, but he was giving it a hundred per cent. Business wanted to be brisker, though. By

November 2006, Soccer Circus was trimming staff and hours. It did seem a slightly queer, dog-eared business for Keegan to have got into, allegedly cutting-edge and yet strangely nostalgic. The modern game, which he had played a large part in defining, seemed to have earned his distaste. When the *Guardian* came to visit in Glasgow he offered a familiar assessment of his feelings from the vantage of self-imposed retirement, though the accent was on the provisional for a change. 'Football is something I really love, but I can take it or leave it,' he told the reporter. 'And I've chosen to leave it at the moment.'

Fortunes could oscillate wildly when the great football clubs of England were bought and sold in a global bazaar. Manchester United had cash in the bank and no debt when in May 2005 the US-based Glazer family acquired the club through a leveraged buyout, despite fierce protest from its match-going support. The Glazers had borrowed £525 million from banks and hedge funds, and they loaded all of that onto the club, then sought new investors via a float on the New York Stock Exchange (having established a new holding company registered in the Cayman Islands).

Over at Liverpool Rafa Benitez had beaten the odds by leading the club to a fifth European Cup in 2005. The Moores family, though, were still of the view that their stewardship could not keep Liverpool competitive. In late 2006 they received a serious and attractive approach from Dubai International Capital, with the promise of money for players and a new stadium, pledges tailored to the support and to public relations. It soon became clear that DIC, too, planned to borrow against their new asset, intended also to sell players, and did not seem rabidly keen to start pricing in the bricks and steel needed to make a new ground. Liverpool's leadership were gripped by misgiving, and in time came a rival bid, from American businessmen George

Gillett and Tom Hicks, which Moores put before the board in January 2007. The Americans pledged not 'to do a Glazer' by loading debt on Liverpool; also that a new stadium would be built 'as soon as reasonably practicable'. The board assented, and David Moores was paid £89 million for his 51 per cent stake in Liverpool FC.

Around this time Manchester City were bought by Thaksin Shinawatra, Thailand's richest man – albeit a man in exile in Weybridge, Surrey, as a former prime minister lately overthrown by the Thai military. Shinawatra had made a business fortune in telecommunications and TV during Thailand's manufacturing-led boom of the 1980s and 1990s, before shifting into politics and striking sufficient voters as the sort of business-savvy leader the country needed, his party Thai Rak Thai (Thais Love Thais) winning a general election in 2001. Aware that Thais love football, too, Shinawatra seemed to take a notion that the ownership of a western football club would be good for his and his party's profile. In 2004 he had made a bid for Liverpool FC, though the pitch was that 'Thailand as a country' would be the purchaser, the government doing the financing. No neutral onlooker could think this entirely above board, and Shinawatra's bid failed, his profile not exactly polished by Liverpool fans waving banners at games that read: 'Say No to Thai Blood Money'. The media had not been slow to scrutinise allegations of corruption surrounding Shinawatra, who was accused by Human Rights Watch of being 'a human rights abuser of the worst kind'. Two years later, however, the board and support of Manchester City were ready to give him a fair crack of the whip. A new manager, Sven-Goran Eriksson, was installed and given £40 million to spend on players.

Since so many of England's famous clubs were getting in step with the new trend in ownership, the question did occur:

what were the odds of a black-and-white Shinawatra, an Abramovich by the Tyne, a Geordie Gillett-and-Hicks? Part of what made those odds long was that in the spring of 2007 Newcastle United had the look of chumps – a club that would fall into the proverbial vat of breasts only to come up sucking its thumb. Ten years on from Keegan's aggrieved departure, despite a revival under the venerable Bobby Robson, they had become Premiership makeweights: a loss-making club with falling turnover, managed by Sam Allardyce, whose teams were made in his own image and so made precious few hearts beat harder. Alan Shearer had retired, and though his number nine shirt had been filled, it was not possible to say that he had been replaced – not even by Michael Owen, who had joined from Real Madrid for £17 million without seeming remotely enthused about it.

Sir John Hall had kick-started the great adventure under Keegan and seen a return of little tangible success but a lot of money. Hall was now urgently keen to cash out of his majority stake in the club, and was travelling down from Wynyard Hall to London to meet with a Malaysian interest, when he received a surprise urgent call from another party. He was met at King's Cross station and driven by Rolls-Royce to the law firm of Freshfields Bruckhaus Deringer, there escorted into a packed meeting room where this unnamed party's financial represent-atives sat ready to frame an offer. Hall would go on to keep his scheduled meeting with the Malaysians, but they insisted on six weeks' grace to do due diligence on Newcastle United; whereas the other party that had shouldered its way into the frame was happy to waive such a right.

The new bidder was Mike Ashley, 42-year-old owner and founder of the madly successful budget sportswear chain Sports Direct. A school-leaver who had built his business from scratch up to the summit of a flotation from which he made £929 million, Ashley appeared to have two objectives in buying Newcastle: the first to extend his brand into the Far East on the back of a Premiership football club; the second to give himself a bit of well-earned leisure at the weekend with his mates, in a football stadium to which he owned the keys. Resolved to this degree, Ashley told the Freshfields lawyer Chris Mort to get the deal done without undertaking lengthy investigations of Newcastle's books.

Ashley bought a 41.6 per cent stake in Newcastle from John Hall's family for more than £55 million. He then launched a £133.1 million offer for Newcastle United, and under stock exchange rules had to make a cash offer for the remaining shares – a stake of around 29.8 per cent belonging to Freddy Shepherd. Shepherd and Hall resigned as directors. Ashley paid off Newcastle's debts amounting to £43 million, cleared its overdraft and loaned the club £100 million on which he waived interest. It was a fast and vertiginous boardroom transformation, and with that much done, Ashley turned his decision-making eye to the football team. He didn't much care for the manager he inherited, Sam Allardyce, on the evidence of mediocre results and a miserable mood among the support. On Boxing Day, as the team were losing 1-0 at Wigan, Newcastle's travelling support had chanted: 'We're shit and we're sick of it.' Knowing little about football but already keen on rubbing shoulders with the fans, clad in a replica shirt and nursing a beer as if to the manor born, Ashley got the picture that very few fans could see a future in Allardyce's cloddish kind of football, and most yearned for the virtues of stylish attack-minded football that they had known so recently. Allardyce's P45 was as good as in the post, though in terms of a replacement the first man Ashley approached was Harry Redknapp; but the Portsmouth boss was not for shifting.

'I got a phone call from Terry Mac,' Kevin Keegan would in time begin the tale of his return to Tyneside, some of its characters familiar from earlier episodes. 'I was up in Glasgow, and he said, "They'd like to talk to you."' Keegan had a second Soccer Circus site on the blocks for a Center Parcs complex near Penrith in Cumbria. But there was no question he could use the remuneration of another Premiership appointment; and this, after all, was Newcastle. McDermott referred him to Chris Mort, now Ashley's Newcastle chairman. Mort arranged a meeting in London in mid-January of 2008 with Ashley and the new owner's good pal Tony Jimenez, formerly a steward at Chelsea, now the director of a small sports agency, and about to be appointed Newcastle's vice-president (player recruitment). 'I quite liked Mike Ashley,' Keegan would recall. 'I thought, "Yeah, this could be good . . ."' Keegan agreed to a three-and-a-half-year contract that would pay him £3 million for the first year, £3.2 million for the second and £3.4 million for the third – so long as he could see it out.

22

The Game in Black and White

2008-09

'Geordie Messiah to be Unveiled as New United Manager!'

Newcastle *Evening Chronicle*, 16 January 2008

'During the continuance of his employment, Kevin Keegan will . . . perform such duties as may be usually associated with the position of a Manager of a Premier League Football Team . . . together with such other duties as may from time to time be reasonably assigned to him by the Board . . . Kevin Keegan will be responsible for the training, coaching, selection and motivation of the Team.'

From Keegan's managerial contract at Newcastle, agreed in January 2008

Keegan's return to Newcastle made for open-goal headline writing, the sceptical sucking of teeth by top-level pundits, and a spectrum of incredulity, perplexity and glee across Newcastle's support. It was certainly showbusiness, the sort of splash Keegan had always loved to make. He was borne on a tide of goodwill through the gold-card executive entrance of St James' Park, a good deal more buffed up and gleaming than it had been on his exit back in 1997. It was match night on the Barrack Road, Newcastle having an FA Cup replay with Stoke to negotiate, and the game had already kicked off, but there were queues of fans pushing through the turnstiles still, having heard the news come down from the mountaintop. Sky, BBC, ESPN – all had been granted standing space by the entrance to wave microphones in the general direction of the Geordie Messiah. 'Kevin, how does it feel to be back at Newcastle for a second time?' shouted one. Keegan, perhaps resisting the instinct to give the questioner his patented 'Behave!' tap on the cheek, offered instead a mildly schoolmasterly wince. 'Third, actually. I came as a player.'

When he met the press for a proper sit-down Keegan said what anyone who knew his record would have expected. 'There is some unfinished business here . . . I love this football club and I don't think anyone would ever doubt that . . . I know what the fans want. As long as they are realistic and patient, we can try to help them have dreams and possibly win something.' Talk of dreams, though, and from the mouth of Keegan, was what inclined the wider football world to scepticism about this second (or third) coming. Keegan's absence from the game had been three and a half years, only half the length of his post-playing sojourn in Marbella, and yet this time the sense of the game having moved on without him felt critical, somehow.

If a new manager very often brought a short-term change of fortune with him, Keegan got no such luck, as if the fates had decided there were no further stocks of romance left for him at Newcastle. His first game was a dire home draw with Bolton, then a 3-0 loss to Arsenal brought back memories of all the failings of his first managerial stint, Newcastle players visibly having no clue whom they should pick up at free kicks or corners.

During the negotiation of Keegan's terms it had been mentioned to him that the club intended to appoint a director of football, and a few names had been bandied around. At the end of January the club made that appointment in Dennis Wise, who quit the management job at Leeds for this new role, defined as executive director (player recruitment), with his friend Tony Jimenez as his deputy. The divergence of views on the wisdom of the appointment would get sharp: Keegan would always maintain that he never believed he would be working under Wise at Newcastle. But on the matter of who had the casting vote with regard to the recruitment of a player, Wise put it in print for the fans that Keegan had 'the final word and then no one else. I'm not gonna do things like bring players in behind his back.'

It was a problem for Keegan's authority, still, that he couldn't seem to buy a win. Newcastle were hammered at Aston Villa, then by Manchester United at St James', where Blackburn turned them over, too, Newcastle hurling all resources at a late winner only to concede a loser as a consequence of abandoning their defensive posts. The idea that Keegan might have returned to Newcastle to take them down a division had a dismaying look for any neutrals with fond memories of his 1990s side. Keegan's salvation came in the return to fitness of Mark Viduka, giving him a big battering forward to play with, alongside the pacier options of Michael Owen and Obafemi Martins. Keegan hit on the tactical stroke of playing all three, and results turned around, wins over Fulham, Spurs, Reading and Sunderland lifting the club out of the long winter's dolour into a version of the old Keegan wonderland.

Keegan had cheered everyone up as only he could yet, as in the last days at Manchester City, he looked a lot less cheery in himself. A particular sickener for him was the loss of a transfer target in Croatian international Luka Modric. The Dinamo Zagreb duo of Zdravko and Zoran Mamic travelled to Newcastle and met with Keegan, Wise and Jimenez. They remembered Keegan as a player, and Keegan could jest with a few Croatian curse words and memories of his old Hamburg muckers Branko Zebec and Ivan Buljan. But Newcastle were low bidders – Modric was not judged by Keegan's colleagues to be worth that much of Ashley's money – and Keegan couldn't disguise his frustration. The idea that any top player would come to Newcastle again having had a picture painted for them by King Kev was evidently fanciful.

With Viduka crocked again, Newcastle ended the season with a couple of defeats, and Keegan used his last press conference before the holidays to give a downbeat assessment of the team's status: 'In my time Newcastle will not be in the Champions League. I do not want to mislead the fans. You'd be mad in my position to say we'll get in the top four next season. The gulf is too big. I can say we will be trying to get fifth and win the other league that is going on in the Premiership. We should make a fist of it next season, provided the owner backs me – which there is no proof of yet. But I have no reason to doubt.'

What Mike Ashley likely heard was a plea for a substantive transfer kitty. But with relegation fears dispelled, Ashley's main feeling seemed to be a grim resolve to stop Newcastle bleeding his money, to get the club on a footing he could understand and that worked to his advantage. Chris Mort hosted 'showdown talks' between Ashley and Keegan in his London office, but the following month Mort quit as chairman to return to his former employment in the law; and as Mort's successor Ashley appointed Derek Llambias, previously a director of London casinos.

Newcastle began the new season in decent nick, drawing at Old Trafford, beating Bolton, and Coventry in the League Cup, with a hardly unexpected loss at Arsenal. But with the close of the transfer window at hand, Keegan was not getting any of the players he coveted. On 30 August 2008, Wise called him to report that he had a fellow worth taking on loan, a Uruguayan named Ignacio Gonzalez. Keegan had never heard of Gonzalez and was none the wiser after an internet search, though Wise referred him to a few YouTube clips. Keegan, though, thought this a poor basis on which to sign a player. In his playing days, the era of Geoff Twentyman at Liverpool, scouting had been done by an intelligence network, a map, and serious mileage on the clock. Now it was video clips, unseemly clusters around the same untested talents, agents holding the cards in undignified auctions. When pressed, Wise explained that the Gonzalez loan would, in essence, be a 'commercial deal' – a favour to the player's representatives, so that they might send more and better talent Newcastle's way in the future. Gonzalez, meanwhile, was not really expected to play, though he would cost the club £1 million in wages over a year's loan.

Keegan weighed up what this arrangement boded for his management of Newcastle and indicated his wish to resign. It was the opposite of what he thought the brochure had promised. Derek Llambias sought to persuade him to stay, but could not say there would be no more 'commercial deals'. And so Keegan walked out, away from football for the final time, leaving Newcastle to discover how many top players could be lured to Tyneside by the dream of playing for Mike Ashley, or Dennis Wise, or Tony Jimenez, or the man Ashley would hire as Keegan's replacement, Joe Kinnear. In a line-up with such characters, whatever the mess Newcastle had got into, there was no one who would seriously pick out Keegan as the party at fault.

In the manner of Dalglish when sacked by both Newcastle and Celtic, Keegan was circumspect for a while on account of legal proceedings afoot: a claim on his part for constructive dismissal, to be settled before the Premier League arbitration tribunal. The burden was on Keegan to show a material breach of his contract by Newcastle, so leaving him with no reasonable course but to quit. Keegan argued there had been an agreement that he would have final say on buying players, though this wasn't explicitly stated in the contract. Newcastle's view was that Keegan had been made aware the club would be operating within a 'continental' structure whereby the director of football made that final decision. Again, though, this had not been written down.

The tribunal came down to the view that if Keegan's contract had not expressly said he would control transfers, nor did it say that he wouldn't; but that deciding which players were recruited was to be assumed as a part of the manager's job, whatever Newcastle's pretensions to continental sophistication. The tribunal also noted that Joe Kinnear had been given final say on transfers within the same structure, and could hardly be said to know players better than Keegan. Thus, in October 2009, the tribunal recognised the Gonzalez loan deal as breach of contract, found in favour of Keegan and ruled that Newcastle owed him £2 million plus interest in compensation. Ashley was by now so reviled that the ruling was largely welcomed by fans who suspected Keegan had more feeling for Newcastle United in his spit than Ashley and his associates could summon between them.

Victory, then, for Keegan; but not such a lot, really, to cheer about. When he was at liberty to speak of his time in the court of King Mike, Keegan did so in tones of real dismay: 'It was a nightmare, an absolute living nightmare . . . If I'd not done that I'd have felt better with my life because of the way it happened and the way I was treated.' The compensation payout was handy, for sure, since by December 2009 the Govan branch of Keegan's Soccer Circus was shuttered and bolted, having failed to drum up enough custom. The larger venture remained alive, with a new Soccer Circus lined up to open in a Dubai shopping centre, Keegan hailing it as 'our flagship attraction'. But this was what Keegan's footballing hobby had come down to, and to many it felt like a poor outcome for what he had done in – done for – the game.

23

The King Is Alive

2009-12

'To be able to bring Kenny Dalglish in the room . . . to have him sat in front of parents as our ambassador was incredible . . . The young kids didn't necessarily know him as Kenny Dalglish the player but their fathers did and their grandfathers did.'

Stuart Webber, former director of recruitment at Liverpool FC

'I think [Mike Ashley] made another mistake bringing back Kevin Keegan. He was yesterday's man, like Dalglish at Liverpool now.'

Sir John Hall, 2011

By 2010 the public profile of Kenny Dalglish was increasingly that of a loyal, wryly serious figure standing at the side of his admirable wife. Following her recovery from treatment for breast cancer, Marina Dalglish had resolved 'to do something to help', founded an appeal, and by formidable efforts raised £2 million towards the construction of a new centre for oncology at Aintree University hospital, which was receiving patients as of 2007. She turned her energies to fundraising for a new radiotherapy centre at Clatterbridge Cancer Centre, and was awarded with an MBE in the New Year's honours list of 2009.

In the summer of that year Dalglish had been offered and accepted a role at Liverpool FC which would give him over-sight of the club's youth academy while also acting as a sort of ambassador for its commercial endeavours. (There was no hiding from the centrality of that second pursuit to the modern game. Manchester United's income from season ticket sales now represented only 12 per cent of their annual turnover of £350 million.) This was all no doubt pleasurable and meaningful for Dalglish – to be involved with young talents, a presence around Anfield, a face at the games, doing the club a good service. Dalglish represented something powerful about Liverpool. In his mind, though, he was quite sure he could yet be more.

By 2010 talk of the Liverpool Way seemed an exercise in nos-talgia. It was a year in which the club were charged £40 million in interest on the debts that the American ownership of Tom Hicks and George Gillett had loaded onto them. But after the club's chief lender Royal Bank of Scotland called time on that loan, Hicks and Gillett were forced to bring in British Airways chairman Martin Broughton, an ardent Chelsea fan, to oversee the sale of the club. Then, in the wake of an underachieving season ending in a seventh-place finish, Rafa Benitez was out. MD Christian Purslow asked Dalglish to get involved in the selection process for a new boss. They drew up a shortlist, and Dalglish came and met the candidates, which can only have been an unusually tough experience for them, facing one of the foremost ex-players and managers in the club's – indeed, the game's – history.

Having weighed the contenders in the balance and found them wanting, Dalglish found he could keep his own counsel no longer and formally put his own name forward to Purslow and Broughton. He was told, however, that what was envisaged for him was a longer-term, back-stage role, the accent very much on player development. Broughton felt Dalglish had been out of the game too long to come back into the firing line of a big Premiership post. In the event it was Roy Hodgson who was lured to the Liverpool job from Fulham, and Dalglish was annoyed to have had his interest spurned. For all the respect implicit in the duties and honorifics sent his way at Anfield, these were just not enough.

Hodgson's tenure got away to a poor start, just one win in eight, including hated defeats by Everton and newly promoted Blackpool. In October Liverpool sat 19th, and looked a negative side with no great hope of turning that around. Liverpool was sold at last, to John W. Henry of Fenway Sports Group, owner of the Boston Red Sox, who did the usual heavy lifting of clearing the debt Hicks and Gillett had brought with them. Martin Broughton moved on, his mission accomplished. The team had got back up to 12th but under the new dispensation it was now Roy Hodgson who didn't fit the business plan. On 5 January, as Liverpool lost torturously to Blackburn at Ewood Park, the travelling support chanted for Dalglish.

Two days later, Hodgson was gone and Henry invited Dalglish to return as manager on a caretaker basis. As with Keegan's return to St James' Park three years previously, it was an appointment that was rocket fuel for the fans and tremendous sport for any football aficionado of a certain vintage. Marina Dalglish expressed her close, personal wonder at the turn of events on Twitter, and with a bit of puckish glee. ('Just a thought! Woke up with Liverpool manager lying beside me! Twenty years since that happened!')

Before he'd had even a chance to hold a training session Dalglish had to take Liverpool to Old Trafford in the FA Cup for an unlikely resumption of hostilities with Alex Ferguson, who inevitably told reporters he wasn't convinced of the wisdom in Dalglish's appointment. On the day there would be no alchemical change of Liverpool's fortunes – United scored an early penalty, then Liverpool had a man sent off – but the team looked better than they had, passing out from the back as if in homage to the 1980s 'red machine', rather than the long-ball game they had sunk into under Hodgson. With maximum lack of romance Liverpool lost the next match at Blackpool, which made for easy carping at the size of task facing Dalglish. But he next oversaw a respectable 2–2 draw with Everton, then the team took flight, winning 3–0 at Wolves with a brace from the unsettled striker Fernando Torres.

Dalglish's first major calls now back in the chair were with respect to a closing transfer window. He moved the clearly out-of-sorts Torres on to Chelsea then broke Liverpool's transfer record twice in as many days to capture two new coveted front men – first signing Luis Suarez for £22 million from Ajax, then spending £35 million on Newcastle striker Andy Carroll. Dalglish had identified certain Shearer-like dimensions to Carroll in terms of presence and power; but in Suarez he was buying a man for the red number seven shirt who could offer the sort of brilliant, transformative element Dalglish himself had brought to Liverpool in 1977.

The trouble with Suarez, though, was one of temperament, made in Montevideo, a long way from 1950s Glasgow. At the time of signing for Liverpool, Suarez was still under suspension in the Dutch league, as a result of a fracas in a frustrating goalless draw with PSV the previous November. In the midst of a gaggle of arguing players, Suarez, the Ajax captain, had made clear his differences with PSV midfielder Otman Bakkal by biting him on the shoulder.

Modern moneybags football had come to be seen as somehow lacking in 'characters'. The top players were supreme athletes, surrounded by courtiers, delivering on the pitch, giving little personality to the fans beyond their packaged appearances in product advertisements. There was precious little drama to the story of Lionel Messi beyond the familiar dimensions of a boy plucked from the slums, his innate gifts intensely hothoused by a retinue of advisors so that the investment would yield to maturity. Journalists struggled to make anything out of Messi's obvious introversion, his boyish love of basketball and a properly cooked Argentine steak. With Luis Suarez, though, there was a little more to bite on, an edge of mania to the young man.

Suarez, yes, had scrapped his way out of poverty in Montevideo, the fourth of seven brothers. His mother had scrubbed bus station floors for money. His father had walked out on the family when Suarez was nine. He hadn't been able to afford a proper pair of boots, a predicament that had seriously impeded his life chances; and at 15 he had seemed set to waste his gift for football with feckless, unfocused behaviour. The cause, however, had been his upset over the loss of a girl with whom he had become deeply enamoured – Sofia Balbi, a bourgeois banker's daughter, whose family relocated to Barcelona. It was a happy reunion with Sofia, whom he would marry, that saved Suarez, by his own testimony.

What marked Suarez as a player – above the fast, direct assaults he could make on an opponent's goal – was his drive to win, which had a kind of furious entitlement about it. If frustrated or impeded in that drive, Suarez could seem shrouded in a sudden fog, behaving in highly eccentric and disagreeable ways. He was a diver, for sure, frequently flailing on the turf after the merest brush of a limb. The biting issue, though, proposed a far bigger problem. 'The adrenaline levels in a game can be so high,' Suarez would explain through the medium of his ghostwriter. 'The pressure mounts and there is no release valve.' He spoke of the forces he could not check in himself as 'pent-up frustration and feeling that it was my fault'.

These were not the greatest of omens. Of course, Dalglish had never had much time for good losers, so Suarez's intensity was a boon in that respect. Moreover, Suarez was every bit as dedicated as Dalglish to his superstitions, his 'magic rituals'.

(He preferred to be last man out of the tunnel, and as a kid he had played with a lucky 50-cent coin down his sock, ever since a good result on the day when the coin got there by accident.) They had that much in common, then. But for all his football intelligence, did Dalglish, nearly 60 and 10 years out of management, have the guile in him to instil better habits into such a volatile specimen of the modern game?

It wasn't just the results but the manner in which they were achieved that spoke of new spirit. Liverpool beat Chelsea at Stamford Bridge, and walked all over Manchester United 3-1 at Anfield, Dutchman Dirk Kuyt scoring a hat-trick, Suarez outshining even Kuyt by his contribution. They saw off Manchester City 3-0 with a brace from Andy Carroll. They salvaged a draw at Arsenal with a stoppage-time penalty, and Dalglish met the disputation of Arsene Wenger with a dismissive hand and a couple of choice expletives. 'In my eyes,' he proclaimed to reporters afterwards – talking as well as acting like a fan – 'we're still the best club in English football, if not world football.'

Liverpool then smashed Birmingham 5-0, Newcastle 3-0, Fulham 5-2 – Maxi Rodriguez notching hat-tricks in the first and third of those. It had been a few free-flowing, attack-minded months for Dalglish's side, Rodriguez in particular seeming to flourish alongside Suarez. And it looked like a triumph of the old Liverpool virtues – pass and move, possession, supply lines from defence to attack. Liverpool climbed from 12th, and on the penultimate match day they had a shot at European qualification if they beat rivals Spurs at Anfield. But Tottenham were the better side, whereas Liverpool looked a lesser team with the high-priced Carroll, who missed the sort of chance he was meant to bury, and whose target-man presence looked less conducive to the pass-and-move ethos. One down at half-time, Dalglish even swapped attire from a tracksuit to the lucky suit worn in the last winning run; but the recourse to magic didn't stop Spurs scoring a second.

Still, Liverpool finished sixth and John Henry gave Dalglish a three-year-deal contract, also to his assistant Steve Clarke who had shored up the defence without deterring attack. To the fans Steven Gerrard gave a statement that sounded like a fan: 'Kenny has lifted the place, the supporters, the players and everyone connected with the club and now we can all look forward to a bright future.' That was the upbeat gloss. The thrill of the hero's return couldn't last, and Dalglish pointed out as much himself in a hastily revised ending to the paperback of his memoir *My Liverpool Home*: 'That romance is gone now . . . It is only right that I be judged solely on results.'

Serious work lay ahead. John Henry knew baseball: his regime had revived the Red Sox, 'sleeping giants', to attain glory once more. Henry also knew sabermetrics, or 'moneyball', the statistical means of ruling on player acquisition and selection, and for that purpose had hired Frenchman Damien Comolli as director of football while Hodgson was still in charge. Henry was trusting Dalglish to replicate Red Sox success in English football by the recruitment of value-for-money players statistically proven to contribute to more goals scored and fewer conceded.

Dalglish, though, was steeped in an older tradition. How could statistics express the things that a football brain could accomplish off the ball, the cleverness of movement and astute positional sense? Dalglish's mindset was well drawn by the sportswriter Michael Calvin in his study of scouts, *The Nowhere Men*: 'Dalglish had been brought up to believe in the subjective judgement of a football man's eye and the timeless quality of peer recognition.' (Calvin also quoted Dalglish's terse response to one sabermetrics devotee in his team: 'At this club we rely only on our eyes and our ears.')

In the close season Dalglish spent big and spent British, rather as he had done in 1987 and again over a couple of years at

Blackburn. It wasn't moneyball he was playing by any measure. He pointedly paid the premium for homegrown talent: £20 million for winger Stewart Downing, £16 million for midfielder Jordan Henderson, £10 million for central midfielder Charlie Adam. Having backed Dalglish to the tune of £113 million, John Henry declared before Liverpool's 3-3 friendly draw with Valerenga of Norway that anything other than Champions League football would be a 'major disappointment'.

Dalglish looked to be building a familiar Liverpool 4-4-2, one wide man tucking in, the other foraging forward. Downing, though, was a rival to the recently inspirational Rodriguez down the left. Henderson was accommodated unusually on the right, vying with Kuyt. A win over Everton, goals from Suarez and Carroll, gave them 13 points from seven games. At Anfield on 15 October they hosted Manchester United and welcomed Gerrard back from injury. The game finished 1-1 but in the changing room Damien Comolli had a query for Suarez. Around the hour mark, Suarez had fouled United's Patrice Evra and a few minutes later Evra came looking for Suarez at a corner, chiding him in Spanish about the foul. There was an exchange. Suarez would attest that the worst thing he had said – to which he thought nothing, based on the place and the game whence he came – was 'Por qué, negro?', 'negro' being, in Spanish, a culturally frictionless reference to a physical characteristic such as stature or hair. Suarez insisted he hadn't meant to be racist, though he'd clearly intended Evra to be on his way. But Evra was alleging a different story, that during an acrimonious exchange initiated by himself, Suarez had sought to denigrate him with reference to his skin colour. It was going to be a matter for football's disciplinary authorities to review.

In early November Liverpool played a goalless draw with recently promoted Swansea, sitting just one place above the Welsh side despite the club's colossal outlay on players. Liverpool were poor – Dalglish's words – and outplayed for long stretches, while Swansea, a credit to their manager Brendan Rodgers, were pacey and passed the ball around the way Anfield liked to see it done. Conversely, the support's lack of regard for Carroll or Henderson was getting very marked. A fortnight later the FA announced it would charge Suarez over the Evra incident with 'abusive and/or insulting words and/or behaviour contrary to FA rules'. Liverpool retorted that Suarez would plead innocent and the club would 'remain fully supportive' of him. One month on, and following a seven-day hearing, the FA banned the player for eight matches and imposed a £40,000 fine for having used 'insulting words including a reference to Mr Evra's colour'.

An independent regulator, then, had considered the matter carefully and decided Suarez had been abusive and insulting, if not explicitly racist. Probably the least painful option was for the player and the club to put up their paws on that point and press on towards the goal of letting their football do the talking. There was no easing Liverpool's niggle that a disputed complaint by a Manchester United player had been upheld. But there was no reason to assume the judgement stained anyone's reputation. Suarez had certain problems with both his mouth and his temper that needed to be addressed. Liverpool Football Club did not have immunity to such infections.

Instead, Suarez was going to pour a load of cement around his position, with Dalglish and the club right alongside him. Liverpool issued a statement claiming to be 'very surprised and disappointed' by the FA's ruling. Dalglish upped the rhetoric within 90 characters on Twitter: 'This is the time when @luis16suarez needs our full support. Let's not let him walk alone.' The following evening Dalglish's players ran out to warm up against Wigan wearing Spartacus-like tee-shirts that bore Suarez's image, name and number. Facing the press Dalglish wore one of these shirts, too, a strange reunion with the number he had distinguished. But such was his customarily fierce loyalty, to his players and to Liverpool, for which Suarez was grateful. 'They will not divide the football club,' Dalglish asserted to reporters, 'no matter how hard they try.' Who, though, were 'they' and what was the grist of their anti-LFC agenda? Possibly the enemy had many faces, but in the way that Liverpool had painted Evra as an unreliable witness one could sense an affront in Manchester United having been the catalyst of the affair.

In returning to management Dalglish had renewed the terse rivalry with Alex Ferguson. The longer and far more pronounced antipathy between Old Trafford and Anfield seemed stronger than ever, and while Ferguson had helpfully tried to adduce some historical reasons, it was hard for any serious observer to see past the old familiar fan-base dispute over top-dog status and bragging rights, based on some imagined but inherent superiority, as unimprovably spoofed by the satirical *Onion* website in 2001. ('[O]ur cities are rivals and have been for quite some time. Your confidence in your team is high, but rest assured, you will suffer humiliation when the sports team from my area defeats the sports team from your area.') But the game Dalglish had returned to was United's to a large degree, and as a Liverpool man he couldn't quite tuck in a resentment.

A proper run to the end of the year had taken Liverpool to fifth and into contention for Champions League football. They were due at Old Trafford on 11 February, the fixture assuming even more import than usual. This was the moment when the implacable Liverpool side Dalglish had graced in the early 1980s would have got in gear and motoring, all the way to the title. But in the cold of the winter of early 2012 the contemporary version of Liverpool came apart.

As things fell, Liverpool first ran into United again in the FA Cup in late January, and knocked them out of the competition. Evra was jeered and booed by the home support, and Dalglish was unbothered. ('The fans are entitled to support their team.

I've got no problem with that and if there's a bit of banter between the teams, that's brilliant. I don't think there was anything untoward.') As well as being in the draw for the fifth round, Dalglish had steered the team to the League Cup final. But the Premiership form record was looking spotty.

Dalglish welcomed Suarez back for a draw with Tottenham, and made sure everyone was reminded of his and the club's concrete opinion. ('He should never have been out in the first place.') Then came the visit to Old Trafford, for which a piece of pre-match theatre had been carefully contrived, such that the players would shake hands down a line-up. But Suarez, having indicated assent to the plan in advance, then shirked Evra's extended hand, leading Evra to clutch at Suarez's arm and appeal in the direction of the authorities. The foul-tempered contest that followed was won by two goals from Wayne Rooney, and when Dalglish was queried afterwards by Sky reporter Geoff Shreeves he expressed surprise about Suarez's snub of the hand-shaking rigmarole.

> SHREEVES: Do you think you have to take a serious look at his refusal to shake his hand and the way it set the tone?
> DALGLISH: I think you are very severe and I think you are bang out of order to blame Luis Suarez for anything that happened here today, right. I think predominantly that both sets of fans behaved really well. They had a bit of banter between each other, no problem, right. How many bookings were there? End of story.
> SHREEVES: Kenny, no, I'm not talking about the fans.
> DALGLISH: What do you mean, 'no'? I can go anytime I want.

Such conduct no longer seemed like a plausible version of the Liverpool Way as updated to modern times. If Dalglish did not see what the fuss was about, or otherwise refused to, John W.

Henry saw it quite clearly from his perspective. Both Suarez and Dalglish ended up issuing formal apologies. The drawn-out nature of the whole affair had left a residual impression, and Lord Ouseley, head of the Kick It Out anti-racism campaign, gave an especially swingeing quote to BBC Radio 5 Live: 'The brand of Liverpool is built on success and dignity but it has been damaged, particularly by Kenny Dalglish's behaviour during the past few months.'

There was no doubting Suarez's worth on the pitch, but he had needlessly led the club into some turbulence, and triggered Dalglish's defensive instincts in the most unhelpful form. As badly as Kevin Keegan's return to Newcastle under Ashley had turned out, Keegan had only won sympathy for how he handled intolerable situations. In his return to Liverpool, though, Dalglish seemed at times to be the manufacturer of such situations. Adversity could conceivably have helped to bond the squad, but the team's form was declining, the formation rarely settled – worst of all a 4-4-2 like Newcastle's, the ball wide and into the box as soon as possible – and the priciest buys weren't delivering.

The Carling Cup was their consolation prize, as they scraped past Cardiff City on penalties, but it had taken the introductions of the relative veteran Craig Bellamy for Henderson, and Kuyt for Andy Carroll, to turn a game Liverpool might have lost in normal time. It was their first silverware in six years; and at Anfield prior to kick-off against Arsenal, Gerrard brought out the cup in red-and-white ribbons, but he didn't appear madly elated. Liverpool lost the game that followed, were beaten at Sunderland, blew up at QPR after leading 2-0 (shipping three goals in 13 minutes against a side that had not won since January), and were beaten at home by Wigan. The nadir was reached with a loss at Newcastle, who were looking better bets than Dalglish's side for a top-four finish. Carroll, who had an especially bad game, derided throughout by the fans of his former club, was substituted 10 minutes from time and fired a few choice words at Dalglish akin to what the gaffer had given Arsene Wenger a year before. This was now Liverpool's worst run since 1953. Carroll recovered with a brave performance to get them through an FA Cup semi-final against Everton but they lost the big Wembley occasion to Chelsea, playing well only when two goals behind, and for only half an hour at that.

Dalglish was stuck in the new bind. His name and stature were insufficient. The results just weren't there. In eighth place Liverpool had finished 37 points behind champions Manchester City, half as many again from a Champions League place. Dalglish went to the US to discuss the situation with John Henry, and came home with his P45.

'Liverpool Football Club have sacked Kenny Dalglish,' wrote *Bleacher Report* blogger Karl Matchett on 16 May 2012. 'The sentence perhaps needs reading more than once to make it clear, absolutely and unequivocally crystal clear, that one of the world's biggest football clubs have actually fired their most revered, loved and loyal servant.' In their parting statement Henry's Fenway Group declared of Dalglish, 'He is, in many ways, the heart and soul of the club. He personifies everything good about Liverpool Football Club.' It was a curious position in which to be found: dispensing with 'the heart and soul' of your business. Was Dalglish, after all his contributions to the Anfield trophy room, to be judged as wanting now because of a season that yielded a solitary trophy? That was still one more trophy than Bill Shankly managed from 1966 to 1970, when the Liverpool Way was born. But that was then and this was now, a long time later; and the new way of doing things had done for King Kenny.

24

Unfinished Business

2013-17

'[T]he best part of your footballing life, definitely, is playing. The managing side or the coaching side . . . is only a poor substitute.'

Kenny Dalglish, July 2001

'After playing football, there's nothing like it again. Management is a pale attempt to hang on to the excitement.'

Kevin Keegan to Stuart Jeffries, *Guardian*, 2011

There can be no hard and fast rule on the likelihood of ex-footballers succeeding as football managers in correlation to the standard they attained on the pitch – be that great, good or indifferent. Johan Cruyff, Franz Beckenbauer and Pep Guardiola, clearly, made the transition with aplomb; Bobby Charlton, Diego Maradona, Lothar Matthaus, very much less so. Conversely, Alex Ferguson, exemplar of the modern boss, only got so far as a player, albeit further than Arsene Wenger or Jose Mourinho.

The special luminosity of having been a supreme player means that Kevin Keegan and Kenny Dalglish will always be greater footballing figures than Ferguson. Yet in the period of years when the three men vied with each other from the dugout and the technical area, there was no question that Ferguson had the upper hand – the steeliness to shape proceedings on the pitch to his will. In this respect, arguably no one in football has done it better than Ferguson. Keegan and Dalglish, driven winners and great haters of defeat, lasted long enough in the game both to be seen off by 'Fergie', who now writes books and delivers lectures at Harvard on 'success and staying power'.

It does seem clear that in modern football the former player requires a drive to succeed equivalent to their playing days and also to be a properly hard thinker about the sport. Kevin Keegan's proud public insistence – even on the very days when he was paraded as new manager of some top club – that he doesn't especially study football or footballers in his spare time says nearly everything about his traditionally English managerial gifts (a horse sense for playing quality, and an ability to motivate) but also his signal deficit in key areas (the sharp edge of thinking on formation and tactics).

Kenny Dalglish's football intelligence is of a different and slightly perplexing order. 'He couldn't really explain why he did what he did,' is the view of Alan Irvine who worked under Dalglish at Blackburn and Newcastle. 'He thought it was simple, but he was a genius. Kenny knew players. He knew the fine details about their habits. He was fascinating because his knowledge was almost unstructured.' The net effect of this – tired clichés about Dalglish's Glaswegian accent aside – was that as a manager he sometimes needed a sort of interpreter; as, perhaps, with the Liverpool system he inherited, or the orderly Ray Harford at Blackburn.

Restored to Liverpool in 2011 Dalglish got Liverpool playing again in varied ways, intelligently conscious of the opposition. But when results declined it seemed unhappily clear that some of Dalglish's priciest buy-British purchases – Carroll and Downing spring to mind – put the team in a poorer shape when they started. And while in Luis Suarez Dalglish had the benefit of bossing another supreme player clad in a red number seven, he had no means of managing Suarez's culpable volatility other than by resorting to a default position, rehearsed since Heysel, as defender and standard-bearer of Liverpool Football Club. He looked exposed, somehow out of time; and not because of his seniority per se (Ferguson, Wenger and Redknapp, managers who finished ahead of him that season, were also older) so much as the years spent out of the game, and the still-burning single-mindedness that had, allied to his genius, made him the player he was.

Nobody, surely, would have blamed Dalglish for harbouring a little bad blood towards the owners of Liverpool FC after his dismissal in 2012. Could he forgive them? Sooner ask if there was blood in his veins. In October of 2013 John Henry invited Dalglish onto Liverpool's board of directors, restoring the dignities – non-executive and ambassadorial – he had enjoyed before taking charge again. This restitutive role had been keenly backed by the man who succeeded him, the assured Northern Irishman Brendan Rodgers. 'When the call came,' Dalglish made it known, 'I had no hesitation.'

And so Dalglish was a face once more at Anfield, a living and very presentable link to still not-so-distant glories. Rodgers' team thrived, and just before Christmas that year the TV cameras caught Dalglish's delight from the stands when young Jon Flanagan – whom he nurtured during his second stint – scored Liverpool's fourth in a battering of Spurs. At the annual commemoration of the Hillsborough disaster at Anfield the following April, the 25th such gathering, Rodgers made an elegant speech in tribute to his predecessor, whom he described as 'an example to us all'. The attendees rose in a standing ovation, while Dalglish remained seated and looked to be keeping a close hold on his emotions. A few weeks later Rodgers' Liverpool side damn near won the Premier League, coming so close they grazed it with their fingers; but down at the wire the crucial results just couldn't be secured, and so it was second place. But then Liverpool FC was a club that over time had, in the words of Yeats, been 'bred to a harder thing than triumph'.

The Hillsborough Family Support Group, led by businessman Trevor Hicks whose two daughters perished in the disaster, had long campaigned for a full re-examination of all documentation relevant to the day's events. In 2009 the Labour government set up an independent panel to undertake this work, and the panel's report in 2012 made plain not just the 'failure of control' by South Yorkshire Police, but also the long-standing inadequacy of response to safety issues at Hillsborough and the efforts by police to modify their official record of the day. The support group now called for new inquests, and the Attorney General agreed: the High Court quashed the original verdicts, and new hearings were convened, beginning at Warrington in late March 2014.

In the week before Christmas 2014 Dalglish gave evidence to the inquest. John Beggs QC, representing the South Yorkshire Police commanders, pursued him over certain observations made in his memoirs, such as references to the numbers of Liverpool fans who had sought ticketless admission to the all-Merseyside cup final of 1986. In a fractious atmosphere the coroner ruled that Dalglish should not be pressed over questions he couldn't possibly answer (such as whether or not Liverpool fans on 15 April 1989 had tickets to the match or had drunk alcohol). Afterwards, Margaret Aspinall, another prominent Hillsborough campaigner who lost her 18-year-old son in the disaster, spoke in praise of the staunchness of Dalglish's presentation: 'Kenny's always been there for the families and he didn't in any way, shape or form let us down.'

Brendan Rodgers was unable to keep Liverpool pushing forward at the pitch of form seen in 2014, and in October 2015 he was replaced by Jurgen Klopp, the characterful and

widely admired boss at Borussia Dortmund. Dalglish blessed
the appointment and liked what he saw, most especially when
Klopp's side achieved a stunning comeback against Dortmund
in a Europa League tie on 14 April 2016. Dalglish, visibly trans-
ported by the spirits of a big European night at Anfield, joined
fellow fans in the singing of 'You'll Never Walk Alone'. The following day was the 27th and final anniversary commemoration
of Hillsborough at the stadium, where Dalglish gave a reading
from the Gospel of John: 'Let not your heart be troubled.'

This marking of the date was now felt to be at a fitting end
in part because the second inquest was due to report; and on 26
April 2016 its jury ruled that Liverpool's fans were unlawfully
killed, victims of gross negligence, and had played no role in
causing the disaster. It was a victory celebrated with solemnity,
the word 'bittersweet' much used to describe the savour of it.
That September, the 96 victims were awarded the Freedom
of Liverpool, as were Kenny Dalglish and his wife. 'I wish we
weren't getting the award,' Marina Dalglish commented ruefully, 'and everyone was still here.' Kenny Dalglish observed his
familiar low-key piety: 'We only did for the families what they
did for us, and that was support us.'

It was clear from his remarks that Dalglish still counted himself as a very lucky individual to whom football had given great
things; who had also seen terrible things he had never expected,
and had coped in the way he'd seen fit, just like he was raised to.
Football had carried on, people caring about the game because
they couldn't do otherwise; and Dalglish remained a football
man, finished with his real dealings in the game, but seemingly
at peace with his legacy, which was considerable. In May 2017
Liverpool FC announced that from the following season the
former Kemlyn Road stand at Anfield would be renamed The
Kenny Dalglish Stand, a gesture to the club's 125th anniversary
and an honour surpassing even the gates named for Shankly and
Paisley. Dalglish, inevitably, professed to be 'extremely grateful'
if 'a wee bit embarrassed'.

Kevin Keegan was also in attendance at Anfield in April 2016 when the tradition of Hillsborough commemorations closed. It was as natural for him to be paying his respects as any of the distinguished players past and present who came, and it signalled, perhaps, a revived connection to the club where he made his greatest achievements in football – a connection that had seemed more undernourished than it might have been over the years. The tenures of Rodgers and Klopp had got Keegan praising Liverpool consistently in his bouts of punditry, to the degree that their managerial virtues corresponded to his own: attacking football, passion, obvious enthusiasm from the fans.

Punditry had been Keegan's most conspicuous activity since the acrimonious end at Newcastle in 2008. He had become the lead voice on satellite sports channel ESPN. At ease before the camera, his analyses and predictions were not consistently on the money, but he had plenty of stories and flashes of old fire about him. Asked during a 2010 broadcast to comment on Mike Ashley's continued stewardship of Newcastle and the likelihood of success there, Keegan's even tone made his contempt all the clearer: 'Mike Ashley doesn't know anything about football. That's the first thing. The second thing is Derek Llambias knows even less than him.'

When the gig at ESPN ended Keegan moved to a role with Qatar-based network beIN Sports, alongside a travelling show of talking football heads made familiar in the Sky era. Keegan the entrepreneur remained in business, and wherever he went now he was pushing a new invention, another interactive foot-ball exercise: 'Sokka', a structure of hinged panels designed for a football workout, their surfaces sensitive to pressure and responsive by flashing lights and data display. 'Interactive stuff is what kids want now,' he told journalists, 'not to see an old football shirt of Kevin Keegan's.' Really, the thing was all about trapping and controlling the rebound of a ball one had just smashed against a flat surface – a practice every ball-playing schoolboy learns to love as long as they grow up anywhere near a handy brick wall. It was easy to see Keegan as the small boy who battered a ball against the garden wall shared with Mrs Wild's place back in Armthorpe, Doncaster. But the price tag for a full set of Sokka panels was an unsentimental £100,000, plus a new Mercedes van. From the outset of his career Keegan had been prodigious in coming up with ways to extract revenue out of ventures derived, however tenuously, from kicking a ball around. Stephen Wagg – whose pioneering social history *The Football World*, published in 1984, remains an authoritative work – described Keegan with acerbity as 'English football's first clone – a persona consciously fashioned with a huge audience of consumers in mind'. He had put money in his purse, and many who had come after had done likewise, in ever greater sums, their progress eased by the path that Keegan forged. But 'clone' was just unkind. He was his own man, and there was no one quite like him within football or without. 'I did all the things I wanted to do, I made my own decisions,' Keegan made plain in 2017 to an interviewer who suspected he must harbour certain regrets. 'No, I enjoyed every minute of it,' Keegan insisted, businesslike to the end. 'And I don't look back much.'

CONCLUSION

'After bringing the [FA] Cup home for the third time in 1955, [Jackie] Milburn recalled, the reward [for the Newcastle team] was handbags for the players' wives: the board bought a job lot for £17 and, stuffed with tissue paper, they were doled out at the official celebration event. "Everybody was howking away inside the bags," Milburn later remembered. "There wasn't a bloody thing in any of them."'

Gordon Burn, 'No More Local Heroes',
Observer, 8 January 2006

"'We were driving back from, I think, Birmingham, when Kieron [Dyer] suddenly shouts out, 'Stop the bus! I've left my diamond earring in the dressing room' ... Can you believe it! Can you imagine in my day a player shouting to Bill Shankly, 'Bill, stop the bus. I've left me earring in the dressing room'?" He is wiping the tears of mirth from his eyes. "It's true. Absolutely true."
'Did they go back for it?
"'Did we, ffff," he said.'

Bobby Robson, interviewed when Newcastle manager,
Telegraph, 15 February 2003

It has become a common complaint among a certain generation of fans that English football itself has lost its integrity, even its innocence – sold its soul, if you like. Kevin Keegan, a consummate self-packager, has had no qualms about characterising himself as 'the bridge between that innocent era of Bobby Charlton, Bobby Moore ... and whatever [football] is now'. *Guardian* football writer Barney Ronay put himself in Keegan's party by writing of a 'peculiar sense of innocence that was still in place throughout the 1970s; the impression, however brief, of something transformed but still unspoilt'. Ronay's feelings are in line with previous sentiments expressed by Stephen Wagg who wrote, a little primly, in his *The Football World* of a game 'less constrained than in the early part of this century by notions of fairness and probity'.

For many of us, the golden age of human affairs is a blanket that settled over the world while we happened to be in our childhoods or teens or early twenties. It is bound up with a person's sense of cherished memories, a buttress against the customary hardening of the self in adulthood. This is not to say that football hasn't got worse in some important respects.

The Premier League is a conspicuous product of an age, its invention overlapping with the popular Toryism of the 1980s, its fame and wealth rising steadily through the three Blair-led Labour governments of 1997-2007. The changes it wrought upon the game – in terms of money, management, presentation – are all glaring and have been itemised many times over. Suffice it to note that in 2015 Rupert Murdoch's Sky paid £4.18 billion for the right to broadcast fewer than half the Premiership's fixtures over a three-year period.

Has the standard of football on offer to the spectator improved or declined in that time? In a sense, the question is negligible. This factor of the quality of what's being served has rarely stopped fans coming to games in the past: football is an addictive mania that way. But many formerly passionate supporters do now declare themselves in retreat from the game, if they have not already deserted it. There are a number of recurrent laments.

One is for the loss of a bond or identification between the player and the average Joe, based on a gulf made by wages and lifestyle, and an attendant sense of players as mercenary celebrities only ever passing temporarily through the club colours they wear. But as we have seen in these pages, such a process had begun earlier than we sometimes suppose – before Keegan and Dalglish, before even George Best and Bobby Moore. Possibly, footballing heroes are not quite what they used to be; but the days of Jackie Milburn, the pitman-player, are not coming back. The players themselves simply wouldn't settle for such a constrained status.

The working-class basis of football endures above all in that the working class is where football talent comes from. Middle-class families still just don't seem to want to put their sons onto pitches in such numbers. And yet, the game's rewards are greater than ever. For all the disapproval of the extreme wealth of modern players, football remains a remarkable vehicle for working-class boys to make it big – their salaries dizzying multiples of those commanded by the increasingly middle-class spectators.

At the end of the day, to be fair – as the pundits say – you're talking about gifted individuals pursuing success, and no one coasts their way there. A young person who seeks to be a professional footballer learns competition the hard way, entering a hothouse, blooded quickly, judged from the first kick. Of those who make it to the top, it's hard to expect these rich young men to be apologetic about the lives they have won for themselves. Elite sportsmen are not natural socialists, and it should be counted remarkable if they manage to be well-adjusted human beings. Kevin Keegan has certainly managed as much, but Keegan is the exemplar of a player who always knew what he was worth, and not only where he was from but where he wished to get to.

The Premiership has its unalloyed admirers, of course. How many really wish for football to be back as it was in the 1970s? Mucky pitches, tackles from behind, ramshackle grounds, bristling hooligans? It should not be controversial to say that it's a fine thing for the game to have shiny all-seater stadiums where you can safely take young kids, because these days at a football match nobody, God forbid, dies. Of course, the steep rises in ticket prices have changed the class profile of football crowds, and many will protest that the game has been taken away from its core supporters. A lot of longtime fans have swallowed the new expense where they can, for the love of football. But evidently for many more the price of match day feels like the dodgy privatisation of a former utility: being forced to pay high for something you really need – and such a price to take one's flip-down plastic seat amid the weirdly muted and domesticated atmosphere of the modern flat-pack ground.

There have been notable revolts, such as at Liverpool after Fenway Sports Group proposed a 30 per cent hike on the top ticket to £77, and an increased season ticket price of £1,029. Towards the end of a home game with Sunderland on 6 February 2016 an organised protest saw fans begin to chant, 'Enough is enough, you greedy bastards, enough is enough', before, on 77 minutes, as many as 10,000 rose and exited the ground. The demonstration drove FSG to a U-turn: a public apology and a pledge to freeze prices for two seasons, together with more reduced tickets for young fans.

There may be more such dissent to come. But in the meantime the Premier League can say that the market is working, the product is successful, the stadia full 90 per cent of the time. People want in, and on that basis it's not surprising clubs try to charge more. The problem arises if one still wishes to think of football clubs as embedded in their communities and conforming to the old story of the game of ordinary working people. Going to the match, though, is clearly no longer a defining form of working-class leisure. The working class is not what it used to be.

Historian Robert Colls has written of how 'fundamental shifts in the pattern of work and residence' led to a state from the 1980s where 'government agencies talked a lot about "community" and employed professionals to foster it, but only as a sign that it was slipping'. 'In the post-war years,' *Economist* writer Jeremy Cliffe observed in 2015, 'people felt united, common and responsible for each other's well-being. Now that is much less the case. One can mourn the passing of that common feeling – as I do – but still acknowledge it as a fact.'

Britain has changed greatly since 1945 – even since the 1980s – and we have to conclude that a great many Britons wished it so. Those changes include the breadth and level of formal education, what people do for a living, average incomes, the ways we consume, the lifestyles we aspire to and respect. In the post-industrial cities – Glasgow, Liverpool, Manchester, Newcastle – vestiges of old industries barely poke through the façades. There is little to be gained from expending great sorrows on this deep, wide, willed transformation. The writer Simon Kuper was commendably tough-minded in the *Financial Times* when characterising 'the many laments for the lost cloth-capped proletarian crowds' of English football as a case of those lamenters 'simply mourning their lost roots'.

Still, the language of expropriation and exploitation dies hard and is readily revived, as in 2000 when sociologist Eric Dunning felt bold enough to write of 'the great social invention of soccer' as a cause to be upheld against 'hooligan fans, complacent politicians, and money-driven owners, managers and players'. Who's left on the good side of that fight, then, except for those who style themselves as true fans? True fans will say football is really about the club, and the club is really about the fans. That's also a view that Keegan and Dalglish have been known to espouse; and it remains true that a football club can be nothing without support.

But what the often eloquent and avowedly leftish fans of football who write blogs and fanzines want the game to be is not where Keegan and Dalglish have helped to take it – to the place where the talented worker is remunerated to the level his ability can command at market. If you want football to be cheap and cheerful, there will always be an amateur game to see in Bootle or Blyth. But that's not why most of us watch football, nor is it the style in which any real ball-player wants to play the game. Fans may speak and write articulately and passionately about wanting to defend a culture of football; but the culture of football, really, is what footballers do on the pitch – and rather a high culture at that, when they play at the heights of their abilities. That, too, is the story of Keegan and Dalglish.

ACKNOWLEDGEMENTS

The making of this book was influenced and abetted by three people in particular: the late Gordon Burn, football being one of the many subjects about which he was wise; my agent Matthew Hamilton, who gave me invaluable input and encouragement from the outset; and my editor Ian Marshall, who embraced the idea and offered expert guidance from beginning to end of execution.

I was also greatly assisted by long conversations with fellow football fans, chief among these Mike 'Biffa' Bolam who runs a superb website devoted to Newcastle United, nufc.com. (I should say, for starters, that the comparison of Kevin Keegan's signing for Newcastle to John F. Kennedy's famous speech in West Berlin is one I owe to Mike.) On the subject of sites devoted to clubs I must also pay tribute to the wealth of statistics and reportage inventoried at lfchistory.net and theceltic.wiki. com. I was also much helped by discussions with Dave Woods about Liverpool FC, and with Stephen Murray about Celtic.

Thanks, too, to Lorraine Jerram who copy-edited the text with diligence.

BIBLIOGRAPHY

Books by Keegan and by Dalglish

Kenny Dalglish with Ken Gallacher, *King Kenny* (Stanley Paul, 1982)

Kenny Dalglish with Henry Winter, *My Autobiography* (Hodder & Stoughton, 1996)

Kenny Dalglish with Henry Winter, *My Liverpool Home* (Hodder & Stoughton, 2011)

Kenny Dalglish, *My Life: A Personal Journey* (Sport Media, 2013)

Kevin Keegan, *An Autobiography* (Magnum, 1978)

Kevin Keegan with Mike Langley, *Against the World: Playing for England* (Sidgwick & Jackson, 1979)

Kevin Keegan, *My Autobiography* (Little, Brown, 1997)

Miscellaneous Books

John Aldridge, *My Story* (Hodder & Stoughton, 1999)

John Barnes, *The Autobiography* (Headline, 1999)

Peter Beardsley, *My Life Story* (Collins Willow, 1995)

Gordon Burn, *Best and Edwards: Football, Fame and Oblivion* (Faber, 2006)

Michael Calvin, *Living on the Volcano: The Secrets of Surviving as a Football Manager* (Century, 2015)

Michael Calvin, *The Nowhere Men: The Unknown Story of Football's True Talent Spotters* (Century, 2013)

Tom Campbell & David Potter, *Jock Stein: The Celtic Years* (Mainstream, 1998)

Lee Clark with Will Scott, *Black or White, No Grey Areas* (Mojo Risin', 2016)

Ged Clarke, *Newcastle United: Fifty Years of Hurt* (Mainstream, 2006)

David Conn, *Richer Than God: Manchester City, Modern Football and Growing Up* (Quercus, 2012)

Bob Crampsey, *Mr Stein: A Biography of Jock Stein CBE 1922-85* (Mainstream, 1986)

Hunter Davies, *The Glory Game* (Weidenfeld & Nicolson, 1972)

Derek Dohren, *Ghost on the Wall: The Authorised Biography of Roy Evans* (Random House 2011)

Eamon Dunphy, *A Strange Kind of Glory: Life of Sir Matt Busby and Manchester United* (Heinemann, 1991)

Tony Evans, *I Don't Know What It Is But I Love It: Liverpool's Unforgettable 1983-84 Season* (Penguin, 2015)

Andrew Fagan, *Joe Fagan: Reluctant Champion: The Authorised Biography* (Aurum, 2012)

Alex Ferguson, *A Light in the North: Seven Years with Aberdeen* (Mainstream, 1985)

Robbie Fowler, *Fowler: My Autobiography* (Macmillan, 1995)

Alan Hansen, *A Matter of Opinion* (Partridge, 1999)

Martin Hardy, *Touching Distance: Kevin Keegan, the Entertainers & Newcastle's Impossible Dream* (De Coubertin Books, 2015)

Simon Hughes, *Geoff Twentyman: Secret Diary of a Liverpool Scout* (Sport Media, 2011)

Simon Hughes, *Red Machine: Liverpool FC in the 1980s – The Players' Stories* (Mainstream, 2013)

Simon Hughes, *Men in White Suits: Liverpool FC in the 1990s – The Players' Stories* (Random House, 2016)

John Keith, *Bob Paisley: Manager of the Millennium* (Robson, 2001)

John Keith, *The Essential Shankly* (Robson, 2001)

Stephen F. Kelly, *Dalglish: The Biography* (Highdown, 2004)

Alan Kennedy & John Williams, *Kennedy's Way: Inside Bob Paisley's Liverpool* (Mainstream, 2005)

Dr Andrew Lees & Ray Kennedy, *Ray of Hope: The Ray Kennedy Story* (Penguin, 1993)

Simon Kuper, *Football Against The Enemy* (Orion, 1994)

Joe Lovejoy, *Glory, Goals and Greed: Twenty Years of the Premier League* (Mainstream, 2011)

Kevin McCarra, *Celtic: A Biography in Nine Lives* (Faber, 2012)

Danny McGrain with Hugh Keevins, *In Sunshine or in Shadow* (John Donald, 1987)

Hugh McIlvanney, *McIlvanney on Football* (Mainstream, 1997)

Archie MacPherson, *Jock Stein* (Racing Post Books, 2014)

David Mitchell, *Life's A Ball: Ian Liversedge: The Highs and Lows Of A Football Physio* (AuthorHouse, 2014)

Phil Neal, *Life at the Kop* (Queen Anne Press, 1987)

Ray Parlour, *The Romford Pelé* (Century, 2016)

Ian Ridley, *Kevin Keegan: An Intimate Portrait of Football's Last Romantic* (Simon & Schuster, 2008)

Bobby Robson with Bob Harris, *So Near and Yet So Far: Bobby Robson's World Cup Diary 1982-86* (Willow, 1986)

Ian Rush with Ken Gorman, *Ian Rush: An Autobiography* (Random House, 2011)

Tommy Smith, *Anfield Iron* (Bantam, 2008)

Graeme Souness with Bob Harris, *No Half Measures* (Grafton, 1987)

Luis Suarez, *Crossing the Line – My Story* (Headline, 2014)

Stephen Sullivan, *Sean Fallon: Celtic's Iron Man* (Backpage Press, 2013)

Chris Sutton with Mark Guidi, *Paradise and Beyond: My Autobiography* (Black and White, 2011)

Adrian Tempany, *And the Sun Shines Now: How Hillsborough and the Premier League Changed Britain* (Faber, 2016)

Paul Tomkins, *Dynasty: Fifty Years of Shankly's Liverpool* (GPRF Publishing, 2008)

Stephen Wagg, *The Football World: A Contemporary Social History* (Harvester, 1984)

Paul Walsh, *Walshy: My Autobiography* (Trinity Mirror, 2015)

Ronnie Whelan, *Walk On: My Life in Red* (Simon & Schuster, 2011)

Jim White, *Premier League: A History in Ten Matches* (Head of Zeus, 2014)

John Williams, Stephen Hopkins & Cathy Long, *Passing Rhythms: Liverpool FC and the Transformation of Football* (Berg, 2001)

Jonathan Wilson, *Inverting the Pyramid: The History of Football Tactics* (Orion, 2008)

Jonathan Wilson with Scott Murray, *The Anatomy of Liverpool: A History in Ten Matches* (Orion, 2013)

Newspaper and Journal Articles

Ian Archer, 'Dalglish walks into the seething dens', *Guardian*, 12 February 2000

Oliver Brown, 'Heysel disaster of 1985 is football's forgotten tragedy', *Telegraph*, 28 May 2015

Daniel Chapman, Interview with David Batty, 'The City Talking', *Yorkshire Post*, 17 July 2015

Carl Clemente, 'Gary Gillespie – Best eight years of my life', lfchistory.net

Robert Colls, 'When We Lived in Communities: Working Class Culture and its Critics', in *Cities of Ideas: Civil Society and Urban Governance in Britain, 1800-2000: Essays in Honour of David Reeder*, edited by Robert Colls and Richard Rodger (Ashgate, 2004)

Andy Cryer, 'I played my part in Blackburn Rovers fairytale, says Atkins', *Lancashire Telegraph*, 11 March 2011

Andy Cryer, 'Jason Wilcox on the Blackburn Rovers revolution', *Lancashire Telegraph*, 25 May 2010

Mani Djazmi, 'Rudi Gutendorf: The colourful life of a "foot-balling missionary"', bbc.co.uk, 2 March 2013

Ian Doyle, 'The Liverpool FC players never talk about Heysel – it's as though we feel partly responsible, says Mark Lawrenson', *Liverpool Echo*, 29 May 2015

Paul Doyle, 'John Giles: Small Talk', *Guardian*, 29 April 2005

Sam Drury, 'Remembering King Kenny's domestic double at Liverpool, 30 years on', *FourFourTwo*, 10 May 2016

Eric Dunning, 'Towards a Sociological Understanding of Football Hooliganism as a World Phenomenon', *European Journal on Criminal Policy and Research* (2000) 8:141

Paul Dykes, 'An Interview With Danny McGrain', *CQN Magazine*, 1 May 2016

Norman Fox, 'Money, money, money man – Jack Walker', *Independent*, 15 August 1992

John Gibson, 'Newcastle United legend Terry McDermott on working with Kevin Keegan and Kenny Dalglish', *Newcastle Chronicle*, 9 March 2015

Norman Giller, 'Wisnae whit? Kenny Dalglish's new witti-cisms', *Sports Journalists Association*, 10 February 2011

Daniel Harris, 'The forgotten story of . . . Rangers' 1972 European Cup Winners' Cup win', *Guardian*, 4 September 2014

Stuart Jeffries, 'The Saturday interview: Kevin Keegan', *Guardian*, 25 June 2011

Ken Jones, 'Six-figure wages destroy reason and self-restraint', *Independent*, 8 October 2003

Neil Jones, 'Dalglish: Klopp and Liverpool are a perfect fit – some of the football is a pleasure to watch', *Liverpool Echo*, 17 December 2016

Simon Kuper, 'How a football tragedy redeemed the game', *Financial Times*, 10 April 2009

Joe Lovejoy, 'Moran gets down to business', *Independent*, 21 August 1992

Joe Lovejoy, 'Keegan besieges King Kenny's castle', *Independent*, 13 February 1993

Daniel McDonnell, Interview with David Speedie, *Irish Independent*, 18 April 2011

Colin Malam, 'Why Keegan's class of '96 blew a 12-point lead', *Independent*, 20 January 2008

Nikki Murfitt, 'We will never escape the ghosts of that day: The daughter of Liverpool legend Kenny Dalglish reveals the toll Hillsborough had on her father', *Daily Mail*, 30 March 2009

Eoin O'Callaghan, 'After Andy Cole left, they were expecting a big signing but they got Jim Crawford', *The 42*, 21 December 2015

Ian Ridley, 'Beardsley bears enduring gifts', *Independent*, 26 March 1995

Paul Rydings, 'China wouldn't interest me, says "millionaire" Keegan', *South China Morning Post*, 10 February 2017

Andrew Slevison, 'Second spell of King Kenny Dalglish vital for Liverpool – Webber', tribalfootball.com

Aidan Smith, 'Jim Kerr on Celtic, Toryglen and playing at Ibrox', *Scotsman*, 13 December 2014

Aidan Smith, 'Look back in wonder: Scotland legend Kenny Dalglish turns 65', *Scotsman*, 3 March 2016

Aidan Smith, 'Tommy Wright on managing, bad knees and cup wins', *Scotsman*, 24 January 2015

Louise Taylor, 'The game that forced Kenny Dalglish to resign as Liverpool manager', *Guardian*, 14 January 2011

Simon Turnbull, 'All aboard the Gullit train', *Independent*, 29 August 1998

Wright Thompson, 'Portrait of a Serial Winner', *ESPN The Magazine*, 27 May 2014

Michael Walker, 'Toon animated by the return of King Kev', *Guardian*, 16 February 2002

Sam Wallace, Interview with Tim Sherwood, *Independent*, 28 March 2014

Paul Wheelock, '"He just had this aura about him" – 25 years ago today Blackburn Rovers appointed Kenny Dalglish', *Lancashire Telegraph*, 12 October 2016

Joyce Helen Woolridge, 'From Local Hero to National Star? The Changing Cultural Representation of the Professional Footballer in England, 1945-1985' PhD thesis, University of Central Lancashire, 2007

Steve Wraith, 'Sir John Hall On Mike Ashley And Future Of Newcastle United', *Toon Talk*, fansonline.net, 10 August 2011

INDEX

Aberdeen FC, 134–5
Abramovich, Roman, 329, 334
Adams, George, 23
Adams, Micky, 288, 289
Adams, Tony, 194, 242, 314, 316
Ajax FC, 68, 122
Al-Fayed, Mohamed, 288, 297, 302, 305, 326
Albert, Philippe, 252–3, 269, 276, 286
Aldridge, John, 190, 191, 194, 204, 209
Allardyce, Sam, 339, 340
Anderson, Viv, 123
Andersson, Andreas, 293, 296, 299
Anelka, Nicolas, 298, 299, 324, 331, 334
Archibald, Steve, 147, 187, 219
Ardiles, Osvaldo 'Ossie', 219, 220, 230, 231, 233
Armstrong, David, 143
Arsenal FC, 51, 190, 194, 269
    KD spotted by, 22
Ashley, Mike, 10, 339–41, 345, 347, 348, 359, 366
Ashman, Ron, 42, 49, 50, 165
Asprilla, Faustino, 9, 268, 269, 270, 271, 276, 283, 287, 288, 290
    injuries to, 290
Atkins, Mark, 249, 260
Atkinson, Ron, 138, 159, 188, 259
Atletico Madrid, 70
Auld, Bertie, 24, 26, 46
An Autobiography (Keegan), 31

Bacon, Anthony, 332–3
Bacon, Christopher, 332–3
Ball, Alan, 37, 128, 322

Barnes, John, 189–92, 193, 203, 209, 214, 215, 261, 270, 286, 291, 292, 303, 307–8, 310–11
Barton, Warren, 264, 269
Batty, David, 249, 259, 265, 269, 271, 275, 285
Baxter, Jim, 22, 44–5
Bayern Munich FC, 92, 121–2, 125, 128, 129 (*see also individual tournaments*)
Beardsley, Peter, 158–9, 164, 189–90, 191, 192, 193, 194, 209, 214, 217, 248, 251, 252, 260, 266, 268, 271, 276, 283, 285, 292, 297
    and Hillsborough, 198, 202
    injury to, 210–11
    testimonial game for, 302–3
Beattie, Kevin, 86
Beckham, David, 263, 306, 313, 314, 316
    product promotion by, 10
Beglin, Jim, 180, 186, 189
Bell, Colin, 86
Benitez, Rafa, 337, 349
Bennett, Reuben, 71
Beresford, John, 239, 245, 260, 266, 270, 287
Berg, Henning, 244, 256
Best, George, 10–11, 46, 64–5, 81, 142
    and alcohol, 64
    business affairs of, 64, 67
    career end of, 67
Blackburn Rovers FC (*see also individual tournaments*):
    and finances, 219–20, 228
    KD becomes manager of, 228

KD quits as football director of, 274
KD quits as manager of, 262
KD's early recruiting to, 229–30
league wins of, 7, 256, 261
motto of, 229
Premier League place for, 237–8
   (see also Premier League)
Shearer clinched by, 238
Blake, Nathan, 292
Boersma, Phil, 82
Boyer, Phil, 133
Bracewell, Paul, 239
Bradford stadium fire, 167
Brazil, Alan, 146
Bremner, Billy, 62, 69, 77–8
   and alcohol, 74
Brooking, Trevor, 142, 146, 153
Brownsword, Jack, 37, 49
Bruce, Steve, 165
Buljan, Ivan, 124
Burns, Kenny, 123
Busby, Matt, 46, 48, 61, 81
Butt, Nicky, 263, 267

Callaghan, Ian, 49, 64, 89
Cantona, Eric, 222, 241, 243, 256, 257,
   263, 269
   fan attacked by, 258
Carroll, Andy, 351, 353, 355, 356, 359–60,
   362
Carter, Jimmy, 211, 217, 242
Case, Jimmy, 89–90, 107, 113, 138, 140
Catterick, Harry, 49
Celtic FC (see also individual tournaments):
   Barnes becomes head coach at, 307–8
   and Beardsley testimonial, 302–3
   disastrous season of, 115
   doubles won by, 26, 45, 70
   and finances, 301–2
   and Hillsborough charity match, 205
   and Ibrox Disaster, 46–7
   KD attempts board takeover of, 301
   KD becomes captain of, 87
   KD becomes operational director at,
      307–8
   KD invited to train with, 28
   KD sacked by, 315
   KD signs to, 29, 40–1
   KD's first-team debut with (as sub), 44
   KD's first-team debut with (whole
      game), 45
   KD's goalscoring prowess with, 59, 61
   KD's hundredth goal for, 93
   KD's Reserves try-out with, 43–4

low-salary problems at, 70 (see also
   players' pay)
North America tour by, 46
Rangers differences with, 25–6, 28
Rangers matches with, 24, 29, 30, 46,
   53, 61, 84, 87, 94, 115, 301, 310–11,
   312
Reserves, treble by, 48
and Scotland's South America tour, 61
Scottish league titles amassed by, 59
slump of, 116
Stein captains, then manages, 26–7
Stein departs, 118
Stein recruited by, 24–5
and Stein's injuries, 87, 88
and Stein's wrath, 44
Channon, Mick, 59, 62, 128, 145, 148,
   152, 154, 253
Chapman, Herbert, 262
Charity Shield, 2, 3, 77–8, 92, 101, 193,
   276
Charlton, Jack, 112, 153, 165
Chelsea FC:
   Abramovich acquires, 329
   Mourinho takes over, 334–5
Chivers, Martin, 62
Clark, Frank, 323
Clark, Lee, 220, 233, 246, 250, 281, 283,
   285–6
Clarke, Allan, 62
Clemence, Ray, 50, 88, 97, 99, 130, 140,
   142, 153
Clough, Brian, 77, 262, 305
Cole, Andy, 245–6, 248, 249, 250–1, 252,
   257–8, 264, 267, 269, 291, 303, 306
Collymore, Stan, 270
Conn, Alfie, 93
Connelly, George, 41, 44
Connolly, Billy, 20, 46, 69
Cowans, Gordon, 230
Cox, Arthur, 149, 152, 154, 155, 159, 165,
   289, 316, 323
Craggs, John, 150
Croker, Ted, 142
Cruyff, Johan, 68, 88, 110, 125, 361
Cumbernauld United FC, KD farmed out
   to, 39
Cunningham, Laurie, 129

Daily Express, KK's column in, 64
Dalglish, Bill (KD's father), 20, 22, 28–9,
   40
   soccer playing of, 21
Dalglish, Carol (KD's sister), 20

Dalglish, Cathy (KD's mother), 20
Dalglish, Kelly (KD's daughter), 106, 199, 203, 204, 206, 211
Dalglish, Kenny:
  and alcohol, 60, 83, 138–9, 212
  apprenticeship of, 27
  birth and early life of, 20–7
  business affairs and endorsements of, 84, 124, 324
  Footballer of the Year awards for, 123, 157
  Freedom of Liverpool award for, 365
  goal-scoring finesse of, 3
  health worries of, 212
  and Hillsborough, see Hillsborough tragedy
  injuries to, 135, 139, 140, 160, 188
  'lost his edge', 158
  Manager of the Year, 210
  marries, 83
  MBE honour for, 172
  memoirs of, 5, 12, 24, 137, 203, 354
  passing skills of, 4
  on players' pay, 11
  pop single of, 84–5
  at PR company, 279
  and Proactive, see Proactive
  as schoolyard hero, 2
  sent off and banned, 172
  stand named after, 365
  superstitions of, 108
  and Tapie, 222–3
  teams associated with, see individual teams
Dalglish, Lauren (KD's daughter), 192
Dalglish (née Harkins), Marina (KD's wife), 60, 83, 86, 93, 100, 106, 211–12, 215, 238, 307, 350
  cancer appeal founded by, 348–9
  cancer suffered by, 330
  Freedom of Liverpool award for, 365
  and Hillsborough, 199, 201, 202, 203, 204
Dalglish, Paul (KD's son), 106, 199, 253, 290, 300
Davidson, Victor, 27, 39, 44, 48
Deans, Dixie, 59, 60
Dinnie, Bobby, 21–2
Docherty, Tommy, 59, 60–1, 69, 182
  Manchester United poach, 61
Doherty, Peter, 49
Donachie, Willie, 97
Downing, Stewart, 355, 362
Duckenfield, Ch. Supt David, 198, 200
Dunning, Eric, 169–70

Eastham, George, 14
Ellegaard, Kevin, 324
Elliott, Robbie, 246, 283, 286
England national side (see also individual tournaments):
  in Argentina, 97
  a 'Dad's Army', 142
  and KK airport-security incident, 73–4
  KK becomes manager of, 306
  KK dropped from, 85, 153
  KK quits, as manager, 317
  KK quits, as player, 153
  KK top-scores for, 126
  KK's first forays with, 62
  KK's first goal for, 73
  KK's first match with, 59
  Revie takes over, 77
  Scotland's matches with, 59, 62, 73, 86, 88, 97, 126
  US tour by, 90
  and World Cup, see World Cup
Eriksson, Sven-Goran, 338
Europa League, see UEFA Cup
European Championships, 59, 90, 126, 153, 274, 304, 309, 313–15, 332
  fan trouble at, 130
European Cup, 30, 45, 59, 70–1, 93, 94, 113, 114–15, 122–3, 125, 127, 128–9, 134–5, 139–40, 156, 162, 163, 172–3, 222 (see also UEFA Champions League)
  and Heysel tragedy, 175–81, 184
  Liverpool win, 337
European Cup Winners' Cup, 30, 58, 82, 95, 110–11, 217
Evans, Alun, 50
Evans, Roy, 173, 177, 182, 215, 252, 253

FA Cup, 49, 50, 51, 71, 72–3, 76, 94, 95, 144, 159, 173, 192, 194–5, 209, 214, 244, 281–2, 291, 293, 296, 298–9, 343, 350, 357, 360
  and Hillsborough, see Hillsborough tragedy
  Liverpool win, 73, 122, 205, 241
  Southampton win, 127–8
Fagan, Joe, 71, 144, 156, 157–8, 163, 171–2, 173, 175, 177, 178
Fairclough, David, 89, 109, 133–4
Fallon, Sean, 26, 27–9 passim, 40, 44, 45, 87–8
  on KD, 6
Ferdinand, Les, 257, 264, 266, 268, 269, 270, 275, 276, 277, 283, 285, 286

Ferguson, Alex, 115–16, 134, 135, 187–8,
    189, 190, 192, 209, 238, 243, 246, 252,
    257, 259, 266–7, 305, 335, 350, 357,
    361–2
  becomes Manchester United boss, 188
  and Hillsborough, 205
  on KD, 187
  KD congratulated by, 262
  KK's spat with, 271–3
  Wenger's rivalry with, 334
Feyenoord FC, 45
FIFA, KK's criticism of, 10
Finney, Tom, 192
Fletcher, Freddie, 216, 221–2, 231, 274,
    277, 278, 286, 299
Flowers, Tim, 249, 256, 259, 260, 261, 269
Fowler, Robbie, 270, 284, 304, 309,
    327–8, 331
Francis, Gerry, 86
Francis, Trevor, 129
Fulham FC:
  divisional win by, 306
  KK becomes operating officer at,
    288–9

Gallacher, Kevin, 244, 259, 260, 261,
    262
Gayle, Howard, 137, 139, 167
Gemmell, Tommy, 46
Gemmill, Archie, 116, 117, 118
George, Charlie, 128
Gerrard, Steven, 314, 316, 354, 355, 359
Giggs, Ryan, 217
Giles, Johnny, 77, 273
Giller, Norman, 59
Gillespie, Gary, 183, 211, 217
Gillespie, Keith, 257, 266, 268, 271, 272,
    283–4, 287, 290, 293, 299
Ginola, David, 264, 266, 268, 270, 272,
    276, 282, 283–4, 285, 296
Glasgow United FC, KD recruited to, 27
Glazer family, 337
Golden Goals (Milburn), 14
Gonzalez, Ignacio, 345–6
Graham, George, 61, 194, 293
Gray, Andy, 116, 117, 272
Greaves, Jimmy, 89, 138
Greenwood, Ron, 97, 126, 130, 142, 148,
    316–17
Grobbelaar, Bruce, 136–7, 143, 144, 145,
    156, 166, 177, 183–4, 185, 186, 187
  and Hillsborough, 201
Gullit, Ruud, 300
Gutendorf, Rudi, 99, 106, 109

Hall, Douglas, 221–2, 231, 258, 278, 284,
    294–6, 299
Hall, John, 9, 220–1, 230–1, 235, 236,
    239, 248, 253, 274, 278–9, 284, 322,
    326, 339, 340, 348
Hamilton, Des, 284
Hansen, Alan, 107, 116, 123, 133, 135,
    136, 183, 187, 188, 191, 205, 211, 215
  and Hillsborough, 198, 201
  as TV pundit, 267
Harford, Ray, 228, 229, 262–3, 271, 299
Harkins, Marina, see Dalglish, Marina
Hartford, Asa, 97, 116, 117
Hateley, Mark, 165
Hay, David, 26, 41, 44, 46, 69, 75
  strike by, 70
Haynes, Johnny, 14
Heighway, Steve, 50, 63, 64, 89–90, 107,
    111, 189, 211, 215
Hemstead, Derek, 42
Henderson, Jordan, 355, 356, 359
Hendry, Colin, 219, 229, 253, 256, 259
Heysel tragedy, 175–81, 184
Hill, Joe, 22
Hillsborough tragedy, 196–205, 252, 363–4
  inquiry into, 207–8
  and Sun's disgraceful report, 201–2, 241
  and unlawful-killing verdict, 365
Hislop, Shaka, 264, 271
Hodgson, David, 156, 246
Hodgson, Roy, 350
Holton, Jim, 70
hooliganism, 54–6, 130, 142, 166–71, 173,
    176, 185
  and Europe ban, 178
  and Heysel tragedy, 176–81, 184
Hottiger, Marc, 252
Houghton, Ray, 190, 214
Howey, Steve, 220, 250, 251, 256
Hrubesch, Horst, 120, 121, 125, 128, 129
Hucker, Peter, 151
Hughes, Emlyn, 50, 65, 71, 79, 122, 131,
    154, 262
Hughes, Mark, 209, 263
Huglin, Victor, 64
Hunter, Ally, 69, 70
Hutchison, Tommy, 75
Hyland, John, 326, 332–3
Hysen, Glenn, 211, 217

Ibrox Disaster, 46–7, 168
Ince, Paul, 209, 263, 314
Inter Milan FC, 30, 59
  Stein studies, 26

Irvine, Alan, 283, 362
Irwin, Denis, 217

Jardine, Sandy, 84
Johnson, David, 92, 135, 136
Johnston, Craig, 136, 160, 163, 177, 187
Johnston, Mo, 216
Johnstone, Jimmy, 26, 29, 44, 45, 46, 73
    and alcohol, 74
Jordan, Joe, 70, 88, 97, 117, 118
Juventus FC, 93, 125, 172–3, 188, 193
    and Heysel tragedy, 175–8

Kanchelskis, Andrei, 217, 263
Kay, Oliver, 335–6
Keane, Roy, 248–9, 267, 334
Keegan, Doris (KK's mother), 34, 213
    death of, 316
Keegan, Frank (KK's grandfather), 9, 32–3
Keegan, Frank (KK's uncle), 35, 36, 150
Keegan (née Woodhouse), Jean (KK's
    wife), 51, 58, 82, 91, 95, 98, 127, 213
    KK meets, 43
Keegan, Joe (KK's father), 33–5, 58, 78,
    81–2, 85, 131, 149
    death of, 93
Keegan, Kevin:
    Ballon d'Or for, 127
    beaten and robbed, 213
    birth and early life of, 34–5, 36–7
    business affairs and endorsements of,
        63–4, 65, 67, 89, 124–5, 131–2,
        213, 325, 336, 366–7 (see also
        Soccer Circus)
    at charity event (2016), 8–10
    charity run of, 37
    charity work of, 11
    European Player of the Year, 8, 122,
        129, 133
    ghosted column of, 64
    Golden Boot for, 146
    injuries to, 133, 146, 147–8, 155
    McMenemy's criticism of, 145
    marries, 82
    media work of, 90, 124–5
    memoirs of, 11, 15, 31, 66, 67, 77, 89,
        96, 153, 327
    Moore's business advice to, 63
    and NoW story, 295
    PFA Player of the Year, 146
    on players' pay, 10, 11
    pop singles of, 64, 125, 131–2
    product promotion by, 10
    retirement announcement of, 160–1

and Shoot! special, 165
in Superstars, 91
teams associated with, see individual teams
as TV pundit, 366
wealth of, 9, 10, 150
Keegan, Laura Jane (KK's daughter), 121, 213
Keegan, Michael (KK's brother), 35
Keegan, Sarah (KK's daughter), 146, 213
Keeley, Glenn, 156
Keizer, Piet, 92
Kelly, David, 231, 233, 236, 245, 247
Kennedy, Alan, 140, 163, 177
Kennedy, Ray, 82, 88, 90, 107, 108, 113,
    126, 138, 140
Kennedy, Stewart, 86
Kilcline, Brian, 235
Kinnear, Joe, 346, 347
Kitson, Paul, 252, 284
Klopp, Jurgen, 364–5, 366

Law, Denis, 22, 69, 89
Lawrenson, Mark, 160, 171, 178, 183, 186,
    190, 276, 278
Le Saux, Graeme, 244, 260
Le Tissier, Matt, 282, 283
League Cup (English), 43, 82, 135, 139, 144,
    158, 162, 190, 243–4, 250, 345, 356, 358
    Liverpool win, 162, 359
League Cup (Scottish), 53, 59, 61, 87, 311, 312
    Celtic win, 83
Lee, Rob, 239–40, 246, 251, 252, 260,
    267, 268, 269, 270, 271, 285, 294, 299
Lee, Sammy, 139, 143
Leeds United FC, Clough takes over, 77
Leighton, Jim, 135
Lennox, Bobby, 27, 45
Lineker, Gary, 185, 186, 187
Liverpool FC (see also individual
    tournaments):
    behind-the-scenes changes at, 189
    and Benitez, 337
    dominance of, 122, 330
    and dressing-room banter, 137
    drinking culture at, 138
    eight straight wins by, 210
    and finances, 89, 123–4, 188, 190–1,
        337–8, 349
    and first KK season, end of, 58
    and Heysel tragedy, 176–8, 184
    and Hillsborough, 196–205, 252,
        363–4, 365
    and hooliganism, 167, 185
    KD becomes manager of (1st time),
        174–5, 180

KD becomes manager of (2nd time),
    350, 362
KD captains, 123
KD joins, 101
KD joins board of, 363
KD overseas youth academy at, 349
KD quits, 214–15
KD sacked as manager of, 360, 363
KD takes player-manager role at, 186
KD trials with, 23, 24
KD's contract renewed by, 163
KD's league debut with, 107
KK joins, 50–1
KK quits, 92
and KK–Shankly bond, 9, 64
KK–Smith fight at, 57
and KK–Toshack partnership, 58
KK welcomed to, 50–1
and KK's fine and ban, 79, 81
and KK's first silverware, 65
KK's first-team debut with, 52–3
and KK's foot injury, 57–8
KK's high goal scoring for, 72
league wins of, 23, 65, 95, 109, 123,
    146, 163, 187, 192, 209
and Molby's driving offence, 193–4
notable European engagements of, *see*
    individual tournaments
Paisley quits, Fagan replaces, 156
Paisley takes over from Shankly at, 76
and players' pay, *see* players' pay
and racism, 191–2, 355, 356
routine at, 56
Rush leaves, 188
Rush returns to, 193
scouting operation at, 49
Shankly quits, 75–6, 79–80
Shankly's success with, 23–4
Souness becomes manager of, 216–17
Southampton's win at, 143
and Spion Kop, 23, 111, 252
stand named after KD by, 365
ticket-price revolt at, 371
training at, 137–8
trophy drought of, 49–50
and Walsall wall collapse, 162
Lloyd, Larry, 50, 65, 71, 123
Lockwood, Dave, 326, 332
Lynch, Andy, 94

Macari, Lou, 41, 44, 46, 48, 59, 61, 116,
    117, 301
on KD, 45
and players' pay, 60, 61

McAteer, Jason, 270
McCreery, Dave, 155
McDermott, Terry, 82, 107, 111, 113, 114, 122,
    135, 140, 142, 153, 154, 232, 235, 240,
    247, 271–2, 281, 293, 308, 311, 340–1
on KD, 7
MacDonald, Kevin, 172, 189
Macdonald, Malcolm, 72, 257
McGrain, Danny, 21, 25, 29–30, 39, 41,
    69, 116
on KD, 23, 41
McIlvanney, Hugh, 196
McIntosh, Peter, 326, 332–3
Mackay, Dave, 138
Mackay, Don, 227, 230
MacKenzie, Kelvin, and *Sun*'s
    Hillsborough story, 202
MacLeod, Ally, 116, 118
McMahon, Steve, 184, 191
McManaman, Steve, 270, 283, 313, 314, 331
McMenemy, Lawrie, 127–8, 145, 148,
    153, 272
McMillan, Ian, 3–4, 21
McNeill, Billy, 24, 48, 79, 87, 115, 174
McParland, Davie, 88
McQueen, Gordon, 97
Magath, Felix, 99, 100, 110, 120, 121, 125, 129
Manchester City FC, 268
    dearth of confidence at, 333
    divisional win by, 324
    and Fair Play table, 328
    and finances, 323, 326–7, 328
    KK becomes manager of, 323
    KK quits, 334
    Pearce takes over, 334
    Shinawatra acquires, 338
    stadium move by, 331
Manchester United FC, 137–8, 185,
    209, 256, 269 (*see also individual*
    tournaments)
    Cole bought by, 257–8
    Glazers acquire, 337
    growing potential of, 217
    and Hillsborough, 205
    and hooliganism, 55–6
    and pitch invasion, 78
    Rooney's move to, 332
    and Stein, 48
Mariner, Paul, 142, 143
Marsh, Rodney, 268
Martins, Obafemi, 344
Martyn, Nigel, 242
Masson, Don, 116, 117
Mathie, Alex, 250

Matthews, Stanley, 36
May, David, 219, 251, 253
Mercer, Joe, 73, 77
Messi, Lionel, 351–2
Miljanic, Miljan, 90
Molby, Jan, 172, 184, 185, 186, 187,
    193–4, 210, 214
Moore, Bobby, 62–3, 153, 265–6
Moores, David, 217, 246, 253, 330, 337–8
Moran, Kevin, 138, 159–60, 185, 219, 227,
    229, 237, 254, 325
Moran, Ronnie 'Bugsy', 51–2, 56, 57, 71,
    161, 173, 182, 206, 215
Moran, Steve, 139, 143, 145
Moreland, Vic, 4
Mourinho, Jose, 287, 334–5, 361
Murdoch, Bobby, 24, 26, 45
Murdoch, Rupert, 218, 223–4
My Life (Dalglish), 5
My Liverpool Home (Dalglish), 354

Nageek Enterprises, 64
Narey, David, 147
Neal, Phil, 82, 97, 133, 135, 142, 144, 173,
    183, 185
    on KD, 6
Netzer, Gunter, 65, 90, 94, 110, 120, 125, 129
Neville, Gary, 263, 266
Neville, Phil, 266, 269, 314
Newcastle United FC, 233 (see also
    individual tournaments)
    Ardiles joins, 220
    Ashley acquires, 339–41
    and Beardsley testimonial, 302–3
    Cole joins, 245
    Dalglish Jr signs for, 290
    and finances, 220–1, 230, 231, 239, 253,
        275, 284, 340
    flotation of, 276–7
    Gullit replaces KD at, 300
    KD becomes manager of, 279–80
    and KK–Ferguson spat, 271–3
    and KK–Hall relations, 235
    KK quits as manager of (1st time), 278
    KK quits as manager of (2nd time), 346–7
    KK quits, as player, 164–5
    KK raises gate of, 155, 233
    KK signs as manager of (1st time), 231–2
    KK signs as manager of (2nd time), 342–3
    KK signs as player for, 9, 11, 149–50
    KK's first match with, as manager, 233
    KK's new manager contract with, 236
    KK's quit threat to, as manager, 235
    KK's sell-out debut with, 150–1

Liverpool buy Beardsley from, 191
    and Magpie Group, 221
    and NoW story, 295–6
    Premier League place for, 247 (see also
        Premier League)
    rising fortunes of, 274
    as selling club, 190
    Shearer signed by, 275–6
    and Stevenage ground, 291, 292–3
    training at, 154
Newell, Mike, 230, 234, 237, 242, 254,
    257, 271
Nicholl, Chris, 133
Nicol, Steve, 183, 189, 215
Nottingham Forest FC, 52, 109, 122–3,
    129, 192, 205
    and Hillsborough, see Hillsborough tragedy

O'Brien, Liam, 233
O'Farrell, Frank, 61
O'Neill, Martin, 315
Ormond, Willie, 62, 69, 70
Overmars, Marc, 298
Owen, Michael, 313, 314, 339, 344

Paisley, Bob, 33, 50, 56, 71, 80, 85–6,
    89–90, 91, 96, 100, 108, 126, 140,
    144, 146, 174, 184, 189, 273, 305
    Liverpool manager role quit by, 156
    Shankly's replacement, 76
    on Souness, 112
Pallister, Gary, 209
Parkes, Tony, 227, 237
Peacock, Darren, 251, 268, 276
Peacock, Gavin, 233, 236, 245, 247
Pearce, Stuart, 285, 287, 291, 334
Pelé, 53
Perryman, Steve, 66
Peters, Martin, 73
Petit, Emmanuel, 298
Pistone, Alessandro, 285, 287, 298
Platini, Michel, 156, 241
players' pay, 10, 11, 13–14, 35–6, 60, 63,
    66, 67–8, 70, 88
Premier League:
    Blackburn enter, 237
    formation of, 223, 369
    inaugural season of, 237
    Newcastle enter, 247
    Newcastle lead, 255
    and subscription packages, 242
    and ticket prices, 371
Preston North End FC, KK eyed by, 48–9
Proactive, 11, 254, 324–5, 326, 332–3

Queen, Tony, 44, 84, 87
Quinn, Mick, 233, 236, 245

Ramsey, Alf, 62, 70
Rangers FC (*see also individual tournaments*):
   Celtic's differences with, 25–6, 28
   Celtic's matches with, *see under* Celtic
   dominance of, 22
   Ferguson joins, 115
   and Ibrox Disaster, 46–7
   KD becomes fan of, 21
   Souness's effects on, 216
   trebles of, 22, 115
Ranson, Ray, 236
Real Madrid FC, 90, 91, 94, 122, 125,
   128–9 (*see also individual tournaments*)
Red Star Belgrade FC, 71
Redknapp, Harry, 27, 340
Redknapp, Jamie, 261
Reid, Peter, 186
Revie, Don, 45, 77, 85, 97, 165
Rioch, Bruce, 97, 116, 117
Ripley, Stuart, 238, 242
Robertson, John, 129, 147
Robinson, Michael, 157, 158
Robinson, Peter, 89, 127, 163, 173, 174,
   194, 201, 210, 214, 216–17, 246, 253
Robson, Bobby, 139, 152–3, 154, 190,
   278–9, 339, 368
Robson, Bryan, 148, 185
Rodford, Neil, 289, 324–5, 332
Rodgers, Brendan, 355, 363, 364, 366
Rooney, Wayne, 11, 12, 325–6, 332–3, 358
   pay of, 10, 11
   and Proactive, *see* Proactive
Rosenthal, Ronny, 209, 211
Rough, Alan, 117
Royle, Joe, 323
Ruddock, Neil 'Razor', 248, 270
Rush, Ian, 136, 137, 144, 145–6, 156, 157,
   171, 176, 184, 187, 188, 193, 194, 205,
   286, 290, 291
   Juventus buy, 188

St John, Ian, 23, 50, 180
Schmeichel, Peter, 243, 252, 269, 324
Scholes, Paul, 263, 306, 309, 310, 313, 314
Scotland national side (*see also individual
   tournaments*):
   in Argentina, 97
   Celtic players reinforce, 69
   England's matches with, *see under* England
   KD captains, 123
   KD selected by, 59

KD's first goal for, 61
and Scottish FA centenary, 62
South America tour by, 60–1
Under-23 squad, KD's goals for, 59
and World Cup, *see* World Cup
Scottish Cup, 59, 61, 84, 94
Scottish Football League, splitting of, 87
Scottish Schools XI, 23
Scunthorpe United FC, 9, 31, 34, 42–3
   KK joins, 37–8
   KK quits, 50
   relegation of, 42
Seaman, David, 310, 314, 331
Sellars, Scott, 219, 237, 246, 251, 256, 257
Shankly, Bill, 15, 23–4, 49–50, 56–8, 71,
   134, 174, 240, 265–6
   and Charity Shield, 77
   and Hillsborough, 196
   KK praised by, for assault, 112
   and KK's business interests, 64
   KK's views on, 66–7
   at Liverpool, *see* Liverpool FC
   and Shankly's Bar, 336
Sharpe, Lee, 217
Shearer, Alan, 151, 164, 238, 242–4, 245,
   249, 251, 252, 254, 256–7, 259, 260,
   261, 262, 271, 275–6, 282–3, 286,
   292–4, 296, 306, 309, 310, 314, 339
   Golden Boot for, 274
   injuries to, 286, 292
Shearer, Duncan, 234
Sheedy, Kevin, 165, 186
Shepherd, Freddy, 231, 278–9, 284,
   294–6, 299, 300, 340
   and *NoW* story, 295
Sherwood, Tim, 233, 238, 249, 259
Shilton, Peter, 72, 73, 123, 129, 140, 145,
   235, 237
Shinawatra, Thaksin, 338
Smith, Alex, 24
Smith, Dave, 24
Smith, Jimmy, 22
Smith, John, 75, 80, 90, 100, 123–4, 127,
   163, 174, 180, 194, 205, 210
Smith, Tommy, 50, 56, 57, 65, 68, 107, 112
Soccer Circus, 213, 288, 336–7, 340, 347
Souness, Graeme, 112–13, 114, 118, 123,
   133, 135, 136, 139, 140–1, 144, 160,
   188, 238, 249, 282
   becomes Liverpool boss, 216–17
   on KD, 6, 7, 174
   Liverpool quit by, 162
   and *Sun*, 241
   unpopularity of, 246

Southampton FC, 131–2
  (*see also individual tournaments*)
  KK signs for, 128
  KK's debut with, 133
  as 'Tip Top Saints', 145
Southgate, Gareth, 316
Speed, Gary, 293, 299
Speedie, David, 185, 187, 188, 211, 217, 229, 234, 237, 238–9
Sports Direct, 339
Srnicek, Pavel, 247, 249, 256, 269
Stapleton, Frank, 219
Staunton, Steve, 189
Stein, Jock, 15, 28–33 *passim*, 39–41, 44–6, 100, 123, 134, 146–7, 210
  birth and early life of, 31–2
  Busby approaches, 46, 48
  car-crash injuries to, 87
  and Celtic, *see* Celtic FC
  death of, 187
  directorship of, 115
  Ferguson studies, 116
  on Ibrox Disaster, 47
  and players' pay, 60
  and Protestantism, 28
  and Scotland's South America tour, 61
  takes over Scotland, 118
Stepney, Alex, 113
stock-market flotations, 156, 223, 275, 284, 301
Strachan, Gordon, 135, 147
Stretford, Paul, 11, 12, 219, 246, 253, 254, 257, 286, 324, 325, 326, 332–3
Sturrock, Paul, 147
Suarez, Luis, 351, 352–3, 355, 356–7, 358–9, 363
Sugar, Alan, 224
Sun, and Hillsborough, 201, 241
Sutton, Chris, 254, 256–7, 259, 260
SV Hamburg FC (*see also individual tournaments*):
  and championship shield, 126
  KK moves to, 3, 96, 98–9
  KK quits, 129–30
  KK sought by, 95
  KK's first match with, 105
  and KK's Lubeck assault, 112, 114
  KK's ultimatum to, 120
  losses of, during KK's absence, 114
  rare Bundesliga title for, 125
  successes of, 95
  top-of-table position for, 128
  Zebec hired by, 120–1

Taylor, Lord Justice Peter, 207–8
Tebily, Olivier, 308
Thatcher, Margaret, 131, 166, 169, 179–80
Thompson, Peter, 50, 52
Thompson, Phil, 71, 79, 88, 123, 142, 144, 153, 189, 215
Todd, Colin, 73
Tomasson, Jon Dahl, 285, 286–7, 290, 293
Toshack, John, 50, 57, 65, 72, 82, 88, 89, 109, 140, 216
  injury to, 58

UEFA Champions League, 274, 285, 290, 332, 357 (*see also* European Cup)
UEFA Cup, 65–6, 78, 88, 89–90, 93, 145, 255, 276, 283, 328, 331, 365
  Liverpool win, 65–6

Varadi, Imre, 150–1, 154, 155
Vega, Ramon, 296
Venison, Barry, 189, 227, 239, 240, 244, 250, 252, 253
Viduka, Mark, 311, 344, 345
Vieira, Patrick, 298, 334

Waddle, Chris, 149, 154, 159, 160, 164, 222, 303
Walsh, Paul, 163, 184, 185, 189
Wark, John, 126, 146–7, 161, 171
Watson, Dave, 128
Watson, Steve, 220, 246, 268, 283
Watson, Tom, 262
Wegerle, Roy, 234, 244
Wenger, Arsene, 298, 334, 335, 353, 360, 361
West Ham United FC, KD trials with, 27
Wharton, Kenny, 154
Whelan, Ronnie, 136, 138, 145, 182, 184, 186, 187, 188, 191
White, Noel, 210, 214
Wilcox, Jason, 252, 256, 263
Wilkins, Ray, 130, 289, 297
Wilson, Paul, 83, 84
Wise, Dennis, 313, 314, 344, 345
Woodhouse, Jean, *see* Keegan, Jean
World Cup, 7, 53, 61, 62, 69–70, 73–5, 90, 93, 97, 109, 116–18, 133, 141–3, 146–7, 172, 187–8, 316
Wright, Alan, 229
Wright, Tommy, 236, 247

Yeats, Ron, 23, 50, 189, 211

Zebec, Branko, 120–1, 125, 154, 344, 364